Planning Office Space

PLANNING OFFICE SPACE

Edited by Francis Duffy
Colin Cave
John Worthington

The Architectural Press Ltd: London
Nichols Publishing Company: New York

Preface

This book is intended to be a practical handbook for the architects and clients who work together to plan office space. Sometimes the problem will be the design of a new building; sometimes merely the shifting of desks and departments in existing space. Whatever the problem this handbook is intended to facilitate the dialogue between those who are concerned with the building and those who are concerned with its use. It is designed to improve the client's understanding of the architect and the architect's understanding of the client.

That it has been possible to prepare a book on planning office space which takes into account both architects' and clients' viewpoints is due to the enormous amount of innovative work which has been carried out over the last few years by a wide variety of people. For example, many ideas in this book can be traced back to Germany—to Alsleben, to the Schnelle brothers, to the Quickborner team and to 'Kommunikation'. Others relate to the tradition of space planning and building management in New York, Chicago and other North American cities. A heavy debt is owed to user requirements studies in this country, particularly those carried out by the Building Research Establishment, the old Ministry of Building and Works and the new Property Services Agency.

Another important tradition goes back via Land Use and Build Form Studies at Cambridge to the Whitehall brief prepared by Sir Leslie Martin. Further British contributions are the work on offices by Peter Cowan and others at the Joint Unit for Planning Research and Peter Manning at the University of Liverpool. Finally, the lead of the 'Architects' Journal' itself in publishing its first Information Library Series on office design in 1964 and in commissioning the subsequent series on which this book is based.

Many thanks are due to all the people who contributed to the planning of this original series of articles in the 'Architects' Journal' including Brian Day, Peter Cowan, Ian Davis, John Deakin, George Gebler, Dean Hawkes, Jerry Hewitt, Colin Jackson, Charmian Lacey, Owen Luder, Bev Nutt, H A Rhee, Geoffry Shuttleworth, Terry Trickett, K Trigwell, Peter Ullathorne, Terry Wyatt. All those who have contributed parts of this book are acknowledged on the appropriate pages.

First published in book form in 1976 in Great Britain by The Architectural Press Ltd

ISBN 0 85139 505 8 (British edition)

Published in the United States in 1976 by
Nichols Publishing Company
175 West 79th Street
Post Office Box 96
New York, N.Y. 10024

ISBN 0-89397-007-7 (USA edition)

Library of Congress Catalog Card No. 76-39810

Filmset and printed in Great Britain by
BAS Printers Limited, Wallop, Hampshire

Contents

Introduction

We are all now on the wrong side of the office boom, consolidating at the bottom of the market as the optimists say. In the sixties it was possible to make a lot of money out of office buildings—so much so that this building type became notorious among architects and the general public as a symbol of profligacy and the destruction of our cities. Fortunately the end of the boom has coincided with a growth in awareness by users of what they want from office space. There is now a breathing space to think out what offices are really for, how well they meet user requirements, what kinds of office space are best for various purposes, how offices are best used and managed. There is also a little time for theory, for generalising about the problems of providing office space, so that when the boom returns, as it undoubtedly will, a strategy will have been thought out by architects and clients which may help to avoid some of the worst faults and limitations of the last one.

One of the great advantages of the current slow-down in new office building, is that it has forced both architects and clients to think more carefully about the more fundamental problem: the planning of office space, that is *any* office space, whether old or new. All office space is a precious resource which should not be squandered. The basic design problem is to use it properly.

This is a handbook for both architect and client. Its major objective is to help both to talk together so that in planning office space the user and client will understand what the architect is saying and vice versa. To achieve this objective the book is laid out to follow the major joint decisions which have to be made:

- The office shell—decisions about how much space and what kind of space is required;
- The office interior—decisions about the layout of office space, the style of office interior appropriate for the organisation, and about how to get it;
- The economics of building offices—decisions about where to spend the money;
- The law and regulations—the constraints within which design decisions must be made;
- The office environment—decisions about the quality of the acoustic and thermal environment and about the interconnections between the various services, the shell and the scenery;
- Office facilities—decisions about entrances and reception areas, meeting rooms, restaurants and vending areas, lavatories and special areas such as those for storage and computers;
- Managing office space—decisions about how to run and maintain office buildings, how to arrange moves, and how to select furniture. Above all this section stresses that the real design problem is not simply the one-off building but fitting a changing organisation through time into a changing stock of space.

The handbook ends with a comparative review of some recent projects, a survey of important trends and a compact design guide.

Looking forward to the probable resurgence of new office building in the late seventies, it is to be hoped that these new buildings will be different and better than those we see around us today. They should perform better technically without necessarily using more of our scarce resources. They should offer a wider range of spaces which, in turn, should be capable of being used by diverse tenants in many different ways. On the user side, the architect should expect a greater consumer awareness, which will probably have the effect of changing roles so that investor developer, architect, project manager, client, user space planner, building manager will work together more closely and to greater effect. We hope so. Perhaps this book will help to make it a little easier to plan office space both now and in future years.

November 1975

SECTION 1: PLANNING OFFICE SPACE

Section 1 : Planning office space

The principles of office design

THE EDITORS review the basic principles of
office design. The major themes of the handbook
are established, some definitions are made, and
the importance of the expected life span of the
various elements of office design is argued. The
place of the architect in the process of office design
is discussed.

1 Objectives

1.01 To managers and architects, planning office space
presents numerous problems. This book is intended to be a
practical guide to solving these problems—a handbook of
space planning.

1.02 To the client, problems come in the form of decisions
about how much space is appropriate, where it should be,
what sort of furniture to buy. Or in another form, problems
present themselves as complaints about overcrowding,
discomfort, draughts or noise, and perhaps even in losing
valued staff to the firm with better premises next door.
Above all, problems are to do with money—how much can
we afford to do this or that, is it worth spending an extra sum
to achieve a marginal gain, are we spending too much on
space?

1.03 To the architect, a major problem is extracting a brief
from the client which is detailed enough to allow him to
design but general enough to allow the client to change and
grow within the new space. Another class of problems is in
coordinating all the specialised contributions of structural
engineers, acousticians, mechanical and services consultants while at the same time meeting client requirements.

1.04 These problems are complex and difficult, particularly so in a period which is very rich in new ideas about
office space and which at the same time is characterised by
violent fluctuations in the economics of development on
which most office building is based.

1.05 The objective of this book is to help architects and
managers face and solve such problems by:

- making clear the principles on which office design is
  based and which all parties should respect;
- showing how the amount of office space required can be
  estimated;
- reviewing the basic types of office space which are
  currently available and relating them to user requirements;
- providing basic information on standards and dimensions for detailed planning;
- explaining the basic issues in designing the services
  which support office space so that architects and users
  know the right questions to put to specialists;
- examining the cost implications of various kinds of office
  design;
- reviewing the legal and planning controls on design and
  use of office space;
- examining the function and design of such specialised
  areas as reception, computer areas, meeting spaces,
  restaurants;
- evaluating the major systems of office furniture against
  functional criteria.

In this way a rational basis is presented for making all the
major decisions in commissioning and designing office
space—from writing out the brief to laying out furniture.

2 The situation today

2.01 Ideas mature so slowly that sometimes it is hard to believe that anything has ever changed in office design. Fortunately this is not exactly true. The extent of the difference between what was considered an acceptable office environment two decades ago in the United Kingdom and what is thought adequate today is very great.

2.02 New speculative and custom built offices present a greater range of sizes of space than the narrow 'speculative' blocks of the 1950s. Spaces range from vast floors hundreds of metres deep to intermediate depths of 20m to narrow bands hardly 5m wide. Some buildings are made up of several depths. Moreover, office buildings vary more in the quality of services and finish. Altogether many more options are open to clients and tenants.

2.03 New experiments are being tried, in plan form particularly, in exploring the consequences of locating fixed elements in various ways in order to increase the utility of the space for various kinds of user. Other experiments are being made in manipulating the section of office buildings. Others are attempts to achieve reversible space, ie office floors which can be made either open plan or cellular.

2.04 New kinds of furniture have been developed which are designed for the open plan and which combine the functions of desk and partition into what are called 'systems'. Such systems, at their best, widen the range of available types of workplace to include accommodation for newer tasks such as programming and project work. Often they are invaluable for group as well as for solitary work.

2.05 New devices have been invented to break office space up into usable units. Sometimes these are part of the building structure; sometimes they are almost as temporary as furniture. Certainly they go far beyond the limitations of the older forms of partitioning. Combined with new kinds of furniture they enormously increase the range of options open to architects and their clients in the design of office interiors.

2.06 A new higher level of servicing is now common and a greater degree of integration in the design of lighting heating and air conditioning has become possible. Such sophisticated servicing opens up many possibilities in the design of office buildings but at a cost: the seemingly inevitable increase in energy consumption.

2.07 New research has thrown light on the way office space becomes obsolete and on how rapidly changing organisations occupy several properties simultaneously, sometimes shedding one space while taking on another. The design problem becomes not just getting a building built once and for all but managing a stock of space over time.

2.08 New kinds of consultancy services have emerged which seem to answer some kind of demand from clients which conventional architectural practice does not seem able to satisfy. The quality of these consultants varies enormously but there is not doubt that they all, in some degree, impinge upon what architects regard as their preserve. Are architects inherently incapable of satisfying this demand or is it possible for them to redefine their area of professional competence?

3 Shell and scenery

3.01 What do all these new developments mean? Are they connected? What significance do they have for the next generation of office buildings? Two themes hold this book together and explain much that appears unconnected and peculiar to office design.

3.02 The first theme—*shell and scenery*— emphasises building elements; discusses how the physical elements of office design relate to one another through time. The second theme—the *process*—describes how the parties involved work sometimes with each other and sometimes independently.

3.03 Some office design decisions are long term while others are short term. If you distinguish long term from short term design, a great many consequences follow. The distinction helps to explain why old buildings can be gutted and entirely redesigned internally; why interior design work is separated from architectural design; why services ought to allow scope for later change; why it is significant when partitions are thought to be part of short life scenery rather than long life building; why the management of a stock of leased space is a vital part of design; why different user information is required to design the building shell and the interior, **1**.

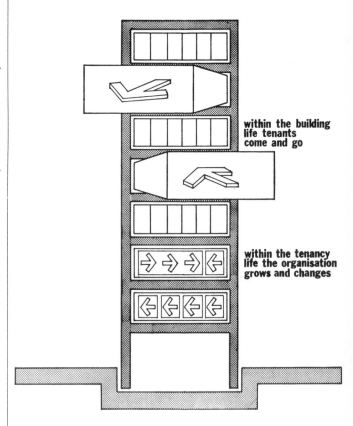

within the building life tenants come and go

within the tenancy life the organisation grows and changes

1 *Cycles of changing use in an office building*

3.04 A speculative office building can be thought of as the site of the building contract—as does the architect; or as so much space to be leased—as does the estate agent; or as a device for making money—as does the developer. It is of course all these things but also very much more. Once the building is complete, tenants come and go changing the interior several times in the building's lifetime; and within each tenancy innumerable minor changes take place—desks and partitions are shifted as the tenant organisation changes and grows. The building is the sum of all these changes throughout its useful life.

3.05 Office design is like design for the stage. The *shell* of an office building is equivalent to the bare stage which is built for as long as the theatre will last. The *scenery* is the assembly of props required for a production ie a tenancy. The *sets* are the various dispositions of scenery needed for the different scenes of the play.

3.06 Office design is several levels of design activity laid on top of one another but carried out independently of each other. Each type of design activity can be distinguished by the length of time the thing designed is meant to last. The architect and developer together design a building *shell* that will be used for (say) 40 years. Shorter term needs—for example those of a tenant with a five- or seven-year lease—are met within the framework of the building shell **2, 3, 4.** Within each tenancy, although certain basic design decisions were fixed in the initial interior design, design continues as departments are moved, equipment is changed and adapted as people come and go.

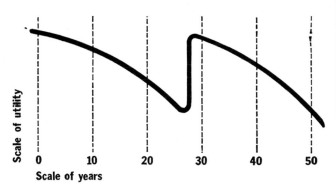

Cycle of the building shell

2 The building shell is useful for say, 40 years—with a refit at 25 years

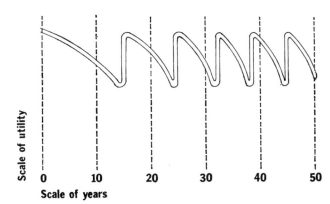

3 The office 'scenery' is replaced at shorter intervals with each new lease

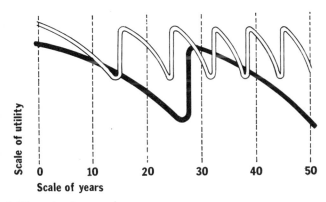

4 Changing 'scenery' can keep an office building useful throughout its life

3.07 Designers must predict because their solutions have to last. Anything which lasts into the future lasts into uncertainty. Some architects are asked by developers to predict 40 years ahead. Their designs, for example, of speculative office buildings (or for that matter of custom-designed ones) must leave open many options for many likely users **5, 6, 7**; the column positions must not be a nuisance either now or in 40 years' time. But the designer of the office interior needs to be less farsighted, for he is asked to predict only for the length of a lease. He can therefore afford to be much more precise about meeting the client's more easily predictable needs. Scenery's function is to take up the tolerance between the shell and what the tenant actually wants.

3.08 Finally, the office manager (who is a designer too) can see far enough into the future to plan three months ahead for the fluctuating needs of his 'clients'. He can see ahead for only a short time but he can see very precisely; he must and can design with a degree of precision impossible for the architect or the office designer.

3.09 Shell design is for (say) 40 years; scenery design for seven years; set design for three months. The designed object is in effect amortised over these periods; it lasts as

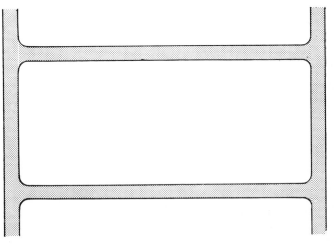

Shell

5 The elements of the shell

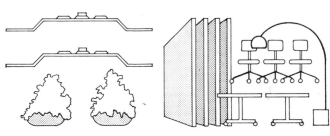

Scenery

6 The five- to seven-year elements of scenery

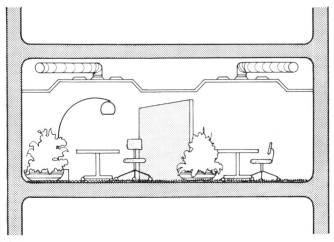

Sets

7 Users' adjustments of 'scenery' create the 'sets' for the office scene

long as it is useful. The design of services can be categorised in the same way using the predicted life of the designed object as a guide. Roughly speaking, basic installations such as lifts and major trunking can be expected to last for 20 years while the various outlets, such as lighting fittings, extracts, power points, need not be expected to last any longer than the scenery with which they are so closely integrated.

3.10 John Weeks[1] grasped the shell side of the shell-scenery argument when he enunciated the duffle coat principle—that as three sizes of duffle coat fit all sailors, so a very limited range of room sizes can accommodate the vast majority of functions in a modern hospital. The scenery side of the argument simply reminds us how important are furniture, partitions and fittings in mediating between the coarse, long life building shell and precise, short term organisational requirements. Interior designers have always understood this. Clients know it very well. Perhaps only architects have tended to overlook the importance of designing with time in mind.

4 The process

4.01 Shell and scenery and set are physical. Equally important in office design is the way things are done: the *process* of office design.

Space management

4.02 Here the organisation's point of view matters more than that of the architect. Organisations grow and change very rapidly. A firm is extremely aware of continuity through time because the problem of what to do when the existing accommodation becomes inadequate or the lease runs out is very pressing. An organisation is not necessarily accommodated in one place or one space; it is quite usual for firms to occupy part of a floor, or half a building, or so many thousand square feet here and so many there. Very rarely is a firm completely 'fitted' to one building; if it is, it is unlikely to remain so for long.

4.03 Architects ought to understand this, for every architect who runs a practice or a group is a manager of space. He is always aware of the cost of space and of how much he needs now and how much he will need in years to come. He rents more space than he needs, sublets for a time, keeps his options open by short leases.

4.04 Letting surplus space is a management strategy. In microcosm it is exactly the same policy as might be adopted by an enormous firm with hundreds of offices of varying quality, sizes and lease conditions in many different places. The choice of such a strategy is as much a design decision as getting a layout straight or choosing a floor covering. It involves finding spaces with certain dimensional and servicing characteristics within which change is possible. Above all it means deciding how long each space is likely to be useful and how much money should be spent on it.

Different kinds of brief

4.05 The architect has often seen the brief as a document which pins the client down. Since it is a statement of client requirements it is the architect's guide. It is a protection against later changes of mind, as well as a means of defining how much design freedom the architect has. A good architect will pay a great deal of attention to getting a brief sorted out before he begins to design.

4.06 It can be strongly argued that in office design a definitive brief is an impossibility; this is true if office design is seen from the client's point of view as one part only of space management. The best that can be hoped for is different kinds of statements of intention which are independent of one another and allow for revision without affecting the others. Thus, each kind of client—developer,

tenant, a firm building its own premises—will issue its own kind of statement.

4.07 The *developer's* statement of intention must leave many options open. His role is to add to the total stock of space in a city in a way that meets the changing demands of the mass of space users. His part in the process is to make the longest guess ahead about the likely uses to which his building may be put, constrained only by his long-term market forecasts of likely type of tenant and by his knowledge of how his development contributes to a total stock of space in a particular locality.

4.08 The *tenant's* statement of intention will be detailed and short term and even then sufficiently imprecise to allow for growth and change. For the tenant, what matters is the pattern of work, the relationship of person to person, department to department. Style is vital. The way the management treats its workers, itself and its visitors is reflected in the layout. Office landscaping is a very good example of how study of work patterns and a particular participant management style results in a very characteristic kind of brief.

4.09 For the *big organisation* looking ahead, information on user requirements need not, and must not, be so detailed; detailed user requirements are of no value at the outset of a new building project, nor is information on which work places will be adjacent. But abstract figures on the statistical distribution of department and work group size are required, and some overall patterns of contact between whole departments. At this level a decision to use office landscaping is irrelevant except to indicate that relatively deep, relatively highly serviced spaces are necessary.

4.10 Yet good judgement at the custom building and developer level, however broad statistically, must nonetheless be based on detailed knowledge of a multitude of individual tenant requirements. Multi-tier market research, able to cope with both individual and mass, short term and long term requirements, is needed. Today, unfortunately, the weakest part of the office design process is the passing of information from user to designer: improvements in office design must come from better use of information.

4.11 Whoever can best understand short-term individual tenant requirements and is able to abstract from them guidelines for the development and design of long-term office shells will be the most valuable person in the office design process.

Information into policy

4.12 'Programme' is a better term than 'brief' because it catches something of the experimental aspect and transience of policy making. 'Brief' is too final, too legal, too much a set of fixed instructions which bind the client and so prevent the architect from understanding what the client really needs or will need.

4.13 It seems inevitable that the more seriously the architect takes user requirements, the more the client will include him in the decision making process. Not only ought he to be near the client as the latter makes decisions, in order to understand their consequences, but the client too needs to be near the architect so that he can digest and really use what the architect offers.

4.14 User requirements are data. The problem is to translate them into policy which both client and designer understand.

The members of the team

4.15 Of course, this method of work and construction means going beyond the service envisaged in the RIBA Conditions of engagement. The method involves unusual juxtapositions of talents—architects working with managers, office managers working with interior designers;

developers with market researchers, space planners with cost accountants. Some of these relationships will be temporary; others will be long term. Some contributions to the total service will be independent of all the others. Some architectural firms will be able to provide a great many of the skills required; others may concentrate on one area alone.

5 The future

5.01 Both architects and clients have a lot to learn from each other. This book contributes to the learning process, firstly by providing some basic facts which will be useful to all parties. Secondly it contributes by looking at office buildings in the light of the concept of *Shell and scenery*, thus distinguishing long and short term design decisions which must coexist but which involve clients and architect in different degrees at different times. Thirdly, it contributes by encouraging architects and clients to be more flexible in their roles in the *process* of designing and planning office space. All parties involved should realise that planning office space is too complex a process to be dealt with satisfactorily by traditional professional procedures.

Office design is prototypical of the future of a great part of all building design. What makes it potentially so rich an example is the close relationship between the workplace and the worker and between the whole stock of space and the user organisation. Feedback from the users in these circumstances ought to be very powerful.

If this feedback is exploited, we may expect in the next decade more important innovation to emerge than in the previous ten years. Rather than the arid confrontation between cellular and open planning, there may be:
- a far wider range of types of office space;
- a greater variety of interior layout;
- more flexible and versatile furniture systems;
- a clearer distinction between shorter and longer term elements in office design;

Above all, we can probably expect a blurring of the boundaries between office space and other building types such as factories, shops, health centres. One consequence of greater precision in understanding and designing for short term needs is that the capacity of long term building shells is likely to be expanded greatly. There is no reason why this flexibility should be limited only to office use. This handbook on the planning of office space establishes the principles which will allow these changes to take place.

Reference

1 WEEKS, J. Indeterminate architecture. Transactions of the Bartlett Society 1963-64 vol 2.

Section 1: Planning office space

Two decades of continuous development

A major idea of this book is the separation of the design of the building shell from the design of the office interior—the scenery. In this review of recent developments the EDITORS examine the shell and scenery concept as well as other important ideas—generic types of space and scenery, the impact of automation on the office, the control of the internal environment, developments in furniture design and how offices relate to their setting.

Shell

1.1 Nature of the shell

The shell is all that is provided for the duration of the life of the building: the structure, the envelope and the basic services.

Empty shell

Shell with scenery

1.2 Range of space sizes

Although deep space is now commonly provided in both the UK and the rest of Europe, the important fact is that there now exists a range of space sizes.

Orenstein—Koppel, Dortmund

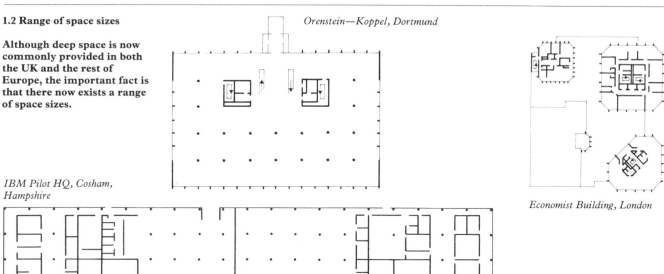

IBM Pilot HQ, Cosham, Hampshire

Economist Building, London

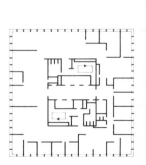

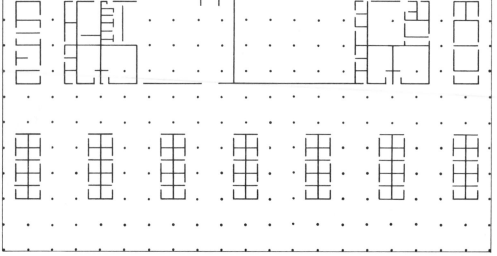

P & O, London

1.3 Planform: location of static elements

It is now realised more clearly that the shape of the envelope, the position of columns and cores not only affects the wall-to-floor ratio but also, more important, how useful the office space will be to the tenants throughout the life of the building.

CIS, Manchester

Europa House, Stockport

Eros House, London

One Charles Center, Baltimore, USA

Zur Palme, Zurich, Switzerland

Cathays Park, Cardiff

1.4 Continuous space

Recently some non-rectilinear plan forms have been designed. The notion of space continuous in section as well as in plan is being explored.

Burroughs Wellcome, N. Carolina, USA

Centraal Beheer, Apeldoorn, Netherlands

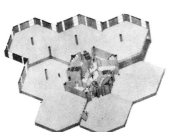

New town hall, Reading

1.5 Reversible space

The notion that the shell
defines the limits of utility of
the office space enclosed is
elaborated in the remainder
of the book. Space capable of
several uses is called
reversible space. In the UK it
is felt that this concept is
constraining. More liberating
is the intention to design
shells in such a way that they
enclose a range of spaces each
of which is capable of several
uses.

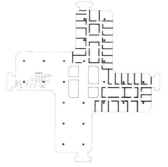

City Hall, Brunswick

Scenery

2.1 Nature of scenery

Scenery has a much shorter
life than the shell. Its role is to
take up the tolerance between
the precise needs of the tenants
and the loose fit of the
building shell.

John Hancock Center, Chicago

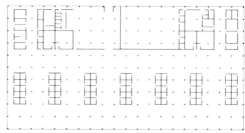

IBM Pilot HQ, Cosham, Hampshire

2.2 Scenery divides

Screens and furniture are
now used to divide and define
space. They have taken over
from the fixed walls of earlier
days as well as from the
demountable partition of the
50s and early 60s.

Open scenery (far left)
Scenery as subdivision (left)

2.3 Generic forms of scenery

There are several patterns of
layout current in office design
today of which the most
common are cellular, open-
plan and Bürolandschaft.
There are variants on each
but these three are the basic
choices available to
architects. It is the architect's
task to choose the most
suitable form; and certainly
he must not get bogged down
in the over-simple 'closed'
versus 'open' arguments of
the early '60s.

Cellular

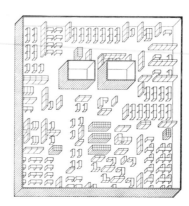

Open plan

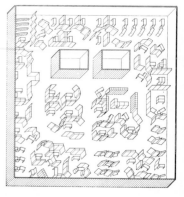

Landscaped

2.4 Quality of scenery

Differences in the quality of scenery usually result from the image the firm wishes to present to its employees and to the outside world. New types of designer have emerged and they have taken over some parts of the architect's role. They specialise to cope with the demands of increasingly specialised buildings. In office design the specialist is the space planning firm which will design, programme and manage a stock of office space.

'Luxurious'

'High style'

'Clerical'

Automation

3.1 Elimination of routine tasks

Some tasks have disappeared, some changed, and some new ones have been substituted, such as data preparation. The gradual change has had two effects: companies have: 1 modified their organisation structure; 2 considered what to do with excessively deep space when the organisations may eventually be just managers and machines.
The telephone and Telex are now only part of the arsenal of communications devices available.
Computers and their associated activities need no longer be physically associated with the headquarters of the firm; decentralisation is increasing.

Post Office Confravision Studio, London

Bell System—Picturephone

Office environment

4.1 Rising standards

In the last decade office workers have come to expect higher and higher standards of illumination and thermal comfort. The developers have been able to provide them because of the greater sophistication of services technology.
A greater degree of control is possible today than was the case 10 years ago. In practice this means centralised control with every worker having to accept an optimum level of environment. Workers of course have to sacrifice the individual control they had before (adjusting the windows and the local lighting).

Lower standards

Landscaped, highly serviced

4.2 Reaction from centralised control

There is a growing reaction against centralised control and in favour of giving back to the office worker the opportunity to manipulate his own workplace environment.

Centraal Beheer, Apeldoorn, Netherlands

4.3 Servicing the work station

Up to 10 years ago, work stations were fed from the building perimeter for power, telephone and (often) heating and ventilation. But now, even in narrow buildings, services are distributed from floors or ceilings. Not only does this mean (potentially) more flexible space but it has also led to the general acceptance of tracked power, lighting and telephone systems, suspended floors, and, more important, to general acceptance of the principle of the floor sandwich.

'Perimeter dependence'

'Ceiling servicing'

'Just field telephones'

4.4 Integrated environmental design

Integrated environmental design (IED) is perhaps the most debated issue in the field of environmental control. The argument is whether the attempt to balance heating and lighting etc in an integrated package leads to unintended rigidities in planning. There are several recent office buildings which embody the principles of IED.

'Environment' UK style

Avonbank, SWEB

'Environment' US style

Europa House, Stockport

Furniture

5.1 Office furniture

Office furniture has changed
dramatically; the impetus for
change has come largely from
planning furniture layouts in
deep office space.
Increasingly, furniture, not
walls, now divides spaces.

Modulo 3

Herman Miller Action Office

Hille

Westinghouse

Multi-national firms

**6.1 Multi-nationals are
invariably in the vanguard of
the field of office design
because they can exercise an
almost renaissance kind of
patronage and compete for
the services of top designers.**

IBM, Havant, UK

IBM, New York

IBM, Florida, US

IBM, Cosham, UK

'Not a setting but an environment'

Office in its setting

7.1 Urban development

City centres have continued to be developed at greater and greater densities.

Cité de la Défense, Paris

City Centre, Atlanta, US

John Hancock Center, Chicago

Model Meteor Center, Toronto

7.2 Urban mixed development

One of the most obvious facets of urban change has been the emergence of mixed developments; the office content is almost always the commercial generator with shops, hotels and now even theatres linked to it.

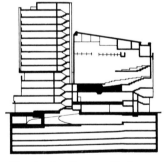

New London Centre, with theatre

Offices over department store, Southend-on-Sea

7.3 Dispersal

Probably the most important trend in office location has been the shift to suburban areas. The factors have been pressures of rents, travel, recruitment, automation etc, as well as those of a political nature such as office development permits.

Station Area, New Malden, Surrey

7.4 Offices in the country

Often firms leapfrog the suburbs to go into the country; the 'office park' has emerged.

Bell Telephones, US   *Heinz, UK*

7.5 Change of use

In the UK more and more buildings originally designed for other uses have now been taken over for office functions; it is commonplace to find offices in warehouses and town houses for example. This has happened chiefly because it is cheaper to convert, but also, in the case of warehouses, because offices now easily accept 'deep space'.

BSD office, San Francisco : warehouse into new office

7.6 The developer

The developer has appeared and grown from strength to strength as he has satisfied the ever-rising demand for office space through the sixties and early seventies. Economic and social factors have now reduced both demand and the importance of his role.

Bootle, Merseyside

Section 1 : Planning office space

Some notes on an activity

These notes by STEPHEN MULLIN emphasise the major themes of this book by looking backwards at the history of office work. He argues that what we now call office work was carried out for centuries in buildings such as cathedrals which we do not normally associate with 'offices'. The invention of the office building is relatively recent and since the patterns of office work are always changing we may well have designed long life buildings too precisely to a short term view of this activity.

1 The word 'office'

1.01 It is only comparatively recently that we have come to associate the word 'office' with a physical location or building type. The Foreign Office and the Holy Office represent tasks, duties, places of authority, greater than the men who perform that office, and which may or may not require some sort of physical framework for their function. We refer to 'the last offices' performed for the dead. We speak of the 'office of the planner' and by that we do not necessarily mean the local planning office as an actual physical entity, but, more often, the duties and functions of the planner. And when we ask an official to 'use his good offices' on our behalf, we are not suggesting that he maximises the use of a particularly well-designed building shell, but rather that he employs his authority to our benefit.

1.02 Indeed, the difficulties of defining the office as a building type are matched only by the ease with which we can identify the function of an office. The concept of the office can be seen as one of the most consistent threads in any culture, for systems of government and manufacture may change beyond recognition, but in any organisation of human beings which extends beyond the smallest group, the word office, and the idea it represents, emerge as stable components of language. The concept may be wholly abstract: in German for example, an office, 'ein Amt', means, literally, 'a vacancy'—a slot, that is, to be filled in the ordered hierarchy of society. Even in this general sense, we can define fairly closely the function of the office. It will not be concerned with the immediate handling of goods or people in physical terms; it will, however, be concerned with their organisation and movement at a distance. Its functions are those of regulation and control, and the precise definition of any particular office rests with whatever is so regulated. Similarly, the demands it makes on any building shell will be governed by the scale and complexity of the organisation it controls, the type of communication, whether physical or non-physical, employed in such control, and the means by which the information so transmitted is assembled, monitored, stored, and accessed.

1.03 Clearly, the smaller the scale of activity, and the more rudimentary the means of communication employed, the less obvious the demands upon buildings as such will be. But the demands will be there and the physical offices will exist. We commonly assume, for example, that the emergence of the large, identifiable office building form dates, at the earliest, from the 19th century. Yet we ignore the existence, all over the western world, of some of the largest open-plan office buildings ever constructed—the cathedrals.

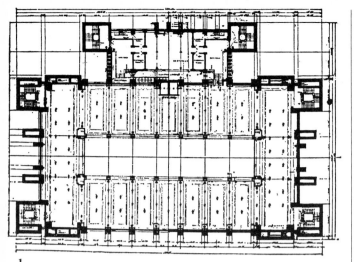

Even if we forget, for a moment, the crowds of small businessmen which thronged the aisles of mediaeval cathedrals, the central activities carried on there were definitely those of an office. The function of the mediaeval Church could fairly be said to encompass the operation of a large celestial telephone exchange coupled with the co-ordination of an enormous goods inward, filing and despatch accounts department. With head offices in every major city and town, and branch offices in the smallest community, the Catholic Church in its heyday formed an international cartel before which present-day trans-national giants pale into insignificance. Seen as a share battle, the Thirty Years War makes the takeover bids of today seem positively trifling. So, though Cowan[1] is correct in pointing out that 'the affairs of the Church could be administered from the cathedral chapter house', his inference, that 'the place of the office was very small indeed' in the mediaeval context, is faulty. Like many others, he has mistaken the building for the function. Indeed, the survival of the aisled form of the cathedral in various guises shows that we have a respectable analogy on our hands. The concept of the central large-span open space 1, clerestory lit, and serving generalised 'clerking' functions, with subsidiary, specialised uses strung along the aisles 2 reappears in the archetypal form of Wright's Larkin Building of 1896, and in a whole host of the other American, British and German hall-type solutions, such as Otto Wagner's Vienna Post Office Savings Bank or the main office building at Port Sunlight (discussed on pages 204–08). It is not entirely fanciful to equate the use of the confessional with a slightly sticky interview with a Branch Manager answerable directly to Head Office.

1.04 In fact, banking and the associated activities of the money market formed one of the earliest secular uses attracted to the shelter of large scale ecclesiastical buildings.

One of the most dramatically documented planning enforcements against illegal change of use occured some 2000 years ago with the expulsion of the money-changers from the Temple at Jerusalem. The reasons for attraction to such a location are obvious. Financial transactions of some complexity can easily be carried out by one person, with the aid of a pad, ledger or tablet to record dealings, and little else.

Provided the structure of society is sufficiently advanced to avoid the need for the actual handling of cash, the only other requirements are some form of physical shelter, proximity to similar office activities, and a known location for such dealings to take place. The pre-Reformation Cathedral or Abbey church possessed all such attributes. It was likely to be a centre for the ambient literate population of the city. It already operated a thriving business in shares in the hereafter through the sale of indulgences and masses for the dead. And it provided an enormous daily catchment area of population. In short, it could be seen as a modern Central Business District in embryo. An illuminating account of the evolution of such activities is given by Stow (1598) in his description of Old St Paul's in the City of London. Originally, he says, the old London Stone (providing location but not shelter) was 'said to be set for the tendering and making of payment by debtors to their creditors set their appointed days and times, till of later times payments were more usually made at the font in Poules Church, and now most commonly at the Royal

1 *Typical working floor, Larkin Building, 1904 (F. Lloyd Wright*
2 *Working Gallery, Larkin Building*
3 *Completely glass-covered vault, Post Office, Vienna, 1904 (Otto Wagner)*
4 *Galleries around court, Coal Exchange, 1846 (J. H. Bunning)*

5

6

7

Exchange . . .'[2]. Thus, the growing complexity of financial activity necessitated the construction of a specialised building—Gresham's Exchange of 1571.

The exchanges
1.05 Though burnt down in 1666, Jerman's subsequent rebuilding preserved the plan-form of the original—an open court (corresponding to the nave of St Paul's) surrounded by cloisters (or aisles). A further fire in 1828 allowed Tite to replace the missing central vault. By then, greater specialisation had produced the Corn Exchange of 1750 and the Stock Exchange of 1802. The Coal and Wool Exchanges followed in 1849 and 1874. Yet it is significant that each of these, in essence, preserved the basilica plan with slight modifications. Where the basic pattern of office activity retains much the same scale, and where the original requirements of physical proximity to similar businesses and good communications alter little, then there would seem little incentive for the building form to alter either.

2 The professions and trade
The law
2.01 We can see a similar pattern at work in the evolution of the English legal system. The office of government was centred around Westminster Palace. The process of direct petition to the Crown for the redress of grievances made Westminster Great Hall an ideal venue for the growing legal trade which used the large enclosure as a ready-made space for carrying on the business of advocacy. In time, the legal functions of the Palace of Westminster expanded by a process of accretion, gathering up new and progressively specialised spaces to match the demands made by new functions. By 1824, Soane had rebuilt the seven courts of law **5** around Westminster Hall; yet by 1832 proposals were already in hand for the bodily removal of the courts from Westminster. It seems that the introduction of specialised office spaces creates its own impetus for renewal: the appetite for 'close-fit' is merely quickened by its immediate appeasement.
2.02 Yet, when the Law Courts finally moved to the Strand in the 1880s, George Edward Street's building remained remarkably faithful to the original Westminster context: an enormous vaulted central hall **6** surrounded by specialist court and office areas. Nor is Street's design a special case. Of the 11 architects chosen to submit designs for the Law Courts competition of 1866, all save a few fixed on this basic plan-form as a generator for their designs: Waterhouse's in particular, proposed halls of even greater grandeur than Street's executed design. Summerson has pointed out that Waterhouse's design 'with its semi-circular roof of iron and glass . . . reminds one a little of the Crystal Palace but even more of the Galleria Vittorio Emmanuele **7** at Milan, just then begun[3]. This is significant. The secular tradition of the large-span market space runs parallel with the use of ecclesiastical buildings for office purposes. The 'factory floor' of the cathedral can be compared directly with the large clear span spaces of the Flemish cloth halls, and indeed with the provincial corn exchanges of 19th-century England.

The office—and other activities
2.03 The physical necessity—or convenience—of proximity of office functions to the process of manufacture, display or storage of goods has meant that these functions have been subject to considerable confusion right up to the

5 *Court of Chancery, Palace of Westminster, 1824 (Sir John Soane)*
6 *Central Hall, Law*
Courts, 1874 (G. E. Street)
7 *Galleria Vittorio Emmanuele, 1865 (G. Mengoni)*

present day, with 'factory', 'shop' and 'office' often used as synonyms for a generalised type of industrial activity. At the one extreme, we have the notorious case of the post-war Board of Trade classification of office functions as 'industrial'—a piece of muddle-headed thinking which effectively masked the London office-building boom of the late '50s.

At the other, consider our use of the words work*shop* or—disparagingly, as architects—plan *factory*.

Perhaps this is pedantry. After all, we all know that 'industrial unrest on the shop floor' is probably not taking place in the premises of a small tailoring establishment in the Burlington Arcade, and that a 'closed shop' does not necessarily describe a bolted grocer's door. But words are powerful and sometimes misleading instruments. Take 'education', for example. We commonly think of teaching taking place only in recognisable school buildings. After all, we have examples of such purpose-built enclosures of far earlier age than 'office' buildings. Yet in the 16th and 17th centuries the local church commonly provided the only school building available for a small parish. Seaborne tells us that 'the school building at Medborne, Leicestershire met in the parish church from at least the middle of the seventeenth century until 1868'.

2.04 It may be argued that resemblances between educational and 'office' usage are only coincidental, made necessary by force of circumstance. I do not think this to be the case. It can certainly be argued that one of the major functions of the large offices of the 19th century was that of education. In the absence of separate training establishments the office, of necessity, was forced to train its junior staff on the spot. Writing in 1924, Robert Atkinson, the then Director of Education at the Architectural Association, recalled that 'in the days of Soane, Street, and Scott . . . the young architect received his training wholly within the orbit of the office of his principal, whose conduct of business was sufficiently leisurely to allow him time to devote to the instruction of the pupils. In the absence of other opportunities, the office provided in itself a small art school . . .'[4].

2.05 On the other side of the coin, we find the Clarendon Commission of 1864 on the English public schools raising an interesting argument against the increasing trend towards specialised and differentiated spaces in educational buildings. 'It is necessary,' the commission pointed out, 'at the Bar and in other careers of life, and in the Houses of Parliament, that much mental work should be done of all kinds, amidst many outward causes of distraction. It would be a matter of regret if public school life should in any way disqualify boys for the conditions under which they must do their work as men'[5]. The fact that politics and the law are specifically mentioned rather than the offices of 'trade' is significant. By the late 19th century, the buildings we think of as the classic office type'—banking, insurance and pension fund buildings which had made a dramatic appearance in America and Europe in the 1830s—were housing functions which the 18th century would not have been recognised, except in part, as those of an office.

3 The images adopted

3.01 With the introduction of the typewriter in the 1870s the major functions of these buildings were those of machine hall, (mechanised clerking) and training college. There is a good case for seeing the 'classic' office building

8

9

10

11

8 *Courtyard, Somerset House, 1776 (Sir William Chambers)*
9 *Courtyard, Uffizi Palace,*
1560 (Giorgio Vasari)
10 *Post-war Lessor Scheme*
11 *The Four Seasons, 1958 (Philip Johnson)*

as an atypical aberration enshrining certain stages of progress in data processing and communications. This would only be of passing interest if it were not for the fact that our present passion for naming, defining and typing particular building forms has led us to apply entirely different performance standards to buildings carrying out very similar functions.

3.02 In fact, the luxuriant 'climax growth' of the 19th century office form has obscured several equally important strands of development in the office function, whose example may perhaps be more pertinent to our own problems today. It is common, for instance, to view the development of Government office buildings as occuring at a comparatively late date. Cowan, for instance, notes that 'even as late as 1793 the Treasury employed only thirty-seven people'[1]. And, indeed, the construction of Somerset House in 1780 still allowed most of the principal offices of the British Government to be united under one roof.

The palace

3.03 To think of Somerset House as a modern prototype is to miss the essential point that its form—it had salons and galleries for learned institutions as well as spaces for the more humdrum activities of the tax office—was a reworking of the Renaissance palace plan. The machinery and office of government had developed within and from the royal palaces of Europe: the Uffizi Palace **9** in Florence of 1558 was named after its principal function. Buildings such as Somerset House and, later, the London Foreign Office and the Quai D'Orsay in Paris rework, on a grand scale, the format of an essentially domestic building. Indeed, Summerson remarks that in the late 18th century, 'the normal habitat for a government department was an ordinary London house. The ordinary house, multiplied, disciplined and enriched, is the basis of Chambers's masterpiece'[6].

The house

3.04 It was not only in government that 'house' could be synonymous with 'office'. The East India Company occupied a private house from 1600 to 1726. Lloyds only ceased to be 'Lloyd's Coffee House' in 1777 when it took up quarters in the Royal Exchange. Indeed, from 1651, when the first City of London 'coffee-house' opened in Cornhill, to the end of the 18th century these particular institutions formed the backbone of much of the City's office function. Between the private houses of the merchants, the coffee-houses, and the new exchanges, the invisible web of commerce spread in an orderly and efficient network.

3.05 In times of particular stress any overload could be taken up by the surrounding streets. During the South Sea Bubble of 1720, for example, 'Change Alley was more like a fair crowded with people, than a mart of exchange, as were all the avenues leading to it; and there was a little hump-backed man, who, seeing this mania, made his fortune by lending his back, as a desk to make transfers on, to those who could not afford time to run to the coffee-houses'[7].

3.06 In just the same way, the offices of the legal profession developed with the domestic 'chambers' of the Inns of Court and the Temple. When the purpose-built small office suites of the mid-19th century began to appear, they were most often called 'chambers'; in the same way that the idea of sharing a single building with other owners of apartments was made palatable to the Victorians by calling it a 'mansion'[8].

No such snobbery appears to have affected the United States, where the use of the word 'building' for a multiple letting of office space appears to have been universal from the 1860s onward.

The three forms, basilica, palace, house, confused

3.07 There is little real difference, except in terms of scale and servicing, between late 19th century purpose-built buildings (four floors of two offices each, lavatory on the second floor and lavatories and closets in the basement) and the European and American office blocks of the 1920s and 1930s, serving new specialised activities such as advertising. Their individual format still springs from the house tradition—the third part of the group: cathedral—palace—house. It may be argued that there is little point in separating these three strands of development, now that they appear to have become so closely intertwined. But there are certain signs that an unquestioning acceptance of the homogeneity of 'the office' has already cost us dear. There is one comparatively recent example of a confusion of the ideas behind these three forms. The post-war British Government launched the £7½ million Lessor scheme **10** in an attempt to solve its London office space problems through private enterprise. The developers were property speculators used to building commercial offices on 'domestic' principles; the 'clients' were government departments organised in 'palace' hierarchy; and the question of which department should inhabit which building was left open until their completion—which implied a 'forum/basilica' solution. The result, by 1950, was 13 buildings and 1 320 000 square feet of inefficient, ill-organised, awkwardly partitioned-off floorspace, satisfying no known functional criteria save the rudimentary one of basic shelter.

'Office', 'school' and 'home'

3.08 Luckily in the post-war school and hospital rebuilding programmes, recognition of the changing requirements of the functions spurred a fruitful and far-reaching research and development programme. The debacle of the Lessor scheme, in spite of the parliamentary furore it aroused at the time, seems largely forgotten today—at the very time when its lessons ought to be most urgently heeded in other fields. It is becoming much too easily accepted that the present format of schools is ideal, and ought to be repeated indefinitely. Yet it is precisely at the point at which a particular specialised building form appears to have crystallised into a steady state that we ought to be on our guard. For the differences between such building types are more apparent than real. The clue to what has happened is that there has been a game of leapfrog between these types as each in turn provides higher and higher performance standards for increasingly similar activities. A personal secretary in a present-day office in London will almost certainly enjoy higher space standards, better furniture and a higher degree of thermal comfort at 'work' than at 'home'. Her boss may leave an office heated at 75°F to attend a Parent Teacher's Association at his child's school where the ambient temperature may be as low as 60° or even 55° if the meeting is held in the school hall. Meanwhile, his child may be doing homework in a bedroom which has furniture chosen from the same catalogue that supplied the father's office. It will be luck which decides whether the bedroom is unheated (local authority cost yardstick standard); heated to 60° (Parker-Morris standard); or to 65° (high-grade private housing standard). The father's 'office' may be no more than a thin 'shell' of space surrounding a large computer installation and the only reason why he may need to be in any physical proximity to this installation is that his working environment provides a buffer airlock to the specialised air-conditioning of the central data-bank. Take all these factors together and the utility of the words 'house', 'school' and 'office' to denote separate concepts becomes increasingly suspect.

In such a context, it might at first seem that any concentration on the pre-19th century office can be of little value today. After all, the exponential growth of office activity, caused by the rapid development of physical communication, allows us to equate the last century of construction with the two preceding millenia. But, by the same token, we forget that the development of non-physical forms of communication is already having as drastic an effect on our conception of office location.

3.09 The giant leap from the essentially man-to-man relationship of the late 19th century office to the swollen clerical hierarchies which the typewriter, postal system telegraph and telephone made possible, and the steam and internal combustion engines made necessary, is eclipsed by the potential of cybernetics and audio-visual communication. If, as seems likely, person-to-person contact is about to re-assume an increasingly dominant role in the office function, then the time has come to disentangle the strands once more, and for that the pre-industrial office may have as much to teach us by way of analogy as the more familiar buildings of the 19th and 20th centuries.

4 Where now?

4.01 Certainly, our focus is at present far too close. How far removed, after all is Lloyd's Coffee House from the tables of the Mirabelle or the Four Seasons **11**? Is the departure lounge of a large international airport so dissimilar as might appear from the aisles of Old St Pauls? Can we really say that the businessman radio-phoning his secretary from his seat in the Metroliner is such a novel phenomenon; or does he not begin to merge with the figure of Brunel carrying his portable surveyor's office on horseback along the route of the future Great Western Railway, or indeed with that of the 'little hunch-backed man' who made such a killing in Change Alley? For the office function, as for all others, the past still contains a wealth of possible futures.

References

1 COWAN, P. and others. The office: a facet of urban growth, London, 1969, Heinemann, p25 [32] £3·15
2 STOW, J. A survey of London. London, 1960, Everyman Edition Dent, p202 [052] £1·50
3 SUMMERSON, J. Victorian architecture: four studies in evaluation. London, 1970, Columbia, p112 [Ac18]
4 ATKINSON, R. Introductory essay. A book of design by senior students of the Architectural Association School. London, 1924, Benn, p4 [Ano] o/p
5 HMSO Report of Her Majesty's Commissioners. London, 1864, HMSO, vol 1, p287 [71]
6 SUMMERSON, J. Architecture in Britain: 1530-1830. London, 1970, Penguin, p420 [9(Ad41)] £7·50
7 BRAYLEY, E. W. The beauties of England and Wales. London, 1810, vol X, part 1, p657 [9(Ad41)]

Brayley quotes 'another' (unidentified) writer. He earlier (p656) notes that 'Persons of quality of both sexes, were deeply engaged' in various South Sea and other Bubbles 'avarice prevailing at this time over all considerations of either dignity or equity; the Gentleman coming to Taverns and Coffee-houses to meet their Brokers, and the Ladies to the shops of Milliners and Haberdashers for the same ends.'
8 For example, Oriel Chambers, Liverpool and Queen Anne's Mansions, London. It is still quite customary for the word 'house' to be used in the description of large British office blocks (eg Bucklersbury House, London). The introduction of the tower block to Britain marked a change-over in nomenclature (eg the Shell and P & O Building, London, or the CWS Buildings, Manchester) which presumably follows the US example through the associational image of the building form.

Section 2: The office shell

The custom-designed office building

Most organisations aspire to be in a building designed specifically for their needs and reflecting how the company wishes to be seen. In reality, many head offices are accommodated in speculative office buildings and the block is then given the company's name—Castrol House, for instance. This study by JOHN WORTHINGTON examines in detail two such buildings—Radiation House and the Co-operative Insurance Society building, both of which were built about 10 years ago. The major points are: how aspects of the brief and the management's preferences affected the form of the buildings and how well the building has been able to serve the company when the latter has changed its organisation and methods.
The conclusions underline the ideas put forward in this book: the more precisely building shells are designed to meet an organisation's immediate needs, the less easy it will be to adapt it for changed work methods. When the design of 'shell' and 'scenery' are treated as part of the same problem, the opportunities for future change are much reduced.

1 Custom design

1.01 When an organisation develops an office to occupy itself (rather than as a speculative venture to be rented to other organisations) it is called a *custom-designed building*. As a half-way situation a property company may develop a building as a speculative venture but bring in a major tenant at the design stage, so allowing the tenant to gain some of the benefits of a custom-designed building **2** (eg, Castrol House **4**). For the firm that decides to build for itself there are these advantages:

1 The possible location choices are wider.

2 It can build-in facilities, either recreational amenities to attract staff or special equipment to serve its special needs.

3 It can develop a building which offers a range of space types relevant to its pattern of work at the design stage and in the future. Many organisations with large departments for clerical work have difficulty in finding speculative blocks which will give 'open-plan' spaces.

4 It can create a distinctive image and yet not hamper its flexibility **6**. The management also has the chance to reconsider its structure and make changes that can be reflected in the form of the new building.

1.02 A company can benefit in many ways by building for itself, but there are possible drawbacks:

1 The form of the building can be too closely designed to fit the organisation's form at the time of design with the result that any major organisational changes may be severely restricted by the building's form **5**. Thus the shell can have built into it many detailed aspects of a firm's present and past requirements so freezing an existing situation.

2 The building can become a monument to particular personalities and attitudes that exist at the design time so that personal styles of management may be built into the form of the building.

1

2

4

5

3

1 *The Shell Centre, London—architect Howard Robertson. Most organisations aspire to be in premises which reflect how the company wishes to be seen.*
2 *New Scotland Yard, London—architects Chapman Taylor & Partners. The Metropolitan Police has adapted a speculative office block to its specialised requirements.*
3 *Hertfordshire Police Force hq—county architect Geoffrey C. Fardell. The organisation can build into custom-designed office any facilities it may require. The HQ houses offices and communications requirements.*
4 *Castrol House, London—architects Gollins, Melvin, Ward & Partners.*
5 *Polytechnic of Central London school of building—GLC architects department. Each block specifically houses a department of the school, so that major changes in the organisation of the school may be severely restricted.*

2 Radiation House, Neasden

2.01 Client Radiation group of companies.
Architect Dennis E. Pugh Associates.
Description of building Thirteen-storey tower block with a central core joined to the existing offices and warehouses by a two-storey block **6**. Each floor is approximately 275 m² with the core as 20 per cent of the area. The average depth from the perimeter to the core is 5 m.
Building costs £250 000.
Building conceived November 1958.
Architect appointed March 1959.
Construction begun November 1959.
Building occupied May 1961.

The decision to build

2.02 The building was originally commissioned by Ascot Gas Water Heaters Limited and Parnall (Yate) Limited who owned the site, which already housed their offices, factory and warehousing. Soon after inception of the project the Parnall Group were taken into the Radiation group of companies, which used the office space to house some of its separate selling companies.

The design process

2.03 From the beginning the client and his architect were determined to create:

1 Independent office space for the different companies in the group; each company had its own separate management, with its own typing pool, filing, storage and communications equipment.

2 A building which embodied the image of the Radiation group and would also act as a landmark in an otherwise uninspiring area.

2.04 Dennis Pugh, the architect, felt the main aims must be: to create a landmark for the Radiation group; to leave the site as clear as possible to allow for future expansion of the warehousing; to produce a visual impact on what, at the time, was a dreary route through factory backlands. The client did not like that solution for he was concerned about people walking past other companies' offices; neither did the massing meet the architect's desire for a tall landmark on that site. The final design was for a thirteen-storey tower block, each floor size being based on the floor area required by a single company. A typical tower floor was very precisely tailored to the concept of independent companies,

each with its own management. Four individual offices of approximately 15·5 m² for executives were ranged along the north side; the other three sides were arranged for approximately 21 personnel and their filing in an open layout.

2.05 In the original plans, the ground and first floor were given over to facilities for all the companies—reception, reproduction, mail and telephone exchange. The second to eleventh floors each housed a separate company or department, the twelfth floor was reserved for main board directors and the thirteenth for a board room and executive dining room **7a**. By the time the block was occupied, half the second floor had been taken over for personnel, and some of the first floor to allow for a new export section **7b**. In 1968, the group was taken over by Tube Investments bringing more directors and new companies into the group. Ascot Sales, which began on the seventh floor of the new building, moved to another floor, then moved across to the old offices, and is now in Birmingham as part of a new heating conglomerate New World (Gas Heating) Ltd **7c**. Other firms within the group have developed with a different relationship of executives to clerical staff so that a firm on one floor has had to use offices on other floors for its managers, thus splitting up its manpower **8**.

Conclusions

2.06 The company secretary, R. S. Martin, said that the floor area of each floor was influenced by site and architectural requirements. With the choice of a tower block and relatively small areas on each floor:

1 The proportion of usable office space to circulation on each floor is abnormally low **9**.

2 There are considerable limitations on the way that the space can be organised and allocated. Mr Martin feels that even when he has spare space on a floor it is often difficult to re-allocate it, owing to the vertical separation of sections within the same company.

Dennis Pugh achieved his objective of creating a good-looking building which contributed to its surroundings (the building was acclaimed in the architectural press at the

6 Radiation House, London—architects Dennis E. Pugh Associates. The site for Radiation House adjoins the company's water heater factory on the North Circular road.

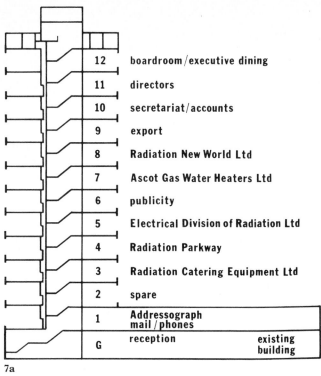

	12	boardroom/executive dining
	11	directors
	10	secretariat/accounts
	9	export
	8	Radiation New World Ltd
	7	Ascot Gas Water Heaters Ltd
	6	publicity
	5	Electrical Division of Radiation Ltd
	4	Radiation Parkway
	3	Radiation Catering Equipment Ltd
	2	spare
	1	Addressograph mail/phones
	G	reception existing building

7a

	12	boardroom/executive dining
	11	directors
	10	directors/company secretary
	9	divisional chief accountant technical development
	8	New World Gas Cookers Ltd
	7	Radiation Creda Catering Eqpt Ltd public relations department
	6	Parkray Ltd/Central Printing Dept
	5	Jackson Electric Ltd Radiation Sunhouse Ltd
	4	Tube Investments Domestic Appl Service
	3	Tube Investments Domestic Appl Service
	2	personnel dept James Gibbons Ltd
	1	Radiation International mail
	G	reception existing Addressograph building

7c

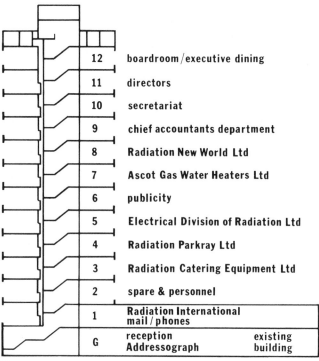

	12	boardroom/executive dining
	11	directors
	10	secretariat
	9	chief accountants department
	8	Radiation New World Ltd
	7	Ascot Gas Water Heaters Ltd
	6	publicity
	5	Electrical Division of Radiation Ltd
	4	Radiation Parkray Ltd
	3	Radiation Catering Equipment Ltd
	2	spare & personnel
	1	Radiation International mail/phones
	G	reception existing Addressograph building

7b

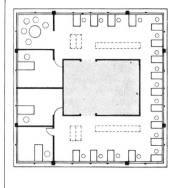

8

7a *Section through building showing location of departments at time of sketch designs.*
b *Section through building showing location of departments at move in May 1961.*
c *Section through building showing location of departments at January 1972.*
8 *Typical floor plan showing layout of desks.*

time). But he may have been too easily influenced by the clear structuring of the group into a number of separate companies which each needed about 230 m² and a constant proportion of managers to staff. The result was a building form closely tailored to a particular organisation form—and inevitably it changed over 10 years **10.**

2.07 The form of organisation that Radiation House was designed to meet is relatively rare. With more usable office space on each floor and a greater depth on the south side from core to perimeter, the problems of allocating space to different companies as they expanded and contracted might have been greatly reduced. In practice, it has been found that the small areas on each floor mean that any spare space is invariably on the wrong floor for the firm or department which requires it and it is difficult to re-deploy staff. The story of Radiation House highlights a classic dichotomy where a sympathetic form for the site conflicts with the requirements for change.

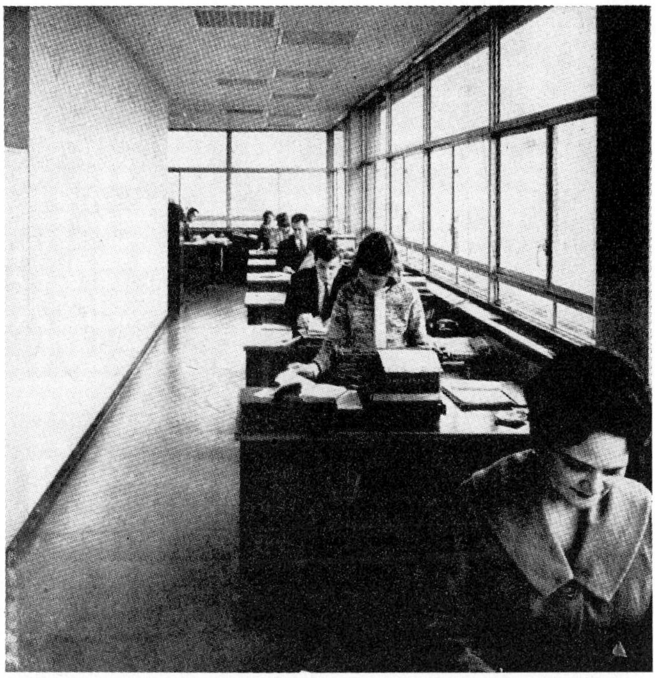

9

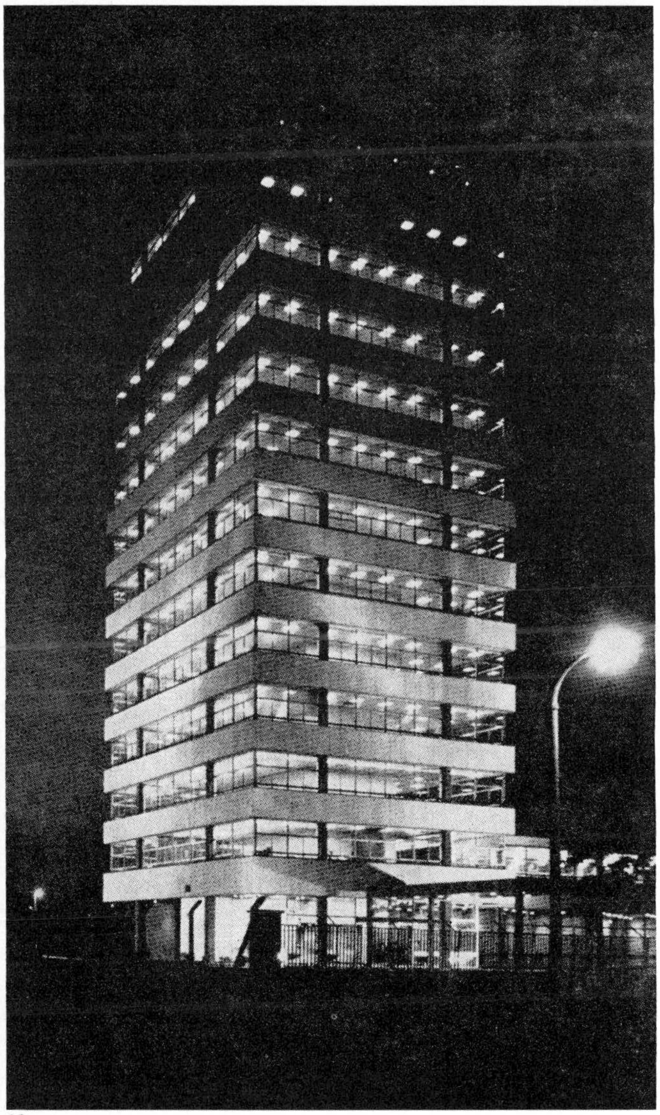

10

9 *General view of Radiation House office space. Narrow width between core and perimeter restricts range of alternative office layouts.*
10 *It was stated at the time of opening the building that because the client firm works in a series of relatively small departmental groups of almost domestic scale, it appeared that the most logical solution was to arrange one department on top of the other.*

3 Co-operative Insurance Society headquarters building, Manchester

3.01 Client Co-operative Insurance Society Limited (CIS).
Architect G. S. Hay, chief architect of Co-operative Wholesale Society (CWS) in association with
Consultants Sir John Burnet, Tait & Partners
Interiors Design Research Unit.
Description of building The building takes the form of a 21-storey tower on a 4-storey podium. Each office floor in the tower is 18 m × 44 m supported by 900 mm square columns on a 7·8 m grid, creating 727 m^2 of space. Each of the podium floors is 75 m × 55 m giving an area of 4125 m^2. The service core is located outside the office tower which offers great flexibility and creates a very favourable percentage of core area to office area **11a, b, c.**
Building costs £3 980 000.
Building conceived 1953 initial discussions with Manchester Corporation.
Beginning of work on site September 1959.
Building occupied October 1962.

The decision to build

3.02 The CIS board of directors decided that a new headquarters building was required to accommodate the 2500 head-office staff (who were dispersed in 10 different buildings throughout Manchester) to ensure that up-to-date methods were used to process their policies and claims. The new building had to be 'a towering advertisement for the prestige and strength of the CIS and the Co-operative movement'. In January 1953, R. Dunnage, the CIS general manager, told his board to begin planning a new head office **12a, b.**
Long negotiations followed with the Manchester Corporation and it was only after four years that permission was obtained to build on the present site. G. S. Hay, the chief architect for CWS in Manchester, was appointed architect for the proposed development, and a brief was worked out for the type of accommodation needed based on a

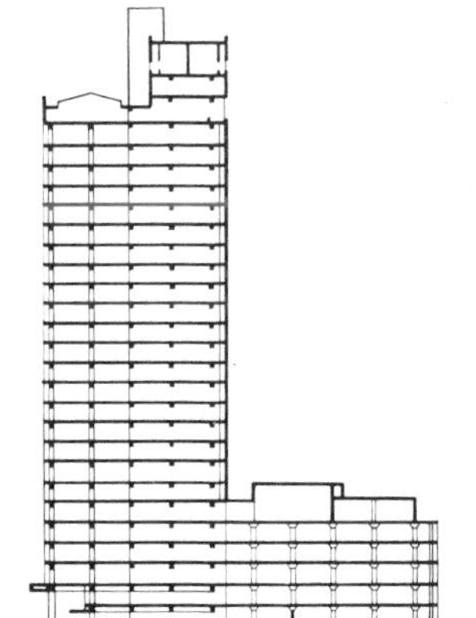

11a

11a, b, c *Plans and section of CIS Building. The building form allows for a combination of deep office space, 75 × 55 m on the podium floors and medium depth office space of 18 × 44 m in the tower block.*

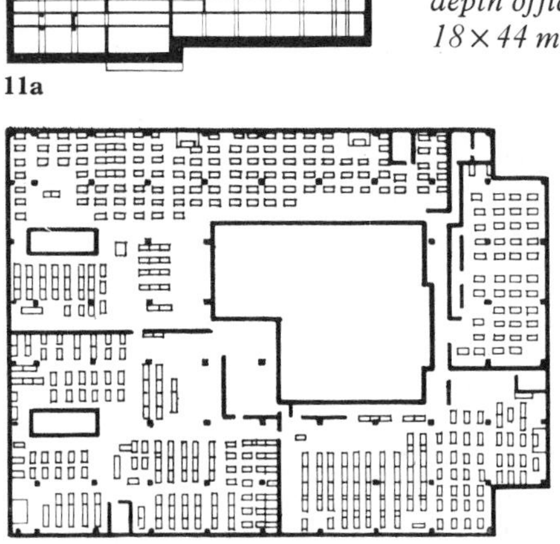

11b

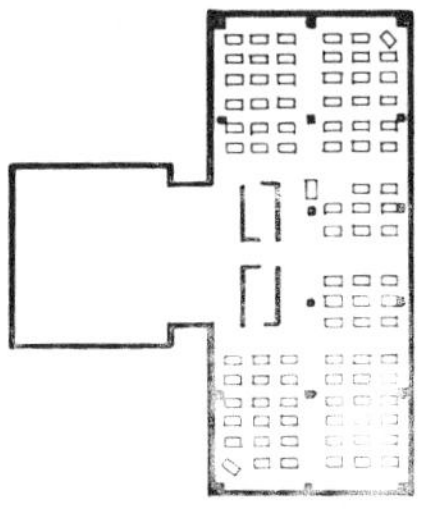

11c

12

13

14

12 *The CIS Building has shown in its 10 years of existence that it has an additional business justification as the visible sign of an active company.*

13 *Desk layout of typical tower floor at the time of move in.*
14 *Desk layout of typical podium floor at the time of move in.*

projection of what would be required in 15 years' time. The general manager summed it up when he said 'It was realised that our new building was likely to be one of the largest and tallest office buildings in the country and would be the subject of much interest and probably criticism. We were anxious that it should be a building of which the CIS in particular, and the Co-operative movement in general, could be proud and which would enhance the society's prestige.'

The design process
3.03 From an early stage, the CIS board had set up a chief office premises sub-committee which, on the appointment of the architect, became the nucleus of the project team. The electrical and mechanical engineer had to become intimately involved with design and construction so that he would know how the building worked when he took up his responsibilities of running it. The project team, after a visit to America to look closely at the Inland Steel building in Chicago, decided to aim for clear open floors unbroken by lift shafts, lavatories, etc, to give maximum flexibility. It was further decided to build with two forms of space:
1 Open-plan office accommodation in the tower **13**.
2 Areas for the machine room in the podium with the large administrative departments who use the computers **14**.

Changes after occupation
3.04 The new CIS building was officially opened on 22 October 1962 and the head office staff and the Manchester branch was moved into the building in September 1962. There were 2575 persons, and space was allocated as follows:
1 The four podium floors were used by the large administrative departments who most used the computers and needed common access to filing.
2 The tower was inhabited by the smaller departments with executives and canteen facilities on the top floors—other restaurants were put in the basement.
3 Space for expansion was spread throughout the building and used for storage.
3.05 Over time, the nature of the work became more mechanised and the demand by the remaining staff for individual offices increased. In 1965–66, the company had a job evaluation survey and head office staff was reduced by 600, the number of grades was reduced and many of the accounting jobs were done by computers. In 1967, the building population had dropped to 1700, with the result that in 1968 it was decided to rent off three floors to the Inland Revenue. But, since 1968, with a greater work load, the population has increased, and the 1972 population was 2164. In the 10 years since building completion the following major changes have occurred **15a, b**:
1 Fewer staff are needed so that it has become possible to lease off space.
2 Work has become more and more mechanised. Since the firm moved in, traditional office machinery has been superseded by automatic data processing and so the original four floors of podium space that were needed for departments with office machinery and access to common filing is now reduced to two floors. Large areas of the podium floors have now been converted for computer suites; in 1970, the company set up its own printing department on one of the podium floors.
3 The grade structure has changed and, with it, the system of space standards. The number of grades has been reduced and the traditional chief clerk's dais has been removed and more people have been appointed at management level so that there are more private offices **17**.
4 New methods of work have created new layouts. At present the o & m department is experimenting with an open-plan layout for the typing pool. Initially, typing was

organised as five separate pools in different parts of the building. In 1963, audio-typing was introduced and it was possible to reduce the typists to three pools. In 1971, the number of typists was decreased to one central pool, which now occupies the whole of one of the tower floors.

5 The desire for cellular offices has grown. In some departments where many staff are entitled to individual offices, the perimeter offices reduce natural light and create air-conditioning difficulties for the open plan areas in the central space.

6 As CIS has sub-let three floors to the Inland Revenue space for expansion and re-organisation is limited; there are small pockets of space left on some floors and other departments use space standards extravagantly, but it would require a major reshuffle to create balanced amounts of space.

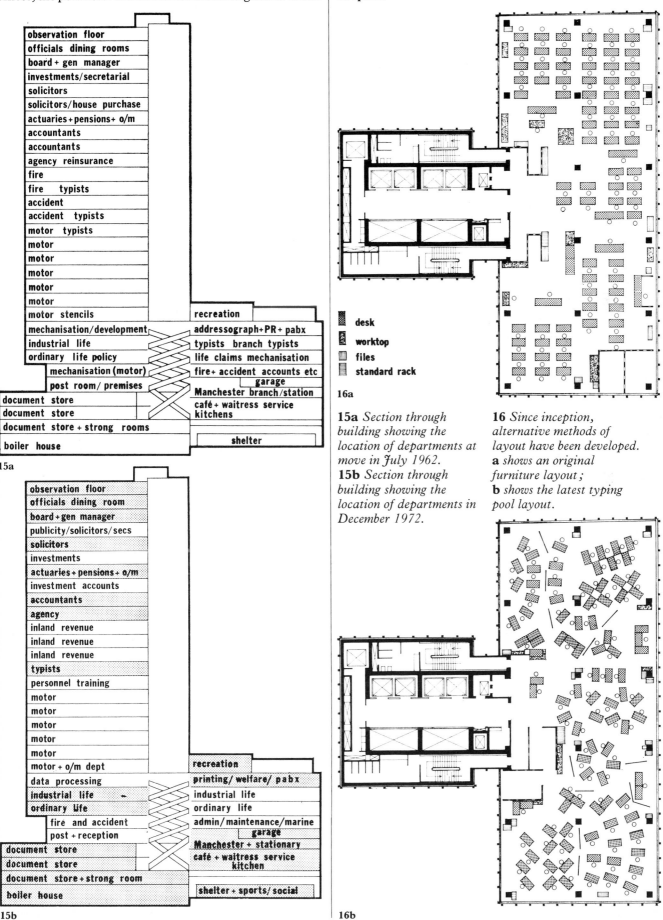

15a

observation floor	
officials dining rooms	
board + gen manager	
investments/secretarial	
solicitors	
solicitors/house purchase	
actuaries + pensions + o/m	
accountants	
accountants	
agency reinsurance	
fire	
fire typists	
accident	
accident typists	
motor typists	
motor	
motor	
motor	
motor	
motor	
motor stencils	recreation
mechanisation/development	addressograph+PR+ pabx
industrial life	typists branch typists
ordinary life policy	life claims mechanisation
mechanisation (motor)	fire+ accident accounts etc / garage
post room/ premises	Manchester branch/station
document store	café + waitress service kitchens
document store	
document store + strong rooms	
boiler house	shelter

15b

observation floor	
officials dining room	
board + gen manager	
publicity/solicitors/secs	
solicitors	
investments	
actuaries + pensions + o/m	
investment accounts	
accountants	
agency	
inland revenue	
inland revenue	
inland revenue	
typists	
personnel training	
motor	
motor	
motor	
motor	
motor	
motor + o/m dept	recreation
data processing	printing/ welfare/ pabx
industrial life	industrial life
ordinary life	ordinary life
fire and accident	admin/maintenance/marine / garage
post + reception	Manchester + stationary
document store	café + waitress service kitchen
document store	
document store + strong room	
boiler house	shelter + sports/social

Legend:
- ■ desk
- ▤ worktop
- ▥ files
- ▦ standard rack

16a

15a *Section through building showing the location of departments at move in July 1962.*
15b *Section through building showing the location of departments in December 1972.*

16 *Since inception, alternative methods of layout have been developed.*
a *shows an original furniture layout;*
b *shows the latest typing pool layout.*

16b

17 *The original layouts for a separate chief clerk's area (above). With the rationalisation of the grade structure and a changing system of space standards, the glazed screens have been done away with.*

Conclusions

3.06 The CIS building was carefully worked out by the architect, his consultants and the client, and this thoroughness and open-mindedness in the early stages has paid off handsomely. Ten years after completion, the building has a great deal of flexibility and has been able to adapt to the changing requirements of the organisation because:

1 The space types originally created allow for a variety of layout patterns.

2 The servicing and partition grid allowed for detailed layout changes and an increase in the number of cellular offices.

3 A clear system of initiating and undertaking layout changes was set up in embryo before the building was completed. Departmental changes are begun by the local departmental management and referred to the management services department which advises on floor layout use. The work is then carried out by the chief office premises controller who has a staff of personnel concerned with the running, maintenance and implementation of adaptation to the building.

4 The design of custom-built offices

4.01 A company which decides to build its own premises must:

1 Think carefully about its future, about how big it is likely to become and about how departments might develop.

2 Consult regularly with all its professional advisers in making decisions about future accommodation.

3 Set up a procedure during the design process for managing the space so that the problems of future use are considered at inception.

4.02 CIS Manchester was a well planned project where the benefits of the client's foresight can be clearly seen. Radiation Tower Neasden is a carefully considered building, but possibly lacks flexibility. Perhaps the real lesson to be learnt from these two examples is that while the form of a building stays constant, the form of an organisation may alter drastically through changing technology, methods of operating, or markets. A too precisely tailored shell will constrain future options.

5 The effect of custom design on the speculative market

5.01 The two buildings discussed, although both custom-designed offices, show how the speculative block might progress. The changes that occurred in both organisations could equally well have happened to an organisation leasing speculative space. The requirements for floor space that allows for changing layouts, alternative methods of sub-division and ease of sub-leasing are relevant both to custom-designed and speculative buildings. The architect's role, whether designing speculative or custom-designed space must be to design a shell form that will allow for change. The organisation that decides not to build but to go into a speculative office block must still take many of the same decisions as the firm building its own premises: the design decisions are here made in the choice of which block to lease out of those available, rather than in the choice of what type of shell to build. Whether the organisation is considering leasing or building, the choice will depend on whether it has properly faced questions of patterns of growth, methods of work and resultant layout patterns, relationships required between departments and the nature of the organisation.

5.02 The designer of the custom-designed office, because the nature of the organisation to be housed is known, can be more adventurous in the type of space he creates. The depth and quality of space created at CIS Manchester in 1962 would never have been built as a speculative venture. In 1972, we have few examples of 20 m deep speculative office space. Custom-designed offices are important in two ways:

1 They exemplify new ideas about the use of office space which filter down to the speculative market, partly because the custom-designed office becomes in part a speculative venture through sub-leasing (eg, the three floors of CIS let to the Inland Revenue, or the Commercial Union and P & O buildings).

2 Their existence increases the range of different types of available office space. The majority of speculative blocks in the country are still predominantly slab blocks 10 to 14 m wide, but now, in that sector, the choice is getting wider as parts of custom-designed offices are sub-let as speculative space.

5.03 The design of both custom-built and speculative offices should be based on separating 'shell' from 'scenery' for the custom-designed office block is speculative in that its future is unpredictable.

Section 2: The office shell

Methods of measuring space: the shell

A very real problem in office design is reconciling the methods of measuring space used by quantity surveyors and estate agents, for example. Here FRANCIS DUFFY defines some of the more common terms used in measuring office space. He goes on to describe a method of sizing an office building, introduces the concept of a stock of space and shows how the utility of office space may be evaluated.

1 Defining terms

1.01 Methods of defining areas vary. The choice may depend on the locality and the particular kind of organisation. Above all the choice will depend upon the particular purpose for which the definition is used. (Table 1.)

For town planning purposes

1.02 *Gross floor area or gross floor space* is the total area of the building from the outside edge of the exterior walls, **1**. This definition is used by the GLC (Greater London Council) to calculate plot ratio. It is also used for assessing office floor space for office development permits (ODPs). Town and Country Planning Act 1971, sections 78–86.

For calculating building costs

1.03 *Gross floor area* is defined differently by quantity surveyors as the basis for calculating building costs. For this purpose the total floor area of the building is measured *inside* the external wall, **2**. Unfortunately the same term is used differently for planning and cost purposes.

For letting and interior planning another set of definitions is used which emphasises the amount of office space that the user actually pays for or occupies.

Table 1 Definitions of terms used to describe office area

Precise definition is difficult in some cases because of different usages, variations in building design (eg slab or centre core), and differences between the letting of floors, parts of floors and whole buildings.

● indicates that the space or structural element is included in the area defined.

Table I

	Gross floor area—for planning purposes in UK. Equivalent to gross outside area used for costing purposes in USA.	Gross floor area—for costing purposes in UK	Net usable area	Rentable area / Lettable area (British practice)	Lettable area (US and European practice)	Building core	Service area
Each office floor							
Thickness of external walls	●						
Columns structure	●	●					
Staircases	●	●		●		●	●
Lifts	●	●				●	●
Lavatories	●	●			option	●	●
Ducts	●	●				●	●
Plant rooms	●	●				●	●
Circulation within the core	●	●				●	●
Public corridors	●	●	●				
Private corridors	●		●	●	●		
Internal walls required for building purposes—not influenced by space use	●	●					
Internal walls—tenant's own subdivision	●	●	●	●	●		
Floor reception	●	●	●	●	●		
Office space/desk area	●	●	●	●	●		
The whole building							
Building plant rooms	●	●		■			●
Building reception	●	●	●	*	*		
Covered parking	●	● (if enclosed) (if enclosed)		†	†		
Storage for whole building eg in basement	●	●	●	*	*		

* option if single letting
† subject to separate rental calculation
■ partially included

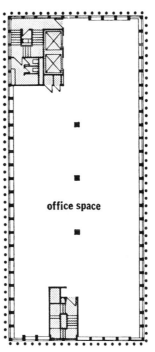

1 *For planning purposes gross floor area is the total area of the building measured from the outside edge of the exterior walls.*

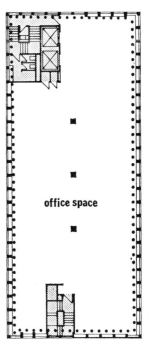

2 *For cost purposes gross floor area is the total area of the building measured from inside the external walls.*

Net floor area (of a building or floor of a building)

1.04 There are two methods commonly used to define net floor area:

1 Definition commonly used in British practice: all internal areas measured from the inner face of the building envelope, excluding main entrance halls, staircases, lifts, lavatories, plant rooms, ducts, internal walls and all corridors. This is sometimes referred to as 'net carpet area' **3**.

2 Definition commonly used in US and by some large corporations. All internal areas measured from inner face of the building envelope but excluding elevators, stairs, lavatories, mechanical equipment rooms, maintenance facilities and any public corridors between the elevators and these facilities **4**.

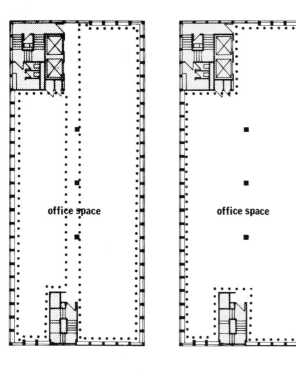

Net floor area U.K.   **Net floor area U.S.**

3 Net floor area—UK practice excludes all corridors between tenancies (dotted).

4 Net floor area—US practice excludes only circulation in the core.

Service area (building core)

1.05 Includes lifts, stairs, mechanical equipment rooms, maintenance facilities and any public corridors between the lift and these facilities. The core includes lavatories **5**.

Rentable area (of a building or floor of a building)

1.06 There are two definitions of this term used by estate agents when negotiating a lease:

1 The term used by estate agents in the UK when negotiating a lease is: the net floor area plus ducts, internal walls and corridors.

2 The term used in the US is: the net floor area plus a percentage of the core area that is pro-rated according to the amount of floor area occupied by the tenant.

Ratio of gross to net floor area

1.07 The relationship between gross and net floor area is critical. The closer the two figures are the more profitable will be the development. The ratio between net and gross varies from building to building and is determined not only by the skill of the architect but also by the physical requirements of the site, and the requirements of the planning authority and of the client or developer.

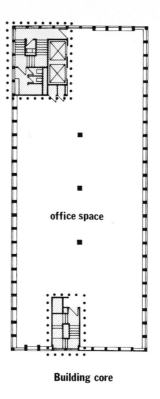

5 Service areas or building cores. This example has a major and a minor core.

office space

Building core

1.08 A 20 per cent difference between gross and net is normal in most UK offices although figures as low as 15 per cent have been achieved with low buildings on large sites. In tall buildings where a relatively small net area is obtained per floor, ratios may be as high as 25 per cent to 30 per cent.

2 Sizing an office building

2.01 One of the problems faced by the architect of a purpose-built office building is how to decide the total area of the building; the architect acting for the developer of a speculative building, however, must decide rather how many people it can possibly house. In either event, the total area is related to the number of people who will occupy the building. However, two factors complicate the equation—first, space standards per person vary widely for different companies; second, buildings house not only people (both at their work places and in restaurants) but also machines. A method of calculating area requirements which take into account both people and machine spaces is presented on p.90 onwards.

2.02 For crude feasibility studies in which the object of the exercise is simply to give a rough but realistic total area to an office building project, a very basic minimum of 10 m² net usable area per head should be allowed for all present or planned personnel. This allowance excludes major circulation, core, and normal support functions*. This minimum may very easily be increased to 20 m² or even more depending on the type of user. See the detailed calculation in Methods of Measuring Space: the scenery, p.90 onwards. To convert the total net area into gross floor area by including major circulation, core and normal support functions, a factor should be added. It is suggested that purely office space should be near 80 per cent of gross floor area (see Table 1).

2.03 These recommendations are reasonably generous They should be compared with the two worked examples in Methods of Measuring Space: the Scenery (p.91) where with quite reasonable assumptions in each case, the figures for NUA per head are 9·25 m² and 21·6 m²; a wider range. It cannot be stressed too much that office organisations

*These may include items such as storage, filing and reception areas. Support functions are dealt with in section 7, p.149 onwards.

Table II Space standards at feasibility stage

Absolute minimum area for a work station	3·7 m² to 4·2 m² (including some access, filing cabinets and desk space). But this is too low for individual offices
Minimum area for reasonable conditions at each work station	4·2 m² to 6·0 m² (14 m³ to 17 m³). But allow more for individual offices with single occupation
Requirements of Offices, Shops and Railway Premises Act 1963	3·7 m² minimum floor area per person if ceiling height is not less than 3048 mm. Where ceiling is less, requirement is 11·3 m³ (400 ft³) per person
Additional space for visitor's chair	Allow minimum 1·8 m² extra for visitor's chair
Recommended allowance for sizing an office building	Between 10 m² and 20 m² per person excluding circulation, wcs and so on, depending on type of user
Completely integrated office plus eating and lounge facilities	At least 14·0 m² per person
Proportion of total floor area to be aimed at for office working space	Nearly 80 per cent of gross internal floor area

vary widely in composition of staff, in space standards and in facilities.

2.04 Some empirical evidence is available for space standards in the open office. Davies* found, after surveying 12 layouts in deep space which altogether housed over 1000 people, that there are variations which relate to user activities. For general office space, an average of 8·9 m² was found; for drawing office staff, an average of 11·2 m². These figures include a proportion of normal support areas such as circulation, meetings, storage, etc, and may not be directly comparable to the figures recommended in para 2.02. Davies's measurements indicate that the proportions of gross floor area occupied by office space were on average 66 per cent for general offices and 69 per cent for drawing offices (table III).

Table III Results from Davies's measurements of space allocation in a number of open-plan offices. General office space is compared with the special case of drawing office space

Category of planned open office	Net work area expressed as % total net area	Net area for support expressed as % total net area	Total net area per person	Net work area per person
General	69%	31%	8·9 m²	6·32 m²
Drawing	72%	28%	11·24 m²	8·08 m²
All	70%	30%	9·66 m²	6·97 m²

The drawing office is included just to make the point of how a specific activity (a marginal office activity) alters the ratios.

3 Methods of evaluating office space

3.01 The following notes suggest two means of evaluating office space. The first is primarily an assessment of building form and applies mostly to open office spaces; the second stems more from an assessment of the requirements of an actual office organisation which was looking at the suitability of some existing buildings available for renting.

Evaluation of office shells for open office planning

3.02 The decision as to whether an office floor is suitable for open office planning depends on
1 the size and proportion of the office floor
2 the size and proportion of each structural bay.
The methods of assessment which are described below were developed by the User Requirements Study Branch (offices) of the Department of the Environment. They contain certain assumptions about the undesirability of open space over a certain size, which may be questioned, although they are shared widely in this country.

Space standards for planned open offices by R. Davies. DOE unpublished internal report, April 1971.

To assess the size and proportions of office floors
3.03 1 Define the proportions of the floor, eg, 1:4, **6**.

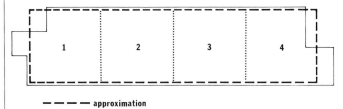

– – – – approximation

6 *Defining the proportions of a floor using approximations of its proportion.*

2 Using the net area and proportion of the space, determine the suitability of the floor for open plan using the chart **7**. If the point of intersection of net area (vertical axis) and proportion (horizontal axis) falls within the shaded area, the whole floor will be considered suitable for open plan.

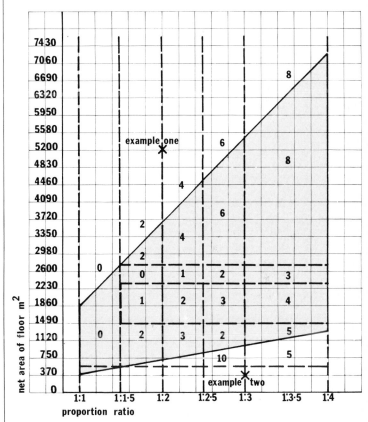

7 *Chart showing office floors which are considered of acceptable area and proportion for open planning. Proposals must fall within the shaded area to be considered* *acceptable. Numbers 0 to 10 placed on both tinted and untinted areas indicate percentage discount—see para 3.04.*

Example 1. An area 5200 m² with a 1:2 proportion would not be satisfactory because the width of floor is more than 43 m. According to Davies, such a deep space, even in the best conditions, would tend to cause apprehension and disquiet because the sense of release created by an external view would be insufficient in the centre.
Example 2. An area of 370 m² with a 1:3 proportion would also be unsuitable because the width of space would be less than 18·5 m. This depth, according to the authors of this method, would not allow the disposition of four work groups plus a main circulation route; less than four work

groups is held to inhibit the desirable attributes of flexibility and effective group working in open plan design.

To assess bay size and proportion
3.04 1 Define the bays into which the office floor is divided by columns, stairs and other fixed elements. Use approximations where necessary **8**.
2 List the area and proportion of each bay in the building to be evaluated.
3 Using area and proportion in a similar way to the method used to evaluate whole floors, classify each bay according to the chart **9**. Co-ordinate intersections falling in the shaded area are considered to be satisfactory for ordinary office use. Those outside are unsuitable except for support services such as stationery and document stores.

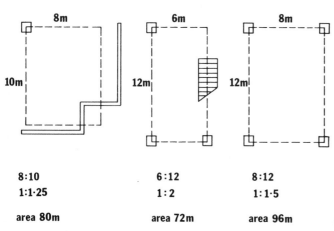

8:10	6:12	8:12
1:1·25	1:2	1:1·5
area 80m	area 72m	area 96m

8 *A method of assessment of the proportion of bays into which an office floor is divided by columns, stairs and other fixed elements, using approximations where necessary.*

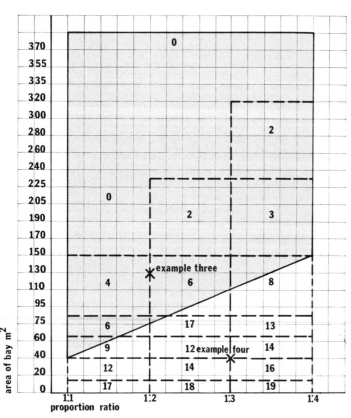

9 *Chart showing bays of office space which are considered to be of acceptable area and proportion for open planning. Proposals must fall within the shaded areas to be acceptable. Numbers 0 to 19 placed on both tinted and untinted areas indicate percentage discount factor—see para 3.04.*

Bays, although falling within the shaded area, are considered less suitable the nearer they approach the boundary. This feature has been expressed as a *percentage discount* factor in the appropriate areas of the chart.
Example 3. A bay of 130 m² with a proportion of 1:2 is acceptable according to the authors. However, it incurs a percentage discount of 6 because it approaches the boundary of unsuitability. It should, therefore, be marked on the layout plan as an area for use when group and intergroup flexibility is needed less.
Example 4. A bay of 40 m² with a 1:3 proportion will not be satisfactory because this results in a column spacing of 3·6 m—less than the minimum requirement of 6·1 m.

To calculate the percentage discount factor
3.05 1 Proceed as in steps 1, 2 and 3, para 3.04, in assessing bay size and proportion.
2 By using the chart **9**, calculate the *effective area* of an acceptable bay (area and proportion shown within the tinted area) by reducing the actual area by the percentage discount factor.

$$\text{area of bay} - \left(\text{area of bay} \times \frac{\% \text{ discount factor}}{100}\right) = \text{effective area of the bay}$$

3 Aggregate the effective areas of all suitable bays. This gives a crude assessment of area which is suitable for open planning and which may be less than the net office area.

To calculate the 'net effective area' on all floors available for open office use
3.06 Reduce the aggregate area by percentage discount factor for the *whole floor* which is shown in **7**.

$$\text{total effective area of bays} - \left(\text{total effective area of bays} \times \frac{\% \text{ discount factor}}{100}\right) = \text{net effective area of the floor}$$

3.07 The effective area method is a means of assessing *not* crude total area of office space but area which is actually likely to be suitable for open office planning. It does this by excluding areas which are unsuitable because of size or awkward proportions and then by reducing what remains by discount factors which reflect the *relative* unsuitability of space.

Evaluation of office shells for organisations requiring many separate rooms
3.08 This method is the reverse of the open-plan evaluation technique described above. It starts not with the building but with the departmental groups and units which make up the organisation which is going to use the space.

Evaluating the suitability of existing cellular space for an actual organisation
3.09 A method is suggested below to compare requirements of an actual organisation seeking space with the characteristics of a number of offices up for rent. The question asked was whether any of the available offices met the requirements of the organisations.
The method is to
1 Decide on the component parts of the organisations
2 Decide the required area of each component part
3 Decide how separate each required area should be from the other
4 Display the resultant required area in a histogram
5 Break down each likely office into a stock of separate spaces
6 Display these spaces in histogram form
7 Compare the histogram of required areas with the histogram of stocks of spaces.
In this way a match can be made between what a client requires and what an estate agent can offer. In the example illustrated, an advertising agency made up of a large number of relatively autonomous working groups is

matched with the stock of space in an 18th-century building in Berkeley Square **10**. This building was composed of too few rooms, most of which were too large. The conclusion that the Berkeley Square building was unsuitable was strengthened by the difficulty of subdividing tall handsome rooms in an old building. Of course, the organisation could have approached the problem in another way by looking at its own structure and hierarchy—and perhaps altering them.

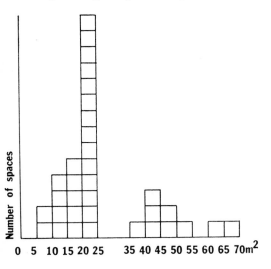

Distribution of Group Areas

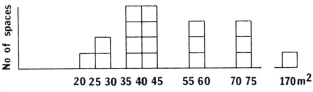

Stock of spaces in 46 Berkeley Square

10 *A comparison of a stock of spaces in an existing building and the requirements for rooms of an actual organisation. Obviously there is a discrepancy in this case between what is available and what is desired. In other words there are too few small rooms.*

Section 2: The office shell

Shell and core

Here the major constraints and options in the design of the office building shell in the UK are reviewed by FRANCIS DUFFY. Readers in other countries should, where appropriate, consult codes and regulations applying to local circumstances. Four depths of space: shallow, medium, deep and very deep are defined. The importance of the location of the core is stressed since it is the relationship of spaces of various depths and the core which determines what a shell can offer.

1 Definitions

1.01 A variety of related activities such as shopping, car parking and housing can be grouped in the same building provided there is proper separation for escape purposes and provided the right conditions are designed for any common access, intercommunication and services. A complex office building project may be difficult to categorise; it is far easier and yields more information if one analyses the parts.

The office shell
1.02 Even an office building which is restricted to purely office accommodation, may be composed of a number of types of office shell. The shell may be defined as the envelope for a floor of office space, and it is possible to classify shells into distinct and recognisable types.

Office spaces
1.03 Most floor plans break down into a number of different kinds of office space—for example, into space which is suitable for ordinary office rooms and space which is suitable for open-planning, spaces and office activities being closely related.

The core
1.04 The term core is applied to the conglomerate of elements which are brought together for ease of services and construction.

The scenery
1.05 To work as offices spaces have to be fitted with partitions, services, furniture, etc. These fitting-out elements, which we call scenery, are dealt with in Section 3, page 90 onwards.

2 Factors that shape shells
2.01 Many factors influence the shape of office shells, eg density; light and overshadowing; fire regulations (means of escape).

Density
2.02 Density of development on a site may be controlled:
1 by restriction of the height of the building;
2 by plot ratio which relates area of built floor space to site area;
3 by fire brigade access (CP3: chapter IV: part 3: 1968, 8);
4 by GLC requirements for Section 20 buildings for perimeter access (London Building Acts).

Light and overshadowing
2.03 With the exception of permitted openings in relation to adjacent buildings (Building Regulations, Part E),

overshadowing of one building by another is prevented by the use of such methods as daylight 'fan' guides[1] rather than statutory controls; nonetheless, these influence the bulk and shape of buildings. The depth of the office building as well as the proportion of glazing in the envelope may be influenced by using daylight factor methods in order to achieve acceptable light levels within the building. However, permanent supplementary artificial lighting of interiors (psali) and the use of even greater proportions of artificial light has liberated the office from the constraint of reliance on daylight and, energy consumption apart, makes deeper buildings acceptable. Various aspects of, and techniques for dealing with the lighting problem are published as follows: the sun and sunlight[1, 2, 3], natural lighting[4], daylight factors, sky components and internally reflected components, BRE daylight protractors, general information[5, 6, 7, 8].

Means of escape

2.04 Specific requirements on escape vary. Applicable regulations for new buildings are:
1 London Building Acts[9];
2 Building Regulations[10, 11];
3 Building Standards (Scotland) Regulations 1963[12].
4 Code of Practice Means of Escape in Case of Fire, Greater London Council[13].
For existing buildings consult:
5 Offices, Shops and Railway Premises Act (1963)[14].
See Table I for where these regulations apply.
The GLC's new Code of Practice on means of escape sets out general principles for the design of new buildings and for alterations to existing buildings to provide satisfactory means of fire escape. The Code is principally intended as a guide to designers and has no mandatory force. However, it does illustrate the conditions likely to be required to obtain the Council's approval for means of escape.
Generally throughout the remainder of this study the British Standards CP3: chapter IV[15] is referred to. This differs in some respects from the GLC Code.
For both new and existing buildings consultation is required. However, certain basic principles have a very great impact on the location of cores, the placing of escape stairs and the depth of office space. No one should have to pass through fire to reach safety[14]; an alternative escape route to a *protected point* must be available, **1**. Limits to the allowed distance from remote positions to protected points are based on the time taken by a person to reach the zone. The result called the *travel distance* is defined as 'the distance measured along the escape route between the furthest point in any office and either the exit door from the storey or the exit door to the open air' (CP3: Chapter IV: Part 3). The numbers and siting of stairways are determined by the principle of the travel distance and numbers of occupants at risk on that floor and the floor above.

Maximum travel distance: escape possible in one direction only

2.05 For ground and first storeys only, the maximum travel distance, according to CP3: Chapter IV: Part 3 (1968), from any point in any office to an exit door from the storey may be up to 30·5 m, **2**, provided:
1 opening windows are available in all offices (minimum dimensions 840 mm × 535 mm wide);
2 the lower level of the opening lights is not more than 3·8 m from the level of the ground immediately outside the window and not more than 915 mm above the internal floor level;
3 the ground beneath the windows is clear of any obstructions which could prejudice escape, such as railings, for a distance of 1830 mm measured horizontally from the building.

Table I Regulations and recommendations for means of escape from fire

	Acts	Regulations	Memorandum
In inner London boroughs	London Building Acts (Amendment) Act 1939	Offices, Shops and Railway Premises Act 1963 (Modification of section 29) Regulations Statutory Instrument 761, 1964	None
New buildings	Section 34 20		
Old buildings	Section 35 36 38 39		
Access to roofs	Section 31		
England and Wales except inner London boroughs but including rest of GLC area	Building Regulations 1972	Offices, Shops and Railway Premises Act 1963 (Modifications of section 29) Regulations Statutory Instrument 761, 1964	None
Scotland	Building (Scotland) Act 1959. Statutory Instrument No 1897 (S102) 1963. The Building Standards (Scotland) Regulations 1963 part V	Offices, Shops and Railway Premises Act 1963 (Modifications of section 29) Regulations Statutory Instrument 761, 1964	Means of escape from fire and assistance to fire service. Building Standards (Scotland) Regulation 1963 explanatory memorandum part 5

Applicable in various parts of UK

Codes of Practice	Other official sources	Administered by
GLC *Code of Practice Means of escape in case of fire* London 1974, GLC, (supersedes GLC publication 3868)	None	GLC Building Regulation Division for approval of plans; HM Factory Inspector for certification of existing buildings
BS CP3: chapter IV, Precautions against fire. Part 3: 1968, Office Buildings	Safety, Health and Welfare New Series. Means of Escape in Case of Fire in Offices, Shops and Railway Premises. HMSO (Department of Employment and Productivity)	Fire Authority Local Authority HM Factory Inspectorate for certification of existing building

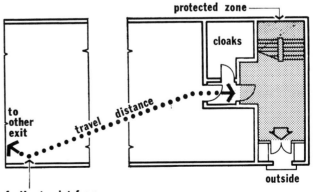

1

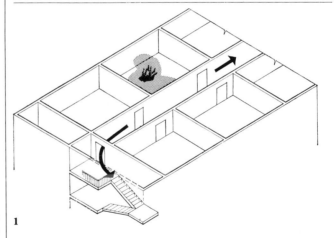

farthest point from protected point

2

1 *Alternative escape routes with a limited travel distance must be available from fire to a protected zone.*

2 *Maximum travel from any point on ground and first floor to a protected zone must not exceed 30·5 m.*

Where these conditions are not satisfied in ground and first floors, and for all other storeys, maximum travel distance from any point in any office to an exit door from the storey should not exceed 12·2 m. In all cases an escape route from an inner office should not pass through more than one access office. Both offices should be in the same occupancy.

Maximum travel distance: escape possible in alternative directions

2.06 Where escape is possible in alternative directions the maximum travel distance from any point in any office to an exit door from the storey should not exceed 46 m. In individual offices, no point should be further than 12·2 m from the nearest exit door from the office, unless a second exit door is provided in such a position that the angle subtended between the lines joining the two exit doors to any such point in the room is 45° or more.

The distance between any point in an inner office and the exit door of an access office should not exceed 12·2 m unless a second exit door is available spaced as above. Where an inner office is provided with alternative escape routes which do not pass through the same access office, the limiting travel distance of 12·2 m in the inner office does not apply, but the exit doors from the inner office should be spaced as described above (45°).

An escape route from an inner office should not pass through more than one access office and both should be in the same occupancy.

The distance between any two adjacent exits from a storey should not exceed 61 m.

2.07 All escape routes should be fully recognisable at all times and should not involve passing through accommodation in a separate tenancy or doorways likely to be locked or obstructed. Any exit door, not in regular use for normal egress, should be clearly indicated by an exit sign and the escape route should be clearly marked until the final exit is in sight.

Second stage of the escape: stairs

2.08 Lifts should be disregarded for escape purposes because of the possible delay involved, their limited capacity and the possibility of electrical failure. CP3 requires that staircases be enclosed with a fire-resisting construction to prevent smoke and heat obstructing the staircase and to avoid fire spreading from one storey to another via the staircase. In a building, or part of building, served only by a single staircase a protected and ventilated corridor or lobby should be interposed between the accommodation and the staircase. In multi-staircase buildings with storeys up to 18·3 m in height, a door at the entry to the staircase enclosure gives adequate protection. Above this height a lobby or corridor should be interposed between the entrance door of the accommodation and the door into the staircase enclosure. In buildings over 18·3 m high some staircases should be constructed as fire-fighting staircases. No store or other fire risk such as a cleaner's cupboard should open directly on to a staircase or lobby, **3**. However, lavatories and protected lifts present a negligible fire hazard and may be planned within a staircase or lobby enclosure.

There is greater risk that a basement staircase will be attacked by heat and smoke. For this reason, basements should preferably have direct access to the open air, either at basement level or to ground level by way of a staircase. Where this is not possible, the basement staircase should be adequately separated from the upper levels.

2.09 Where staircases are to be used for escape they must remain free from smoke and heat. Even though staircases are enclosed, smoke and heat may still be admitted when the doors opening into them are used. It is therefore desirable to provide openable windows at each storey;

where this is not practicable, a permanent vent with an area equivalent to 5 per cent of the staircase enclosure should be provided at the top of the staircase. With unfenestrated staircases, a ventilation shaft is sometimes used as a means of clearing smoke from the staircases. In sealed, air-conditioned buildings, it may be possible to clear smoke from staircases and lobbies by maintaining an increased air pressure.

2.10 All buildings with floors over 18·3 m above ground level should have at least one fire-fighting access staircase. Such staircases should:
1 be continuous throughout the entire building:
2 have access at ground level from the street to both staircase and fireman's lift;
3 have openable windows at each landing level;
4 have permanent ventilation at the top of the enclosure of at least 5 per cent of the enclosure area; and
5 have a protected and ventilated lobby between it and the accommodation on each storey.

The lobby should be at least 5·5 m² and should be planned to allow easy manipulation of hoses. Ventilation should be provided to the open air by openable windows of not less than 1·4 m². A permanent free opening of 0·05 m² should be provided for pressure release. The internal hydrants and rising mains required for fire-fighting may be accommodated in this lobby.

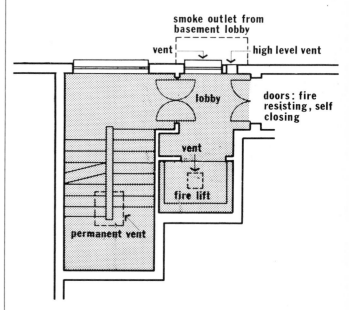

3 *In buildings over 18·3 m high some staircases should be constructed as fire-fighting staircases, with smoke outlets, vents, and fire-resisting, self-closing doors.*

Table II Minimum staircase width for multi-storey buildings with more than two storeys above ground level (from CP3: chapter IV, part 3)

Gross floor area of the storey (calculated at 9·3 m² per person) not exceeding m²	Number of persons in the storey	Minimum width for each staircase		
		2 staircases mm	3 staircases mm	4 staircases mm
230	25	765	765	765
930	100	1070	1070	1070
1070	115	1220	1070	1070
1210	130	1370	1070	1070
1350	145	1525	1070	1070
1490	160	1680	1070	1070
1630	175	1830	1070	1070
1860	200		1070	1070
2140	230		1220	1070
2420	260		1370	1070
2700	290		1525	1070
2800	300		1525	1070
2980	320		1680	1070
3210	345		1680	1220
3260	350		1680	1220
3630	390			1370
4050	435			1525
4470	480			1680
4890	525			1830

Width of staircases
2.11 For single staircase buildings the minimum width (CP3) should be 765 mm for staircases serving storeys whose gross floor area does not exceed 230 m² and 1070 mm above this floor area (Table II). In two-staircase buildings with only one floor above ground level, each staircase should have a minimum width of 1070 mm for the first 1860 m² of gross floor area plus 152 mm for each additional 280 m². For buildings having only one floor above ground with more than two staircases, the width can be calculated from the following formula if y represents the number of staircases less one:
each staircase should be at least 1070 mm wide for the y × 1860 m² floor area plus 152 mm for each additional y × 280 m².
For multi-staircase buildings with two storeys or more above ground floor, Table II gives required widths.

Third stage of the escape route: from the foot of an escape staircase to an exit from the building
2.12 The external exit door should be reached from the foot of the escape staircase without passing through any door other than one provided to form a draught lobby. The space between the staircase and the exit should be treated as part of the staircase enclosure and should be subject to the same conditions (para 2.08). The width of the entrance hall should not be less than the width of those doors nor less than the required width for the staircase. Final exits should:
1 be free from fire risk from the basement or adjoining accommodation;
2 discharge into a street or open space leading to a street;
3 have a width not less than the minimum required for the entrance hall, lobby or corridor leading to them; and
4 open outwards and be capable of being opened at all times.
2.13 The requirements listed above are based on CP3: Chapter IV: Part 3 (1968). The first amendment to the Building Regulations became operative on 1 September 1973 and required means of escape to be included in the Building Regulations. CP3 (offices) was adopted, as deemed to satsify 'under certain conditions', for new buildings. The London Building Acts and the Building Standards (Scotland) Regulations 1963 differ in certain respects from CP3. The Offices, Shops and Railway Premises Act 1963 makes certain requirements for means of escape in existing buildings and requires inspection and certification of office premises.

3 A basic grammar for office shells

3.01 The aim of this section is to provide a basic grammar for office shells; concentrating on location of the core, position of major circulation routes and depth of space.

Locations of the core
3.02 The location of cores is determined by:
1 means of escape;
2 the type of subdivision and the degree of adaptability required. The strategic location of cores can facilitate the multi-tenancy of a speculative building, create a range of space and/or allow for privacy in certain departments;
3 lifts—first the access required at ground level and then the circulation pattern required at each floor.
3.03 Core location is important because it is the origin of main circulation.
Cores can be put into three categories:
1 internal core;
2 semi-internal core; and
3 external core.

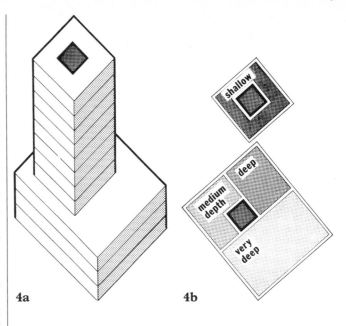

4a   4b

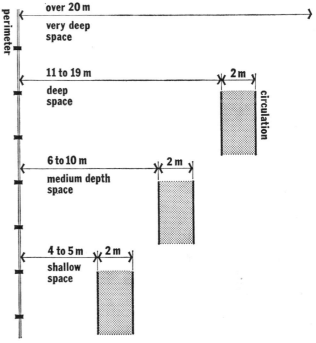

5

4a, b *Illustration of how different types of office space with different kinds of use can be provided in one office building by the simple device of core placed asymmetrically in the podium.*

5 *Four basic depths of space. In all cases (except very deep space) depth is measured between building shell perimeter and primary circulation across uninterrupted office space. Circulation is assumed to be 2 m deep.*

For the purpose of this survey, core generally means the primary core. In some examples, however, secondary cores are shown because they may be necessary to provide alternative means of escape and also because their location affects the use of the office space. For example, a core placed asymmetrically allows a variety of types of office space to be created in the same shell, **4a, b**.

Main circulation
3.04 There are two basic arrangements:
1 single zone—circulation to one side of office space only; and
2 double zone—circulation serving office space on both sides.

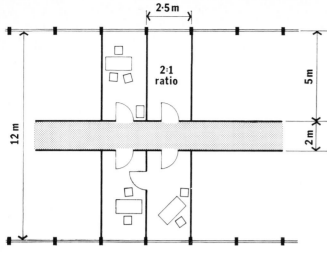

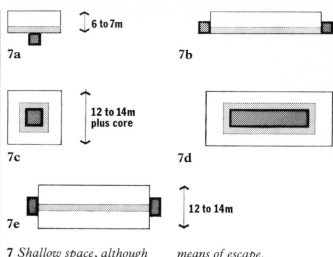

6 *Shallow floors often depend upon perimeter ventilation and permit reasonably shaped rooms. If 2:1 is accepted as a suitable* *proportion and if the minimum acceptable width for a single room is 2·5 m, then a shell depth of 12 m results.*

7 *Shallow space, although essentially linear, can be provided in a variety of office shell forms.*
a *Single zone.*
b *Single zone—alternative*

means of escape.
c *Single zone—central core.*
d *Single zone—elongated central core.*
e *Double zone.*

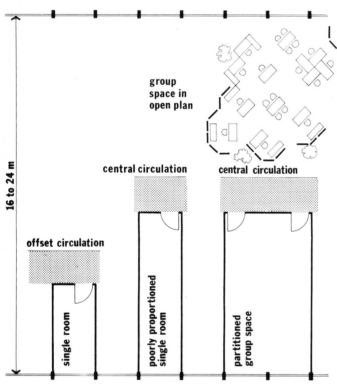

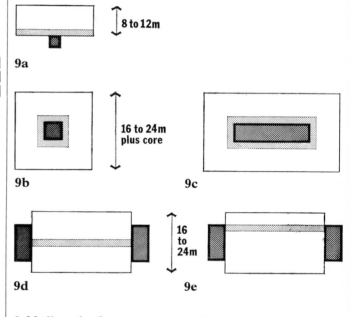

8 *In office shells of 16 m to 24 m depth (double zone medium-depth space) acceptable single rooms can only be provided with an offset corridor. The use of an* *offset corridor greatly enhances the adaptability of shells of this depth because it enables more than one depth of office space to be provided.*

9 *Medium-depth space can be provided in a range of office building shells. If, as in **e**, the position of circulation is not fixed (eg by central columns) both shallow and medium-depth space can be provided in a shell which can also provide two zones of medium-depth space.*

a *Single zone.*
b *Single zone—central core.*
c *Single zone—elongated central core.*
d *Double zone—fixed central circulation.*
e *Double zone— asymmetrical position of circulation providing shallow and medium-depth space.*

Depth of space
3.05 Depth of space is defined as the distance from the main core or main circulation to the perimeter. Four basic depths may be distinguished, **5**.

Shallow depth
3.06 Perimeter ventilation will suffice for shallow depth space, which permits reasonably proportioned single office rooms (no more than 2:1 ratio). Double zone spaces will produce a shell depth of about 12 m. Shallow office space is essentially linear, though linear space can be provided in a non-linear shell. The most common use of such space is a series of small rooms linked by a corridor. Floor plans of this kind are usually well suited to subdivision into separate tenancies. Small suites can be formed for individual tenants by opening rooms directly into each other. Subdivision into small rooms is a method most suitable for individual and small group working, but generally unsuitable for large groupings **6, 7**.

Medium-depth space
3.07 Medium depth spaces mean that some work places will not be adjacent to the window wall. This depth varies from 6 m to 10 m and double zone spaces will provide a shell depth of about 14 m to 22 m.

In medium-depth space it is possible to adopt a freer attitude towards planning than with either shallow or deep spaces. All kinds of office activities can be accommodated

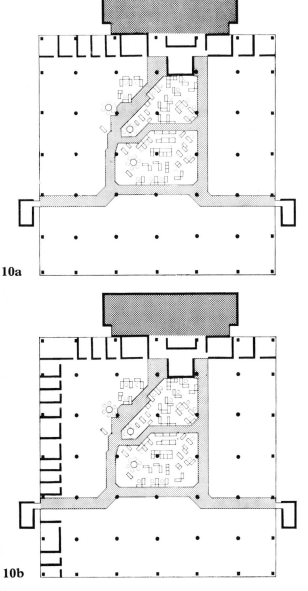

10a

10b

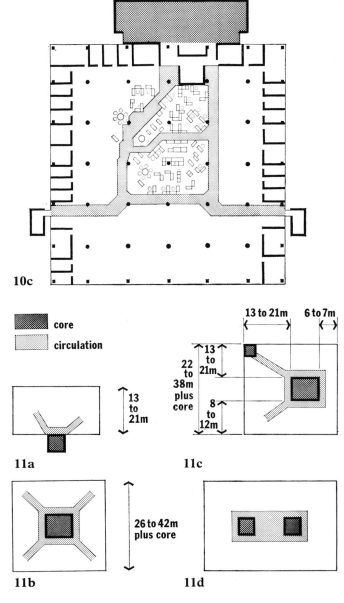

10c

■ core

▨ circulation

13 to 21m   6 to 7m

13 to 21m

22 to 38m plus core

13 to 21m

8 to 12m

11a

11c

26 to 42m plus core

11b

11d

10 *The consequences of increasing the proportion of enclosed offices at the perimeter of a deep office space are shown as follows:* **a** *(8·4 per cent of the area) hardly affects the quality of the open space;* **b** *(16·8 per cent of the area) has begun to reduce the aspect from some workplaces;* **c** *(25·2 per cent of the area) provides barely acceptable conditions for many workplaces. It is important to realise that although 25 per cent of the area is cellular, enclosed workplaces are provided for only approximately 10 per cent of the workforce.*

11 *Some examples of deep space. In* **11c** *the asymmetrical placing of the core creates a mixture of deep, medium and shallow space.*
a *Single zone.*
b *Single zone—central core.*
c *Single zone—asymmetrical core.*
d *Double zone—split core.*

in medium-depth space. In addition medium-depth space may usually be subdivided into separate tenancies without undue difficulty. A disadvantage is that it is not always possible to achieve well-proportioned single rooms. Space is often wasted unless the corridor is offset to permit single office rooms on one side and deep office space on the other, **8**. As with shallow space, medium-depth space can be provided in a variety of shell forms, **9**.

Deep space
3.08 Deep offices range from 11 to 19 m but really come into their own at about 15 m. A double zone space will provide a shell depth of about 32 m. Deep space can be subdivided into small offices, or group spaces or be left undivided. If internal rooms are not allowed, the proportion of enclosed to open space depends entirely upon the configuration of the building and may lead to an imbalance between cellular and open offices, **10**. The larger deep spaces are only suitable for organisations which can use open planning on a large scale, **11**.

Very deep space
3.09 Very deep offices may be defined as any which are deeper than 20 m. At this depth, several main internal circulation routes are necessary; the relationship with the perimeter is less critical and the options for locating main circulation far greater, **12**.
3.10 Combinations of shallow and medium-depth space can be used to good effect if it is anticipated that a combination of cellular and open or group space will be useful throughout the life of the building. Combining shallow and deep space in a single building is a more difficult design problem.

The shell and the user
3.11 Office buildings should not be designed too closely to the needs of any one user at any one time because organisations change rapidly. In this sense, all office buildings can be called speculative. Nevertheless, some general organisational factors may be taken into account in the design of a shell.

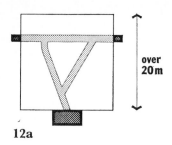 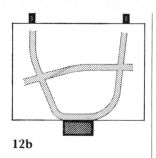

12a **12b**

12a, b *In very deep space so many choices are available for locating circulation that* *the concept of zones of space defined by circulation is no longer useful.*

3.12 *Custom-built offices :* in a large firm, department size may range from two or three people to several hundreds; there may be very good reasons for many of these departments to be in contact with each other or to be connected with some centralised services, and this may suggest buildings with single central cores and with large floors at each level.

3.13 *Single-tenancy speculative offices :* these buildings will, it is hoped, be rented by one tenant; but the developer is not likely to risk building deep, air-conditioned space and so reduce the possibility of subletting each floor separately if he fails to find that single tenant. There is a fundamental conflict here between what benefits the developer most and what the larger occupier wants and needs.

3.14 Speculative office buildings aimed at a single tenant may exhibit a fundamental conflict between the developer's fear of building deep space which has to be air-conditioned and may be difficult to sublet, and the tenant's requirement of central access and servicing. Once the developer has decided to let office space in small parcels, the need for centrality and single access disappears or at least becomes less urgent.

3.15 *Multiple-tenancy speculative offices :* similarly with multiple tenancies, the need for large spaces, centrality and single access is less pronounced. The appropriate building is subdivided into a variety of different-sized areas, each with direct access to one of, perhaps, several cores.

4 The design of the core

4.01 The size and content of the core depends upon:
1 the area and population served by each floor which affects the number and size of lifts, stairs and lavatories required;
2 the number of floors—which affects the number of lifts;
3 additional elements, such as tea stations and mechanical conveyors, within the core unit; and
4 cleaning and maintenance space. The requirements for cleaning and maintenance areas total about 1 per cent of the gross area of the whole office building subdivided into:

cleaners' stores	40 per cent
cleaners' locker-room	10 per cent
maintenance workshops	15 per cent
maintenance store	15 per cent
refuse storage	10 per cent
housekeeper	10 per cent
	100 per cent

It is desirable for the cleaners' stores to be distributed on every floor of the building in the core. Heavy equipment can be stored centrally and moved round the building while day-to-day supplies can be stored on each floor.

References

1 DOE Welsh Office *Sunlight and daylight—planning criteria and design of buildings*, London, 1971, HMSO, 40p.
2 BURBERRY, P., 'The sun' manual edited by AJ, 12.1.66, p105, [(N7)]
3 LYNES, J., 'Sunlight: direct and diffused', *AJ Handbook : Building environment*, Section 2, AJ 16.10.68, p879, [(E6)].
4 *BS CP3 : Daylighting*, Part 1, chapter 1, 1964, British Standards Institution, Sales Branch, 101 Pentonville Road, London, N1 9ND, [(N7)] £7.
5 LONGMORE, J. *Daylight protractors*, British Research Station, 1968, HMSO, [(N7)].
6 HOPKINSON, R.G., PETHERIDGE, J. & LONGMORE, J. *Daylighting* London, 1966, Heinemann, [(N7)], £4·20.
7 BUILDING RESEARCH STATION, *Daylight and building* 1, BRS Digest no 41, 1964, February, HMSO, [(N7)].
8 BUILDING RESEARCH STATION *Daylight and buildings* 2, BRS Digest no 42, 1964, January, HMSO, [(N7)].
9 GLC *Constructional Bylaws* London Building Acts 1930-39 London Building (Constructional) By Laws 1972 London 1973 GLC.
10 *The Building Regulations 1972*, London HMSO.
11 ELDER, A. J., *The Guide to the Building Regulations* 1972, London 1972, The Architectural Press.
12 Statutory instrument No 1897 (S102) 1963, *The Building Standards (Scotland) Regulations* 1963, part V HMSO.
13 GLC *Code of Practice for Means of Escape in Case of Fire*, Publication No 7168-0573-1. London 1974 GLC.
14 *The Offices, Shops and Railway Premises Act 1963 A General Guide*, London 1971 HMSO.
15 BS CP3, chapter IV, part 3 (1968), British Standards Institution, London 1968.
The reader is referred to Section 5 of this book, page 113 onwards, for a general review of law and regulations controlling office building.

Section 2: The office shell

Office shells: a comparison

Nine office shells are broken down into their component parts so that activities can be related to the kinds of spaces which can be provided. RICHARD DAVIES isolates three basic kinds of space—small, medium and large. These spaces are defined because they are likely to relate to activities; they are not the same as depth of space which is used analytically in 'Shell and Core'. Some shells provide the whole range of spaces; some more large than small; some more small than large. If it is possible to characterise an organisation's requirements in terms of the size of working groups which can then be related to kinds of space, then this method of analysis is an important step towards either choosing or building the stock of spaces an organisation needs. This analysis was prepared with the help of BARRY BOOTH and JOHN FRANCIS.

1 Method of evaluation

1.01 A typical floor of each building is evaluated for its potential for subdivision into different *types* of space; screens and partitions etc are mainly ignored because the layout shown may be only one of several possible ones. These are the categories into which the spaces have been placed:

Small spaces
1 For one person, but will often be shared by two or three people
2 Maximum depth from the perimeter 6 m; maximum area 40 m². This means that small spaces may rely on windows for light and ventilation
3 A minimum room size is postulated; minimum length (or width) 2·6 m and thus minimum area 8 m².

Medium spaces
1 For groups of (say) five, where team working or frequent supervision is needed.
2 Area from 40 m² up to 150 m².

Large spaces
1 For several working groups.
2 Area over 150 m².

1.02 Where fixed elements—columns or cores—are within 6 m of each other or the perimeter, they make a 'boundary' to a large space, for they form a significant constraint upon the layout—and may reduce the efficiency of use. Columns are not generally considered a major constraint in the planning of medium or small spaces as the size of these spaces will inevitably restrict freedom of layout.
1.03 It has been assumed in defining the subdivision of a plan that spaces will have windows on at least one side and that their proportion on plan ought not to exceed two to one. For comparison of areas, allowance must be made for the fact that large spaces always include provision for intergroup circulation and escape routes—a function satisfied by corridors in buildings used mainly for small spaces. Half the width of any corridor is added to any office which it serves.
1.04 With these criteria it is possible to define the options for subdividing any floor by assessing the percentage of the

gross area that may be used for small, medium or large spaces. It is important to use the term 'gross area' because 'net area' does not mean the same thing for all buildings as it excludes the corridors, also if office spaces were expressed as a percentage of the gross area we have a useful indicator of the efficiency of building form. The effect of, say, the height of the building and its consequent effect on core area is thus automatically taken into account.

Corner rooms

1.05 L-shaped rooms going around the corners of the building are considered as in **1**. In other words, the room is 'straightened out'. It is recognised that in terms of saving primary circulation space this form of layout is more efficient than straight rooms.

Constant spaces

1.06 Where the form of the building exactly determines how a space may be used (see plan of Whitgift Centre this sheet) the area of this space (or spaces) is calculated as a percentage of gross. This is called constant space. The percentage will, of course, always be included as part of the overall figure for small, medium and large spaces.

Tenancies

1.07 It is assumed when discussing the potential of a building (or a typical floor) for separation into tenancies that:
1 Each tenancy is self-contained (thus potentially secure) and so has no through traffic from other tenancies; it also has direct access to at least two escape exits.

2 When the building is divided into separate tenancies the layout does not duplicate the primary circulation.

2 Conclusion

2.01 The major constraint on the use and change of use of any office building is the degree to which the shell shape prohibits and determines its subdivision.

2.02 Even the most traditional pattern of office work demands some flexibility—for group working and clerical support. This traditional pattern of office work (it probably applies to most office organisations) can be used to illustrate how well some of the examples work.

2.03 The Economist Building was tailored to the needs of one client and user, and even if that firm moved it is unlikely that an office in such a location as St James's, London would remain unlet even though it cannot provide any medium space.

Britannic House, which can provide only 10 per cent medium space, is just a speculative office block in a rather less prestigious city location—and thus in such circumstances could be much less easily let.

2.04 In Marsham Street 9 per cent of the gross area can only

The problem of the L-shaped room.

Table 1 Possible space combinations

	Small (%)	Medium (%)	Large (%)
Economist	74	—	—
Britannic House	1·6 to 79	0 to 84	—
DOE, Marsham Street	0 to 53·5	9 to 62·5	—
Whitgift Centre	0 to 82·5	0 to 82·5	—
Commercial Union	0 to 18	0 to 63·7	0 to 50·5
Robert Bosch	13 to 29	0 to 61·2	0 to 66·75
IBM	0 to 10·7	0 to 38·8	49 to 90·9
Kew	5·4 to 39·5	15 to 60·3	17·5 to 71·4
CIS	0 to 34·5	0 to 65	0 to 65

2 This histogram compares the inherent flexibility of each of the following examples. The profiles show the maximum proportion of the area in each building which can be used for 'small', 'medium' or 'large' spaces. Superimposed on this in tone is the proportion of space which can only be used in one way. Thus in the example at Kew there is a certain amount of the floor which can only be used for small spaces, some only for medium spaces, and some only for large spaces; the remainder of the floor can be used in any way.

Table 1 sets out in tabular form the information displayed in the histogram figure 2

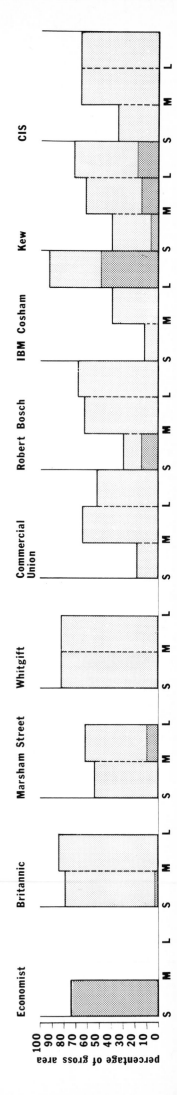

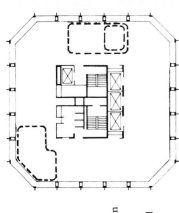
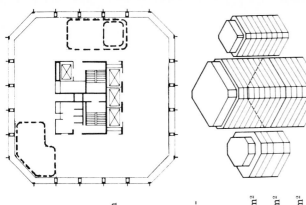
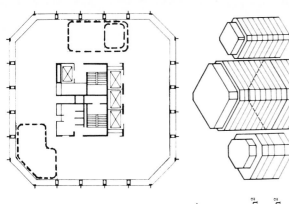
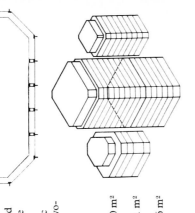

The Economist Building, London SW1

Completed 1964
Location Urban. The office tower is one of three buildings—bank, residential tower and The Economist's own editorial staff offices.
Cost £979 027.
The shell form was constrained by the GLC regulations on the ratio of office to residential buildings. There was a specific requirement in the brief for two-man editorial staff offices.

Space

Total gross area of building (tower)	6310 m²
Total gross area of selected floor	421 m²
Net area of selected floor	286 m²

Percentages of gross area

Minimum amount of small spaces	74 per cent
Maximum amount of small spaces	74 per cent
Medium spaces	none
Large spaces	none
Perimeter module	3·2 m
From core to perimeter	5·2 m

Analysis
The building was tailored for a small organisation with a specific work pattern. It can be subdivided for subletting into complete floors.
For the small capacity of each floor (30 to 40 staff) the corridor width of 1·3 m is probably adequate. The distance from this corridor to the perimeter is comparatively short (4·1 m) and results in a generous amount of window space in each office. This shell can only provide small spaces for one to six people.

if maximum small spaces are used (percentage of gross area — S M L)

if maximum medium spaces are used (percentage of gross area — S M L)

if maximum large spaces are used (percentage of gross area — S M L)

Flexibility of the typical floor plan. This diagram shows how this building can only provide 'small' spaces.

**In the nine shells which follow, the plans (except for that of IBM Cosham) are to the same scale.
The key isometric drawings are not to a constant scale.
The broken lines within the plan areas indicate the range and variety of small, medium and large spaces which may be obtained. For example, the Economist Building cannot be divided into spaces larger than 40 m² (rooms for one to three people).**

Architects

Cooperative Insurance Society, Manchester	G. S. Hay of the Cooperative Wholesale Society Ltd
The Economist Building, London SW1	Alison and Peter Smithson
Government Offices, Kew, Surrey	MPBW now DOE/PSA
Whitgift Centre, Croydon, Surrey	Fitzroy Robinson & Partners
IBM, Cosham, Hants	Foster Associates
Robert Bosch, Stuttgart	Company architect
Marsham Street, London SW1	MPBW now DOE/PSA
Commercial Union, London EC4	Gollins Melvin Ward & Partners
Brittanic House, London EC4	Joseph F. Milton Cashmore & Partners

---

be used as medium spaces and this limits its use; more important a large amount of space is wasted on circulation—the maximum that can be used in any circumstances as work space is 62·5 per cent (see table I).

2.05 The Whitgift Centre satisfies the normal spectrum of need: over 80 per cent of the gross area can be subdivided into either small or medium spaces. In this type of building it may be best to allow for future change by an initial provision of a fixed ratio of different sized spaces evenly distributed throughout, and thus avoid the disturbance of moving partitions later.

2.06 When an organisation's hq needs a certain number of large spaces as well as medium and small spaces, office blocks such as CIS will perform better than the Commercial Union Building. CIS can provide up to 35 per cent small spaces, 65 per cent medium and 65 per cent large. Commercial Union fails because it does not provide sufficient small spaces. On the other hand it is a new, air-conditioned office block in the city; and in an area of such high demand this disadvantage may be overcome if work positions are cut off from the windows by small offices on the perimeter. On the other hand this type of block, with an internal core, does provide for subdivision into tenancies better than CIS.

2.07 The Robert Bosch building, the only foreign example, is interesting in that it allows more than 60 per cent of the floor space to be used as small or medium spaces. Alternatively it can provide 29 per cent small spaces with either 41 per cent medium or 41 per cent large (see 2). This excellent range of options comes from using units of comparatively deep building space with service cores at each end.

2.08 At the other extreme from the Economist Building (only divisible into small spaces) is the IBM building at Cosham; but this single storey, lightweight, short life shell is unlikely to create a precedent. It may be a very economic way of housing a large organisation but it is really only viable as a series of large spaces; it cannot satisfy the normal requirement for small spaces unless work places without windows are accepted.

2.09 Kew is a far more practical office building for large organisations which need the maximum flexibility; it can be arranged for up to 40 per cent small spaces and up to 60 per cent medium spaces. The use of internal cores precludes the use of more than 70 per cent of the area for large spaces.

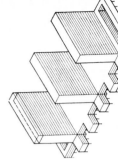
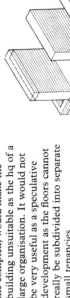

2 Marsham Street, London SW1

Completed 1970
Location Urban
Cost £4·4 million
The complex has three identical towers on a linking podium.

Space

Total gross area of building	40 500 m²
Total gross area of selected floor	913·8 m²
Net area of selected floor	555·6 m²

Percentages of gross area

Minimum amount of small spaces	0 per cent
Maximum amount of small spaces	53·5 per cent
Minimum amount of medium spaces	9·0 per cent
Maximum amount of medium spaces	62·5 per cent
Large spaces	none
Perimeter module	1·2 m
Between central columns	1·8 m
From columns to perimeter	5·2 m

Analysis

Each tower can be divided in two ways: by central or offset corridor. Either way can contain small and medium spaces; large spaces are not possible because of central columns. The limited options for subdivision and the degree of separation that occurs between units in separate parts of the complex, would make the building unsuitable as the hq of a large organisation. It would not be very useful as a speculative development as the floors cannot really be subdivided into separate small tenancies.

if maximum small spaces are used

percentage of gross area — 100 90 80 70 60 50 40 30 20 10 0 — S M L

if maximum medium spaces are used

percentage of gross area — 100 90 80 70 60 50 40 30 20 10 0 — S M L

if maximum large spaces are used

percentage of gross area — 100 90 80 70 60 50 40 30 20 10 0 — S M L

Flexibility of the typical floor plan.

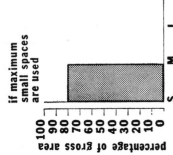
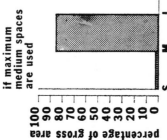
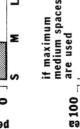

Britannic House, London EC4

Completed 1967
Location City of London
Cost £12 million
The tower block is 35 storeys high: there is a six-storey office podium alongside it plus an exhibition hall and cinema, with underground parking for 200 cars.

Space

Total gross area of tower block	45 000 m²
Total gross area of selected floor	1300 m²
Net area of selected floor	910 m²

Percentages of gross area

Minimum amount of small spaces	1·6 per cent
Maximum amount of small spaces	79 per cent
Minimum amount of medium spaces	0 per cent
Maximum amount of medium spaces	84 per cent
Large spaces	none
Perimeter module	1·3 m
Between central columns	5·6 m
From columns to perimeter	6·8 m

Analysis

The shell allows small spaces and medium spaces with a capacity of up to seven people — but does not allow large spaces. One option provides medium space which takes in part of one perimeter zone and part of the central area of the building normally used for storage or other support services; this is unlikely to be used however, as it inhibits primary circulation.

Because it has two corridors (one either side of the core) each floor of the building can easily be split into two tenancies for about 40 staff.

if maximum small spaces are used

percentage of gross area — 100 90 80 70 60 50 40 30 20 10 0 — S M L

if maximum medium spaces are used

percentage of gross area — 100 90 80 70 60 50 40 30 20 10 0 — S M L

if maximum large spaces are used

percentage of gross area — 100 90 80 70 60 50 40 30 20 10 0 — S M L

Flexibility of the typical floor plan.

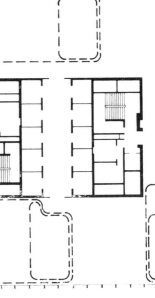

Commercial Union Building, London EC4

Completed 1969
Location City of London
Cost £8·3 million
The building is part of complex which includes the P & O building.

Space
Total gross area of building — 35 150 m²
Total gross area of selected floor — 1406 m²
Net area of selected floor — 842 m²

Percentages of gross area
Minimum amount of small spaces — 0 per cent
Maximum amount of small spaces — 18·4 per cent

Minimum amount of medium spaces — 0 per cent
Maximum amount of medium spaces — 63·7 per cent

Minimum amount of large spaces — 0 per cent
Maximum amount of large spaces — 50·5 per cent

Perimeter module — 2 m (approx)

From core to perimeter — 7·2 and 11·4 m

Analysis
The main circulation area passes around the core and creates the two zone depths — one for small and/or medium spaces, the other for medium and/or large spaces. It is possible to increase the size of offices in a few places by increasing the circulation area within them — these larger spaces must then become access offices. This form provides the possibility of a variety of spaces from 20 m² to 242 m². It also allows some separate tenancies on each floor (more if there is a doubling of primary circulation). The existing layout of this building (eg on the seventh floor) breaks a number of the rules set out in para 1.01. It allows spaces that are deeper than 2:1 and some spaces do not have direct access onto an external window.

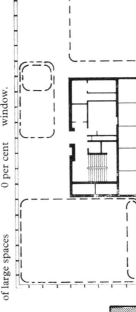

if maximum small spaces are used

percentage of gross area

if maximum medium spaces are used

percentage of gross area

if maximum large spaces are used

percentage of gross area

Flexibility of the typical floor plan.

Whitgift Centre, Croydon, Surrey

Completed 1968
Location Urban in outer suburb
Cost not available
The complex has three identical office towers over shopping precinct and multi-level car parking.

Space
Total gross area of building (one block) — 11 798 m²
Total gross area of selected floor — 878 m²
Net area of selected floor — 627 m²

Percentages of gross area
Minimum amount of small spaces — 0 per cent
Maximum amount of small spaces — 82·5 per cent

Minimum amount of medium spaces — 0 per cent
Maximum amount of medium spaces — 82·5 per cent

Large spaces — none

Perimeter module — 1·4 m
Between central columns — 1·6 m
From column to perimeter — 5·4 m

Analysis
The 'corridor' columns are closer together than 6 m and thus significantly constrict an 'across corridor' layout. Main circulation is fixed, as are spaces in four corners of building. These account for about 20 per cent of gross area.
The largest office would house 10 staff, the smallest one person quite economically.
The form allows for two separate tenancies on each floor; each would be 313 m² for 30 to 40 people. All rooms could be perimeter dependent.

if maximum small spaces are used

percentage of gross area

if maximum medium spaces are used

percentage of gross area

if maximum large spaces are used

percentage of gross area

Flexibility of the typical floor plan.

the number of small spaces is tiny. Not only must large spaces always form the major part of the accommodation, they must inevitably be *very large* (well over 800 m²).
Typical layout variations are:
1 *The maximum amount of small and medium spaces*
2 *The maximum amount of large spaces.*

IBM, Cosham, Hampshire

Completed 1971
Location Suburban, on reclaimed estuary land
Cost not available
The building is a one-storey, low cost, temporary office. Air is heated and cooled.

Space

Total gross area of building	10 658 m²
Total gross area of selected floor	10 658 m²
Net area of selected floor	9202 m²

Percentages of gross area

Minimum amount of small spaces	0 per cent
Maximum amount of small spaces	10·7 per cent
Minimum amount of medium spaces	0 per cent
Maximum amount of medium spaces	38·8 per cent
Minimum amount of large spaces	47·0 per cent
Maximum amount of large spaces	90·9 per cent
Perimeter module	1·8 m
Overall dimensions	73 m × 146 m

Analysis

The existing layout breaks some of the rules laid down in this Information sheet—eg rows of cellular offices with glazed fronts are situated back to back. These rows are used to create large spaces with a greater than 2:1 ratio. Large spaces are broken up to some extent by carrels; so most work positions have no view of the outside world. This is a serious failing in a building of this size where personal identity for workers is important.
The potential disadvantages of such an enormous building may be defined by using the rules in para 1.01; while the number of medium sized spaces is limited,

Flexibility of the typical floor plan.

if maximum small spaces are used — percentage of gross area (S M L)

if maximum medium spaces are used — percentage of gross area (S M L)

if maximum large spaces are used — percentage of gross area (S M L)

---

central strip on each wing can be used for storage or similar purposes not requiring access to external walls, maximum proportion of gross area that can be used for small spaces is low (28 per cent).
Even with limitations this is a useful plan, for it allows several options.

Robert Bosch Building, Germany

Completed 1970
Location Suburban/rural
Cost not available
The complex has three similar wings radiating from a central core, varying from eight to ten storeys.

Space

Total gross area of buildings	48 600 m²
Total gross area of selected floor	1438 m²
Net area of selected floor	830 m²

Percentages of gross area

Minimum amount of small spaces	13 per cent
Maximum amount of small spaces	29 per cent
Minimum amount of medium spaces	0 per cent
Maximum amount of medium spaces	79·9 per cent
Minimum amount of large spaces	0 per cent
Maximum amount of large spaces	66·7 per cent
Perimeter module	1·8 m
Between columns	7·2 m
Columns to perimeter	7·5 m

Analysis

Unless each wing is used as one large space, there will be a corridor running along length from one core to the other.
The position of this corridor is governed by internal columns. Any combination of columns and corridor walls will produce gaps of less than 6 m and they will be a constraint upon layout if large spaces are demanded. A 6 m gap is not considered a significant constraint in medium or small spaces.
Around the cores are areas (13 per cent of total) which can only be used as small spaces. Unless a

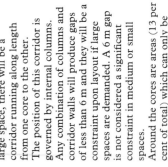

Flexibility of the typical floor plan.

if maximum small spaces are used — percentage of gross area (S M L)

if maximum medium spaces are used — percentage of gross area (S M L)

if maximum large spaces are used — percentage of gross area (S M L)

Cooperative Insurance Society (CIS) Building, Manchester

Completed 1960
Location Urban (in Manchester's commercial centre)
Cost Contract price £3 980 000
Total gross area of the total complex 51 480 m²
A group comprising large office tower on four-storey podium, smaller office tower and conference hall. Escalators give access from ground to fourth floor of podium.

Space
Total gross area of the large tower   27 500 m²
Total gross area of selected floor   1100 m²
Net area of selected floor   712 m²

Percentages of gross area
Minimum amount of small spaces   0 per cent
Maximum amount of small spaces   34·5 per cent
Minimum amount of medium spaces   0 per cent
Maximum amount of medium spaces   65·0 per cent
Minimum amount of large spaces   0 per cent
Maximum amount of large spaces   65·0 per cent
Perimeter module   1·6 m
Between columns   7 m

Analysis
Although there is the distinct limitation that it is only possible to use 35 per cent of the gross area for small spaces, this shell gives a wide range of options for all sizes of offices; there are many ways of laying out these spaces, and only a selection is shown in the diagram. The enormous columns, 1 m square, hinder flexibility. They are almost as large as smaller spaces and take up same space as small room.

if maximum small spaces are used — percentage of gross area — S M L

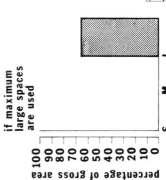
if maximum medium spaces are used — percentage of gross area — S M L

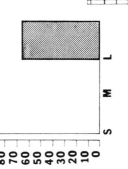

if maximum large spaces are used — percentage of gross area — S M L

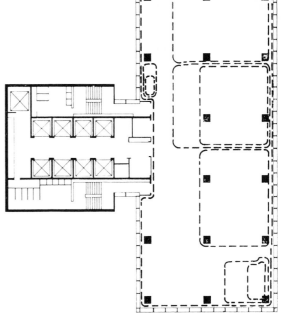

Flexibility of the typical floor plan.

Government Offices, Kew, Surrey

Completed 1969
Location Suburban on the outskirts of London
Cost £217 000, excluding fittings
A two-storey building with parking and support areas on ground floor. It was built as an experimental building for the Home Office—as a model of one floor of an office tower.

Space
Total gross area of building   1748 m²
Total gross area of first floor   1369 m²
Net area of first floor   1102 m²

Percentages of gross area
Minimum amount of small spaces   5·4 per cent
Maximum amount of small spaces   39·5 per cent
Minimum amount of medium spaces   15·0 per cent
Maximum amount of medium spaces   60·3 per cent
Minimum amount of large spaces   17·5 per cent
Maximum amount of large spaces   71·4 per cent
Perimeter module   1·21 m
Overall dimensions   37 m × 37 m

Analysis
The shell can provide spaces from 8 to 740 m². There is a limited number of layout options to take care of various combinations from this range.
For example it can be subdivided so as to provide simultaneously one-man offices, medium spaces for about 10 people and a large space, containing possibly 70 people. Escape stairs, well over 6 m from perimeter only slightly inhibit the layout.

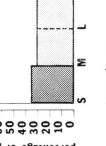
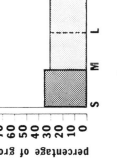
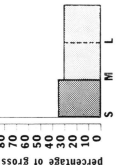
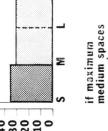
if maximum small spaces are used — percentage of gross area — S M L

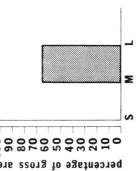
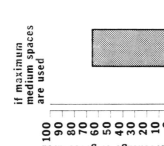
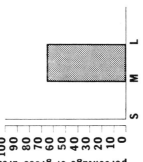
if maximum medium spaces are used — percentage of gross area — S M L

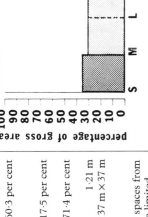
if maximum large spaces are used — percentage of gross area — S M L

Flexibility of the typical floor plan.

Section 2: The office shell

Grids

FRANCIS DUFFY discusses how grids may be used as a dimensional discipline. The aim is to review some of the more important dimensional disciplines that architects must respect when designing office buildings. While the various kinds of grids are often unified in design into a supergrid which relates every building element, there may also be a case for disengaging grids so that, for example, the scenery may be, to some extent, liberated from structure and servicing. In this way buildings may be designed to respond more flexibly to the changing needs of users.

1 The function of grids

1.01 Grids in office buildings are of two kinds. The first kind is concerned with layout planning and the second with the elements of which the building is constructed. The two kinds of grid are not unconnected; many difficulties in using a layout planning grid stem from earlier inept choices of structural, constructional or servicing grids **1, 2**.

1.02 Grids are dealt with in this study under four headings which highlight their functions:

1 *Structural grids* define zones for the major elements of the building, such as structure, and the major areas used by services. These zones will be located in the horizontal and vertical plane

2 *Constructional grids* locate and co-ordinate subsidiary building elements such as partitions and windows within the overall discipline of the structural grid

3 *Servicing grids* assist the distribution of service points throughout the building

4 *Planning grids* guide the location of workplaces and workgroups.

2 Structural grids

2.01 The structural grid is the dimensional discipline which relates the biggest and most permanent parts of the building shell to one another. The choice of an internal structural grid depends on:

1 The types and sizes of spaces which are required in the building. The analysis of nine buildings by Davies on pp. 45-51 illustrates how office spaces of various sizes are demarcated by structure.

2 The economic spans of structural system chosen, eg, flatplate, two-way waffle, precast plank, composite, space-frame.

3 Floor loadings; variations in loading occur in different parts of office buildings.

2.02 This is not the place to discuss in detail all the reasons for preferring one type of structural system to another. Economic structural grids at normal office loadings may vary as much as from 5 m to 9 m. In planning deep office spaces, 5 m is generally too constraining and becomes 'a forest of columns'. Columns or structural elements at 3 m centres constrict office layout almost as much as cross walls. The notes which follow illustrate some planning consequences of typical structural grids.

Typical structural systems
Columns
2.03 From the point of view of the planning of office layouts, columns should be placed as far apart as possible.

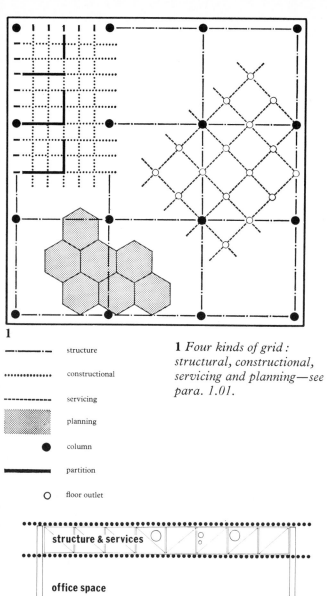

1 Four kinds of grid:
structural, constructional,
servicing and planning—see
para. 1.01.

—·—·—·—	structure
··············	constructional
- - - - - -	servicing
▨	planning
●	column
▬▬▬▬	partition
○	floor outlet

2 Grids cannot be considered
in plan alone—the section
must be considered.

The placing of columns is critical in both conventional and deep offices. In the conventional cellular office, the main problem is that columns fall in inconvenient places and do not coincide with likely lines of partitioning. Since the minimum usable width for a single office room is 2·4 m (and should be nearer 2·75 m), the column grid should be a multiple of this dimension so that a desk can be placed across the room **3**. The depth of single office rooms may go up to 5 m but is best at 3-4 m. Larger rooms occupied by two people, one at the window and one in an inner position, may be 6 m deep or more.

2.04 In the open-plan office, the column grid should be related to one of the basic units of open layout planning—workplace, aisle and workplace, ie, at least 5·1 m **4**. The flexibility required in planning complicated layouts which are non-rectilinear, which contain elements besides desks, such as filing cabinets, and which allow for

workplaces larger than the minimum (3·75 m²), demands a wider spacing of columns.

2.05 There are three common peripheral locations for columns in relation to the envelope.

1 Outside the envelope. This arrangement has the advantage of freeing the wall from internal projections, thus allowing workplaces to be placed adjacent to the envelope and avoiding the problem of special partition units against columns. However, this solution is expensive and may lead to problems of maintenance **5**.

2 Within the thickness of the envelope **6, 13, 14a**. Arrangements may complicate the partition system, as well as service runs, which are very often taken round the perimeter of the building.

3 Within the office space **8, 12**. This last arrangement complicates partition systems, can be wasteful of space at corners and also limits layout options.

2.06 If the office is to be open-plan, the distance between the perimeter and the first line of columns should at least allow for one workplace plus an aisle (2·4-2·75 m) **9a**. If this column condition is planned for cellular offices, the distance between the perimeter and the first line of columns should allow a sensible room depth (at least 3 m). Naturally, this dimension is clear floor area and excludes sills, etc. Whether open-planned or not, the larger dimension (3 m) should always be chosen. Beyond 3 m, the next suitable depth of cantilever is 4·5 m to 5 m, which allows for another workplace, or corridor if the building is to be cellular.

Structural mullions

2.07 The use of structural mullions avoids some of the problems of columns. However, the spacing of the mullions determines where partitions can be placed **7**. This is true even if not all the mullions are structural, because it is the structural members which determine the module **10**. In general, the modular discipline created by structural mullions may result in room sizes which can be increased or decreased only in increments of 6·0 m². This may be too great for economy if room sizes are to be tuned to finely graded space standards **10**. The spacing of window mullions is important in cellular offices because it determines room widths and because room width (with room depth) leads to efficient use of cellular buildings. Table II shows the consequences of adopting a 1200 mm basic fenestration module in a building with a standard 4800 mm room depth.

2.08 A mullion module of 1350 mm is preferable to 1200 because it permits an 1800 mm desk to be arranged comfortably either across the room or parallel to the long axis **14**. A width of 4050 mm is likely to provide a convenient large single office and 5400 mm a convenient shared room.

Loadbearing external walls

2.09 These have the great advantage that they provide a grid with zones of freedom for the location of partitions **11, 13**. Room sizes can easily be adjusted within the fixing zone to give a large range of possible areas. As the ratio of window to wall increases, locating partitions becomes less flexible. Since many people like their desks by the window, the building with loadbearing walls can result in wasted space. Desks may be placed by windows only and the solid wall areas underused.

54

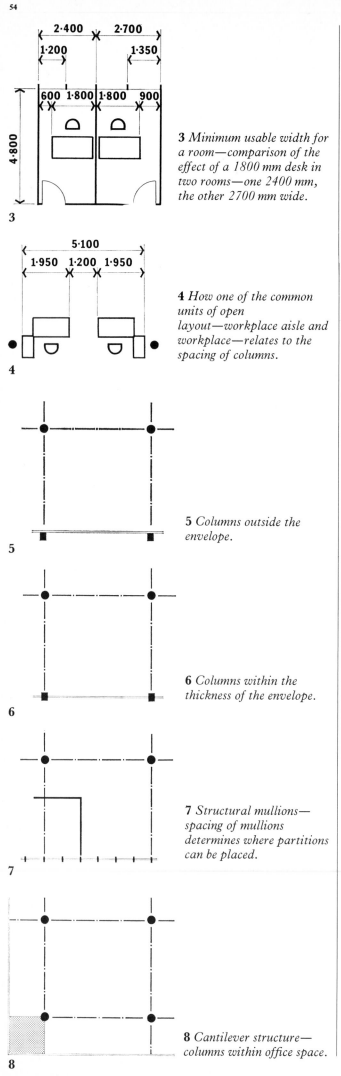

3 *Minimum usable width for a room—comparison of the effect of a 1800 mm desk in two rooms—one 2400 mm, the other 2700 mm wide.*

4 *How one of the common units of open layout—workplace aisle and workplace—relates to the spacing of columns.*

5 *Columns outside the envelope.*

6 *Columns within the thickness of the envelope.*

7 *Structural mullions—spacing of mullions determines where partitions can be placed.*

8 *Cantilever structure—columns within office space.*

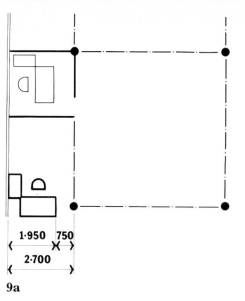

9a

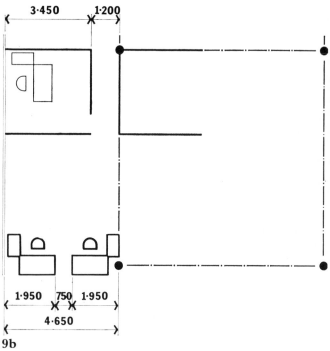

9b

9 *Planning office layouts with cantilever condition—cantilever should allow either **a** minimum room depth or workplace and aisle between column and perimeter. After that*

*condition has been satisfied, the next step **b** is to accommodate two workplaces and an aisle or a room and a corridor: this step means a considerable increase in the cantilever.*

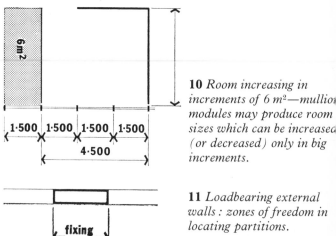

10 *Room increasing in increments of 6 m²—mullion modules may produce room sizes which can be increased (or decreased) only in big increments.*

11 *Loadbearing external walls: zones of freedom in locating partitions.*

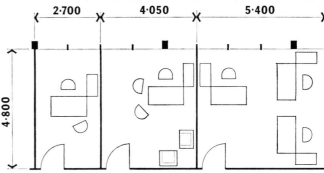

14 *Room arrangements. Furniture arrangements in rooms ranging from width of 270 mm for one person to* *5400 mm for three people. The increment is determined by the 1350 mm mullion spacing.*

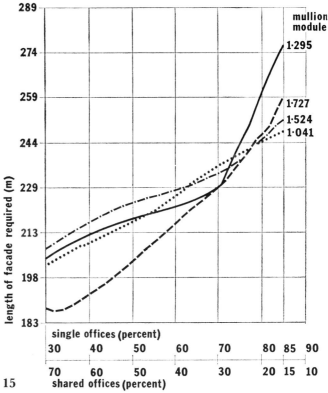

15

15 *This graph shows some of the implications of the information in table II. It makes several assumptions: for instance how status is to be shown and seen (will, say, three bays well enough establish a status grade against two bays?). The smallest mullion spacing is not necessarily the best—the rooms cannot grow by big enough steps. Thus, with 1295 mm, even single* *rooms can grow only by 1295 mm, becoming 2590 mm, 3885 mm, 5180 mm wide. And with a larger module, 1727 mm, it would be unthinkable to give relatively junior management 5182 mm rooms, so they are forced to stay in rooms 3454 mm which gives a 'saving' in facade length. This is based on work done by G. Shuttleworth.*

3 Floor loadings

3.01 Floor loadings in office buildings vary. Table I illustrates some of the most common conditions. The tendency to use the lowest possible figure should be resisted as this is likely to inhibit planning flexibility. However, superimposed floor loading can be costly. To design for full flexibility, ie, permitting concentrated loads such as registries and libraries, to be moved to any part of the office may add 5 per cent to the total cost. The core of

12

13

12 *Cantilever structure—New Zealand House. Architects Robert Matthew, Johnson-Marshall & Partners.*
13 *External walls with limited fixing zone. Office building in London W8. Architects Chapman Taylor Partners.*

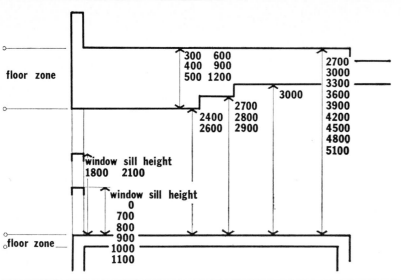

16 *Ceiling-height dimensions related to floor-to-floor heights and floor thicknesses. Window sill height to be considered. For visual comfort of workers sitting at desks.*

the building can sometimes provide space with a high load rating. But placing heavy loads on the office floor itself is sometimes necessary. The inherent problems are to decide how big the zone of heavy loading should be on any given floor and where it should be placed to provide maximum flexibility.

Table I Typical loadings

	N/m²
Normal office loading	3·830
Punched card accounting machines	5·270
Four-drawer foolscap filing cabinet	7·182
Lateral filing cabinet	9·576
Punched card storage cabinets	17·237
Address plate storage cabinets	21·067

These figures are based on research by the Office Management Division of ICI (AJ 12.2.64 Information sheet 1237).
Always check concentrated filing and storage loadings as well as such special loads as GPO PABX equipment.

Table II Office width and bay module—allocation of accommodation and total space required. Bay module 4800 mm and mullion centres 1200 mm assumed. These are not recommended, but simply an example.

Designation	No of people	Single room or sharing	No of cases	Office widths*			General office multiples of 3600	m² per person
				2400	3600	4800		
Senior managers	2	Single	2			2		23·23
Middle managers	6	Single	6		6			17·84
Junior managers	10	Single	10	10				11·89
Senior assistants	18	Sharing 2 in 3600	9		9			8·92
Senior clerks	24	Sharing 3 in 4800	8			8		7·90
Junior clerks	40	In general office at 4 in 3600	10				10	4·46
Total no of offices				10	15	10	10	
Facade length (m)				24·5	54·9	48·8	36·6	164·6

* All 4800 mm deep

4 Structural grids in the vertical dimension

4.01 For minimum floor-to-ceiling height for an office which is in inner London, the London Building Acts stipulate a minimum of 2·438 m on the top floor and 2·591 m on other floors. Recommendations for vertical controlling dimension for office buildings are contained in *Dimensional co-ordination for building*, documents DC4, DC5, DC6 and DC7, and in BS 4330: 1968. These recommendations are illustrated in **16**. In general, the deeper the office space the greater the floor-to-floor dimension, because of the greater depth required between ceiling and slab for the service ducting. This is still likely to be so despite such forms as the two-way waffle which are designed to avoid deep beams. In addition, there are many who will argue strongly for a great floor-to-ceiling height as

the depth of the space increases in order to compensate for what they consider to be an oppressive 'sense of ceiling' which occurs in the open plan. 2·70 m is currently thought to be a comfortable floor-to-ceiling height for deep spaces. Minimum ceiling height should be avoided in deep open offices.

5 Constructional grids

5.01 Planning must take account of apparently insignificant elements such as fluorescent tubes, as their cumulative impact can have a profound effect on planning. The solution to this kind of problem is not necessarily to reduce the grid to the lowest common denominator of all the systems to be accommodated. If this were so the resultant grid would be extremely fine. However, the need for constructional grids is determined by the fact that building products and materials are made in a limited range of sizes.

Lighting fittings and ceilings
5.02 Fluorescent lighting fittings may be 600, 900, 1200, 1500, 1800 or 2400 mm long. However, the total length of the fitting is often slightly more than this nominal dimension and can conflict with the ceiling tile grid which is most likely to be based strictly on 300 mm increments, especially if it is intended to use flush fittings. Fluorescent lighting fittings can also be surface-mounted, or suspended, or fitted in tracks which provide a degree of adjustment **17**. More sophisticated types of ceiling which avoid the dimensional discipline of fluorescent tubes include:
1 *Illuminated ceilings*. Translucent ceilings above which the lighting fittings are suspended. This type of lighting is inefficient, giving low illumination at high brilliance **18**.
2 *Integrated ceilings*. These include lighting as well as air-conditioning and, in some cases, other services. Some are based on a 1500 mm grid **19**.
5.03 A basic decision on lighting which is particularly important in open-plan offices is whether the lighting pattern is to be directional. Since many open-plan offices have equal freedom in both directions, non-directional lighting is preferable. This explains why 600 mm square fittings in non-directional patterns are often used in the United States. Another device favoured in Europe is to suspend a two-way baffle beneath tubes which can then be of any number or length.

Partitions
5.04 Partitions are of two kinds:
1 *Assembled on site*. Many partition systems are fitted together on site. They are based on standard studs and are covered with a wide range of materials, including plaster-

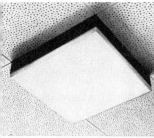

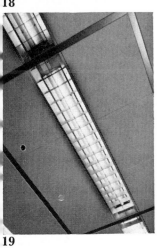

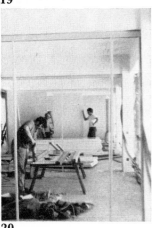

17 *Ceiling tiles and lighting.*
18 *Illuminated ceiling.*
19 *Integrated ceiling.*
20 *Site-constructed partitioning.*
21 *Steel partition.*

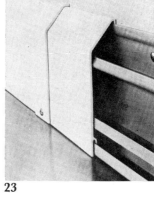

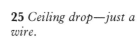

22 *Floor outlet with field telephone.*
23 *Skirting trunking.*

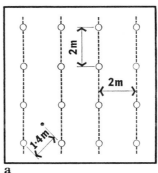

24 *Unequal outlet grid:*
a *2 m × 2 m service outlet grid achieves an overall coverage such that no position in the layout is further than 1·4 m from an outlet.*
b *To economise on outlets, a 3 m × 3 m could be used. This means that the farthest position on the layout from an outlet is 2·1 m. This may be too far if the aim is to serve each workplace with its own outlet.*
c *A compromise solution is an unequal grid which needs fewer outlets than the 2 m × 2 m grid but which ensures that no position is farther than 1·6 m from an outlet. Unequal grids, in this respect, provide more effective coverage than simple rectilinear grids.*

25 *Ceiling drop—just a wire.*

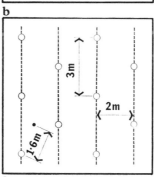

board and glass. They can usually be trimmed to size. The only modular discipline inherent in them is the size of standard sheet materials—often 1200 mm, but this is not great since cutting can often be done on site **20**.

2 *Assembled in the factory*. These partition systems are based on factory-assembled units **21**. The dimensional discipline which they impose is thus stricter. The usual module is 1200 mm, but infill pieces are usually available. Some more sophisticated partition systems can be made to measure for a particular job.

6 Servicing grids

Perimeter-dependent

6.01 In cellular office buildings, power and telephone wiring is usually carried either in the partition or in skirting trunking **22**. The dimensions of such wiring are subordinate to the partitioning.

Open layout grid

6.02 Although several types of under-floor ducting are in use, not all of which demand a strict grid of outlets for power and lighting, a decision must be made on the spacing of these outlets because they relate so closely to the planning of layouts **23**. Leads longer than 2 m—with their increased nuisance value and danger of people tripping over them—should be avoided.

6.03 Grids of power outlets vary between 1200 and 2500 mm. Not all outlets need be activated at any one time. Some economy is achieved by using unequal grids **24**. The choice of grid is also affected by the structural grid, the proportion of staff using telephones and by the density of occupation. Ceiling grids provide power and telephone outlets independent of partitions and floor but at the price of wires dropping from the ceiling or the use of poles **25**.

7 Planning grids

7.01 Much of office layout consists of a process of joining one workplace to another until everyone is accommodated. The basic increment is the workplace. Planning grids are devices which impose an overall order and maintain individual and group space standards. In cellular office buildings, the planning grid most affects the location of partitions relating to space standards for various grades of staff. Space standards as explained in Methods of Measuring Space; the Scenery, p.90 may exhibit few or many grades. The planning grid for the partition layout may, therefore, be fine or coarse to allow the right kind of distinction between grades. This is equally true whether rooms are occupied by one or by more people. In open-plan layouts, the planning grid is less evident but no less important. Here the grid has to preserve the territorial identity of groups, to discipline routes through large open spaces and to guard space standards so that some workplaces do not gain space at the expense of others. It must do all this without the aid of any physical barriers like partitions. Another method is to use an overall grid like the hexagonal grid for laying out some screen-based furniture systems.

7.02 Many discussions of office space planning grids never get beyond dimensioning the workplace unit but in most offices, libraries, meeting areas, storage and machine rooms must be accommodated too and the planning grid should also help the layout of these. Planning grids are related to and constrained by:

1 *The structural grid*, eg, bay sizing and column and mullion location

2 *The constructional grid*, eg, lighting, ceiling tiles

3 *The servicing grid*, eg, the distribution of power points and telephone outlets.

8 Conclusions

8.01 1 Planning implications should always be taken into account when selecting structural, constructional and servicing grids.

2 It is not usually possible, and sometimes a waste of time, to try to achieve a complete match between planning, structural, constructional and servicing grids.

3 Although the open plan may liberate the architect from the discipline of partition grids, this freedom is achieved at the expense of the difficulty of relating a planning grid to a grid of service outlets.

SECTION 3: THE OFFICE INTERIOR

Section 3: The office interior

Bürolandschaft: A science of office design?

Office landscaping revolutionised the design of office shells and scenery when it was first introduced over twelve years ago. Experiences since then have ranged from the early enthusiasm, to extravagant claims, to commercial imitations, and to the final inevitable disillusionment. It is now possible to step back a little and assess objectively the claims made for office landscaping without undue enthusiasm or disparagement. BEVIS FULLER focuses on one aspect of office organisation; he does not attempt to explain how this particular solution to office organisation was generated.

1 Background

1.01 In Germany, about 17 years ago, a group of management consultants, who called themselves the Quickborner Team, invented a new approach to office design, which became known as *bürolandschaft*[1]. The characteristics of offices designed in this way are their large, open floor areas, provided with relatively sophisticated environments, which are furnished in a 'free' rather than a rectilinear geometric way **1**.

1 *The obvious characteristics of bürolandschaft offices are their large floor areas furnished with less formality than traditional open offices. For instance, carpets and planting help to provide a sense of luxury. Layout can easily be rearranged without structural alterations.*

2 A unique approach to office design

2.01 The originators of bürolandschaft claim, however, that their invention cannot be understood in terms of its obvious characteristics but must be appreciated as a unique approach which applies scientific knowledge to office design. Lorenzen and Jaeger,[2] for example say '. . . the term *office landscape* is, in fact, catchy—but if focuses only on the visually perceptible result of a very complex planning approach.'

2.02 What, then, is remarkable about this complex planning approach according to its practitioners? An examination of a number of articles written by members of the Quickborner Team shows that it is claimed as unique in at least four distinct ways. First, it is a team approach; second, it is a way of meeting future needs as well as present ones; third, it embraces organisational improvement as well as building design; and fourth, it provides a set of specific design prescriptions drawn from modern organisational theory.

The team approach

2.03 Bürolandschaft is described as an approach '. . . in which systems analysts, architects, and interior designers plan, as a team, the optimum layout[3] and work environment for an organisation. . . .'

'Team, as understood in this context, is the simultaneous working together of various specialists with the possibility of instantaneous face-to-face communication'.[2]

Now this is a very specific definition of team working, which stresses interaction, but it is no more: Bürolandschaft has no monopoly of team-working or of the use of specialists. To recommend team-working is commendable but to claim that it confers uniqueness is unjustified.

Meeting future needs

2.04 'The Quickborner Team's professed aim to plan office buildings which not only meet fully the requirements of office procedures, but also environmental and "work-needs" of the office personnel—not only for today, but for the entire life span of the building. We do this by drawing, in a systematic way, on all applicable knowledge available.'[2] The quotation implies that the approach has some special means of predicting the future which is unknown to others. The only way, in fact, in which bürolandschaft provides for the future is the obvious one, through the inherent flexibility of its large, well-serviced spaces. The claim to use 'all applicable knowledge' is therefore specious.

Organisational improvement

2.05 '. . . not only were better office buildings designed, but also improvements in the organisational system were implemented. The latter is of paramount importance, because it makes no sense to put an obsolete system into a new building.'[2]

An example, the analysis of filing systems, is used to imply that other design approaches do not allow for organisational improvements.

'Investigations in offices show that there are an average of from 15 to 18 feet of files per person. At this point, we differ from the conventional approach by not providing equipment and space for that type of storage.'[2]

2.06 However, the next passage provides a welcome (and rare) admission that there is a distinction between organisation and building design:
'We question the necessity of the material. The volume of paper used is excessive for efficiency at the individual work places and requires too large a portion of valuable space. . . . We, as consultants, consider it our task to identify and solve such problems with new systems and methods before we begin to plan space.'[2]

If, indeed, as Lorenzen and Jaeger say, they 'solve such problems . . . before we begin to plan space', then, clearly, the two activities are independent. Organisational improvement is no more a monopoly of bürolandschaft than is team-working.

Design prescriptions

2.07 If the above claims to uniqueness, namely, the team approach, meeting future needs, and organisational improvement can be dismissed, the case that bürolandschaft is a unique approach which applies scientific knowledge to office design must rest on its specific design prescriptions for buildings. The importance of the office building is indeed explicitly set out.

'The most decisive effect to be achieved by such office planning is the improvement in office efficiency. We are not just thinking here of routine work, but even more of decision-making processes. Traditional "space planners and designers" are insufficiently equipped to cope with this task. Traditional management consultants, on the other hand, have failed to realise that their knowledge is highly essential if optimum solutions are to be achieved in this field. Quickborner Team, as management consultant, was successful in filling this gap. We realised that the office building is, in effect, management's most important tool. . . .
'The effective functioning of the organisation is decisively determined by the type of office building and/or office layout used. The office building is the main tool for our administrative work and decision-making process. As of today, it is more costly and affects more people than even the computer.'[2]

2.08 Thus bürolandschaft, as a form of design, is claimed decisively to affect organisational efficiency. It is the substance of this claim and its articulation which is examined in most detail below. Can it be shown that specific organisational knowledge is related to particular design features? To examine this case, and to allow the reader to judge for himself, the discussion below is set out in sections each headed by a particular assumption of bürolandschaft theory. First, an account of the design prescriptions of the bürolandschaft practitioners, including translated quotations from their articles, is presented. This is followed by a discussion of this material.

3 Organisational ideas and office design
Communication in organisations requires large undivided floor areas

3.01 Organisations are described as 'information processing centres':

'The administration of a concern can be considered as a "stock exchange" of information processing' which is the key-work in administrative work. Paper-flow, communication, and the decision-making process are terms which characterise information processing. In the administrative organisation, . . . most of the exchange of information is between persons but can also be between man and machines.'[4]

Having established the basic premise that organisations are for information processing, communication is presented as a central design problem. The need for communication is one argument used in favour of large, undivided floor areas:

'A great many man hours are lost in work involving cooperation among personnel who are spread throughout many floors and individual rooms. . . . The building must allow for the close positioning on one undivided area of those groups connected by strong lines of communication.'[4] **2**

Discussion

3.02 What must be questioned in this part of the 'bürolandschaft' theory are the assumptions made about organisations. Are all office organisations well described by the term *information processing centres* with its suggestion of a ceaseless traffic of paper, speech and decisions? Are there not many cases of small groups of people working within close confines, perhaps with material coming in and going out by post twice daily, and with little need for intensive communication? Are there not office jobs where a particular task is of long duration, so that the person doing it has only infrequent need for communication? If there are, in fact, great variations in the type of work performed in office organisations, then there should be more interest in finding out about these kinds of work, and *a priori* assumptions should be avoided. Indeed, the techniques used by the Quickborner group themselves provide examples of the empirical study of communication. It is grossly misleading to assume that all organisations are communication-intensive. Further, even in cases where there is considerable communication in organisations, it does not follow that there is an indisputable case for large, undivided areas. Most communication may take place within relatively small work groups. Communication between the groups may be slight, and is quite often conducted by one person, not by the group as a whole. In such cases, sub-division into small areas need not cause significant loss of man-hours.

Staff should be arranged on the basis of communication analyses

3.03 The importance of communication in organisation does not merely call for large, undivided floor areas. It should also determine the arrangement of staff. A more obvious way of planning the arrangement would be to follow the firm's departmental hierarchical structure, but it is suggested that this structure does not coincide with the pattern of communication:

'The following example shows the results which would have occurred had one started from the point that the organisational areas within an enterprise actually contained the highest frequency of communication. . . . There are the following large organisational units in a machine factory:
1 Purchasing department
2 Drafting department
3 Design department
4 Sales department
'In the planning of a four-storey office building the result would be that the distribution of the departments would result in the following schematic layout. . . . **3**
'. . . Tallying the actual running communication shows, however, that the individual sub-departments within the main department have a low frequency of communication and that the greatest frequency of communication is between the groups of the various departments. . . .
'. . . The arrangement of the groups within the building must follow a corresponding pattern.'[5] **4**

Discussion

3.04 The comments made above about communication are again pertinent: the pattern of communication is a matter

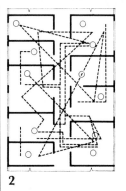

2 *The bürolandschaft case rests on assumptions about the nature of office work, especially about communication. This diagram entitled 'Unorderly work systems' is used to suggest that the subdivision of all office buildings into small rooms must inevitably frustrate communication.*

2

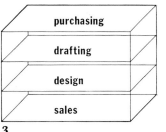

3

	design
drafting	design
purchasing	sales
drafting	design
purchasing	sales
drafting	design
purchasing	sales
drafting	design
purchasing	sales

4

3 *This represents the result of a conventional design approach. It accepts without question the subdivision of the organisation into separate departments which are accordingly placed on four separate levels.*
4 *Alternative layout to* **3**, *resulting from communication analysis. The communication analysis consists of a count of telephone calls, visits, and paper passed between individuals. The subsequent layout brings into proximity those between whom there is most communication. It is*

asserted that frequently there is more in 'horizontal' than 'vertical' communication; that is, more between equal than between different ranks. Thus the departmental structure becomes dispersed as shown. It seems questionable whether communication analysis would frequently provide a significant basis for office layout, since the departmental structure is usually devised to contain the most regular communication operations.

for empirical study, not for *a priori* assumptions that communication *must* determine arrangement. No doubt cases can be found where 'horizontal' communication is of greater significance then hierarchical, but the suggestion that this is common is questionable, since the hierarchical structure is frequently devised to contain much of the communication pattern. This criticism is not intended to deny the usefulness, in many cases, of arrangements, in whatever kinds of buildings, of working groups according to known patterns of communication. It is simply intended to cast doubt on the over-generalised position taken by the 'bürolandschaft' practitioners.

Working groups should have group spaces

3.05 It is claimed that membership of a group increases output and that each group should have its own space:

'. . . the feeling of belonging to a group increases work performance, a fact clearly proved by many investigations. Each group must have . . . its own particular and specific "working space". . . .'[4]

Discussion

3.06 The assertion that group membership increases work performance, which is said to have been 'clearly proved by many investigations', is incorrect. A simple refutation of the statement could be made by pointing to other investigations of work groups which seem to show that they can restrict output (Lupton,[6] Sales[7]) but this is not at issue. The essential point is not whether group membership increases or decreases performance, but *that there is no direct connection between work-group membership and performance* of any kind, or at any time. To make this clearer it is necessary to appreciate that 'organisations' are not self-contained entities.

3.07 'Work performance' is not an isolated phenomenon contained within work boundaries but is motivated by the meanings which people attach to their actions, **5, 6, 7**. These meanings are products of life experience, which shapes expectations and demands. The way in which people are involved in their work can vary from intense devotion, through indifference, to positive loathing. A car worker may loathe his work on the assembly belt but may perform is assiduously because the pay is high and buys him satisfactions in the world outside. A married female clerical worker may be indifferent to her work but derive satisfactions from social contacts in work and from earning pin-money. A political worker may display intense devotion because of identification with his party; that identification itself may result from experience of a particular position in society. It is to explanations of these kinds that we must turn to understand human action, not to objective features of the environment, whether physical or social.

Supervision requires undivided floor areas

3.08 Problems of control are also raised as a reason for having large undivided areas, and although not explicitly stated, for not separating the managers from the managed. In a section headed 'Advantages of office landscape in open plan offices'[4] several statements occur which are here analysed:

1 'Unnecessary or prolonged visits are avoided': it is implied that in conventional buildings time is lost through certain kinds of visits. One form of 'unnecessary' visit would presumably occur if a person seeks to visit another who is absent from his room but cannot be seen to be absent because of the walls. There may be other forms also. A 'prolonged' visit presumably occurs when people carry on a conversation beyond the duration required for official purposes. It is suggested that openness can obviate these visits.

2 'Punctuality and self-discipline are encouraged': it is implied that in a conventional building people are likely to be unpunctual or lazy because their activities are concealed by the walls and that undivided areas obviate this tendency.

3 'There is an optimum of orderliness at each individual desk and throughout the entire office': again it is implied that people are disorderly when concealed by walls, and that an effective way of producing order is to have undivided spaces.

Discussion

3.09 In so far as this argument in favour of undivided areas rests simply on the idea that where activities can be seen and heard they are easier to control, there is no dispute. 'Bürolandschaft' areas are not, of course, wholly undivided, nor are conventional offices wholly divided, so that this aspect of control cannot be thought of as absolutely polarised.

3.10 However, what subjects people include in their conversations, how long the conversations last, 'punctuality', 'laziness', 'orderliness', are not consequences of physical causes but, as argued above, are aspects of meaningful human action. Thus, it is not possible in principle to show that undivided areas *cause* any of these things. A simple 'mental experiment' shows that it is really as easy, for instance, to envisage undivided areas causing an *increase* in non-work-related interaction as a decrease. For

6

7

5, 6, 7 The bürolandschaft writers tend to assert that work performance can be influenced by changing office design. But work performance, whether in the office or elsewhere, is not something that can be separated from a person's whole experience.
There are several different kinds of involvement in work depending on the ends which people pursue and the means by which they achieve them.
5 It is possible to loathe the job but perform it assiduously because the pay is high and satisfaction is sought elsewhere. The worker in this situation is described by some as 'alienated'.
6 Many people are indifferent to the job itself but perform it for supplementary finance and perhaps for the social contacts it brings. This attitude may be described as 'instrumental'.
7 Work may be a source of intrinsic satisfaction where there is commitment to the work itself. This involvement may be described as 'moral'.

8 *Bürolandschaft writers assert that seeing the work and performance of others is stimulating and reduces negative group thinking.*

The validity of such assertions is doubtful. Seeing the work and performance of others is not necessarily stimulating.

example, there may well be increased collaboration on crossword puzzles.

Avoidance of 'organisational conflict' requires undivided floor areas

3.11 A further aspect of the case made for undivided areas is that tendencies to various forms of conflict are obviated:

'Seeing the work and performance of others is stimulating and reduces over-intense negative group thinking. . . .
'Intrigue is reduced and better, more businesslike, contact results between superiors and other office workers.'[4] **8**

Discussion

3.12 The arguments outlined above have sufficiently demonstrated both that the statements made are not good social theory (eg, seeing the work of others is not necessarily stimulating) and that it is wrong to move from physical 'causes' (undivided floor areas) to behavioural consequences.

3.13 This approach may sound like a counsel of despair if it is taken to mean that a psychological approach at the level of individual experience is needed. But this is not what is meant; a valid approach which emphasises meaning can be found in a social-action approach, which starts, not with individuals, but with representative actors. It must be emphasised that if use is to be made of ideas drawn from organisation theory in relation to design, it must be from theory which can itself withstand critical examination.

3.14 This argument is not stated with the aim of decrying the provision of identifiable space in offices, which may be a good thing to do for various reasons. It is stated to show that the basic premises of the assertion that 'each group must [or should] have its own particular and specific work space' are misleading. There also seems to be an implication that group feeling can be produced by providing group spaces. Physical arrangement cannot generate social arrangements; one has only to imagine a collection of people, with deeply conflicting interests, orientations and expectations, being placed in a particular space, to dismiss the idea that they can. It is quite a different matter that a group of people may attach meanings of cohesion, identity and so on to being together in a certain space. Broady[8] has repeatedly attacked architectural (or environmental) determinism, yet statements of a deterministic kind continue to be made. Even Broady, despite his energy and eloquence[8], does not state the attack in its most radical form. It is not that 'the exact consequences of any particular space cannot be predicted', but that spaces do not have human behavioural consequences. This is not hair-splitting or pedantic; it is a fundamental distinction about the sources of human action.

Managers should not be separated from their staff

3.15 Not only is communication in general advanced as a reason for having undivided areas, but it is argued that managers, in particular, should not be cut off from those they manage because positive separation will cause tensions:

'Managers also belong to a group, to a small work group as well as to a larger one: the department or division. And in the long run there is no advantage in erecting barriers between certain selected employees and others. Such separation would break down the feeling of belonging together, and undesirable tensions would easily arise. It is really essential, therefore, that executives should not work in private rooms but in the same room as all the other employees, separated from them only by small movable partitions.'

Discussion

3.16 Criticism of this part of bürolandschaft theory can also be made on the dual grounds of first, being invalid organisation theory, and second, arguing behavioural effects direct from physical 'cause'. In the organisation theory relied on, the avoidance of tensions is taken to be desirable and attainable. Such a view ignores the meaning of tensions to the participants, and substitutes instead, a reified (falsely concrete) concept of 'organisational health' as a desirable state, free from tension and conflict. But 'organisations' cannot be sick or well; only people are sick or well, and tensions and conflict are not pathological organisational states, but are endemic features of human relationships, especially where interests differ and power is exercised.

3.17 Apart from this, relationships between executives and employees, of whatever kind, are not caused by their being or not being in the same room. This is not to deny that meanings may be attached to such things, but what matters is the way the participants view their being in the same room; there is no direct link between the external 'fact' and a behavioural outcome. Again, in making these points, it must be stressed that it is a separate matter whether or not it is desirable in particular cases for design to provide, or not provide, separate rooms.

Organisational change requires undivided floor areas

3.18 Lastly, organisations are taken to be subject to rapid changes in information processing, resulting in changed patterns of communication. The changing patterns should continue to determine the arrangement of staff. This will entail the formation of different-sized groups in different relationships which, it is suggested, can be achieved only within undivided spaces, because fixed constructional elements such as walls prevent rearrangement:

'A change in the rules of processing means, however, that the working stations will change and that new communication connections come into play. The space principle must make it possible to change the arrangement of working places without having to resort to changes in the building. Carrying out such organisational demands in an office building can only be realised in large, undivided office areas.'[5]

Discussion
3.19 As a simple argument in favour of a particular kind of flexibility this might be unexceptionable. What must, however, be questioned is the assumption of change and of the significance of communication as a general problem rather than an examination of change and communication as variables. Some organisations change rapidly (eg, electronics firms), others much less so (eg, legal firms). Internal communication processes are important for some (eg, the stock exchange) **9**, for others much less so (research institutions). Can there not be kinds of change which could be realised quite satisfactorily in subdivided buildings? If legitimate issues like these are raised, there should be answers to them. The 'bürolandschaft' theory which ignores them, cannot be acceptable.

4 Bürolandschaft: Background of ideas
Human relations
4.01 A long discussion of the background of ideas held by the bürolandschaft writers would be inappropriate here. However, a brief discussion of the subject is justified because, as noted earlier, the support of organisation theory is loosely invoked to give a 'scientific' base for ideas about design.

4.02 Characteristics already noted in the above discussion, such as the strong emphasis on communication, on feelings of belonging, on the avoidance of organisation conflict, on high work performance, and so on, are associated with the 'human relations' school of the '30s, with 'neo-human relations', and with the 'organisational psychology' of more recent years. In his introduction, in *Kommunikation*, of a report on a conference held in Pittsburgh in 1966, Wolfgang Schnelle refers to McGregor's *Human side of enterprise* and to Likert's *New patterns of management* as sources of ideas on participative management which were central to the discussion, confirming that organisational psychology is indeed the source of many of the ideas used by the Quickborner Team.

Hierarchy of needs
4.03 Put simply, the organisational psychologists, who also include Herzberg, Argyris and others, use the concept that people have a hierarchy of needs, an idea developed first by the psychologist Maslow, to revive the idea 'that workers are similarly motivated and can be understood in any unique situation by reference to general assumption about human behaviour. . . .'[9] According to Maslow, people first seek to satisfy lower needs, ie, physiological needs, then safety needs, then social needs for acceptance by others, and finally, at the highest level, needs for 'self-fulfilment'. These needs are taken to be universal attributes of human beings, at least within the boundaries of Western culture. Having made this basic assumption, the organisational psychologists go on to argue in favour of arranging organisations in ways that will provide for the satisfaction

9 *The intense communication activity of a stock exchange. Bürolandschaft practitioners make their design prescriptions on the assumption that offices are,* *in effect, stock exchanges of information, but not many offices are like stock exchanges. Many workers seldom communicate in the course of their work.*

of these needs. Job enrichment, job rotation, responsible group autonomy through the delegation of decision making, are among the recommendations which they make.

Conclusion: disputed ideas
4.04 This is very much the conventional wisdom of contemporary management but it has been shown to be basically unsound by many critics. The most cogent objection is that the supposedly universal needs cannot be shown to exist. Empirical studies, such as that of affluent workers by Goldthorpe *et al*,[10] find that they are not dissatisfied, although work is perceived as lacking richness, change, autonomy and any share in decision-making. Clark[9] advances subsidiary critical points: that the organisational psychologists assume that work is a central life interest, and that they also assume that hierarchical relationships are of central importance. But it has been shown that for many people work is not a central life interest (Dubin[11]) and there are studies of organisations (eg, Crozier[12]) which indicate that in some instances horizontal relationships matter far more to individuals than do hierarchical ones. Faced with criticism of this type, supporters of this point of view such as Blauner[13] and Argyris[14], are driven to argue that workers 'ought' to have the needs that they claim exist.

4.05 The main point that should be made here is that the background of 'bürolandschaft' ideas is not a well-established, uncontroversial, body of knowledge, called organisation theory, but a particular variety of ideas in a much disputed area, already subject to very potent criticism of which bürolandschaft practitioners show little awareness. Their unawareness is no doubt due to their location in the field of management consultancy, where organisational psychology still provides a legitimating ideology.

Footnotes and References

1 The team's name is derived from the place in Germany, Quickborn bei Hamburg, where their office was situated and the term *bürolandschaft* can be translated as *office landscape*.

2 LORENZEN, H. J., and D. JAEGER. The office landscape, A systems concept. *Contract magazine*, January 1968

3 The assumption that there is an optimum layout is made all too easily. Such an assumption is open to serious objection.

4 GOTTSCHALK, O., and H. J. LORENZEN. The new shape of office buildings. *Kommunikation* 111/1, 1967 [32]

5 LORENZEN, H. J. Organisational aspects in planning office buildings, *Kommunikation* 111/1, 1967 [32]

6 LUPTON, T. On the shop floor, Oxford, 1963, Pergamon [(Afk)]

7 SALES, L. R. Behaviour of industrial workgroups 1958 Wiley [(Afn)]

8 BROADY, M. Planning for People, 1969, Bedford Square Press

9 CLARK, P. A. Organisational design 1972, Tavistock [(Af)]

10 GOLDTHORPE, J. H., D. LOCKWOOD, F. BECKHOFFER and J. PLATT. The affluent worker in the class structure, 1970, CUP [Afk)]

11 DUBIN, R. Industrial workers' worlds, *Social Problems*, January 1956 [(Afk)]

12 CROZIER, M. The bureaucratic phenomenon, 1964 Tavistock [(Af)]

13 BLAUNER, R. Alienation and Freedom, 1964, Chicago University Press

14 ARGYRIS, C. R. Integrating the individual and the organization, 1964, Wiley

Section 3: The office interior

Bürolandschaft: an appraisal

FRANCIS DUFFY and COLIN CAVE continue the appraisal of office landscaping begun by **BEVIS FULLER**. They examine the reasons for its attraction, raise questions about its definition, size, assumptions on status, flexibility and the kind of furniture it is said to require. Good and bad points are evaluated and special attention is given to the many innovations in office design stimulated by office landscaping.

1

2

3

The attractions of office landscaping

Older architectural magazines reveal with cruel clarity the prevailing standard of office design in the late 50s and early 60s. Advertisements display more vividly than editorial what seems to us now to be an astonishingly uncomfortable internal physical environment—hard floor finishes, lots of glazed partitioning, surface mounted light fittings, bulky steel desks, **1**.

In the UK even admired buildings of the time: Castrol House, the Vickers Tower on Millbank, the CIS building in Manchester—show that technical problems rather than user requirements or experiments in plan form were what obsessed architects.

The demountable partition, the thin skin, the window module were the problems of the day since it seemed that by playing with all three an effect could be achieved which resembled American prototypes, **2**. That these prototypes were entirely different in scale, in plan form, in depth of space, in degree of air-conditioning and in design organisation is not, perhaps, fully realised even today, **3**.

It was against this background that office landscaping was presented to British architects in the early 60s. Originating in Germany in the mid 50s, an invention of the Schnelle brothers, bürolandschaft first reached this country in 1962 via the international architectural press on the one hand[1] and the multi-national corporation on the other.[2] By that time in Germany the concept had already reached its mature form. There are three essential features about the early reports. First, they presented managerial and physical arguments in parallel. The apparently idiosyncratic layout was not an arbitrary design whim but, so it was argued, an inevitable physical concomitant of a certain managerial style. Second, the arguments had a distinct moral edge. Not only must you have office landscaping but you *ought* to adopt this managerial style.

Third, the package was complete. Once the decision had been made, the techniques for applying office landscaping were already codified (in 68 rules) and ready to be put into effect.

Given the intellectual climate of architecture in the early 60s, the appeal of office landscaping was inevitable. User requirement studies were highly valued: they were even incorporated into the RIBA *Management handbook*. If schools could be planned round a brief based on user requirement studies, why not an office building? Management, in which architects were said to be weak, had enormous prestige. Any crumbs of management consultancy which could be fed to architects were bound to be gratefully received. Remember also, those were the heady days of design methodology, of matrices and adjacency studies. Not only did office landscaping depend upon these techniques but it was said to be their inevitable result. Office landscaping, whether or not it satisfied the user, fitted our intellectual needs like a glove.

The appeal to management is no harder to explain. The package quality of office landscaping was extremely attractive. Like many other glittering management consultancy packages, office landscaping was something you could buy from the shelf and then command the expert to apply. To decide you wanted it was a progressive, dynamic step—a bit like ordering Blue Streak but on a smaller scale. Moreover, it added something to your range of choice.

Previously you had only two choices: either the cellular office you had always known and loved, or the cold hard efficiency of the American open plan. With office landscaping the choice was much richer. Above all—and this was really serious for architects—office landscaping seemed the closest approximation to a service which it was felt architects and interior designers were failing to supply—the detailed planning of interior space by people who understood something both of design and organisational structure.

Meanwhile, a number of fundamental changes were taking place. One was that air-conditioning and suspended floors had become available and reliable permitting deep space to be used for offices. In other words, an advanced building technology was an essential antecedent to office landscaping. Another vital factor was that there was enough industrial patronage around to encourage experimentation. In Europe office landscaping flourished partly because purpose built office buildings were (and are) common and speculative development was less so.

Finally, gradually and quietly, standards of office accommodation were rising and the expectations of office staff, particularly in lower grades, were increasing. Whether this was because of rising standards of living, better home conditions or prior experience of well built, well planned schools, is not certain. What is clear is that a comparison of today's advertisements showing office accommodation with those of 10 years ago shows a real improvement in standards. Office landscaping is partly responsible for this but conversely office landscaping is possible only because of these heightened expectations, table I.

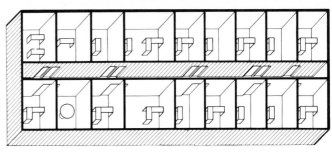

4

1 *Conventional office of the late 50s. Surface mounted lighting.*
2 *High class American office interior of around 1960.*
3 *Typical British bürolandschaft office of late 60s.*
4 *Traditional cellular arrangement of offices.*

Date	Key British buildings	Relevant events	Publications	Key foreign buildings
1960		Late 1950s Quickborner team formed in Germany		CBS Building New York (USA) Continental Center, Chicago (USA)
1961	Ford building, Warley Birds Eye Foods HQ, Walton			
1962	West Midland Gas Board, Solihull	Conference on design methods—Papers edited by Christopher Jones and D. G. Thornley	*Baumeister* No 5 1962: 'Das rationelle Büro': series of articles on open planned offices	
1963	Robinson building, Bristol		RIBA *Management handbook Kommunikation* magazine of landscaped offices first published	Nino, GmbH Nordhorn, Germany
1964	Heinz Foods, Hayes, Middlesex		F. Duffy, article on bürolandschaft, *Architectural Review* February 1964 (UK)	
1965			Peter Manning (ed), *Office design: a study of environment* (Liverpool University)	Place Bonaventure, Montreal
1966			F. Duffy, *Office landscaping: a new approach to office planning* R. Illig, *Office planning, layouts, facilities and buildings*	GEC Mail Order Office, Kameu, Germany Osram GmbH Munich, Germany Yamanashi Press Centre, Kofu, Japan
1967	BP headquarters, Harlow	Office landscaping symposium, Chicago Whitehall plan	Whitehall Development Group MPBW *The office brief* (internal)	Du Pont & Co, Wilmington, USA
1968	Building Design Partnership offices, Preston Northern Gas Board, Killingworth	Integrated environmental design discussed at Electricity Council conference at RIBA	R. Probst, *The office, a facility for change* (USA)	GAKO Building, Gothenburg, Sweden
1969	Experimental offices for DOE at Kew Boots HQ offices, Nottingham Lever Bros, conversion of offices at Port Sunlight	MPBW, Supplies Division, prototype furniture	Philip Tabor, *Pedestrian circulation in offices*, LUBFS W.P.17 (UK) *Office landscaping*. Based on articles in *Office design* 1967–68 (USA) J. Shelton, 'Landscaped offices', *Architects' Journal*, 5.3.69	
1970	Fred Olsen offices, London			
1971	Offices for Norman Frizzell, Poole SWEB Avonbank, Bristol	Herman Miller holds first UK seminar on AO2 furniture system	Axel Boje, *Open-plan offices*, first English edition *Planned open offices*, cost benefit analysis, DOE *The planned open office*, a primer for management, DOE	
1972	Hambro Life, Swindon. Use of Herman Miller AO2 in traditional speculative office shell Penguin Books, Harmondsworth IBM Greenock IBM Cosham			Centraal Beheer, Apeldoorn, Holland
1973	Europa House, Stockport			
1974	Burmah Oil HQ, Swindon Halifax Building Society, Halifax GLC island block, London CEGB Engineering Division HQ, Gloucester			

Table 1 *Chart of key buildings and events in the last 15 years for office landscaping.*

What is office landscaping?

Very often 'pure' office landscaping is compared with an adulterated version in much the same way a seventeenth-century Anglican divine would compare 'pure' doctrine with teachings tainted by Geneva or Rome. Purity is an interesting notion. It has the great advantage of calling attention to the importance of first principles and to the danger of compromise. But is office landscaping an idea sufficiently simple to be 'pure'? Several streams in the argument for office landscaping can be traced to source. The emphasis for example on increasing patterns of communication as a cue for layout design was not, despite its cybernetic trappings, a new idea. You can find similar arguments in Taylor-inspired American office manuals[3, 4] of the early years of this century—and similar diagrams showing how important it is to trace a flow of work before a layout of office desks or departments can be successfully designed, 5.

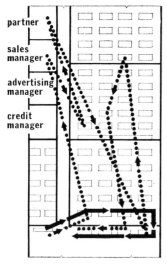

5 *Early example of open plan layout by Galloway. Dotted line shows original course of an order, solid line the course of the same order after reorganisation.*

Take another example: the argument for an easy going, non-hierarchical, participative management style which finds its physical expression in layouts where functional relationships matter more than hierarchical links and in which status distinctions are played down. These ideas stem directly from American human relations management thinking of the 30s and 40s which was itself partly a reaction against Taylor's implied treatment of men as simply units of production. Or take another important theme in office landscaping: the old idea, which stems back to the elimination of cholera by clean water and good drains in the nineteenth-century, that a good physical environment will create good work. Much

human relations thinking was inspired by the dramatic contradiction of this idea by the famous Hawthorne experiments of the 20s[4] in which human factors were found to be more significant than environmental factors in motivating men to work.

The origins of office landscaping ideas are not only complex. They verge on the contradictory. Latter day Taylorism vies with updated human relations; human relations thinking conflicts with environmental determinism. Perhaps the only common factor to these ideas is that they are all slightly out of date.

More recent thinking on the structure of organisations, particularly in this country, stresses the interdependence of social factors and the technology of the work that has to be done. This is essentially a relativistic, comparative approach which recognises that different kinds of work may demand different styles of management. Once this is recognised another implicit argument behind office landscaping is shaken—that all office organisations are essentially the same and so all layouts should be equally landscaped. Logic and common sense suggest the opposite.

Let us examine in rather more detail some of the arguments in office landscaping which relate physical rules to organisational prescriptions. How well do these stand up?

The bigger the better

The central theme of the protagonists of bürolandschaft, and one to which other management consultants as well as architects and interior designers were particularly susceptible, was the proposition that offices (viewed as factories) required large undivided spaces. Offices are factories in the sense that information, transmitted on paper or tape, fed along telephone lines, encapsulated in recorded decisions and so on is the raw material for processing rather than a soup of chemicals or minerals. To the early bürolandschaft writers this theme was the central issue. Suddenly all organisations were described as being communication-intensive and the only way to meet this requirement was for designers to provide space as large and as column-free as possible.[5, 6] This argument is an oversimplification. It is probable that interaction between people and between people and machines is not as pervasive as we were asked to believe. Tabor,[7] for example, did not find a massive network of functional communications but rather a delicate web of small scale social contacts.

More significant for architects was the *dogma* that planning or designing for communications

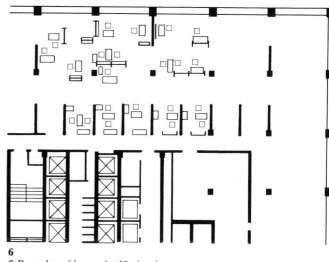

6

6 *Part plan of layout for National Education Television showing how fin walls can be used to structure* space.
7 *Carrels in use at Boots hq Nottingham.*

7

required open spaces—the bigger the better. The fervour with which this fundamental *non sequitur* was (and is) propounded is extraordinary. By the 1970s architects had learned more about organisations. Though it is possible to generalise about them, each is unique—differing from its neighbour in the number of levels in the hierarchy, the range of group sizes, rhythm of work, the management style and so on. If the office landscapers had convincingly demonstrated that the sizes of groups were constantly and unpredictably in flux then the case for large undivided spaces would have been better made.

Designers felt the need to enlarge the vocabulary of spatial responses to organisational requirements beyond cellular and open requirements. In the civil service, for example, the concept of group spaces for teams of 8-12 persons was investigated, as a means of using older buildings more effectively and also as a way of avoiding large depersonalising spaces. Other designers sought to structure large spaces with fin walls, accommodate office

workers in carrels and so on, **6, 7**. There were other reasons for prescribing large individual spaces than communications. Issues such as output, organisational conflict and supervision were raised and pronounced as being improved by office landscaping[8].

The experience of the last 15 years has shown that the requirement of openness is frequently in conflict with other requirements such as changing space usage, the need for privacy in some work activities and differing office management structures.

Methods now exist to identify different types of space.[9, 10] When these analytical tools are paired with enhanced knowledge of organisational requirements designers can refute the idea that big and open are always best and can demonstrate that there are situations where a large undivided space is inappropriate.

Large spaces can become redundant too easily. The client's philosophy behind the design of the Hamburg Electricity Company building by Arne Jacobson was to avoid building possibly redundant large spaces because it was argued that increasing automation would eliminate routine work leaving only 'thinkers' who would require individual offices. Would it be possible to adopt the same policy and further cellularise the GLC building, **8**, Europa House, **9** or Avonbank, **10**? Apart from the planning difficulties what would happen to the services? The consequences of extensive cellularisation of deep space are shown in **11**. Perhaps the most important single decision in the design of offices is the location of the core. Notice how the core at Kew, **16**, has been located to produce a range of spaces. It is by such simple means that *space types* of different qualities and capacities are made.

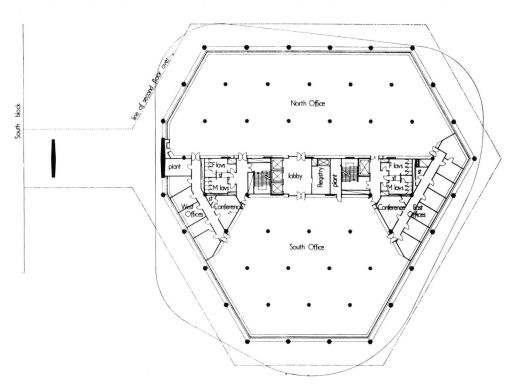

8 *Plan of first floor, GLC island block.*

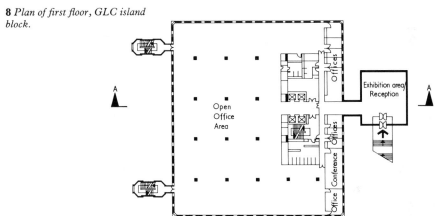

9 *Plan of typical floor of Europa House.*

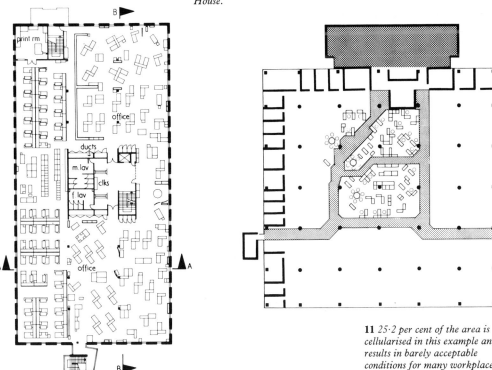

10 *Plan of typical floor of SWEB at Avonbank.*

11 *25·2 per cent of the area is cellularised in this example and results in barely acceptable conditions for many workplaces. The enclosed 25 per cent of the area would house only 10 per cent of the staff.*

72

Egalitarianism rampant

Status in offices was traditionally very important. Hierarchies gave order and structure to organisations. An individual's status was usually made very clear by such devices as giving him as he moved up the firm more space, more carpet, his own office, a bigger desk and so on.

All this was swept away by the new breed of bürolandschaft office designers. It was held to be inconsistent with the aims of modern organisations run along democratic rather than autocratic lines. Participation and joint responsibility teams had been substituted for armies of workers governed by supervisors, junior, middle and senior management. The pyramid was being flattened. This egalitarian argument was very seductive to both the wily captains of industry and architects.

Egalitarianism was worn conspicuously as a badge of progress. This resulted in the early days in undifferentiated layouts where all workplaces were similar and it was not obvious who was general manager and who was clerk, **13**, **15**. Some of these have mellowed. Compare how the stamp of hierarchy has returned to the most recent layout of Dobson House, **12**, **14**, **18**. See also this trend over time at Kew, **16**, **17**.

However in this gadarene rush one important function of status was overlooked. Status makes communication within an organisation authentic and intelligible[11] and this was a strange omission on the art of those who elevated communication to a central design problem.

It is now clear in both organisations which intercommunicate massively and those which intercommunicate less that status is very important and to neglect it is foolish. In the late 60s two important members of the Quickborner team writing in *Kommunikation* had also accepted this fact and were now seen to be proposing a 'scientific' method of distributing the

13

13 *Typical egalitarian bürolandschaft layout with few screens.*

12, 14 *Plans of Dobson House : see how the stamp of hierarchy has appeared in the later layout.*

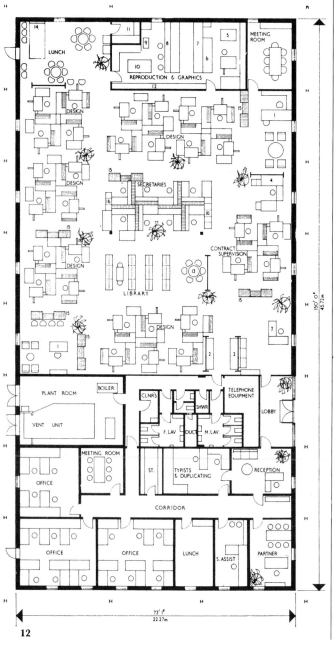

12

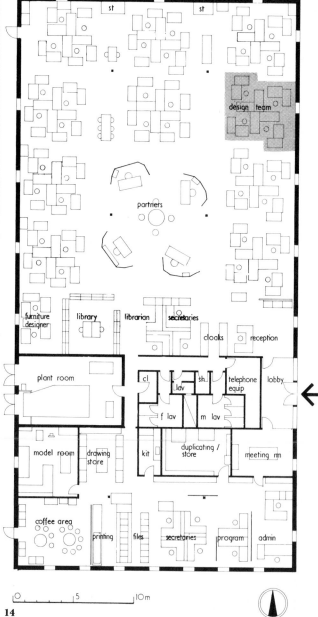

14

symbols of status.[12]

Today our attitudes are more pragmatic. Whatever setting a person needs to enact his particular role should be provided for him. It is now considered good practice for furniture and equipment to be allocated on a need-to-have, as well as on a grade basis thus respecting the structural division *and* levels of hierarchy in an organisation.

15 *Ford Building, Cologne.*
16 *Plan of government office at Kew.*
17 *Plan of government office at Kew showing how cellular offices were added.*
18 *Partners' area at Dobson House.*

15

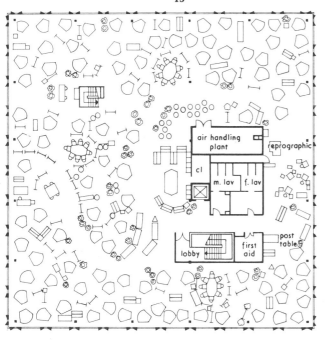

16

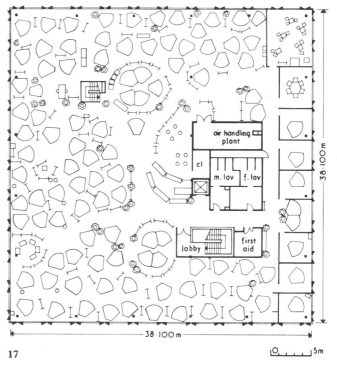

17

18

19

20

Everything should move

Linked with the theory that all organisations are in a state of flux and require large undivided spaces is the laudable notion that if change can be facilitated without building effort then it is desirable. One consequence of this was the belief that within the large open shell everything had to be mobile.

This idea of total mobility was taken up and actively promoted by furniture manufacturers who saw the potential of new and expanding markets. But furniture has always been mobile. Change happens less than we imagine and demountable partitions (though troublesome and costly) had already been with us for some time.

Why then was it necessary to have all these new ranges of furniture? The answer is that the old office furniture was not anyway very suitable for the job it had to do and was not sympathetic to landscaping. Two furniture systems had a great impact on office design in the UK. Neither of them came from Germany. First was the screen based system Action Office **20** by Herman Miller, **19, 20**, which took on some of the subdivision functions normally performed by the shell, and which showed designers how to break with the right angle in planning furniture layouts. The influence of its design was felt in this country long before it was actually marketed. The second example was the civil service prototype furniture the Mk 2 version of which was used at Kew, **21, 23**. Both these systems are built round the idea that different people and different jobs require different items of furniture which can be accreted on the basis of need. Both designs rejected finally the 'duffel coat' philosophy of the pedestal desk. In practice AO2 and similar screen based systems gave architects and designers the means to overcome the emergent problems of exposure and lack of privacy. If it had been generally available, the civil service furniture would have made it possible to create organic multi-directional layouts, which did not rely on regular, rectilinear or hexagonal geometry, truly independent of the building envelope, **16, 17**.

Bürolandschaft increased knowledge and awareness of organisations and their requirements and eventually enabled sophisticated judgments about fit between buildings and organisations to be made. In the same way it heightened sensitivity to individual requirements and

19, 20 *Herman Miller Action Office furniture layouts*

21

differences at the level of the workplace and this, combined with the large range of furniture available, now has permitted sophisticated design of role settings. Consider how precisely tailored are the carrels at Boots, **7**, and the workplaces at Dobson House, **24** to the needs of the occupants. It is interesting that at Dobson House as at the Preston offices of Building Design Partnership we find that day-to-day change is accommodated by moving people not furniture. The now well-established relationships between mobile furniture, deep spaces and workplace design has given rise to a new skill; the management of building spaces. Though generally a problem for the occupier and not the architect, the initial spatial design controls the limits of use of the space through the life of the building.

In Europa House, for example, it will be vital that the occupier has a definite space management programme. In Fanum House (AJ 11.12.74) it is less important, as the spaces are smaller. In Centraal Beheer, **22, 25, 26**, as in early office buildings such as Castrol House or Millbank, space management is largely taken out of the hands of the occupier because the building shell is so positive.

21, 23 *Civil service office furniture at Kew.*
22 *View of Centraal Beheer (see 25, 26).*
24 *Typical workplaces at the Faulkner-Brown Hendy Watkinson Stonor Dobson House.*

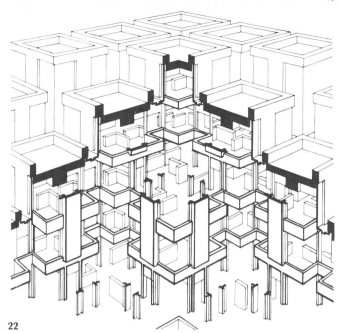

22

23

24

The real value of office landscaping

Office landscaping, which appeared to be such a luminous, tangible, hard edged concept, turns out to be a bundle of rather ill-assorted ideas which can be rearranged and developed in different ways with varying physical consequences.

To us this realisation came gradually. Nagging doubts about the extent to which 'purity' as a criterion could be applied gave way to scepticism, a scepticism which was reinforced by the arbitrary nature of the *rules* on the one hand and on the other by the empirical evidence that not all organisations are similar nor do all function well in similar spaces. Nevertheless the realisation was a

shock. Had the enthusiasm been completely wasted? Had all the vast amount of design effort and persuasion been for nothing? We do not think so. Office landscaping has had a tremendous success and that in itself is an achievement. Moreover it has fostered a large number of important design inventions; it has raised fundamental questions about the relation of social facts to design; and it has taught us a great deal about the nature of design concepts and how they help us to communicate with clients. In science a strong hypothesis is one that boldly attempts to explain a very large number of disparate facts. Office landscaping is a little like such an hypothesis: it may be, in the long

term, an inadequate formulation but it is certainly bold. It has attempted to bundle together a great many previously unrelated notions, and in doing so it has succeeded in illuminating a vast uncharted area of design activity.

Improvements in design stemming from office landscaping

Office landscaping has certainly encouraged innovation in the design of office furniture. The first office landscaping furniture was designed to be light and portable with minimum storage attached to the work-station and proper provision for filing elsewhere. What seems to have happened later is that, in the

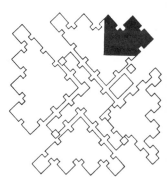

25 Outline plan of typical floor of the Centraal Beheer Insurance Company building, Apeldoorn, Netherlands (Architects H. Hertzberger in association with Lucas & Niemeijer).
26 A part of the Centraal Beheer plan which shows the planning principles which make this building so interesting. It is broken down by

cruciform voids, structure (solid black) and shape into a series of interlocking modules of space. These are connected by a fixed grid of circulation (shown tinted) which is consistently reflected by a change in ceiling height. Within this dominantly architectural framework there is paradoxically great freedom in arranging

workplaces and groups. Compare this with a typical office landscape plan where the job of defining group boundaries is left first to furniture and second to management. Centraal Beheer has many faults but by bringing architecture back into office planning it suggests many new possibilities for meeting user requirements.

25

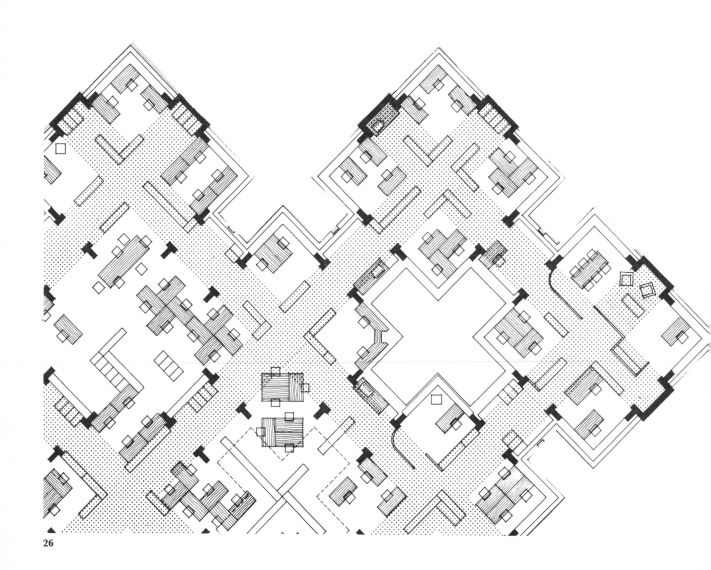

absence of partitions, furniture has aggregated to itself many of the functions of the wall. Herman Miller AO2, although it was developed in the US, is almost certainly a response to office landscaping. So are the several British furniture systems derived from AO2 and carrel systems such as Hille's. But the process of invention is not over yet—see, for example, recent ideas about intermediate linking pieces which permit several desks to be linked in various formations.

Equally fertile has been the stimulus to the design of services. High lighting levels were part of the basic assumptions of office landscaping and to provide these in deep space was in itself a technical achievement. Later, integrated environment design (IED) was extensively promoted, only, in its turn, to be attacked because it introduces unnecessary rigidities into the replanning of space and because it assumes a high overall illumination level which may waste energy and be inappropriate for many office tasks. It seems likely that many future offices will have a low level of overall illumination and great deal of task lighting at the workplace but it would be a disaster if the recent obsession with energy saving were to sweep away all the benefits of deep space. Developments in the design of power and telephone outlets in floor grids and ceiling drops or the great improvements that have been achieved in design for acceptable acoustic conditions in the open plan office are further examples of technical advances stimulated by office landscaping.

Improved understanding of the use of space

Debate about office landscaping has sharpened our understanding of the use of space by office organisations. We have been forced to study offices in detail—the patterns of communication between individuals and between groups, the size of groups, the various kinds of work carried out by different firms. Constantly the question is—what relevance does this or that piece of information have for design? If this organisational fact is so, which design variable should be modified?

To answer this question, the major office design variables have been categorised. We can distinguish between different depths of space which are suitable for various kinds of desk layout. We know that some organisations are composed of small groups, others of large. Some firms are highly integrated; others are composed of parts which have very little to do with one another. We know more, now, about the life span of what we design. The basic office building shell lasts 40 years; the scenery within five or seven. When an organisation takes a space or builds a building, it is necessary to ask how long its

present organisational structure will last. How might it change? How many scenery options does the shell leave open? The first huge office landscaping shells precluded too many later options by being too closely tailored to one kind of scenery. We will not make that mistake again. Office landscaping has inspired many excellent studies of user satisfaction. As a result we know more about the function of windows, about reactions to air conditioning, about noise. Without the shock of this novel idea, it is hard to believe that our understanding of offices would have grown so much.

Improved understanding of the design process

In the end office landscaping will benefit the consumer. This is not just because it gives him another choice. The implications of office landscaping go deeper than that. Office landscaping is a rare example of a generic design concept which is intimately allied to an organisational idea. One cannot approach it from design without implying an organisational directive or vice versa. This quality seems to us to be a prototype of a possible, far more intelligent briefing method in which both architect and client discuss strategic design options at a very early stage before design work has properly begun. If both are able to discuss the same basic concepts—which must be sufficiently robust to survive scrutiny from both sides—then we shall have taken an enormous step forward from the present situation in which the client is expected to express his requirements abstractly but completely, so that he is pinned down, while the architect has complete freedom to perform his own mysteries. The trouble with office landscaping is very largely that it is the *only* concept of this kind at the moment. Another fundamental lesson about architect/client relations is that office landscaping has come to imply a thorough examination of user requirements. It has done this only because such thoroughness was rare in office design ten years ago. Now, perhaps, we take for granted requirement surveys, a sense of designing with time and a more relativistic approach to possible design solutions. We may expect a host of other generic solutions to arise but it should never be forgotten that office landscaping was the first impetus to such developments.

Conclusion

The principal defect of office landscaping is its glamorous packaging. The danger of packaging, despite its consumer appeal, is that it stops intelligent questions being asked about the limitations of what is inside. In the end this is fatal because the result on the one hand is disillusionment and on the other the stunting of the proper development of the concept. Architects have a great advantage here because their basic professional ethic is still one of personal service to their clients. Were they able to combine this with a greater sense of how to involve themselves in their clients' organisational choices *and* a greater capacity to abstract valid generalisations from their own work, then the result would be formidable. Instead of one office landscaping we would have many concepts which both architects and clients could grasp as a basis for a dialogue about strategic design options.

If office landscaping was a mistake, then it was a relatively happy mistake since it shows us how truly popular architectural concepts can communicate between users and architects. Meanwhile it has given birth to a whole progeny of developments and new ideas. We have come to the end of simple office landscaping and perhaps to the beginning of a more complex period in office design. A new series of challenges is being met:
better understanding of the different styles of organisation;
greater interest in providing a range of space types;
exploiting a much wider range of furniture options;
using building services in a more sophisticated manner;
the spatial challenge of using the building to structure office space.
New ideas are cropping up in various forms and in different places: different space types in a single envelope (at Kew); the idea of reversible space (in Germany); spatial modules (by Hertzberger in Holland). These ideas are evidence that a new period of experimentation, variety and greater success in meeting user requirements is about to begin.

References

1 *Baumeister*, July 1962. (Special issue on office landscaping).
2 Through G. Shuttleworth and BP's new landscaped office in Hamburg.
3 W. H. LEFFINGWELL, *Office management: principles and practice*, A. W. Shaw & Co. Chicago, 1925.
4 GALLOWAY, L., *Office management in principles and practice*, The Ronald Press, New York, 1921.
5 LORENZEN, H. J. & JAEGER, D., 'The office landscape, a systems concept', *Contract Magazine*, January 1968.
6 GOTTSCHALK, O. & LORENZEN, H. J., 'The new shape of office buildings', *Kommunikation*, iii/i, 1967.
7 TABOR, P. 'Traffic in buildings' Working Paper Nos 17-2. Centre for Land Use Built Form Studies, University of Cambridge, 1970.
8 These ideas are critically evaluated in A. B. Fuller. 'Bürolandschaft: a science of office design', pages 61-66.
9 DUFFY, F. & CAVE, C. 'The organisation and the shell' and 'The organisation and the scenery' on pages 78–83.
10 DAVIES, R., 'Office Shells: a comparison', pages 45–51
11 DUFFY, F., 'Status and the design of civil service offices', 1972, unpublished.
12 TREBESCH, K. & JAEGER, D., 'An analysis of the significance and distribution of status symbols in bureacratic organisations', *Kommunikation*, vii, 4, 1971.

Section 3: The office interior

The organisation and the shell

FRANCIS DUFFY and COLIN CAVE show how an organisation's structure and method of working limit the range of building shells in which it can be accommodated. The exercise develops an argument implicit in the two previous chapters: that there are many different styles of management and types of office work. Correspondingly we should expect several distinct and different kinds of office layout.

1 Preface

1.01 To illustrate the argument that organisations make demands on office building shells, this study has been cast in the form of an exercise where the object is to fit four organisations into four shells.

2 Four organisations

2.01 Four types of organisation have been chosen to represent a range of user requirements. One thing, however, that all four organisations have in common is a need for a total of 370 m² of office space.

Design office
2.02 This type of design office is not uncommon. Four groups are each composed of four or five designers who work together closely on long-term projects. Each group is closely integrated but the working links between groups are weak; general togetherness, however, is valued. The two partners cluster together yet remain as nodes to the design groups they control; all are served by the usual support functions—secretaries, library, messengers and accounts **1**.

Advertising agency
2.03 An advertising agency is essentially co-ordinative. A likely structure for a small agency is four account groups who have little to do with each other since each runs its own accounts. Each account group is under pressure to meet very tight deadlines and competes for the services of the vitally important specialist groups: creative, ie, copy-writers and art directors; studio; and media. The finance department and the progress chasing department struggle for attention amid these warring bands. The directors, whose role is to control and to seek new business, keep their distance **2**.

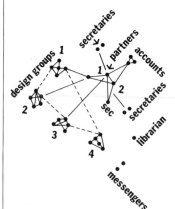

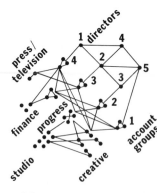

1 *Design office, structure and interactions—dotted lines are for weak links, continuous for strong.*

2 *Advertising agency, structure and interactions. Directors control finance through the account groups.*

Top management

2.04 Top management is essentially a pyramid. A chairman is at the apex. Under him are the directors who, in this case, are each assumed to have major responsibilities. To each director, divisional managers report. The divisional heads are supported by assistant managers and may call upon the services of a variety of specialist staff groups. Secretarial assistance is personal and well distributed. Links between personnel are regularised rather than constant **3**.

Clerical

2.05 Such a clerical structure may be found in a bank. Paper processing is the vital function and a number of groups are set up to perform routine computation and checking of figures. Each group—accounts, reconciliation and control unit, cash, clearings and bills—operates internally in a strict sequence of paper-passing. There is little face-to-face contact between groups but much movement of paper. Overlaid on this simple pattern are strict supervision, some security areas where cash and documents must be protected, and a small but noisy accounting machine room **4**.

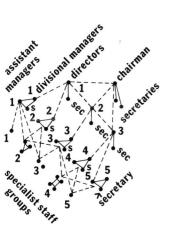

3 *Top management, structure and interactions.*

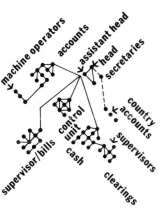

4 *Clerical office, structure and interactions.*

3 The requirements of an organisation

Stock of spaces

3.01 Each organisation requires a number of separate spaces. The space requirements of the design office are shown in **5** and **6**, and **7** shows how these can be expressed in histogram form—basically a few big spaces and a few little spaces. Similarly **8, 9** and **10** give the space information for the advertising agency, top management and the clerical office. The variation is acute between the big demand for small rooms of top management and the clerical office's requirements for big space.

Clustering of spaces

3.02 Some organisations work better if their component parts are dispersed; others if all departments are clustered for easy access. The advertising agency, for instance, consists of departments which need to be together but yet

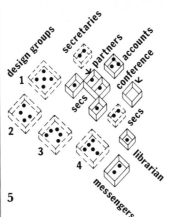

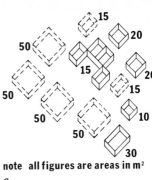

note all figures are areas in m²

6

5, 6 *Space requirements of the design office.*

A Librarian
B secretaries
B₁ partners' secretaries
C partners
D conference
E accounts
F messengers
G design groups

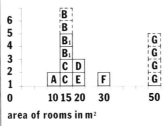

7 *Histogram of the space requirements of the design office—dotted lines show spaces which can be combined. Letters refer to different types of space.*

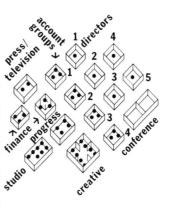

8 *Space requirements of the advertising agency.*

9 *Space requirements of top management.*

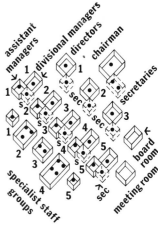

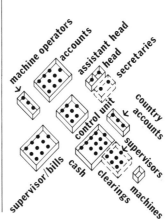

10 *Space requirements of the clerical office.*

have to be separated from each other. In table I three kinds of departmental clustering are distinguished:
—little interaction (top management).
—interaction with separation (advertising agency and design office).
—much interaction (clerical office).

Table I Organisational requirements

Organisational requirements	Stock of spaces	Clustering of spaces
Design office	Small spaces, medium or large spaces	Interaction or interaction with separation
Advertising agency	Small spaces Medium spaces	Interaction with separation
Top management	Small spaces	Little interaction
Clerical	Small spaces Large spaces	Much interaction

4 Capacity of office shells

4.01 Each office shell has an inherent capacity to meet some but not all organisational requirements. Here two kinds of capacity are highlighted because they reflect the kinds of requirements stressed in the description of the four organisations:

Space stock capacity
4.02 Any shell is capable of being divided up to a certain extent into small (up to 40 m²) medium (40 m² to 150 m²), and large (above 150 m²) spaces. Some shells cannot provide small spaces; others cannot provide large. Of course, area alone is inadequate to describe the characteristics of spaces. In each case, it is assumed that the proportion of length to breadth of each space is no more than 2:1. (See page 45 onwards).

Clustering capacity
4.03 Some shells have the capacity to allow for spaces to be brought together. A large, open-plan floor is an example of this because several departments can be grouped round each other; other shells are inherently divisive, inhibiting continuity between spaces. Some, particularly large old houses, can allow for a number of separate spaces to be close but divided. These varying capacities are a reflection of the organisational requirements: interaction is provided by the open plan which can be fully continuous, while separation is guaranteed by the narrow central core type. Thus the open plan suits the design and the clerical office but not top management. On the other hand the narrow central core type is likely to be favoured by top management. Perhaps the advertising agency which needs interaction with some separation may prefer the large old house.

Requirements and capacities
4.04 Consider four kinds of office shell. In **11** the requirements of the four organisations for a stock of spaces of certain sizes is tested against the capacity of the four shells. In **12**, the requirements for continuity or division between spaces are tested. Not all shells meet all the tests. Some are more versatile than others. Some meet certain requirements outstandingly well.

5 Conclusions

5.01 The conclusions to be drawn from this exercise are:
1 Organisational requirements vary widely.
2 Not all office building shells are equally good at meeting organisational requirements.
3 Some office building shells are more 'specialised' than others. The 'spec' type is good for most requirements but it is not as good as the open plan for the clerical office or the

narrow central core type for top management.
4 A process of matching shells against organisational requirements protects potential tenants against choosing the wrong kind of space.

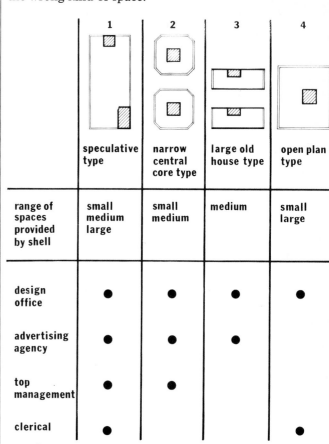

	speculative type	narrow central core type	large old house type	open plan type
range of spaces provided by shell	small medium large	small medium	medium	small large
design office	●	●	●	●
advertising agency	●	●	●	
top management	●	●		
clerical	●			●

11 *The requirements of the four organisations tested against the spatial capacity of the four shells.*

	speculative type	narrow central core type	large old house type	open plan type
degree to which spaces are continuous or divided from each other by the shell	spaces partially divided or fully continuous	spaces highly divided	spaces highly or partially divided	spaces partially divided or fully continuous
design office	●		●	●
advertising agency	●	●	●	
top management	●	●		
clerical	●			●

12 *The requirements of the organisations for division between spaces is tested.*

Section 3: The office interior

The organisation and the scenery

The need for a clear distinction between shell and scenery is best realised when an exercise is carried out to accommodate a range of types of scenery in a range of shells. Here COLIN CAVE and FRANCIS DUFFY explore the relationship between four organisations and four generic types of scenery: cellular group spaces, open plan and office landscaping.

1

2

1 Preface

1.01 The previous chapter, the organisation and the shell showed the relationships between four organisations or parts of organisations and the spaces provided by four, building shells. In a similar way, this technical study will illustrate the next stage of the shell/scenery argument: that scenery design must be related to organisational requirements. (The same four organisations are used here—a full description of each can be found on pages 78–9.

1.02 This facet of the argument is important because scenery design is important. Some forms of scenery can only be used in certain building depths and thus need different shell forms. Decisions of shell form and building depth are taken early in the design process and are often irreversible. Equally with any existing building whose suitability is being evaluated; the form of the building, and particularly the depth of the space, determines the range of scenery options.

1.03 Scenery design demands a knowledge of the organisation, not simply of how many members it comprises, but how it hangs together and works. Answers to such questions as: what are the processes involved?; do its members work in groups?; if so what is the nature of inter- and intra-group communications?; what are the environmental and service demands of particular sectors of the organisation?, are required long before detailed furniture allocations or anthropometric and ergonomic data can be used.

2 Scenery arrangements

2.01 The scenery arrangements illustrated in this article are neither definitive nor exclusive and can exist in combination either on different floors or even on the same floor of a building. The arrangements vary from small to large spaces and should be treated with some caution because a multitude of variations of each exists.

Cellular

2.02 This traditional form is most often found in narrow buildings up to 12 m deep and is characterised by spine corridors with many small rooms leading off them. Commonly the rooms are perimeter dependent for all services. They may be augmented with permanent supplementary artificial lighting. Although the rooms vary in size, it is unlikely that they contain more than five persons.

Group spaces

2.03 Group space is a term which has been recently coined for medium-sized rooms containing 5-15 persons who work together. For this arrangement to be satisfactory, slightly deeper buildings of 15-20 m are needed.

Open plan

2.04 This is just a traditional way of laying out a large deep space. There is usually a complete absence of any form of sub-division and the work stations are arranged according to a rigid geometry, **1**.

Office landscaping

2.05 This concept has come into being in the last 15 years and is characterised by an apparently random layout, a fully controlled artificial environment. The work station layout reflects the structure and method of working of the organisation. Screens, plants and storage furniture are used to mark circulation routes and give territorial definition and identity to the working groups **2**.

3 Organisations and scenery design

3.01 In table I, these four scenery arrangements are displayed on a matrix against the four organisations, and suitability or fit is noted where they interact. It can be seen that the design office is best accommodated in landscaped scenery, the advertising agency in group space scenery, the clerical office in an open-plan or landscaped arrangement and top management in cellular scenery.

4 Conclusion

4.01 A note of caution was struck earlier regarding the selection of scenery types. This is underlined by the lack of precise fit in the matrix. In spite of this, the following conclusions can be drawn.

1 The range of scenery arrangements is wide and selection of an arrangement which 'fits' is important. The wrong choice can greatly hamper easy working.

2 It is important to consider scenery design early in the design process because certain arrangements require different building depths. For example, 'landscape' requires a much deeper space than 'cellular' or, again, certain deep spaces just cannot be satisfactorily compartmentalised.

3 Scenery design demands a knowledge of management style as well as organisational structure; for example, if supervision is vital, the clerical office would be better accommodated in open plan rather than landscaped scenery.

Table I Interaction: types of services and organisations' needs

Type of scenery	Design office	Advertising agency	Top management	Clerical office
	Intensely interactive project-based groups in loose touch with each other. Serviced by normal support functions. Visitors at all levels. Partners in close touch. Concentrated work with occasional confidentiality.	Isolated work groups, co-ordinative work. Two kinds of groups; working group competes for the services of the other. Usual support services. Directors not involved in day-to-day work; concerned with clients.	Isolated executives with secretarial and PA support. Confidential and contemplative work. Visitors.	Large supervised groups—paper and/or machine intensive. Highly intra-active groups. No public entry.

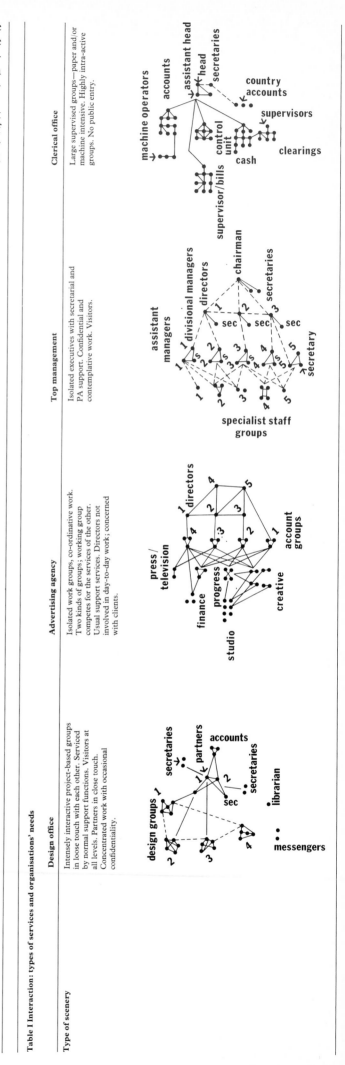

Cellular	Unsuitable for large groups—isolation incompatible with supervision requirements.	Suitable; permits confidentiality and suitable reception of visitors. Special arrangements required for board room.	Unsuitable because of group size and informal interaction. Separate rooms breed isolation.	Unsuitable because of group size though could be made to work.
Group space	Possibly suitable—depends on space and group size, though similar problems as cellular.	Possibly suitable but spaces may be too large.	More suitable than cellular, though still not ideal.	Most suitable. Groups prefer this degree of territorial definition.
Open plan	Suitable, accepts group size fluctuations, supervision and high interaction.	Unsuitable, incompatible with status management style and requirement for confidentiality.	Inappropriate for method of working, management style and occasional need for privacy (meetings).	Inappropriate for method of working and management style.
Landscaped	As open-plan but supervision restricted.	Unsuitable. Top management too exposed.	Probably very suitable. Group identity and territorial definition sustained—with day-to-day rearrangement potential. Allows easy access for visitors.	Not very suitable. Frenetic and competitive mode of working disturbs others.

Section 3: The office interior

Layout in open-plan offices

Large scale office layouts (especially in deep space) are often highly complex and difficult to plan. The form of the building shell limits what can be done; departmental and workplace relationships must be respected; each piece of furniture must be related to other furniture, to circulation and to service outlets. On a large floor with perhaps two or three hundred workplaces, the exercise is like city planning in miniature.
This study by COLIN CAVE discusses the stages involved in office layout planning and describes some of the techniques and rules which can make planning easier.

1 The importance of office layout

1.01 The architect tackling the problem of fitting a large and complex organisation into a building can no longer simply put the top man on the top floor and move down the building, floor by floor, accommodating successive grades in the hierarchy **1**. This method is inadequate because it fails to recognise that organisations comprise groups of people performing specific and interrelated activities. The designer must not only recognise this fact, but also, obviously, must develop ways of detecting significant working relationships before he can devise office layouts which support these relationships.

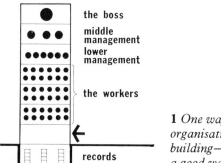

1 *One way to fit an organisation into a building—not always a good way.*

2 Growth of layout planning

2.01 In the UK many office buildings are between 10 m and 15 m deep, with rooms, either side of a corridor, each of which accommodates one person or a small group. For such buildings layout planning has largely been a question of allocating people to existing rooms. This approach to layout has often been facilitated by space standards which are closely related to building modules. In other words, the organisation has to adapt itself to the building. Interaction between people and facilities has been underplayed. Tomorrow's buildings will probably be different; they may be deeper, as they will be able to rely on artificial means for environment control; they will have to allow for changes in user requirements, not impede them.
2.02 Analyses of movement and interaction were used in the design of office layouts as early as the end of the first world war. By the 1940s, several textbook methods of office layout had been published in the US[1-4]. These were influential in the UK too. Most of these early layout methods assumed that the best way to arrange workplaces was through analyses of pedestrian movement or paper flow in the office **2, 3.**
2.03 The most difficult form of office layout problem is found in deep rather than cellular office space. This is because the building itself provides little help in arranging

workplaces. This study concentrates on layout in open space, although the principles apply to both deep and narrow offices.

2.04 There are two kinds of layout method; those concentrating on *movement* (whether of paper or goods or people) and those concentrating on *communication* (usually based on frequency of face-to-face contact, telephone or other means of transmitting messages). The 'movement' methods grew out of the work done in planning plant layouts. The 'communication' methods derive from the human relations school which emphasised human values as well as stopwatch control. If movement can be detected in the rigid, rectilinear, open plan layouts of the early large offices, the human relations school, with its emphasis on communication, finds expression in bürolandschaft layouts 4[5].

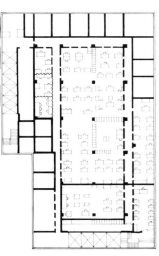 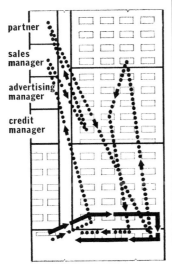

partner
sales manager
advertising manager
credit manager

2 *Schultze's detailed layout for a shipping company's purchasing department, based on intensive workflow studies 1919.*

3 *Early example of open plan layout based on workflow studies by Galloway. Dotted line shows original course of an order, solid line the course of the same order after reorganisation.*

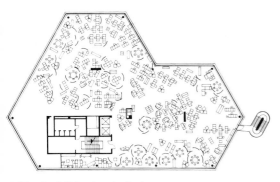

4 *Typical Bürolandschaft layout.*

3 Methods of layout planning

3.01 All methods of layout planning have the same fundamental stages:
1 Data collection, gathering information by questionnaire or structured interview
2 Analysing that information (often by computer)
3 Drawing diagrams of the relationships between individuals and groups
4 Translating these into a layout.

4 Data collection

4.01 Information is needed to make layout decisions. These data can be gathered by interviewing management and staff, by questionnaires, or by a mixture of both techniques. The questionnaire does not easily yield nuances of information but tends to be best at eliciting simple matters of fact from many different sources. Also, it may easily result in a description of the *status quo*. Interviews, necessarily selective, avoid the problem of just collecting a mass of facts. They have the very great advantages that the interviewer can probe and follow up, that he can investigate more complex problems, and that he can get people to give and discuss the highly qualified judgments which are the chief clues to the pattern of future growth. On the other hand, interviews are selective and can be biased.

4.02 Whatever techniques are selected, information is needed on:
numbers of staff in groups and departments, now and for some years ahead
grades of staff
planned changes in method of work, eg new equipment
patterns of contact within groups
patterns of contact between groups
patterns of contact with visitors
use of meetings of various kinds
use of communications devices
management style
equipment used by individuals
equipment shared by groups
existing method of work
informal social groupings among the staff.

5 Analysing information

5.01 Analysis takes various forms. It is usual to end the whole process manually, so that numbers and area requirements are tabulated; overall relationships between departments and groups are established in order of priority; individual workplace relationships are understood; and a list of key issues and problems can be prepared for solution by design. Throughout this process, good judgment is necessary so that strategic issues are isolated from trivia. A sense of scale is necessary in dealing with the vast amount of data which can accumulate.

5.02 To reduce the labour of manual sorting, several computer programs have been devised, usually for editing the data supplied in response to a questionnaire. Two programs which do more than just edit are discussed here—the first *RMA Comp 1*, was developed by Richard Muther & Associates in the US and the second by SCICON in this country[6, 7, 8].

5.03 *RMA Comp 1* is part of SLP (Systematic Layout Planning), a methodology developed earlier by Richard Muther & Associates. *RMA Comp 1* was developed to make easier some of the more tedious mental/manual processes of SLP. It follows the same stages as the mental/manual method. The data base consists of plotted 'closeness ratings', recorded on a matrix called a relationship chart 5. Each 'closeness rating' has to be supported by a reason. To the relationship chart are added the physical details of space required by each activity or facility. The computer then produces a two-stage 'theoretical best relationship diagram'. First, the computer selects the activity with the greatest 'total closeness rating' and, placing that in the centre, arranges all others in relationship to it. The computer also acknowledges activities which should *not* be placed next to one another, and separates them. The second stage is when area is added to the model. This 'theoretical best relationship diagram' is then adjusted manually to fit into the building space (if it exists)

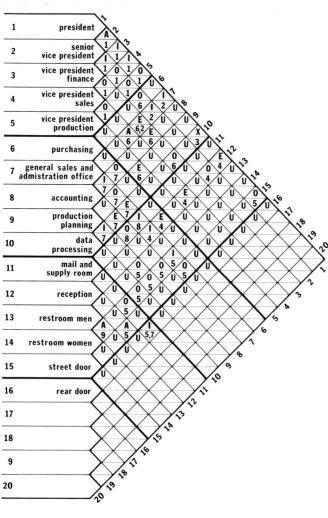

1	president
2	senior vice president
3	vice president finance
4	vice president sales
5	vice president production
6	purchasing
7	general sales and admistration office
8	accounting
9	production planning
10	data processing
11	mail and supply room
12	reception
13	restroom men
14	restroom women
15	street door
16	rear door
17	
18	
9	
20	

reasons which govern closeness value	code	reason
	1	personal contacts
	2	use of steno pool
	3	noise
	4	number of visitors
	5	convenience
	6	supervisory control
	7	movement of paper
	8	use of supplies
	9	share same utilities

5

closeness rating	value	closeness
	A	absolutely necessary
	E	especially important
	I	important
	O	average satisfies
	U	unimportant
	X	undesirable

5 Relationship chart for a small firm
6 Stages in Scicon's program

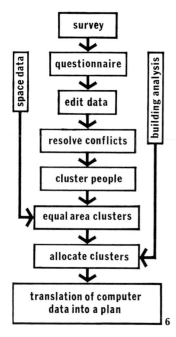

6

or used as a planning basis if a new building is required. Two limitations of this program that judgement has to be used at first on the data to make its order sensible; and that the program usually only handles up to 45 activities at a time.

5.04 The SCICON computer-aided office layout program is more versatile. Some of the subroutines can and have been used for analysis of organisations as well as layout planning. The strength of the method is that it uses information gained by questionnaire about the frequency of face-to-face communications between members of an organisation. The drawback is that it only takes account of face-to-face relationships, therefore neglecting work flow which is not reflected accurately in the face-to-face contact date. The stages through the program passes are shown in **6**.

5.05 'Editing the data' is the point at which it is tabulated in various ways, revealing the gaps or conflicts, which are then resolved. A typical conflict is that person A claims he visits person B five times a week, whereas B may claim he only sees A once a week. These conflicts can be resolved mathematically by averaging both results or by asking someone from management to resolve the difference from his experience. Clustering people is fairly complex mathematically. A quite arbitrary decision has to be made at the outset about how many clusters there are to be in the end. The computer than produces the best clustering of that arbitrary number. Any number from five to fifty has been used, and usually the best number is when each cluster has an average of five to six people. Each cluster is then assigned a value based on the interaction between the members; a high number indicates a cluster with intense interaction. Once the clusters are chosen, the problem is to equalise the areas of each for the next stage of allocating the clusters on the plan. Large ones have to be broken down, and high communication values assigned to ensure that they remain adjacent through the next stage. Some clusters are lumped together. Now is the time to use the space data which have already been fed in, based on space standards for individuals. The clusters are grouped within a series of spaces, which conform to the blocks of space in the building. Choosing these blocks which must each be the same area requires a high degree of skill in dividing up the available space. This is obviously a weak point in the process, as the diversity of plan forms and locations for static elements within them can make this very difficult. The clustered clusters are then allocated to the blocks of space by the computer; manual adjustment is required in order to work this up into a detailed plan. Obviously several different sized blocks of space can be used and thus several layouts are generated which can be evaluated against each other on the basis of a total communication value.

5.06 Both computer methods share a strong emphasis on face-to-face communications as the most important determinant in layout design. But can communications be reliably measured by face-to-face interaction? What other factors are involved in layout? How is change and regrouping accounted for? These questions still leave much room for individual judgment. However, with all their limitations, computer methods certainly reduce some of the labour involved in analysing data and the preliminary sorting out of relationships.

6 Drawing diagrams of relationships

6.01 Although computer methods can assist in this process, constructing a good relationship diagram between groups and activities is usually a manual and graphic process. Some graphic techniques are inappropriate for office design for two reasons: first because graphical simulation is good for illustrating, say, industrial production lines which generally exhibit a simple work sequence but is inadequate for an office because office traffic is like a complex web of delicately balanced major and minor strands of interaction; second, because office traffic relies on different *modes* of communication as *distance* increases. For purists, these objections may lead to a rejection of this method in favour, say, of mathematical modelling[9]. However, relationship diagrams have one great virtue—that they make the planning process accessible to accommodation and O & M officers who will have the responsibility of maintaining and modifying the layout during the time the building is occupied. The modelling approach is valuable because the model can be manipulated, the original structure does not have to be assumed and new structures of relationship can be generated.

6.02 Perhaps the best way of illustrating the main stages in planning a layout is by means of a worked example such as the following: The organisation to be housed is a large department (200 people in 15 groups) of a large highly stratified organisation. All groups do similar work. There is great interaction in the form of consultations, meetings, paper passing, reference to files. There are two main problems—the location of the department's main working groups; and the arrangement of working positions within the groups. There are a few typists, a photocopier, a registry and three shared conference rooms. (There are also seven staff who, for a variety of legitimate reasons, require a partitioned room.)

6.03 These structures can be depicted either as bubble diagrams, or by a single or two-way interaction matrix. These relationship diagrams can be further developed, and clusters of highly interacting groups isolated. For example, in 7 groups 13-15 form a highly interactive cluster and only one work group interacts with any other in the department. Obviously, if it was necessary to divide the department into several clusters or put on cluster on another floor, then the

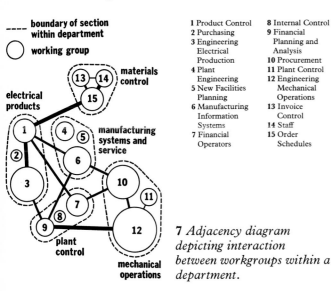

- - - - boundary of section within department

◯ working group

materials control (13, 14, 15)

electrical products (1)

manufacturing systems and service (4, 5, 6)

plant control

mechanical operations (12)

plant control (8, 9)

1 Product Control
2 Purchasing
3 Engineering Electrical Production
4 Plant Engineering
5 New Facilities Planning
6 Manufacturing Information Systems
7 Financial Operators
8 Internal Control
9 Financial Planning and Analysis
10 Procurement
11 Plant Control
12 Engineering Mechanical Operations
13 Invoice Control
14 Staff
15 Order Schedules

7 *Adjacency diagram depicting interaction between workgroups within a department.*

work pattern of this cluster would not be seriously affected by doing so. However, it should be noted that separation not proximity may be required[10].

6.04 By this stage the designer will have a good idea of how much space he requires. He must now apply this to his knowledge of relationships. He will have to estimate the space required not only for 'people' spaces but also for 'non-people' spaces. This information is usually recorded graphically or in schedules (see table I). Each group is now examined in detail to see how individual workplaces should be related to each other. Are there any peculiarities? For example, does one secretary serve two people in different groups? Or is one person acting as a 'gatekeeper', that is, does all communication out of that group go through him?

Table I Space requirements for a department

Workplace / Total / Group total cells are shown as "No / m²". Unit sizes shown in header: A 25.3, B 11.3, C 11.3, D 11.3, E 9.0, F 11.3, G 6.8 (m²).

Group description	A	B	C	D	E	F	G	Total	Sec. circ. (m²)	Total 1 (m²)	Files	Work areas (m²)	Meeting areas (m²)	Others (m²)	m² total	Sec. circ. (m²)	Total 2 (m²)	Total 1+2 (m²)	Main circ. (m²)	Group total
Product manufacturing	1 / 25.3					1 / 11.3		2 / 36.6	3.7	40.3								40.3	6.0	2 / 46.3
Financial operations General accounting		1 / 11.3	1 / 11.3	9 / 61.2			1 / 6.8	12 / 90.6	13.6	104.2	25	6.8			31.8	3.2	35.0	139.2	20.9	12 / 160.1
Cost accounting			1 / 11.3	8 / 54.4				9 / 65.7	9.9	75.6		6.8			6.8	0.7	7.5	83.1	12.5	9 / 95.6
Financial plan and cost control		1 / 11.3	1 / 11.3	3 / 20.4				5 / 43.0	4.3	47.3								47.3	7.1	5 / 54.4
Budgets			1 / 11.3	3 / 20.4				4 / 31.7	3.2	34.9	11	6.8		2.2	20.0	2.0	22.0	56.9	8.5	4 / 65.4
Financial analysis			1 / 11.3	2 / 13.6				3 / 24.9	2.5	27.4								27.4	4.1	3 / 31.5
Internal control			1 / 11.3	1 / 6.8				2 / 18.1	1.8	19.9	1.0				1.0	0.1	1.1	21.0	3.2	2 / 24.2
Meeting areas													70.0		70.0	7.0	77.0	77.0	11.6	88.6
Department total	1 / 25.3	2 / 22.6	6 / 67.8	26 / 176.8		1 / 11.3	1 / 6.8	37 / 310.6	39.0	349.6	37.0	20.4	70.0	2.2	129.6	13.0	142.6	492.2	73.8	37 / 566.0

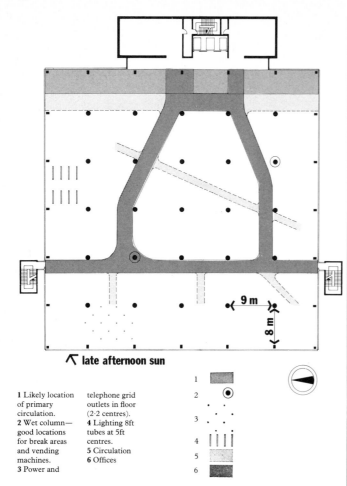

↖ late afternoon sun

1		▨
2		⊙
3		· · ·
4		‖‖‖
5		░
6		▓

1 Likely location of primary circulation.
2 Wet column— good locations for break areas and vending machines.
3 Power and

telephone grid outlets in floor (2·2 centres).
4 Lighting 8ft tubes at 5ft centres.
5 Circulation
6 Offices

8 *Analysis of the constraints the building may impose upon the organisation.*

7 The physical layout
Building constraints
7.01 Analysing the building constraints **8** is a very important process and involves looking at and making decisions about the contents and implications of the core location; location of service areas around the core (are they suitable for such facilities as libraries, filing etc?);

m² net usable area

floor service	break area	landscaped offices			
	conference rooms	finance	audit		floor 4
floor service	break area	landscaped offices			
	conference rooms	sales	marketing	manage -ment	floor 3
floor service	break area	data processing communications	repro	landscaped offices	
	confnce rooms			operations	floor 2
cafeteria	kitchens	education	landscaped offices		
			personnel	spare	floor 1
recption	confer -ence	archive	storage	manufact- uring	ground floor

m² net usable area

9 *How major areas are distributed on each floor of the building.*

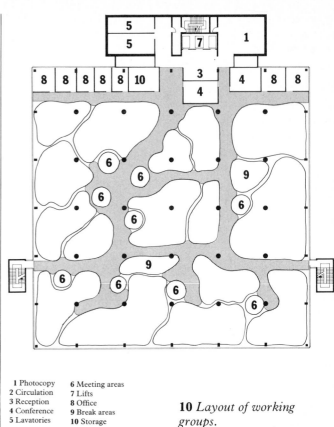

1 Photocopy
2 Circulation
3 Reception
4 Conference
5 Lavatories
6 Meeting areas
7 Lifts
8 Office
9 Break areas
10 Storage

10 *Layout of working groups.*

the service distribution, structural and construction grids. Once the building constraints are understood, the next stage can be completed within them.

Stacking plan
7.02 Diagrams are now prepared of relationships between groups and department and, at a lower level, between workplaces within groups and departments. Area requirements are also known. Layout design usually is done in two stages—first, the 'stacking plan' **9** or arrangement of groups and departments in appropriate horizontal and vertical relationships within the building shell and, second, **10** the 'layout' which shows groups in relationship to each other which will be worked up into the final layout with every workplace and indeed every piece of furniture positioned. The stacking plan must precede the layout because to operate at these two entirely different scales simultaneously is practically impossible.

Furniture
7.03 Furniture requirements must be known, a choice made, and the constraints inherent in that choice realised before detailed layout can begin. Choosing the right furniture is not easy because many kinds of office furniture, even the most sophisticated, contain hidden limitations and tacit stereotypes. Action Office, for example, is usually found on a hexagonal grid with workplaces facing outwards, from the centre of the group, an arrangement which is not very good for clerical work, although excellent for some other activities. The geometrical properties of the furniture can be an enormous constraint on any layout. It is quite possible, for instance, that there are certain ways in which units of furniture cannot be combined which may prevent the right kind of relationships between individuals[11].

Organisational requirements and detailed layout
7.04 Matching the organisational requirements with the layout of furniture in the space or vice versa involves several stages. First in the analysis of building constraints **8**, the location of cores, escape points, areas of heavy

loading, sources of noise, shallow or deep space will probably lead to natural paths for the primary circulation. When the primary circulation routes are established, workgroups can be located—taking care to fracture as few relationships as possible. This process will probably throw up several alternatives which must be evaluated. The working requirements of individuals in each group need to be considered next, taking account of particular work patterns. In a clerical intensive workgroup, for instance, it is quite possible that although a lot of intra-group interaction takes place, interaction between that group and others is channelled through a single person. Again, several options may be generated, all of which have to be evaluated.

Final layouts

7.05 Working up the final layouts in which each workplace is positioned in final relationship to other workplaces, to service outlets and to the building, is extremely time consuming **11**. A useful guide at this stage is that if moving one workplace affects more than six or ten others, the layout is too tight and future layout flexibility will be compromised. Certain rules will be formulated during this process—keeping circulation routes 'clean'; being careful about overlooking of circulation routes and other people; and carefully distinguishing between primary and secondary circulation routes. (These rules should be recorded and passed on to those responsible for managing the layout.)

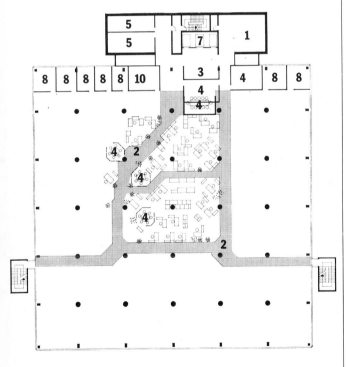

11 *Final layout, showing some furniture—refer to* **10** *for key.*

8 Conclusion

8.01 This technical study has not attempted to be exhaustive or to present a detailed, rigid guide; instead, it has tried to illustrate the broad stages in the process of making office layouts, discussing issues as they arise. There are several conclusions to be drawn:
1 Effective layouts depend on good design information and suitable building spaces.
2 Design information is only good if it accurately models patterns of interaction. Information gathered on (say) face-

to-face contact may only reflect social contact in some organisations.
3 Buildings and furniture are not neutral. Building spaces, structural and service grids do constrain the range of layout options. In the same way, some furniture systems have a far greater range of possibilities than others. Architects should be aware of the limitations which an early, normally cost determined, decision such as columns spacing can place on the use a building can be put to throughout its life.

References

1 LEFFINGWELL, W. H. Office management: Principles and practice. Chicago, 1925, A. W. Shaw & Co [(Alf)]
2 SCHULZE, J. W. Office administration. New York, 1950, McGraw Hill [(Alf)]
3 IMMER, J. R. Layout planning techniques. New York, 1950, McGraw Hill [320]
4 GALLOWAY, L. Office management. Its principles and practice. New York, 1921, The Ronald Press [(Alf)]
5 FULLER, A. B. Bürolandschaft, a science of office design? pp.61–67.
6 MUTHER, R. & ASSOCIATES. A computer program for making office layouts. London, *The Office*, 1971 June [320 (Ago)]
7 SCICON Computer aided office planning SCICON, 1971 [320 (Ago)]

8 There are several examples of computer-aided layout programs 9 below.
9 TABOR, P. Traffic in buildings. Working papers 17-20. Centre for Land Use and Built Form Studies, University of Cambridge, School of Architecture. 1970 [91 (E2p)]
10 DUFFY, F. A method of charting and analysing relationships in the office. *The Architects' Journal* 12 March 1969 [(E2p) (Ao)]
11 Furniture configuration is covered on pages 187–190.
12 DUFFY, F. and WANKUM. Office landscaping. London, 1967, Anbar [320]
One of the few good books on layout planning is RIPNEN, K. Office Space Administration, New York 1974, McGraw-Hill

Section 3: The office interior

Methods of measuring space: the scenery

Detailed information is provided by the EDITORS on space standards for different kinds and grades of staff, on how the area requirements of an organisation can be built up using these standards in conjunction with other factors, and finally on the dimensions which are essential in planning office layouts.

1 Space standards

1.01 In Methods of measuring space: the shell, it was proposed that for crude feasibility study requirements an overall area allowance of between 10 m² and 20 m² net per person is a reasonable range of possibilities. However, later on in the development of the project, when more information may be available on the status of the occupants and activities to be accommodated, and when the allotment of space to the various areas within the building becomes necessary, this range will be seen to be too crude. This section demonstrates how widely allowances may vary—25·9 m² to 11·1 m² in the examples given—according to the nature of the organisation to be accommodated.

2 What are space standards?

2.01 Space standards are the means of controlling the allocation of space in office buildings to individuals or activities. They are one aspect of the formal expression of status in organisations. Organisations may express status in three ways.
1 Allocation of space: most organisations have codified space allocations. Broadly speaking, space is allocated to individuals in increasing amounts as they progress up the organisational hierarchy.
2 Enclosure: usually grades above a certain level are entitled to a separate room.
3 Furniture: frequently entitlement to items of furniture is codified and stratified in relation to the organisational structure.

3 Why were space standards developed?

3.01 Space standards were developed to safeguard the interests and entitlement of individual workers as well as to facilitate the expression of status. Status makes communication within an organisation authentic, authoritative and intelligible[*]. This is because it confirms the source from which an order derives, what its importance is, and what area of activity it concerns. The symbols of status are also used as an incentive or a reward system.
3.02 Highly codified expressions of status are based on an administrative model of organisation structure which is highly stratified with strongly delineated lines of command. Although this form of organisational structure is far from dead, new kinds of office work with project groups, new specialists and new machines are increasingly eroding the old expressions of status. New, more relaxed, forms of management have also been reflected in simpler space standards. The old, highly codified forms were closely related to cellular office building forms; the introduction of open office planning has been yet another factor of change. In the present situation, a wide range of space standards is found in different organisations. What these standards look

[*] *Status and the design of Civil Service offices* by Francis Duffy, Department of the Environment Internal report, 1971

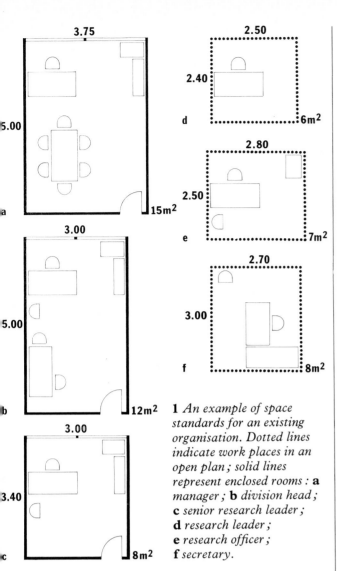

1 *An example of space standards for an existing organisation. Dotted lines indicate work places in an open plan; solid lines represent enclosed rooms:* **a** *manager;* **b** *division head;* **c** *senior research leader;* **d** *research leader;* **e** *research officer;* **f** *secretary.*

like on plan is shown in these diagrams of typical workplaces **1**. These particular examples were used in a study for the Central Electricity Generating Board.

4 Value of space standards in planning

4.01 The value of space standards depends, first, on how accurately they reflect the organisation to be accommodated, and second, on how precisely they are met. **2, 3, 4** and **5** express some typical space standards as histograms. They show a wide variety of management styles with varying degrees of closeness between executive and clerical levels.

4.02 It is evident that, with finely graded increments, dimensional problems are going to arise when space standards have to be expressed as rooms bounded by walls or partitions. In general, space standards are more difficult to meet in narrow than in deep buildings, because the former impose greater constraints. This is in spite of the fact that there are problems of territorial definition in deep space.

4.03 Given these limitations, space standards are essential in devising how much space is required by an organisation at detailed layout design. How they are used is shown in the example which follows.

4.04 The average area per person, of course, depends on whether an organisation is peopled largely by clerks or executives.

5 Contrasted examples

5.01 Two examples are shown in table I. The first illustrates the requirements of an organisation with generous standards, many high-level personnel and many special areas. The second illustrates an organisation with relatively mean standards, lowly personnel and few special areas. The cumulative area per person is of very great interest. Table II shows space standards for special facilities.

Table I Calculating office area requirements

	Action	Example 1 Accumulating area allowance per person—m²	Number of personnel	Accumulating total area required	Example 2 Accumulating area allowance per person—m²	Number of personnel	Accumulating total area required
1	Take sum of workplace areas	10 m² per person	862	8620 m²	5 m² per person	525	2625 m²
2	Add 10% for access to workplaces (circulation within departments)	10 m²+10% =11 m² per person	862	9482 m²	5 m²+10% =5·5 m² per person	525	2887 m²
3	Add area for special, within-department facilities; eg meeting and conference rooms, display or exhibition areas etc	11 m²+2·5 m² (say)=13·5 m² per person ★1	882 (additional 20 serving special facs)	11 907 m²	None provided	—	—
4	Add 15% for inter-departmental circulation	13·5 m²+15% =15·5 m² per person	882	13 671 m²	5·5 m²+15% =6·3 m² per person	525	3318 m²
5	Add area for support facilities to office areas—filing registries, archives, vending machines etc	15·5 m²+3·3 m² (say)=18·8 m² per person ★2	882	16 581 m²	6·3 m²+2·2 m² (say)=8·5 m² per person	525	4462 m²
6	Add areas for special facilities—computer rooms, restaurants etc. Provision varies so much from company to company that no general rules apply. Areas must be determined by preparing rough layouts						
	Special facility A	18·8 m²+1·5 m² =20·3 m² per person ★3	882	17 904 m²	Non provided	—	—
	Special facility B	20·3 m²+1·3 m² =21·6 m² per person ★4	882	19 051 m²	8·5 m²+0·75 m² =9·25 m² per person	525	4856 m²
	Net usable area (NUA) (all the above)	21·6 m² per person	882	19 051 m²	9·25 m² per person	525	4856 m²
	Gross overall area (NUA+core and columns etc—allow 18%-20%)	21·6 m²+20% =25·9 m² per person	882	22 844 m²	9·25 m²+20% =11·1 m² per person	525	5827 m²

NB
Area allowances in items 1-4 above are based on the numbers of people to be accommodated.
Area allowances in item 5 and 6 are based on the requirements of machinery and plant.

Example 1:
A multi-national corporation having a high proportion of high status personnel and providing high quality space standards and a high level of special facilities

Example 2:
A largely clerical organisation providing minimum space standards and few special facilities

Table II Space standards for special facilities in office buildings

Floor lobby (floor receptions) when required	10·75 m²–15·60 m²
Building lobby (main ground floor reception)	37·00 m²–70·00 m²
Switchboard room (size to be determined by laying out in conjunction with GPO)	—
Cafeteria/dining rooms (depends upon standard of service—see *AJ Metric Handbook* table I p. 102)	0·75 m²–1.4 m² per person sitting
Kitchen and serving area (determine by laying out; a rule of thumb is 60:40 relationship between full kitchen and dining accommodation	
Conference and meeting rooms:	up to 10 persons 1·58 m² per person
	up to 16 persons 1·39 m² per person
	up to 25 persons 1·30 m² per person

Bulk storage of paper and filing—accommodation varies according to storage capacity required, disposal policy and method of storage.
NB Possibility of centralised warehoused storage off site. See pp. 160–168.

Computer rooms—see pp.179-184.

Notes on table I

*1   The area allowance for within department meetings and conferences varies between organisations depending upon meeting size and frequency. Accommodation may be based on the following: 10 person rooms allow 1·58 m² per person, 16 person rooms allow 1·39 m² per person, 25 person rooms allow 1·30 m² per person. Accommodation for display and exhibition spaces etc can only be determined by roughly laying out.

*2   The area allowances for support facilities vary depending on storage capacity required, disposal policy and method of storage. Accommodation to be determined by rough layouts.

*3   The staff located in special facilities such as computer rooms are not included in the original personnel numbers (item 1) as it is assumed that accommodation for them is included in the layout of the machinery.

*4   The staff located in special facilities such as restaurants are excluded as in *3 above. Areas to be allowed for in dining areas may vary from 1·4 m² per diner per sitting for table service to 0·75 m² per diner for minimum cafeteria standard.

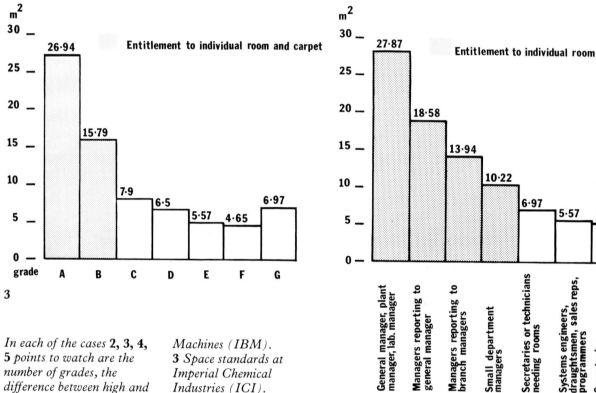

3

In each of the cases **2, 3, 4, 5** points to watch are the number of grades, the difference between high and low grades, and the steepness of the slope between high and low.
2 *Space standards at International Business Machines (IBM).*
3 *Space standards at Imperial Chemical Industries (ICI).*
4 *Space standards at British Petroleum (BP).*
5 *Standards of entitlement in the Civil Service.*

Desk space
6.01 Space standards vary from one user to another. Partly they are composed of space required for furniture; partly of space for circulation immediately adjacent to the workplace; partly of space for planning flexibility; and partly of space used to express relative rank or status.

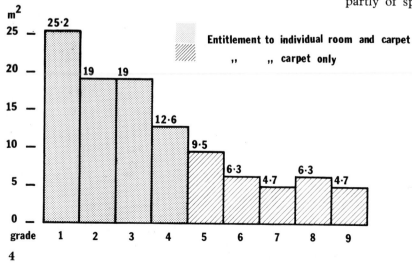

4

1 **General manager**
2 **Department manager**
3 **Divisional manager**
4 **Branch manager**
5 **Technical assistant draughtsman**
6 **Grade 7 and above**
7 **Assistants grade 6 and below**
8 **Secretary**
9 **Typist**

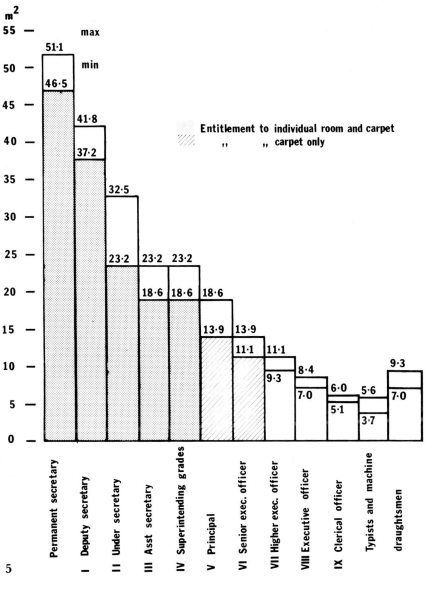

m²

max

min

51·1
46·5
41·8
37·2
32·5
23·2 23·2 23·2
18·6 18·6 18·6
13·9 13·9
11·1 11·1
9·3
8·4
7·0
6·0
5·1
5·6
3·7
9·3
7·0

Entitlement to individual room and carpet
„   „   carpet only

Permanent secretary
I Deputy secretary
II Under secretary
III Asst secretary
IV Superintending grades
V Principal
VI Senior exec. officer
VII Higher exec. officer
VIII Executive officer
IX Clerical officer
Typists and machine
draughtsmen

5

However, the irreducible minimum is space for furniture.
What follow are some basic dimensions which are vital in
detailed layout planning.

Desks, tables and chairs

Swedish standards Swedish recommendations for office flat
top desks, based on A4 paper, are shown in **6** to **12**.
Suitable typing desks are shown in **13**. Other possible desk
sizes based on the Swedish standards are listed in table III.

Table III Possible desk sizes based on figures 6 to 13

Executive/manager	1500 × 750 mm plus extension 750 × 500 mm
Clerk	1300 × 700 mm or 1000 × 700 mm plus extension 1000 × 500 mm
Secretary/typist	1300 × 700 mm plus extension 1000 × 500 mm
Typist	1200 × 700 mm

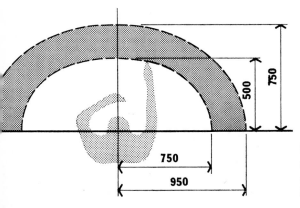

6 *Average reach of person
sitting at desk. To reach
outer area, the user has to
bend but not stand up.*

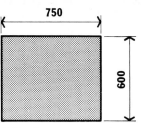

7 *Basic space for writing
and typing.*

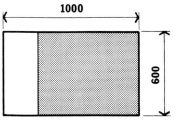

8 *With space for paper on
one side.*

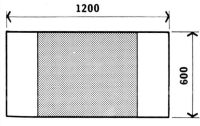

9 *With paper on both sides.*

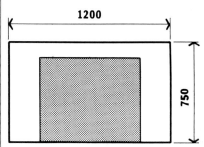

10 *Paper plus space for pens
and telephones.*

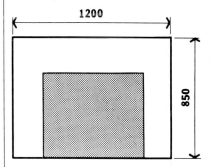

11 *Generous amount of
space for paper.*

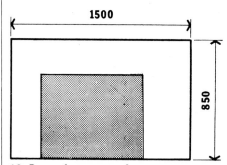

12 *Space for papers plus
area for references.*

6.02 *British standards* Specifications for office desks, tables and seating given in BS 3893:1965 are summarised in Tables IV to VI below with the recommended range given in exact metric equivalents. Suggested rationalised metric dimensions, not contained in the BS, are shown in brackets.

Table IV Office desk sizes (translated from BS 3893)

Work surface			Use
Minimum depth (mm)	Minimum width (mm)	Height (mm)	
686 (700 or 750)	1067 (1050 or 1100) 1143 (1150 or 1200) 1372 (1400) 1524 (1500 or 1550)	711 (710)	General purpose and executive
610 (600 or 650)	1067 (1050 or 1100) 1372 (1400)	648-711 (650-710)	Typists: single double pedestal
762 (750 or 800)	1219 (1200 or 1250)	711-762 (710-760)	Machine operator

Table V Office table sizes (translated from BS 3893)

Minimum depth (mm)	Minimum width (mm)	Height (mm)
533 (550)	914 (900 or 950)	
610 (600)	1067 (1050 or 1100)	
610 (600)	1143 (1150)	
686 (700 or 750)	1219 (1200 or 1250)	711 to 762
686 (700 or 750)	1372 (1400)	(710 to 760)
762 (750 or 800)	1524 (1500 or 1550)	710 recommended
762 (750 or 800)	1676 (1700)	
838 (800 or 850)	1829 (1800)	

Table VI Office chairs (translated from BS 3893) Sizes in mm

a Executive and clerical
Heights:	432 desirable for fixed chairs (430)
	432-508 for adjustable chairs (430 to 510)
Widths:	min 406 (400)
Depths:	356-470; recommended 381 (380)

b Typists and machine operators
Adjustable through 102 (100) in one of the following ranges:
406 to 508 (400 to 500)
483 to 584 (480 to 580)
559 to 660 (560 to 660)
635 to 737 (640 to 740)

Filing cabinets
6.03 Space requirements for drawer cabinets and lateral filing are shown in **13** and **14**, with circulation requirements in **15**. See also minimum space requirements listed in table VII.

Space requirements
6.04 Space required per employee will depend on type of work; use of equipment or machinery; degree of privacy; and storage needs.

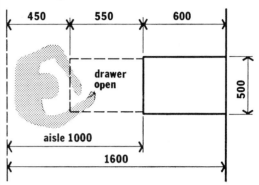

13 *Space requirements of drawer filing cabinet.*

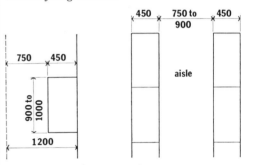

14 *Space requirements of lateral filing units.*

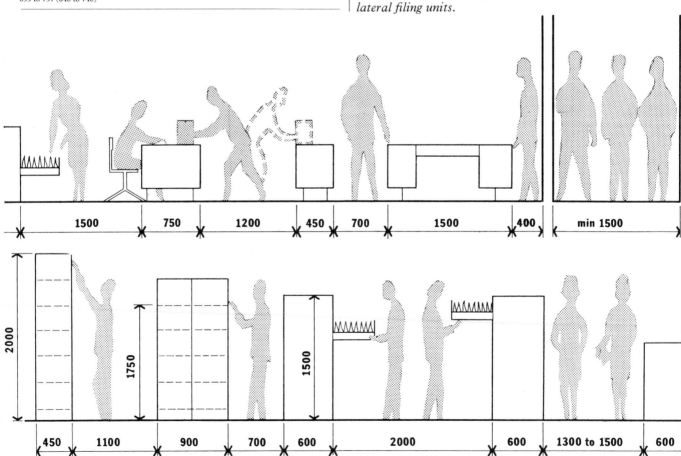

15 *Typical space and circulation requirements of filing and other office equipment.*

Work spaces for individuals

6.05 Spaces required for different desk and table layouts are shown in **16** to **21**.

Desk spacings and layouts

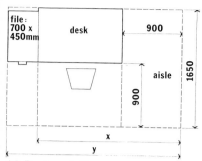
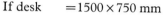

16 *Desk and file.*

If desk $= 1500 \times 750$ mm
x $= 2400$ mm and area $= 3 \cdot 96$ m²
with file y $= 2850$ mm and area $= 4 \cdot 71$ m²
If desk $= 1200 \times 750$ mm
x $= 2100$ mm and area $= 3 \cdot 47$ m²
with file y $= 2550$ mm and area $= 4 \cdot 20$ m²

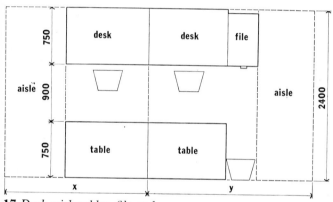

17 *Desk with tables, file and chair.*

If desk and table $= 1500 \times 750$ mm
x $= 2400$ mm and area $= 5 \cdot 76$ m²
with file y $= 2850$ mm and area $= 6 \cdot 84$ m²
If desk and table are 1200×750 mm
x $= 2100$ mm and area $= 5 \cdot 04$ m²
with file y $= 2550$ mm and area $= 6 \cdot 12$ m²

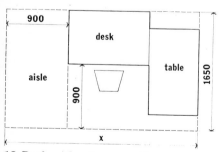

18 *Desk with adjacent table.*

If desk $= 1500 \times 750$ mm
x $= 3150$ mm and area $= 5 \cdot 20$ m²
If desk $= 1200 \times 750$ mm
x $= 2850$ mm and area $= 4 \cdot 70$ m²

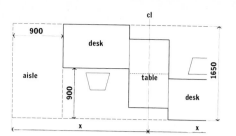

19 *Desk with shared table.*

If desk $= 1500 \times 750$ mm
x $= 3600$ mm and area $= 5 \cdot 94$ m²
If desk $= 1200 \times 750$ mm
x $= 3300$ mm and area $= 5 \cdot 45$ m²

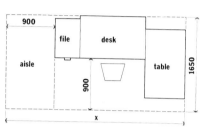

20 *Desk, table and file.*

If desk $= 1500 \times 750$ mm
x $= 3225$ mm and area $= 5 \cdot 33$ m²
If desk $= 1200 \times 750$ mm
x $= 2925$ mm and area $= 4 \cdot 83$ m²

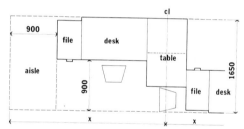

21 *Desk, shared table and file.*

If desk $= 1500 = 750$ mm
x $= 2775$ mm and area $= 4 \cdot 58$ m²
If desk $= 1200 \times 750$ mm
x $= 2475$ mm and area $= 4 \cdot 10$ m²

Desk spaces and layouts

Table VII gives recommendations for spacing office furniture.

Table VII Recommendations for minimum spacing of office furniture (mm)

a Distance from back to front of desks in a row (chair space)	
When each desk is on an aisle	900
When each desk is not on an aisle	900 to 1370
b Aisle widths	
Major aisle (large general office)	1500
Normal general office aisle	900
Minor general office aisle	750
c Distance required in front of filing cabinets	
Single row	900
Two rows facing	1220
When filing cabinets face an aisle, the width of the cabinets when open (1370 mm) should be added to the normal aisle width	
d Distance required in front of shelving	
Two-row facing	750 to 900
When shelving faces an aisle, the width of the shelving should be added to the normal aisle width	

Note Desks should not be placed tightly against and facing a solid wall or opaque glass partition. Rules for good layout are discussed in section 8.

Section 4: The economics of building offices

Building finance

Building costs are only one part of the economics of developing and letting the commodity we call 'office space'. BERNARD WILLIAMS explains why certain cost relationships which seem stable are in fact variable and depend greatly upon non-architectural factors. This is a particularly helpful insight in understanding office design since offices are the building type most obviously influenced by market forces.

1 General economic background

The rental syndrome

1.01 The practice of renting gives rise to a somewhat unique cost/value relationship for the product on hire. For the product is the source of investment income, rather than a once and for all capital profit. If the rent obtainable for the product can be varied during its life then so will the product's value to its owner.

1.02 The decision to rent rather than buy a product—be it tv, tower crane, etc or office premises—is governed mainly by economic factors:
1 financial liquidity
2 tax allowances
3 flexibility.
Conservation of liquid funds is obviously a major determinant, but liquidity problems can frequently be overcome by hire-purchase or loan. Tax allowances and grants also influence the decision, but probably the principal factors are:
1 the amount of capital cost involved
2 the need to easily change the product on hire for a more suitable one
3 the need or desire to offload the problems of servicing and repair.

1.03 The problem which the would-be occupier/owner of new property, particularly commercial property, faces is that it is not readily available to buy; the purchaser has to create it. It cannot be bought from a shop or a catalogue and its performance matters less than its location. To create a tailor-made property involves the buying of the site and the organisation of its development. The process is a formidable prospect and in many locations is just about impossible in the face of competition from property specialists: therefore, 85 per cent to 90 per cent of office space is rented.

The office as an investment

1.04 What distinguishes the office as an investment from a tv set or a tower crane is its life-span, capital cost and relative freedom from competition from other forms of marketing; those commodities have to be written off over a short period with increased costs and reduced profits—and the rental charges have to compete in the capital sales market and with hire-purchase and loan facilities. An office building, once erected and let, will remain a valuable trouble-free asset long after its cost is written off—provided that customers are prepared to compete for it.

1.05 Because customers in the UK are usually competing for office space, leases tend to be short and rents are renewed at the end of each period. Whereas the tv rental company may get, say, 50 per cent extra life-span (usually at reducing rental) after writing off the cost of the set, the property investor can expect to get 200 per cent or more extra life-span with rents which increase with general inflation and supply and demand.

2 The asset value of an office building
Valuation of investments
2.01 Property is considered a safe investment and attracts investors such as insurance companies, pension funds, trusts and other institutions concerned with repaying sums of money entrusted to them for a long period. Apart from keeping pace with inflation, the investment also produces a good profit income. It is in some ways comparable with equity shares in sound trading companies though rather less susceptible to the vagaries of our economic climate. Like stocks and shares, the value of a property investment derives from the rate of interest expected on the capital invested. This interest rate varies with the degree of risk involved. For example, a 'blue chip' share such as ICI (Rolls-Royce?) is considered a very low risk. The investor, therefore, looks for a nominal rate of interest—say 5 per cent—because he believes (a) that his money is secure and (b) that if the company continues to flourish, his original investment will appreciate. The second factor is explained thus:

1 100 shares valued at £100 producing £5 per annum today for the investor will probably be producing £6 per annum in five years' time

2 someone purchasing his shares in five years' time will still look at them as a 5 per cent investment and will therefore offer £120 for the same block of shares. (£6 per annum = 5 per cent × 120). On the other hand, more speculative shares, eg commodities, might be considered a higher risk and the investor will want to see a 10 per cent return on his capital

3 the value of a block of such shares producing £5 per annum would be therefore only £50 (£5 per annum = 10 per cent × £50).

2.02 It can therefore be seen that the capital value of a long-term asset is calculated by the following formula:

$$\text{Capital value} = \frac{\text{annual income} \times 100}{\text{rate of return per cent}}$$

In our previous examples:

1 $£100 = £5 \text{ pa} \times \dfrac{100}{5 \text{ per cent}}$

2 $£120 = £6 \text{ pa} \times \dfrac{100}{5 \text{ per cent}}$

3 $£50 = £5 \text{ pa} \times \dfrac{100}{10 \text{ per cent}}$

Years purchase
2.03 The multiplying factor is thus the reciprocal of the rate of return and in the property world the factor is called the years purchase (YP); it is applied to the net income from renting to produce a valuation of a commercial property. This principle is only varied where the investment has to be written off over a short period—less than 21 years. In those circumstances, for example where a building held on a short lease is modernised and sub-let until the expiration of the head-lease, the YP multiplier incorporates the writing down allowance (sinking-fund payment), i.e.:

$$\frac{100}{\text{interest rate } \% + \text{sinking fund}} \times \text{annual income}$$

$$= \text{capital value on short leasehold}$$

The equity's rate of return is formed by the stock market's assessment of (a) the current and potential demand for the company's products and (b) the chances of continued profits; both are influenced by management and its ability to increase prices to keep pace at least with inflation.

2.04 The office building's rate of return is governed by the same principles. The only difference is that the periodic rent review has to embrace at one step the combined effects of inflation and supply and demand which the equity share has to cope with almost on a day-to-day basis.

2.05 Returns on a property investment, like equities, are never true rates because they anticipate future growth. If let without rent reviews, the required rate of return would settle at the same sort of level as fixed interest non-convertible stock. As things are, the best office investments with five-year rent reviews may change hands for as much as 14·29 YP or 7 per cent; those in less desirable areas with less substantial tenants and 7 to 14-year reviews currently average about 8 YP (12½ per cent). The lower valuations reflect both the higher risk and the diminished growth potential—they go hand in hand. Even with substantial growth on the cards, 14 years is a long time to wait for a rise in rental income which must be 'discounted to present worth' in the valuation calculation. 'Discounted to present worth' merely means that the compound interest the extra rental income *would* have earned in the first 14 years is knocked off the value when you actually get it. This technique is however a refinement which does not concern the architect—other than in principle.

3 The development budget and land valuation
3.01 When he decides to buy a site for office development, the developer must of course determine the maximum sum he is prepared to pay for it in order to be sure of his profit on the whole development. He normally does this by working backwards from the estimated income, deducting all development expenses and his profit—leaving the land as a residual figure.

3.02 As an example, a proposed office building may produce £347 000 per annum after landlord's running and management expenses have been deducted. The developer estimates that the building will be valued on completion on an 8½ per cent basis giving a capital asset value of

$$£347\,000 \times 11\cdot76 \quad \text{YP (ie } \frac{100}{8\cdot5 \text{ per cent}}) = £4\,080\,000$$

If he wants to make 20 per cent profit on his outlay it leaves £340 000 (83⅓ per cent × £908 000) for land and development costs.

3.03 If his development costs come to £2 068 000, this leaves £1 332 000 for the land, bridging finance and acquisition fees. It will be clear that, whereas rentals and the YP multiplier fluctuate widely between locations, the actual building costs are comparatively stable: for this reason the value of the land will increase automatically with increased rental income.

3.04 Quite frequently land owners retain the freehold so as to gain a share in the development profits; local authorities, British Rail and others prefer to grant the developer a long head-lease and the initial ground rent is set at a proportion of the annual income, worked out on the capital budget formula. If the residual value of the land arising from the developer's calculation was £780 000 and the calculation had been made on 8½ per cent (11·76 YP), the annual ground rent expected would be in the order of

$$\frac{£780\,000}{11\cdot76} = £66\,327 \text{ per annum.}$$

3.05 The complication with this kind of deal is that in order to hold a stake in the equity of the scheme, the landlord wants a review of the ground rent at the same time as, and related to, the developer's own beneficial review.

3.06 In the high rental areas, the land forms such a high proportion of the development costs that unless the landlord's proportion of the increased rent is considerably less than his original proportion (ie 'reversely geared') the equity to the developer becomes insufficient in relation to the risk involved. When the developer is asked to include a new library or give the station a facelift then the deal becomes really rather difficult to set up.

4 Financing the development

Bridging finance

4.01 The developer usually needs to borrow the capital required to buy the land and pay the costs of development—he gets a bridging loan. The interest charges, normally quite high, depend on how viable the scheme is and the borrower's status, and must be allowed for in the budget. The usual sources are the merchant bankers but occasionally, when there is plenty of money about, the stock banks and the institutions will lend. If the developer is lucky enough to have his own liquid funds for the development, he will still need to charge a rate of interest against the budget. This rate is based on what the money could earn if employed on some other of the company's projects or invested elsewhere at an equivalent risk; it is known as 'opportunity costing', ie the cost of the loss of opportunity to invest elsewhere. Most financiers will only lend a proportion of the bridging finance; 100 per cent bridging finance can be got but only by parting with up to half of the developer's profit—with the financier.

4.02 The finance for the land is usually on the whole amount at compound interest right through to completion of the buildings. The builder and the design team, however, require only stage payments so money is only borrowed as and when required to pay the certificates and fee accounts. The actual amount can be calculated using a cash flow forecast but rule-of-thumb is usually adequate for feasibility studies.

4.03 By this rule, it can be taken that building finance works out to about half the amount that would be needed if the building costs were all paid out when the contract was signed:

$$x\% \times \frac{\text{contract sum and fees}}{2 \times \text{contract period (years)}} \text{ compound.}$$

It follows, therefore, that the larger the land costs become in relation to the whole budget the more important is the need for speedy completion to minimise the costs of finance on the land purchase. The converse is also true but it is not wise to make too much of this to a prospective client.

4.04 On completion the developer has two choices. He may find a tenant (if an ODP is required he cannot start a large scheme without one) and agree the terms of a lease. If, taking the previous example, the rent is fixed for five years at £385 000 per annum he can offer the building, tenant and all, to an investor for a capital sum. The developer will hope that a pension fund or insurance company will decide that an income of £347 000 per annum (landlord's expenses already deducted) from this tenant is worth a return of $8\frac{1}{2}$ per cent on its investment. If so it will pay the developer £4 080 000 and he will have made his projected profit provided that his costs have not overshot their budget. If the building is valued on say $6\frac{1}{2}$ per cent basis, a greater YP, he will make a greater profit, ie

$$\left(\frac{100}{6 \cdot 5} - \frac{100}{8 \cdot 5}\right) \times £347 000 \text{ pa}$$

$$= (15 \cdot 4 \text{ YP} - 11 \cdot 76 \text{ YP}) \times £347 000 \text{ pa}$$

$$= £1 263 080 \text{ extra dealing profit.}$$

A 10 per cent valuation (10 YP) will reduce his projected profit by $\frac{100}{8 \cdot 5} - \frac{100}{10} \times £347 000 \text{ pa}$

$$= (11 \cdot 76 \text{ YP} - 10 \text{ YP}) \times £347 000 \text{ pa}$$

$$= £610 720 \text{ reduced dealing profit (in fact almost a break-even in this example).}$$

Terminal finance

4.05 Many companies for various reasons (taxation is one) do not wish to make a capital profit by selling off the development; they therefore retain the office building as an investment. Unless they are prepared to use their own funds it is then necessary to arrange what is called 'terminal finance' to repay the development costs.

4.06 There are two main methods of acquiring terminal finance—mortgage or sale-and-leaseback.

Mortgage

4.07 The financier has a charge—a mortgage—on the property in return for lending a proportion of the ascertained value. The mortgage payment per annum is a sinking fund payment on the loan plus the interest payable on the outstanding capital loan; at the last instalment the sinking fund will have accumulated at compound interest to the amount of the original loan, and the property is released from the mortgage. Most financiers will only lend the developer a proportion of the property's value which makes it very important that his costs do not exceed the amount of the mortgage. If they do, he must finance the difference from his own pocket. The object of mortgaging is that the annual repayments should be substantially less than the income from the letting of the office building. With frequent rent reviews, a relatively moderate outgoings/income differential (profit rental) may be worth tolerating until the first rent review. Fixed interest mortgages for a long term are almost impossible to get for office buildings.

4.08 More frequently these days the merchant banks and some institutions join forces with the developer from the outset, and provide both bridging and terminal finance and retain an interest in the equity of the scheme. Although this makes the deal less attractive to the developer it does overcome one of the main problems of mortgages: that is that mortgages are granted only on a valuation on completion but bridging finance at a reasonable rate is not normally available without guaranteed terminal finance. The chicken-and-egg situation with a vengeance.

Sale and leaseback

4.09 The sale and leaseback arrangement means simply the sale *at cost* of the finished building, normally to an institution; it then leases the building back to the developer on a long lease at rental equivalent to a lowish interest rate on the actual cost of the development. As an example: a development costs £1 000 000 for land, building fees, etc. An institution agrees to pay the developer £1 000 000 for the freehold and to lease it back at say 7 per cent—so the developer's initial annual payment will be £70 000 per annum—less than he would pay on mortgage. The developer will have to have found a tenant for the building at an initial rent of say £90 000 per annum to make an adequate 'profit rental'. There are two main snags in this arrangement; first the institution is sure to insist on a rent review on the head-lease at the time the developer reviews his sub-tenant's rent; second, the developer may have committed himself beyond the useful life of the investment.

4.10 It is quite common with this method of terminal funding for the prospective purchaser to provide the bridging finance at reasonable rates of interest.

Financing the DIY operation

4.11 The company seeking to build its own office finds the problem of funding well-nigh insuperable; the best it can normally hope for is to effect a lease-back deal and be vulnerable itself to rent reviews on its own building. In less favourable circumstances the company will have to lend its name to an ODP application in consideration for just some say in the design or a concessionary initial rental.

4.12 The company which can sort out its own finance and get favourable mortgage facilities starts with a mortgage repayment just about equal to the comparable rental. Provided that the building is not unsaleably unique it will add considerably to the company's assets as other peoples' rents escalate.

5 Economics of building design

5.01 The building cost in relation to the capital value is sometimes surprisingly insignificant; this often leads developers and their agents to believe that the actual building process is relatively unimportant. The process certainly bores them—a necessary evil they cannot understand. The reality of the situation is that although the land cost sometimes overshadows the building cost, the land is still merely a residual figure; its value is created by the skills of the developer's advisers in creating a building at a reasonable cost good enough to attract a profitable rental.

Floor space economics

5.02 The plot ratio 'game' is well understood by architects who specialise in office design. It is most effective when played after the site has been bought. Then the income from the extra floor space which has been wrung out of the planners is only reduced by the extra development costs, ie building cost, fees, and finance—not by land costs.

5.03 The architect will aim to create out of the gross area the maximum lettable floor area: the area in the UK is measured between external walls and excludes staircases, structural walls, circulation space, toilets and amenity areas, plant rooms and any other space in which it is not possible to put a desk and rent as working area. (Columns are normally included in the lettable area in the UK but the practice varies in other parts of the world.)

5.04 It is obviously desirable to avoid secondary staircases, and external fire-escapes will please the developer in spite of their high cost; to put lavatories and washrooms on alternate floors can sometimes help the economics of a scheme. The extra cost of high-speed lifts is usually justified if the number of lifts is reduced—a valuable floor area saved for letting.

The external wall

5.05 Curtain walling systems with their problems of heat loss and solar gain have the overriding commercial merit of being fixed to the outside of the structure; thus the space otherwise occupied by the solid wall can be used as lettable floor space. The problem of environmental control arising from the use of curtain walling can of course be minimised by careful orientation but on restricted city sites air-conditioning is normally the only possible counter. Fortunately for the developer City offices with air-conditioning are let at higher rents; in fact failure to provide in an important location (regardless of environmental need) can reduce a block's letting potential and its rent by around £40 per m², per annum. As that £40 is just about the extra capital cost of an air-conditioning system over and above plain central heating it is clear that the developer can recover his extra outlay on air-conditioning in the first year or two.

Parking

5.06 The problem of where to put the car plays a big part in office design and economics. Its principal effect is that it restricts floor space, especially where there are height problems. Although it is not normally included in the gross floor area for plot ratio purposes car space usually has to be found: outside the building; under the building; in the

building; or on top of the building. Below is a rough index of the extra *building* cost of a parking space in various locations.

Option	Index
External hardstanding	100
Open ground floor	700
Open roof	750
Basement	2000

5.07 The decision the developer must make is simply whether or not the income to be derived from getting the maximum permitted office area on the site is enough to cover his cost and profit in providing the extra car space. External hardstandings are always economic and where the rent is over about £30 per m² the roof or open ground floor should pay its way. But basement parking is only worthwhile where the office rent is more than about £60 per m². (The use of double stacking systems can show savings per car space particularly in basements where the cost of the second 'doubled-up' car space has an index of about 600—see the table above.) The car parking calculation is, of course, integrally bound up with the planning requirements for numbers of cars in relation to gross floor area.★

The building cost

5.08 'Floor space economics' is virtually the only aspect of building economics developers and their agents can understand and to only a very limited degree. They tend to budget on the high side for the building cost when doing the residual land valuation; this gives them a contingency sum and covers up for the universal ignorance of the effects of shape, size and specification on the eventual cost of the office building. Their architects usually manage to fritter away the latent contingency in providing 'redundant performance'.

Redundant performance

5.09 'Redundant performance' in a building is money spent without benefit, commercial or architectural; the crime can be committed at any level from the choice of materials to the shape of the building. The actual building cost, even where only a lowish proportion of the budget, is still far and away the most difficult part of the budget to control. Whereas the developer's skill and effort may save $\frac{1}{2}$ per cent on finance or 2 per cent on fees a skilful design team can really reduce the building budget; an unskilful team can, as suggested, make a large hole in the developer's profit.

5.10 Materials specification must always be discussed with the qs or cost consultant who may be able to suggest the least expensive specification to meet the designer's performance requirements; most architects and many qss would be surprised to find what high quality can be obtained within a modest budget by adopting a value-engineering approach.

Shape and form

5.11 The shape of the building and number of storeys may be greatly determined by site restrictions. This however is no excuse for whimsical designs which by their very geometry produce the greatest quantity of the most expensive elements. The hoariest illustration is the effect of wall/floor ratio. The farther a building of constant area and number of storeys departs from a square the longer is the perimeter in relation to the floor area it encloses. When he works to a commercial budget the architect might consider at least whether aesthetics may be better served by a square building clad in marble or a cruciform one clad in whitewashed blocks.

★ It is fairly usual now for a developer in lieu of providing the actual physical car spaces to make a financial contribution to the local authority.

5.12 Most large buildings have a structural frame for one or more of these reasons:
1 The width is too great for free-spanning from external wall to external wall
2 Structural safety in certain conditions
3 The space occupied by loadbearing external walls is too valuable to the developer
4 Spine wall solutions deny flexibility, and so prejudice letting
5 Force of habit—in the architect and structural engineer. This said, it is worth noting that a frame makes no other contribution to the building. It can cost from £15 to £25 per m² of gross floor area which represents upwards of 10 per cent of the total cost.

5.13 Provided that the building works structurally with a load-bearing external wall, that will invariably give best value except in the high rental area where it occupies valuable space. Even then the cost/value calculation is worth doing especially with spans of 10 m or less.

5.14 If ground conditions are difficult it may be worth thinking about concentrating the load on a smaller area by building higher because the cost of an engineering solution to satisfy ground conditions for a high block may be overall cheaper than a low block due to the smaller area; there is of course a trade-off to be done with other elements which will cost more because of the increased height.

The external wall

5.15 A solid outside wall will in certain conditions help reduce the nuisance of traffic and the load on the air-conditioning plant and the thicker floor slabs can improve the insulation. The rather 'extreme' use of solid perimeters in the 'windowless' type of shell increases the need for environmental control; however, it then becomes feasible to go for the deep square shape with its very low wall/floor ratio. The benefit of the economical perimeter of the 'square' shaped office is sometimes negated when the depth entails use of permanent artificial lighting as well as air-conditioning. However, in locations where air-conditioning is a sales requirement regardless of absolute environmental need the possibilities of the deep, square, window-type of shell are worth considering. The amount of internal division is likely to vary in inverse proportion to the amount of external wall. But although unlikely to affect the rent one way or another it will affect what the owner/occupier or tenant can do.

5.16 The lifts element will rarely cost more than about 2 per cent of the total. As previously stated the cost of the lifts lies not so much in their capital costs as in the loss of floor space.

Successful commercial design

5.17 Some architects in recent years have been particularly skilful at the plot ratio 'game' and manipulating floor space economics; in very many cases, however, the effects of inflation on rental values has masked the uneconomic design of many commercially successful office buildings.

6 Floor space as a commodity

The role of the letting agent

6.01 When space is in short supply the quality of the space tends to be overlooked. Neither agents nor prospective tenants are trained to assess the true quality of office space; the result is that most new office space is valued entirely by location and demand.

6.02 In the unlikely event of agreement amongst architects on a method of assessing the quality of space they could still find it almost impossible to get the estate agency profession to adopt it.

6.03 Incidentally, the agent's fee for selling space is about 25 per cent of the architect's fee for designing it and supervising its construction.

Valuing the quality of space

6.04 Among the items which ought to be taken into account in evaluating the quality of office space are:
1 Adaptability
2 Ease of circulation and transportation
3 Environmental control
4 The capital cost of scenery likely to be inherited from the type of shell provided
5 The running costs of the building and services.
While an intelligent estimate can be made of 4 and 5, the other features can really only be subjectively evaluated.

7 Cost in use

7.01 It is much easier for the designer of a tailor-made office building to suit the requirements of an eventual owner/occupier. One benefit which the commissioning occupier has is that he can regulate cost-in-use. As suggested above there is no rent reduction for prospective high running costs; the owner/occupier is certainly in a better position to consider capital costs and running costs and his tax position before finalising the design team's brief.

7.02 There are two hoary old myths which must be exposed when discussing the general subject of cost-in-use. 1 that capital expenditure is always justifiable because it saves running costs. 2 that it is always necessary to spend more capital to save running costs.

7.03 It can be argued that a stud partition is nearly as flexible as a demountable one and at 10 per cent of the capital cost; and plastic rainwater goods do not rust and only the most fickle architects have them painted on installation.

7.04 The most important thing to remember is that whereas capital costs of offices carry finance charges from the outset, maintenance and running costs are deferred to some time in the future. In any event it is the occupier who pays and he is not often the owner; whoever pays will get income-tax relief anyway.

Organisation

7.05 Office building economics is a study on its own. To be effectively applied in practice it is thus essential not only to understand the principles but also to have actual costs and values constantly monitored by a specialist. If the designer can grasp the economic principles along with the many other aspects of office design that is really all that can be asked of him. With that grasp of the principles and with the advice of the building economics specialist his chances of achieving successful and good commercial architecture will be immeasurably increased.

Section 4: The economics of building offices

The residual method of land valuation

This is an example provided by BERNARD WILLIAMS of how a developer in the UK calculates the maximum price he can allow himself to pay for a site for an office building.

1.01 *Example* An office building of 6500 m² gross of which 5500 m² is lettable floor space at £70 per m² per annum.

Estimated capital value

1.02 5500 m² lettable floor area at £70 (pa exclusive total income)	£385 000
Less landlord's management expenses etc (pa)	£38 000
Net income (pa)	£347 000

Capital value assuming $8\frac{1}{2}$ per cent return on purchase price. (Multiply by $\frac{100}{8\frac{1}{2}}$ ie × 11·76 YP)

Capital value at 11·76 years' purchase	£4 080 000
Developer's overheads, profit, risk, say 20 per cent on capital invested ie 16·67 per cent of selling price	£680 000
Permissible development cost	£3 400 000

Building costs

2.01 6500 m² gross floor area at £250/m²	£1 625 000	
Professional fees $12\frac{1}{2}$ per cent	£203 000	

Building finance

3.01 (monthly cash flow basis) at 15 per cent pa

Assuming 21 months contract
∴ 50 per cent × £1 828 000

$\times \frac{15}{100} \times \frac{21}{12}$	£240 000	
	£2 068 000	
		£2 068 000
Total building and finance		
Residual amount		£1 332 000

Letting fees

4.01 Deduct agent's letting fees 10 per cent × rental	£38 500	
		£38 500
Residual amount		£1 293 500

Land acquisition costs

5.01 Agent's fees say 4 per cent and solicitors' fees and stamp duty £52 000	£52 000
Residual amount	£1 241 500
Deduct finance charges on land at 15 per cent pa compound for say $2\frac{1}{4}$ years say £461 500	£461 500
Residual amount	£780 000

Land value

6.01 Residual value of land	£780 000

Section 4: The economics of building offices

Office building: variations in shape

In this exercise BERNARD WILLIAMS sets out in detail the effects that the configuration and heights of an office building have upon the economics of a development. The cost of six different ways of providing 5000 m² of office space are compared element by element.

1 Introduction

1.01 It is hardly possible to illustrate the effects of every design decision on every size and type of office building; but the main principles are illustrated and explained below for a 5000 m² building. Type 1 is taken direct from a cost analysis up-dated to the first quarter of 1976. Types 2 and 3 are theoretical shapes adjusted element by element from type 1 for changes in quantity brought about by their shape; the specification has not varied from type 1 except when it would have been totally unrealistic not to change.

1.02 Building type 2A (the 'windowless' variation of type 2) has been adjusted for specification to take full advantage of the potential economy of structure of the square's shape; this variation requires air conditioning, so for comparison the 'traditional' types 1 and 3 have also been analysed as if they had air conditioning incorporated. For simplicity minor variations in cost have been ignored.

Definitions

1.03 *Ratio*—The quantity of the element expressed as a decimal fraction of the gross floor area; this is sometimes also called the quantity factor.

EUR (element unit rate)—The total cost of the element expressed in terms of its quantity. This is normally calculated as element cost ÷ element area in the case of elements having a plane surface, eg walls, finishes, roof. For this exercise the unit rate of elements such as frame, services, etc, has been expressed in terms of the area served by the element.

1.04 The principal reasons for each variation in element cost have been annotated. Variations in the ratio (quantity factor) are set out *alphabetically*; variations in the element unit rate are set out *numerically*.

1.05 The variations in the above element costs relative to building type are explained thus:

Ratio variations

a Reduced area of ground floor
b Increased area of upper floors
c Reduced area of roof
d Wall height increased because of greater storey height to fit in air conditioning
e Economical plan shape reduces total perimeter
f Need for maximum natural lighting increases window area and so reduces solid wall area
g Minimum natural lighting reduces window area and so increases solid wall to a relatively high area for the shape
h The rectangle, although more regular, encloses a smaller area, giving a greater ratio of perimeter wall-to-floor area
i With suspended ceilings the greater storey height does not produce an increased area of wall finishes.

Specification variations

1 The more economical rectangle has shorter length of perimeter foundation thus reducing the total cost of substructure
2 Increased load on foundation
3 Cost of columns increased because of increase in storey height: total cost of frame increased

4 Columns on perimeter omitted: external walls are loadbearing

5 Increased load on framing members because of increase in total height

6 Construction strengthened in taller building

7 Shorter perimeter reduces overall cost of roof element

8 Construction strengthened in tall building

9 Construction changed to faced loadbearing brickwork

10 Suspended ceilings mask air conditioning equipment

11 Increased storey height increases cost of vertical pipework

12 Plumbing costs higher in taller building

13 Lower perimeter area/floor area ratio potentially reduces heat loss from building

14 Need for increased glazed area for natural lighting increases heat loss from building

15 High proportion of cavity walling reduces heat loss from building

16 Higher heat loss (because of wind action) likely through perimeter wall of taller building

17 Increased air-changes for air conditioning increases heating load

18 Increased heat output from artificial lighting reduces heat load

19 Regular plan-shape reduces costs of trunking

20 Additional power loading for air conditioning

21 Increased artificial lighting due to greater depth

22 Increased artificial lighting due to reduced window area

23 Increased travel on lifts due to extra storey height

24 Increased lift speed needed for increased total travel

25 Increased cost of fire mains for increase in storey height

26 Wet risers needed for taller building

27 Increased cost of fire mains due to increased pipe sizing demanded for taller building

28 Type 1A building, not type 1, is basic building for consideration of air conditioning costs.

Additional notes

A Rental value of each type could be greatest factor on which was the most economical overall

B External works and services could be greater with types 3 and 3A; extra cost might be up to 5 per cent of the building cost with a 1·5:1 plot ratio

C Variations in pattern of circulation would alter amount of usable floor space; and would affect both cost per office worker and of course value of building as an investment

D Variations in performance of any element in above examples could easily alter balance of figures; they should therefore only be used to follow *principles* of effects of shape, size and specification on performance and so the cost of elements

E Variations would be as marked for a change in gross floor area as for the changes in the shape—but controlled by exactly the same geometrical and physical principles.

Table 1 Brief specification

Element	Building types 1	1A	2	2A	3	3A
Substructure	Bored piles, ground beams and pile caps; in situ rc slab	As 1	As 1	As 1	As 1 but heavier loading	As 1 but heavier loading
Frame	In situ rc columns and beams	As 1	As 1	As 1 but no columns on perimeter	As 1 but heavier loading	As 1 but heavier loading
Upper floors	Precast rc units with structural topping. Loading 295 kg/m²	As 1	As 1	As 1	As 1	As 1
Roof	Precast rc units with structural topping. Loading 244 kg/m². Asphalt, screed and insulation board. Cast iron roof outlets. Precast rc parapet units	As 1	As 1	As 1	As 1	As 1
Stairs	In situ rc with tile finish, metal balustrade and hardwood handrail	As 1	As 1	As 1	As 1	As 1
External walls	Precast rc window/wall units (80 per cent area). Faced cavity wall (20 per cent area)	As 1	As 1	Faced loadbearing cavity wall	As 1	As 1
Windows and external doors	Anodised aluminium double hung windows with tinted glass; hardwood veneered flush doors; fully glazed aluminium entrance doors	As 1	As 1	As 1	As 1	As 1
Internal walls and partitions	In situ rc loadbearing walls to core area and escape stairs; block partitions; patent wc cubicles	As 1	As 1	As 1	As 1	As 1
Internal doors	Veneered flush doors generally; patent doors to wc cubicles	As 1	As 1	As 1	As 1	As 1
Wall finishes	Plaster and emulsion paint (70 per cent cost); glazed wall tiling (20 per cent cost); hardwood panelling to main public areas (10 per cent cost)	As 1	As 1	As 1	As 1	As 1
Floor finishes	Cement/sand screed and vinyl tiles generally (70 per cent cost); mosaic tiles in cloakrooms and marble in entrance foyer (30 per cent cost)	As 1	As 1	As 1	As 1	As 1
Ceiling finishes	Plaster and emulsion paint generally (80 per cent cost); hardwood suspended ceiling to entrance foyer	As 1	As 1	As 1	As 1	As 1
Fittings and furnishings	Powder shelves and vanitory units with mirrors over in wcs; under-sink units in kitchens	As 1	As 1	As 1	As 1	As 1
Sanitary appliances	White glazed fittings	As 1	As 1	As 1	As 1	As 1
Disposal installation	Pvc rainwater goods; cast iron waste and soil goods; copper overflows	As 1	As 1	As 1	As 1	As 1
Cold water services	Copper	As 1	As 1	As 1	As 1	As 1
Hot water services	Copper (heat source not included)	As 1	As 1	As 1	As 1	As 1
Space heating	Oil-fired boiler; sill-line finned pipes	As 1	As 1	Similar to 1	As 1	As 1A
Ventilation and air conditioning	Extract ventilation to wc areas	Air conditioning to whole area	As 1A	As 1A	As 1	As 1A
Electrical installation	Power and lighting including fittings	As 1	As 1	As 1	As 1	As 1
Lift installation	Two passenger lifts serving five floors	As 1	As 1	As 1	Two high-speed lifts serving 10 floors	As 3

Floor area: 5000 m²
Rates: first quarter 1976
Gross

Building type diagrams (isometric):
- Type 1 (basic analysis): 39 m, 13 m, 52 m, 16 m
- Type 2: 18 m, 32 m, 32 m
- Type 3: 32 m, 16 m, 32 m
- Type 1A: 39 m, 13 m, 52 m, 16 m
- Type 2A: 18 m, 32 m, 32 m
- Type 3A: 16 m, 32 m, 36 m, 16 m

Key to column abbreviations: EQF = Area to gross floor area ratio; EUR = Per m² of element (£); EC = Per m² of gross floor area (£).

Type 1 (basic analysis) — Perimeter floor area 0·59

Element	EQF	EUR £	EC £	Notes
Substructure	0·20	50·40	10·08	
Frame	1·00	12·60	12·60	
Upper floors	0·80	15·12	12·10	
Roof (including rooflights)	0·20	42·84	8·57	
Staircase			3·02	
External walls	0·39	60·11	23·44	
External doors and windows	0·19	62·34	11·84	
Partitions			5·80	
Internal doors			2·86	
Wall finishes	0·45	3·36	1·51	
Floor finishes	1·00	11·09	11·09	
Ceiling finishes	1·00	15·88	3·28	
Sanitary appliances			1·26	
Fittings and furnishings			—	
Waste and overflows			1·76	
Cold water services			1·51	
Hot water services			2·27	
Heating			11·84	
Ventilation and air conditioning			0·25	28
Electrical			26·21	
Lifts			5·29	
Protective installations			1·51	
Preliminaries			9·49	
Total			**£167·58**	m² gross floor area

Type 2 — Perimeter floor area 0·46

Element	EQF	EUR £	EC £	Notes
Substructure	0·20	44·10	8·82	1
Frame	1·00	13·86	13·86	3
Upper floors	0·80	15·12	12·10	
Roof (including rooflights)	0·20	40·32	8·06	7
Staircase			3·36 d	
External walls	0·19	60·11	11·42 cf	
External doors and windows	0·27	62·34	16·83 ef	
Partitions			6·80 d	
Internal doors			2·86	
Wall finishes	0·45	3·36	1·51 i	
Floor finishes	1·00	11·09	11·09	
Ceiling finishes	1·00	15·88	15·88	10
Sanitary appliances			1·26	
Fittings and furnishings			—	
Waste and overflows			2·02	11
Cold water services			1·76	11
Hot water services			2·52	11
Heating			17·14	13, 14, 17
Ventilation and air conditioning			49·64	28, 19
Electrical			41·58	20, 21
Lifts			5·54	23
Protective installations			2·02	25
Preliminaries			14·16	
Total			**£250·23**	m² gross floor area

Type 3 — Perimeter floor area 0·61

Element	EQF	EUR £	EC £	Notes
Substructure	0·10	55·44	5·54 a	2
Frame	1·00	18·90	18·90	5
Upper floors	0·90	17·64	15·88 b	6
Roof (including rooflights)	0·10	47·88	4·79 c	8
Staircase			3·02	
External walls	0·40	60·11	24·04 h	
External doors and windows	0·21	62·34	13·09 h	
Partitions			5·80	
Internal doors			2·86	
Wall finishes	0·45	3·36	1·51	
Floor finishes	1·00	11·09	11·09	
Ceiling finishes	1·00	3·28	3·28	10
Sanitary appliances			1·26	
Fittings and furnishings			—	
Waste and overflows			2·02	11
Cold water services			1·76	11
Hot water services			2·52	11
Heating			13·86	16
Ventilation and air conditioning			0·25	28
Electrical			28·98	21
Lifts			6·80	24
Protective installations			5·80	26, 27
Preliminaries			10·38	
Total			**£183·43**	m² gross floor area

Type 1A — Perimeter floor area 0·65

Element	EQF	EUR £	EC £	Notes
Substructure	0·20	50·40	10·08	
Frame	1·00	13·86	13·86	3
Upper floors	0·80	15·12	12·10	
Roof (including rooflights)	0·20	42·84	8·57	
Staircase			3·36 d	
External walls	0·46	60·11	27·65 d	
External doors and windows	0·19	62·34	11·84	
Partitions			6·80 d	
Internal doors			2·86	
Wall finishes	0·45	3·36	1·51 i	
Floor finishes	1·00	11·09	11·09	
Ceiling finishes	1·00	15·88	15·88	10
Sanitary appliances			1·26	
Fittings and furnishings			—	
Waste and overflows			2·02	11
Cold water services			1·76	11
Hot water services			2·52	11
Heating			18·65	17
Ventilation and air conditioning			54·43	28
Electrical			37·04	20
Lifts			5·54	23
Protective installations			2·02	25
Preliminaries			15·05	
Total			**£265·89**	m² gross floor area

Type 2A — Perimeter floor area 0·46

Element	EQF	EUR £	EC £	Notes
Substructure	0·20	44·10	8·82	1
Frame	1·00	11·09	11·09	3, 4
Upper floors	0·80	15·12	12·10	
Roof (including rooflights)	0·20	40·32	8·06	7
Staircase			3·36 d	
External walls	0·35	18·00	6·30 eg	9
External doors and windows	0·11	62·34	6·86 eg	
Partitions			6·80 d	
Internal doors			2·86	
Wall finishes	0·45	3·36	1·51 i	
Floor finishes	1·00	11·09	11·09	
Ceiling finishes	1·00	15·88	15·88	10
Sanitary appliances			1·26	
Fittings and furnishings			—	
Waste and overflows			2·02	11
Cold water services			1·76	11
Hot water services			2·52	11
Heating			12·85	13, 15, 17, 18
Ventilation and air conditioning			49·64	28, 19
Electrical			45·36	20, 21, 22
Lifts			5·54	23
Protective installations			2·02	25
Preliminaries			13·06	
Total			**£230·76**	m² gross floor area

Type 3A — Perimeter floor area 0·69

Element	EQF	EUR £	EC £	Notes
Substructure	0·10	55·44	5·54 a	2
Frame	1·00	20·41	20·41	3, 5
Upper floors	0·90	17·64	15·88 b	6
Roof (including rooflights)	0·10	47·88	4·79 c	8
Staircase			3·36 d	
External walls	0·48	60·11	28·85 dh	
External doors and windows	0·21	62·34	13·09 dh	
Partitions			6·80 d	
Internal doors			2·86	
Wall finishes	0·45	3·36	1·51 i	
Floor finishes	1·00	11·09	11·09	
Ceiling finishes	1·00	15·88	15·88	
Sanitary appliances			1·26	
Fittings and furnishings			—	
Waste and overflows			2·27	11, 12
Cold water services			2·02	11, 12
Hot water services			2·77	11, 12
Heating			19·66	13a, 16, 17
Ventilation and air conditioning			49·64	28, 19
Electrical			37·04	20, 21
Lifts			7·31	23, 24
Protective installations			6·05	25, 26, 27
Preliminaries			15·48	
Total			**£273·56**	m² gross floor area

Note The letters and figures in this table refer to the lists. **Key to abbreviations: EC** Elemental cost; **EQF** Element quantity factor; **EUR** Element unit rate.

Section 4: The economics of building offices

Scenery costs

The costs of office scenery are examined by BERNARD WILLIAMS. The spectacular range of possible expenditure on interior fittings is highlighted and a comparative exercise shows where the money goes in several different types of layout.

1 Preface

1.01 The principal reasons for each variation in element cost have been annotated. Variations in the ratio (quantity factor) are set out *alphabetically*; variations in the specification are set out *numerically*.

1.02 The variations in the above element costs relative to scenery type are explained thus:

Ratio variations

a   Reduced area of new partitioning
b   Reduced area of existing partitioning
c   Internal wall height decreased due to lowered ceiling
d   Reduced area due to introduction of self-finish partitioning

Specification variations

1   Demolition of internal partitioning and subsequent supporting construction to achieve desired layout.
2   Lower room perimeter to floor area ratio.
3   Decreased area of the more expensive finishes.
4   Increased making good.
5   Decreased number of doors and openings.
6   Absence of new partitioning and doors.
7   Introduction of movable screens.
8   Increased usable space.
9   Introduction of landscaping.
10 More economic use of existing services.
11 Increased modifications to existing services.
12 Decreased cost of mechanical ventilation.
(NB. Base is quality 1 cellular office.)

2 Definitions

2.01 Ratio The quantity of the element expressed as a decimal fraction of the gross floor area; this is sometimes also called the quantity factor.

EUR (element unit rate) The total cost of the element expressed in terms of its quantity. This is normally calculated as element cost ÷ element area in the case of elements having a plane surface, eg walls, finishes, roof. For this exercise the unit rate of elements such as frame, services, etc, has been expressed in terms of the area served by the element.

EC Elemental cost sometimes expressed in relation to the unit of gross floor area.

EQF Element quantity factor The quantity of an element expressed in terms of its ratio to the gross floor area, eg where external wall area is 2000 m² and gross floor area is 5000 m² the EQF is

$$\frac{2000}{5000} = 0.4$$

Table I Elemental costings

Element	Cellular				Group spaces				Open plan				Landscape			
	EQF* Area to gross floor area	EUR* Per m² of element £	EC* Per m² of gross floor area £	Notes	EQF Area to gross floor area	EUR Per m² of element £	EC Per m² of gross floor area £	Notes	EQF Area to gross floor area	EUR Per m² of element £	EC Per m² of gross floor area £	Notes	EQF Area to gross floor area	EUR Per m² of element £	EC Per m² of gross floor area £	Notes
Quality one																
Structural alterations			4·20				4·20				16·46	1			16·46	1
Floor finishes			3·70				3·46	2			3·36	2			3·36	2
Wall finishes	2·74	3·10	8·50		1·65	2·48	4·09	a3	0·25	1·33	0·33	b3	0·25	1·33	0·33	b3
Ceiling finishes			1·68				1·68				1·93	4			1·93	4
Internal divisions and doors	1·79	3·43	6·13		0·70	3·04	2·13	a5			—	6			3·36	7
Furniture and fittings			16·79				17·63	8			18·06	8			18·47	8, 9
Extension and adaptation of services			3·69				3·36	10			8·40	11			8·40	11
			44·69				36·55				48·54				52·31	
Quality two																
Structural alterations			4·20				4·20				16·46	1			16·46	1
Floor finishes			8·13				7·60	2			7·38	2			7·38	2
Wall finishes	0·82	2·01	1·64	cd	0·82	2·00	1·64	cd	0·20	2·01	0·40	bc	0·20	2·01	0·40	bc
Ceiling finishes			8·46				7·91	2			7·69	2			7·69	2
Internal divisions and doors	1·54	9·96	15·33	c	0·62	9·18	5·69	ac5			—	6			5·04	7
Furniture and fittings			38·62				41·14	8			41·98	8			43·24	8, 9
Extension and adaptation of services			13·86				12·59	10			29·38	11			29·38	11
			90·24				80·77				103·29				109·59	
Quality three																
Structural alterations			4·20				4·20				16·46	1			16·46	1
Floor finishes			16·28				15·19	2			14·78	2			14·78	2
Wall finishes	0·82	32·14	26·36	cd	0·82	32·14	26·36	cd	0·20	27·72	5·54	bc3	0·20	27·72	5·54	bc3
Ceiling finishes			31·14				29·97	2			28·54	2			28·54	2
Internal divisions and doors	1·54	27·08	41·71	c	0·62	24·37	15·11	ac5			—	6			8·40	7
Furniture and fittings			74·14				70·59	8			80·59	8			83·01	8, 9
Extension and adaptation of services			49·53				49·02	10			47·01	11, 12			47·01	11, 12
			£243·36				£210·44				£192·92				£203·74	

NB Rates as for 1st quarter 1976. These are only four examples taken out of a large range of configurations.

Notes: The letters and figures refer to lists in para 1.02 *Key to abbreviations: EC Elemental cost, EQF Element quantity factor; EUR Element unit rate.

Table II Three scenery qualities

Brief specification of office area Element	Quality 1	Quality 2	Quality 3
Structural alterations	Demolition and modification of existing internal structure according to layout	As 1	As 1
Floor finishes	Corded carpet	Low-quality pile carpet	High-quality pile carpet
Wall finishes	Preparation and emulsion paint to existing surfaces. Plasterboard, skim and emulsion paint to new partitions	Preparation and high quality fabric wall covering	Preparation and high quality finishes, eg, hardwood and suede panelling, polished marble
Ceiling finishes	Preparation and emulsion paint	False ceiling	Patented suspended ceiling
Internal divisions and doors	Stud partitioning; flush doors	Self finish dry partitioning veneered flush doors	Self finish demountable partitioning with insulated core and partial glazing; hardwood doors.
Furniture and fittings	Basic quality office furniture and fittings	Medium quality	High quality
Extension and adaptation of services	Utilisation of existing services including adaptation, repairs and servicing where necessary	As 1 but with equipment added to provide a level of environmental control	As 2 but with introduction of mechanical ventilation system

3 Notes on the figures

3.01 The quality example, table I and table II, is based upon the conversion of an existing floor area that has large rooms ideally suited for group spaces and a basic minimum standard of servicing. This is reflected at the lower qualities in that the cost of converting to group spaces is the cheapest, owing to:

1 Minimum structural alterations.
2 Minimum amount of additional divisions and doors.
3 Minimum alteration and adaptation of services.
The layout of the existing area plays an important part in determining the conversion cost levels to space categories.
3.02 Although the cost patterns of quality One and quality Two imply that the conversion to open-plan/landscape offices is more expensive than to a more traditional layout, quality Three reverses this trend. This is explained by the fact that certain elements become more costly as the quality increases, but the quantity of these elements varies according to space type. For instance, wall finishes become a very expensive item under quality Three but this extra mainly affects only cellular and group spaces. The wall finishes element in open plan/landscape is obviously not cost-sensitive, so increased quality here is not likely to have overall significance. As with all building cost patterns, the permutations of quality, quantity and cost are virtually limitless.

4 Ratio of fitting-out to other costs

4.01 It is quite normal for the developer to ignore the cost of fitting out an office shell, though costs are often as significant as the cost of the shell. The large number of permutations of internal arrangement and specification makes it impossible to generalise on costs but it is interesting to consider the possible extremes of elemental costs with a compartmented interior.
4.02 The figures (at 1st quarter, 1976 levels) in table 1 represent a typical range which the tenant can choose from. Costs below the minimum are unlikely except when rock bottom specification is demanded.
Designers can easily exceed the suggested maximum but it is extremely difficult to justify such excesses on performance grounds.

4.03 The borrowing rate and the length of the lease define the ratio of the fitting out cost to the other overhead costs. Table III illustrates the equivalent annual expenditure for the two extremes of capital cost at the interest rate extremes and with varying length leases.

Table III Ratio fitting out costs to other costs

Capital cost of fitting out	£33·00/m² GPA				£270/m² GPA			
Interest rate and sinking fund %	8%	8%	12%	12%	8%	8%	12%	12%
Length of lease in years	5	21	5	21	5	21	5	21
Annual repayment of the capital sum per m² £	8·26	3·29	9·15	4·36	67·62	26·95	74·90	35·70

4.04 One point which is worth noting here is that telescoping the design and construction periods in interior works contracts often leads to a complete breakdown in cost control at all stages; many of the higher costs given result more from this than from any increase in performance.
4.05 The figures exclude fees but do not take into account tax relief. The relatively high repayment over the five-year terms is caused by the high sinking fund payment to write off the capital expenditure; over 21 years the sinking fund payment fades into significance seen against the annual interest on the loan.

SECTION 5: THE LAW AND REGULATIONS

Section 5: The law and regulations

Legislation on the quantity and location of development

The architect works within a web of constraints which define the space within which he must find his solutions; many of these constraints are legal. BILL THOMAS sets out the legislation which affects office development in the UK, discusses why the legislation is needed, distinguishes the parties involved and shows how far they can negotiate.

1 Outline

1.01 There are broadly three sets of laws and regulations in office development:

1 legislation which controls whether or not an office building will be permitted at all in a given context, and if so what total floor area will be allowed; this is controlled by economic, social and political decisions

2 legislation specific to or specially relevant to office building

3 general building regulations.

1.02 This study does not deal with all building regulations which apply to all building types—only with permitting and controlling legislation for offices. See table 1.

2 Intention of control

Consents

2.01 Any office development has to be compatible with local, regional and national strategies; consent has to be obtained at up to three levels:

1 the town planning or local level

2 in the case of Greater London at regional level

3 in the case of Greater London and South-east and other areas where so designated, at the national level.

2.02 These are physical and then economical and eventually political strategies as the scale of consideration widens. They are broadly concerned with balancing amenities such as pleasing environment and convenient communication for a local population as against economic and functional advantages for employers and those who benefit from the success of those employers—obviously where the employer is local or central government the beneficiaries are, in theory, the local population and the costs and benefits are thus, to some degree, relevant to a single set of people. The chief criteria of an office development strategy are:

1 the amount of office space that should be built (in any given future period)

2 the distribution of that office space.

Both these criteria control plans, and in areas outside the South-east applications to develop land as office space are to a large extent determined by the development plans; the problem is made easier because there is seldom a desire to build more office space than the development plans allow.

London and the South-east

2.03 In London and the South-east the problem is entirely different: there is continuous pressure to build offices in all parts. The national strategy as stated in the *Control of Office and Industrial Development Act* 1965 (now consolidated into the *Town and Country Planning Act* 1971) was to disperse office development away from London and the South-east: 'In exercising his discretion to issue or withhold office development permits, the Secretary of State shall have particular regard to the need for promoting the better distribution of employment in Great Britain' (*Town and Country Planning Act* 1971 *Part IV Section* 74 (3)). The strategy for this region is by far the most carefully, if narrowly, worked out assessment of how much office development should occur and where. It is explained in the GLDP paper *Industrial and office floor space targets for* 1971-76 (and the accompanying background paper B452). The relevant statement, quoted in part below, clearly expresses both the strategy which, for the GLC at least, will underly control of office development, and the factors which will determine whether a particular application is successful or not:

2.04 'A plan for getting a balanced distribution of office space throughout London so that jobs and workspace match up. . . . The criteria, which will apply from today, will give London the benefits of better distribution of jobs, will ease the transport problems and also help to make jobs available locally for married women and part-time workers. It will also improve the economic viability of boroughs outside the central area. . . . We also recognise the importance of the City of London where there is a need to retain and attract those enterprises which make such a big contribution to our invisible exports. The City must continue its major role, a role which will become even more significant when Britain enters the Common Market. . . . When considering priorities, the council will be able to pay special regard to general planning advantages gained by particular developments, for example, getting residential accommodation as part of development and improvements to the public transport system.'

3 Office development permit

3.01 In London and specified areas in the South-east (and in any other area which the Secretary of State may decide), an office development permit (ODP) has to be obtained before a planning authority can even consider a town planning application for the construction of more than 15 000 ft² gross of office space **1**. An application for an ODP is made to the DOE stating the amount proposed and what other accommodation is planned in the development. If a permit **2** is granted, two copies are sent to the applicant and he submits one to the planning authority with the planning application. If this application gets consent, the ODP is 'spent' and cannot be submitted with any other planning application. ODPs fall roughly into three groups:

Replacement ODP
3.02 An application is made to replace existing office space by new building, either on the site of the existing one or by amalgamating dispersed offices into a new building on a new site. The existing buildings have to be demolished or their use changed before the new space may be occupied; replacement ODPs are generally non-controversial and readily obtained.

ODP specific to the user
3.03 An office user may need more offices within the Greater London Area; as an alternative to obtaining existing space on the market he may make a case to the DOE for permission to develop and if the DOE accepts then an ODP will be given which is not specific to any particular location or project, but which can be used only for a development of offices which the applicant himself will occupy.

1 *Areas in which an ODP is required are shown with a dark tint.*

2 *An Office Development Permit.*

ODP for a specific site

3.04 A developer may have a site on which he wishes to build offices. He applies to the DOE to build on that site and if he can produce good enough evidence in support of his application he may get an ODP. This is the most difficult way of getting a permit; the developer will need specialist advice and help with the 'case' to support the application.

4 (Outline) town planning consent

4.01 An office building proposal must have planning consent in the normal way; the first stage is an outline consent.

4.02 In practice, the chances of an application succeeding can again be discussed according to type. Theoretically, consent to an outline application will be given if the application conforms to the type and intensity of use set out in the development plan.

Zoning by type of use

4.03 In the (then) MOHLG *Development plans, a manual on form and content,* offices come under the broad urban zoning category 'commercial use', which may 'distinguish, where appropriate, 'between': shopping, office and warehousing uses, or may be non-specific 3.

4.04 A site zoned 'non-specific commercial use', therefore, stands a reasonable chance of obtaining planning consent for office development: in certain commercial areas, such as centres the authority wishes to keep for shopping, there will be limits on the proportion of offices.

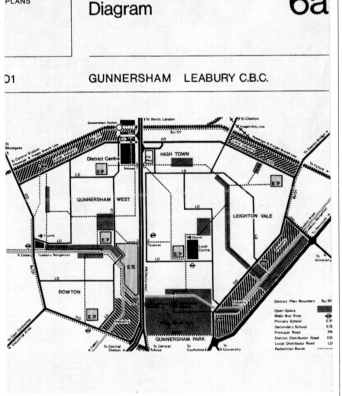

3 *District plan for urban area.*

Zoning by intensity of use

4.05 For all uses other than residential, intensity of development is controlled by the 'plot ratio'; the ratio of 'gross built floor area' to 'overall site area' within the site boundary. To determine plot ratio (and ODP area) the gross built floor area is taken to include the area occupied by walls, columns, stairs, life shafts (at every level), lavatories etc, but it excludes external covered areas, road

areas, car parking, plant rooms and service ducts. There is still scope for argument as to what does constitute the gross floor area in any given project. For example, in a building with recessed windows, is the overall width of the building taken to the outside glass line, or to the line of the furthest projection of the façade, or to some intermediate point? Thus if a site of two acres is zoned at a plot ratio of 2:1 (fairly common in inner areas of London), a maximum gross floor area of four acres will be allowed, the four acres to be distributed among whatever uses are planned for the site.

4.06 But there is an ambiguity when, as often, dwellings are included, for, theoretically, residential accommodation is not included in the plot ratio calculation in the above example and they, at whatever residential density permitted, may be allowed on the site as well as the four acres of non-residential use. Naturally, planning authorities have exploited this ambiguity and their interpretations may vary with the particular project, eg when it is a case of replacement of a non-conforming user in an area zoned residential, the authority may allow that replacement but then ask for dwellings to be included with the total the development plan has allowed for.

Application to replace an existing office

4.07 This is unlikely to be controversial whatever the development plan intention for the site. All that must be agreed is the gross area of the existing office building. The owners' only viable alternative to redevelopment with offices is most probably retention of the existing building; a new building is almost certainly more desirable for the planners as it at least gives the authority scope for improvement on siting, light angles, car parking, etc. Therefore, unless the planning authority is prepared to buy the existing building or wants it to be preserved, an application simply to replace is likely to succeed. But it is possible that the authority will ask for additional development in line with the development plan if the offices to be replaced do not conform.

Application to build a new office

4.08 It is highly unlikely that an authority will consent to office use in areas not zoned on development plans for such use. Outside London, development which conforms to a development plan is a relatively straightforward matter although the authority may seek the replacement of any residential space on the site. Within London, however, commercial zoning is no guarantee of outline consent for new office space (nor is the existence of an ODP). Applications to develop sites as offices in large units within Greater London are referred by the local authority to the GLC for consideration under the GLDP. The applicant normally discusses the development proposal with the GLC; at the same time he talks about it with the local authority. The GLC considers each case in terms of the criteria quoted in the GLDP Paper 1 *Industrial and office floor space targets for* 1971-1976.

Change of use

4.09 Another way in which office space can be 'created' is by changing the use of a building from one planning category, eg 'residential' or 'shopping' to another—in effect 'office use'. This may seem of marginal relevance to architects but, such is the pressure to create office space, that developers have briefed architects to design buildings called and categorised factory buildings, but really designed as offices. Thus a 20-storey, air-conditioned factory building may be designed and built and then let as offices.

4.10 What the developer wants is to rent out the buildings as office space, perhaps by finding a tenant who has a suitable ODP and then applying to the planning authority for change of use, or a tenant who can categorise his major use as one which conforms to the planning consent, eg, research categorised as industrial use. However, such machinations may not be necessary. The developer who is interested primarily in long-term investment may be content initially with an industrial tenant confident that in the long run he will be able to convert to office use.

4.11 Finally, a developer may negotiate with a planning authority on the basis of a non-office use and work out all the details of a satisfactory building with the authority—but delay construction until some circumstance allows a change of use to offices.

Appeal

4.12 If an authority refuses an outline application, the applicant can appeal to the Secretary of State, as with any planning refusal. No appeal will be considered if the scheme requires an ODP but has not obtained one. Any matter having a bearing on the considerations outlined above is relevant to an appeal, as are all discussions with the planning authority concerning the project.

5 Effect of legislation on extent and location of office development

5.01 Legislation since 1965 has had two major effects:

1 It has definitely reduced the amount of new office space developed in London, so that the expressed intention of the '65 Act has been met despite various loopholes. It has also succeeded in relocating within the London area the concentration of office building—away from the City and towards less favoured parts of London and the suburbs. This has been achieved simply by the allocation of office development permits.

2 It has strongly stimulated the replacement of old office areas with new building; an enormous amount of rationalisation and amalgamation of old offices has taken place. Any company with an old office building with huge corridors and imposing staircases, or with branch offices scattered around London, is well advised to assess its collected total gross office floor area and to consider the commercial potential of a replacement ODP. There is also another effect; there is no doubt that restriction of office development has inflated the cost of office space **4**. In London it is vastly more expensive than in other capital cities such as New York, with prices in the City reaching astronomical figures, and £80/m² being commonplace in the West End.

5.02 All this has obviously increased the commercial good sense of vacating office space in central London; an old-established firm which can operate successfully from outer London or elsewhere can vacate rundown Victorian premises in town and move into new air-conditioned offices outside the pressure areas and make a considerable profit just by doing that.

Side effects of legislation on the design of office space

5.03 Legislation controls gross building area, exclusive of ducts, plant rooms, and car parking, but the developer is concerned about 'net lettable' area, ie the amount of space he can rent to a tenant. This generally means the floor area the tenant can carpet, and hence excludes wall area, columns, lavatories, escape stairs, lift shafts, etc. The tenant in his turn is concerned about 'net productive' area, which is roughly the space he can use to put desks, chairs and people working, ie, space with an acceptable working environment. Legislation which restricts the quantity of office space built has had the interesting side effect of greatly increasing the importance of the architect's skill as a building planner and detailer.

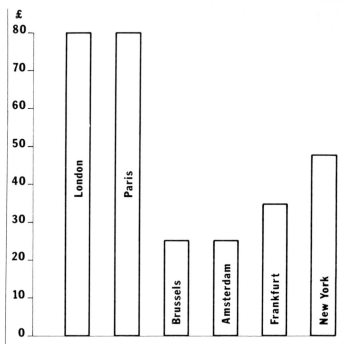

4 *Comparative rents of office space per m² in 1973.*

5.04 Clearly, for the developer, the best building is one which maximises the ratio net lettable/gross floor area; for the tenant, assuming a given rental, the ratio net productive/net lettable must be the best possible, and the two ratios are linked by adjustments in the negotiated rent per net m² lettable. The overall consequences are: 1 very carefully planned buildings (and an increased appreciation by the developer client of his architect's planning skill), 2 probably inferior fabric and environmental control because of this artificial pressure to produce hardware which takes the minimum floor area.

6 Ancillary use

6.01 A building or occupancy may be categorised in planning law in terms of its major use: the space allocated to a shopkeeper's office within his premises is described as 'shopping'. A caretaker' flat in an office building may be categorised as office space. But a building comprising a shop and containing offices where business to do with other branches of the retailer is carried out, ie his 'head office' may be called mixed offices and shops.

It is therefore of prime importance in both assessment for redeveloping existing premises and in new development to clarify and record the legal description of various spaces. The planners' view on this may well determine a client's best policy, both on the viability of redevelopment and on the provision of ancillary uses such as staff amenities.

7 Permitting and controlling legislation

Table 1 Permitting and controlling legislation

Subject of legislation	Act which controls	Explanatory text	Control body	Time scale of negotiations
Office Development Permit	*Town and Country Planning Act, 1971 Part IV Section 73-86 (Town and Country Planning (Amendment) Act 1972)*		DOE	These negotiations must be completed before any further work begins—if an ODP is refused then further work is wasted and money 'down the drain'.
Outline town planning consent	*Town and Country Planning Act 1971 Part III Section 22-35, 42, 169*		Local planning authority	Allow 2-6 months, see section 37 of 1971 *Town and Country Planning Act*
Demolition or alteration of buildings (and listed buildings) in conservation areas	*Town and Country Planning Amenities Act 1974*		Local planning authority	Allow 2-6 months, (see above)
GLDP Policy in GLC area	(not yet formalised)	GLDP Policy documents. See para 2.03 above	GLC	Simultaneously with town planning negotiations
Appeal against planning refusal	*Town and Country Planning Act 1971 Part III Section 36 (37)*	*Planning appeals, a guide to procedure* MHLG 1969 HMSO	DOE Inspector hears evidence submitted	Allow 12 months

Section 5: The law and regulations

Here BILL THOMAS deals with the regulations which apply after consent to develop a site has been given. He looks at the regulations which govern the quality of a building—the constraints which guard both the public and the workers within a building on matters such as the safety of a structure.

Regulations controlling the office shell

1 Definitions

1.01 This section focuses on some controls which are shaping office buildings, and does so in the context of the theme which governs this series—that of 'shell' versus 'scenery'.

1.02 The 'shell designer' is the developer's client company's architect; his job is to produce a building which 'passes' all the legal requirements as cheaply as can be with a maximum nett/gross ratio, and will, so far as he can tell, attract tenants. The scenery designer is the tenant's interior designer and/or office manager/house architect/office use consultant; his job is to take the empty shell which his firm proposes to lease and organise its interior for his company and not flout the legislation which controls both the building fabric and his alterations.

1.03 There is no way of avoiding some conflict of interest between the two parties, but essentially the onus rests on the developer and his shell designer to predict the needs of a user, and to weigh the economic cost of providing more than the 'legal minimum' against the marketing benefit of being able to sell his product either to a wider range of possible tenants or to more selective tenants who are prepared to pay higher rents.

Table 1 Qualifying legislation

		Subject	Act/Regulation	Explanatory text	With whom negotiated
General legislation	a	Detail town planning consent, 'approval of reserved matter'	*Town and Country Planning Act* 1971	Local and national design policies (eg as to tall buildings)	Local planning authority
	b	(Sunlight and daylight guides, not legislation)		DOE bulletin *Sunlight and daylight*. HMSO 1971	Local planning authority
	c	Established rights of light			Adjoining owners
	d	Public health generally (safety and health)	*Public Health Acts* 1936 et seq,		Local authority public health officers
	e	Provision of sanitary accommodation and adequate environment in work places	*Offices, Shops and Railway Premises Act* 1963	(Explanatory book for employees HMSO 1965) *General Guide* HMSO 1969	Medical officer of health (Dept of Health and Social Security)
Legislation operating outside the GLC area	f	Generally	*Building Regulations* 1972 *The Building Standards (Scotland) (Consolidation) Regulations* 1971	*Building Regulations*	Building inspector
	g	Nature of enclosures with reference to protection from fire	*Building Regulations* 1972 *E7*	Explanatory bulletin, appendix to building regulations	Building inspector
	h	Means of escape in case of fire	*Offices, Shops and Railway Premises Act* 1963	DOE *Means of escape in case of fire in offices, shops and railway premises. New series No* 40 HMSO 1969	Fire brigade
Legislation operating within the GLC area	i	Generally			District surveyor
	j	Nature of enclosures with reference to protection from fire	*London Building (Constructional) By-laws* 1972		District surveyor
	k	Minimum amount of windows	*London Building (Constructional) By-laws* 1972 *Part XIV*		District surveyor
	l	Means of escape in case of fire. Tall and large buildings	*London Building Acts (Amendment) Act,* 1939 *Section 20*	*GLC Code of Practice, Means of escape in case of fire Section 20 London 1974*	GLC architects department in collaboration with London fire brigade
	m	Means of escape in case of fire other than Section 20 buildings, above	*London Building Acts (Amendment) Act,* 1939 *Section 35*	*GLC Code of Practice, Means of escape in case of fire Section 34, London 1974*	GLC architects department

1.04 In what follows, the speculative building developer and his architect control the shell and the user and his advisers the 'scenery'.

At the outset, it may be useful to compare the developer's attitude towards qualifying legislation with his approach to legislation constraining quantity. Permitting or quantifying legislation dictates whether a developer, having perhaps acquired a site will be allowed to build office space on it, and if so how much. Qualifying regulations are designed to ensure that a development, once approved in principle, conforms to certain standards of safety, appearance, health etc. Conflicts of interest between the law and the developer are clearly less likely to arise in this second category of control. Those that do occur predictably focus on what is 'satisfactory'; on the whole, the differences between the two are minor, although they do tend to be exacerbated where legislation, inevitably, lags behind technology. Few successful modern developers want to put up unsafe or insanitary buildings—they will be difficult to let.

2 The regulations

2.01 The 'quality controls' are:
1 Detail town-planning control
2 Control of circulation in offices
3 Control of space use in offices
4 Control of fabric design.

3 Detail town planning control

See table I reference a, b, c.

Building envelope

3.01 The planning authority will consider the office envelope in terms of its appearance, its effect on daylight and sunlight reaching other buildings, and the lighting conditions on the building face itself; the authority may also have a policy on the building height. There is no legislation on some of these matters but there is strong guidance on lighting in the code of practice, the DOE bulletin *Sunlight and daylight*, and in Sunlight for residential buildings, technical study AJ 11.4.73 [8 (N7)]. There are also common law rights of light, but these are generally safeguarded by adhering to the code and design bulletin. Usually detail is resolved by informal discussion before the scheme is submitted for formal approval.

Access

3.02 These negotiations on town planning control clearly must be part of the architect's role but his decisions and negotiations with the planning authority will be affected by 'scenery' criteria in at least two ways; the first is on building bulk, where the authority may press for a lower building resulting in deeper office space; the second, fenestration, where module, window/wall ratio, and window frequency all affect the flexibility of possible internal arrangements, particularly where these 'mesh in' with constraints of the public health acts and building by-laws (see para 5 Control of space use).

4 Control of circulation in offices

See table I reference h, l, m.

4.01 The regulations on protected means of escape and on access for fire fighting constrain the 'core' more than any other plan element in an office block; the larger and higher the building is, with all but the simplest buildings, the more advisable it is to negotiate core design with the enforcing agency for, even with regulations and codes of practice, interpretation of written guidance in the light of the particular design and location of each case is what really determines what will be permitted.

4.02 Here the 'scenery' designer is in the hands of the shell designer: the architect's aim in working out a design with the authority will be to minimise the number of cores and their size, both to reduce cost and increase net/gross ratio, and to achieve a floor plan with cores placed as far from ends and edges as the legislation permits in order to maximise the area served by any core—a plan which may not at all suit the 'scenery' designer.

4.03 The shell architect must decide whether fire escape lobbies form part of general circulation routes or separate spaces used only for access to means of escape; the latter is, in the main, wasteful. The 'scenery' designer works with a floor plan with circulation routes implied by the core position or relationship between cores, and if lobbies are planned as part of the general circulation, then that part of the route is already built. When two cores are as far apart as possible (maximum efficiency for the architect) the 'scenery' designer must define, with partitions or furniture, a straight route between them. This kind of restriction is unlikely to become apparent until the building is let unless the 'scenery' designer is involved very early in the leasing of office space.

5 Control of space use in offices

See table I reference d, e, g, j, k.

5.01 The *Public Health Acts* 1936 *et seq* and *Offices, Shops and Railway Premises Act* 1963 control the population of an office and its distribution and subdivision by enclosures. The shell controls the 'scenery' designer's options in these ways:

Lavatories

5.02 The architect has to make an assumption about likely maximum office population. The requirements of the *Offices, Shops and Railway Premises Act* 1963 are stated in number of fixtures per person rather than per m². If he guesses too high a population he will put in too many lavatories and reduce the lettable area; if he puts in too few, then the tenant will not be able to accommodate his staff as densely as he wishes and the office space will be less valuable (unless the tenant installs more lavatories). In practice the architect must err on the high side, as the loss from too many lavatories can only be a small one; but if the developer can know his tenant in advance, then in high-rental sites it will pay to be exact.

Office subdivision

5.03 Subdivision, whether on a module or in a less formal way, is to some extent controlled by the window pattern; for maximum flexibility, the tenant needs continuous windows on a smallish module, say about 1·20 m. (He may also want maximum glass area per module.) The developer, on the other hand, will probably not want to exceed the maximum window area permitted by the by-laws or regulations, even if he knows that this is negotiable, because glazing is expensive to build in and involves high servicing and climate control costs.

5.04 The developer can have no direct effect on the density of occupation of office floor space. The scenery designer has to conform to the *Offices, Shops and Railway Premises Act*.

6 Control of fabric

See table I reference d, h, m.

6.01 The shell designer will choose all the finishes in areas controlled by means of escape regulations, and the enforcing agent, building inspector or district surveyor, will check them. Inevitably, therefore, the style of office interiors tends to differ in these public areas from other parts of the building, partly because of the legislative control and partly because of differences in style between architects and 'scenery' designer. Again, there is no way around this problem short of the 'scenery' designer adopting the style used in the controlled areas.

6.02 The architect will keep the floor-to-floor height to the minimum to reduce bulk and save cost; that minimum will include a likely suspended ceiling depth as well as the legal minimum floor-to-ceiling height and the depth of the structural floor; a 'scenery' designer may find that the depth allowed by the shell is inadequate for the particular system he wishes to use.

SECTION 6: THE OFFICE ENVIRONMENT

Section 6: The office environment

Integrated services for office buildings

In the USA in 1925 mechanical services accounted for less than 20% of total office building cost. By 1965 they accounted for 46%. As the space that services occupy and their effect on other building sub-systems increases, architects depend to an increasing extent on the specialist advice of the consulting engineers. Consequently ANDREW RABENECK argues for closer collaboration between the architect and the engineer, particularly since engineering is increasingly inaccessible to non-engineers.

1 Co-ordination and predetermination

1.01 The approach to integrated services design outlined below can be loosely termed a systems approach. This simply means viewing a problem as a set of interrelated parts, and finding a way to make them work together more effectively.

To do this involves relating resources and needs to performance, cost and time. In this process the levels of performance sought for the different building subsystems, and the costs of achieving them, are made explicit as early as possible in the design process. The aim is to avoid the erosion of project objectives through costly compromises of space or servicing, either in later stages of the design or during the life of the building.

1.02 It is inevitable that a discussion of *integrated* services design should be conducted on a broad front because the cost of the services element is only part of the costs associated with services decisions. The incidental cost effects of servicing on structure, external envelope, space division and other elements are significant. It would not be unreasonable to suggest that services subsystems decisions influence about 80% of the cost of the building.

1.03 Designing buildings with any degree of servicing is rather like assembling a hi-fi system. The components and subsystems need to be 'balanced' to obtain the desired performance without unnecessary expense. Poor performance of one component is likely to drag the overall system performance down to its level, thereby wasting the expensive high performance of the other components. Before buying a hi-fi system, the cost and performance of each component is evaluated, bearing in mind any planned future changes. It should be the same in building. The choice of a good technical solution depends on prior knowledge of cost and performance of alternative solutions or strategies.

1.04 The operation of making a balanced choice is known in systems jargon as *trade-off*, **1**. It is literally a bartering procedure between cost, performance and quality in terms of constraints of time and budget for each subsystem of the building and between subsystems. The data used in trade-offs are generated by the specialists in the design team.

The process described in this article, although not linear, contains six basic steps:

1 Determine basic user amenity needs independent of space planning.

2 Develop range of building configurations and structure/service models to suit project criteria.

124

3 Analyse alternative hardware to arrive at preferred subsystem solutions.
4 Test hardware against preferred configurations.
5 Trade-off configurations and hardware.
6 Detailed space planning.

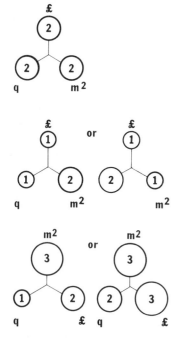

1 The trade-off.
Basic equation between money (£) quality (q) and area (m²).
If money is reduced then either quality must be reduced to provide the same area or area must be reduced if quality is to be maintained.
If more area is sought then: either quality must reduce if budget is fixed or more money is needed if quality is fixed.
If higher quality standards are sought then: either less area will be built or more money will be needed.

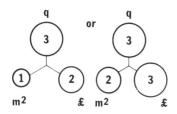

2 Compatibility

2.01 Data is reduced to manageable proportions by recognising the hierarchical nature of decisions about the compatibility of building and systems, **2**. The hierarchy of decisions relates to the concepts of shell and scenery because it recognises that primary decisions will relate to the expensive long-life shell subsystems, and that secondary decisions will depend on these earlier decisions. For example, the decision about the relationship between structure and services (together accounting for 45%-60% of first cost, while services alone account for 40%–55% of alteration costs) precedes the secondary decision about the ceiling/lighting or partitioning **3**. Structure/services is primary because it encompasses, together with the external wall, the most important permanent building element. A discussion of integrated services design must include discussion of the choices to be made for the other major shell subsystems.

2.02 The critical decision areas are:
Building configurations.
Structure/services relationship.
Services distribution and floor sandwich.
Routing control and reserved zones.
Delivery to the workplace.
Using the discussions of these critical decision areas, an architect should be able to:
Brief his consultants on the basic data required.
Determine the hierarchy of decisions for a particular project.
Set up the appropriate trade-offs.
Derive a set of optimum technical solutions for the main subsystems.

3 Building configuration

3.01 Factors external to the technical subsystems choices most influence building configuration. For example, site planning, the type of organisation to be housed and whether the building is speculative or custom built.
In the case of the custom built building, the configuration is a response to the needs of the organisation to be housed, over time, including the scope for change in scenery during the life of the building. For speculative offices, configuration is the response to the expected patterns of tenancy.
3.02 These basic briefing data are used to determine a range of possible configurations with respect to:
1 Space relationships (eg clerical to executive)
2 Horizontal movement of people
3 Vertical movement of people
4 Vertical movement of services
5 Horizontal movement of services
A range of alternatives for 2 and 3 can be generated **3**. The alternatives for each configuration factor are then per-

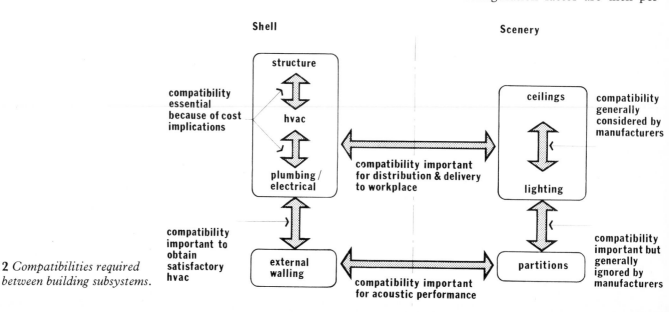

2 Compatibilities required between building subsystems.

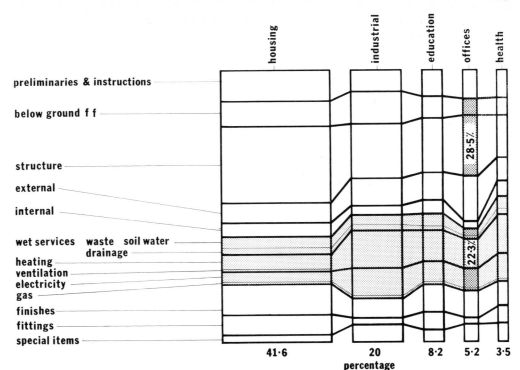

3 *Breakdown of annual national new building output showing relative importance of structure/services in office buildings. Analysis prepared for Building Research Establishment, Garston by Building Systems Development, May 1972, using AJ and BSIC data. Unpublished.*

mutated to isolate those configurations that satisfy the space planning and brief criteria. These are then grouped for easy comparison **4**. At this stage no technical solutions are considered. The next task is to trade-off the preferred configuration against the preferred structure/services options.

4 Structure/services relationship

4.01 The high proportion of first cost attributable to structure/services has already been mentioned. This cost is especially high in the case of adding services as distinct from modifying them. It is highly probable that today's office buildings will need additional electrical and communications services. With this in mind, constraints on service routes must be considered in conjunction with structural systems. Assuming a rectilinear form, the number of geometric relationships of physical components is limited: there are four alternatives for relating horizontal services to horizontal structure, **5**.
These four categories encompass all horizontal conditions. Five alternatives for vertical movement of services are shown in **6**.
4.02 Certain of these vertical and horizontal alternatives cannot be combined into workable solutions: for example, an interior shaft of services cannot easily connect to a horizontal perimeter movement. The most useful conditions are shown in **7**. These two sets of conditions, relating structure and services vertically and horizontally, can be developed into building element solutions. A decision to use a given approach determines the range of building methods applicable, which further implies a range of building products. Conversely, where the building method is predetermined, say by special site conditions or client's preference, this will imply both a range of products and a limited choice of solutions.

5 Services distribution and floor sandwiches

5.01 Total services distribution patterns are not as simple as the basic models. Total patterns may consist of combined and overlapping or combined yet distinct

patterns for different services elements. Although more complex than the basic models, the number of combinations of distribution patterns compatible with one another and with structure is large but limited. These patterns are defined and tested by basing assumptions about technical solutions on the comparative data assembled by the consultants.

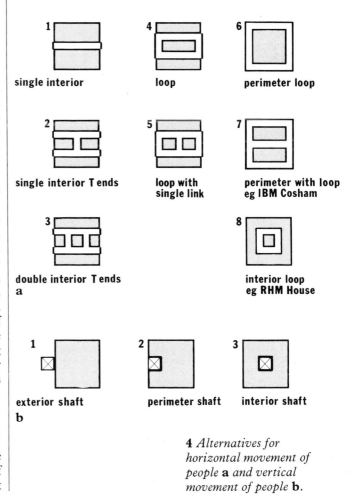

4 *Alternatives for horizontal movement of people **a** and vertical movement of people **b**.*

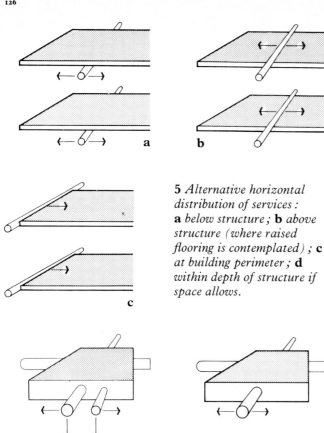

5 *Alternative horizontal distribution of services:* **a** *below structure;* **b** *above structure (where raised flooring is contemplated);* **c** *at building perimeter;* **d** *within depth of structure if space allows.*

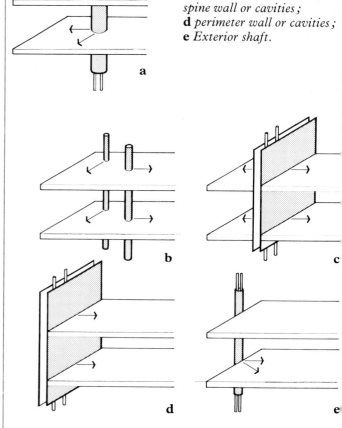

6 *Alternative vertical distribution of services:* **a** *Central interior shaft;* **b** *Random shafts;* **c** *Interior spine wall or cavities;* **d** *perimeter wall or cavities;* **e** *Exterior shaft.*

5.02 This is a key step in the process. Its aim is to narrow the range of useful alternative solutions for subsystems hardware. Criteria of acceptability are determined by the preferred building configurations, and the range of structure/service models that satisfies them.

To find an optimum overall system the structure may be considered in two parts, horizontal and vertical. For horizontal structure the main points would be economic bay sizing, permeability by services and depth. Vertical structure alternatives will be judged according to plan area taken up by structure, lateral restraint provided, height limits and permeability by services.

5.03 The key questions to be answered in services distribution studies are:

How do services mains distribute around the building?
Where do services enter the floor/ceiling space?
How do services pass through the floor/ceiling space?
How do services leave the floor/ceiling space?
How are services delivered to the workplace?

To answer these questions it is necessary to perform many small trade-offs relating to each preferred basic structure/services model. For example, a good return air system for one model may not suit another.

5.04 To avoid overlooking reasonable possibilities and to illustrate the trading-off process, it is valuable to use the floor sandwich as an example of the characteristics and arrangement with respect to one another of all subsystems in the horizontal plane. Manipulation of the sandwich provides information about the cost and performance of the sandwich and its implications for other design elements, **8a–c**.

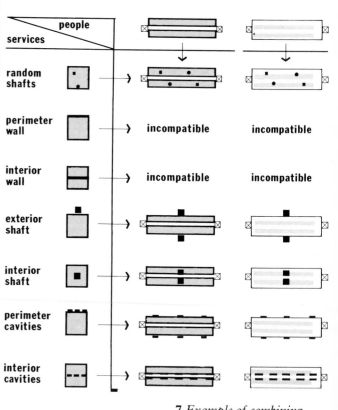

7 *Example of combining vertical movement options with a preferred arrangement of people movement.*

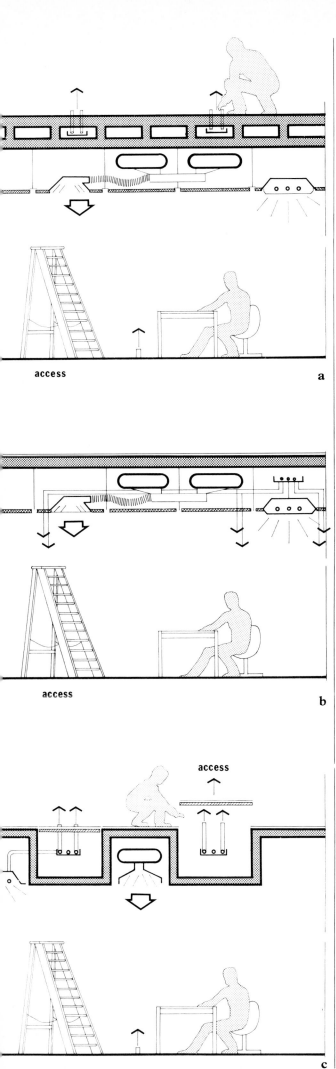

access

a

access

b

access

c

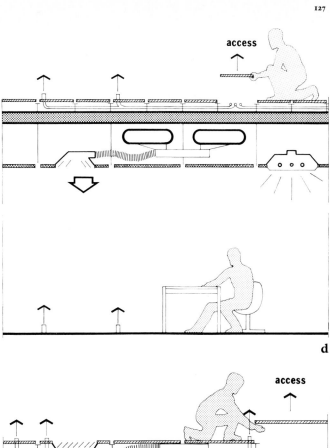

access

d

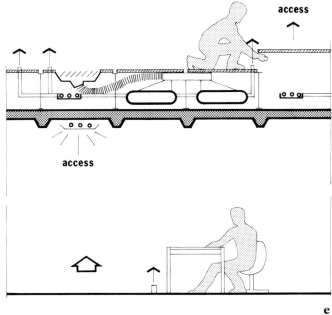

access

access

e

8 *Different forms of floor
sandwich :*
a *Electrics feed from floor
upwards to suit open
planning ;*
b *Electrics feed down into
partitions or power poles ;*
c *More complex integration
of structure with services,
lateral distribution limited,
but structure may act as
ducts ;*
d *Simple raised floor for
electrics and communications
distribution ;*
e *Full raised floor eg in
computer areas.*

5.05 Factors of major importance for each subsystem in the sandwich are shown below:

Structure	Depth and permeability (in relation to HVAC supply and return). Bay size (column free space).
HVAC	Depth of distribution and return system.
Power/light	Type and output of lighting (heat generated). Power distribution and outlets.
Communications	Location and accessibility.
Wet services	Depth for falls.
Ceiling	Loading from partitions and service columns, plenum sub-division, choice of panel type (lighting, luminous, HVAC outlets, acoustic, plain).

The main objectives of floor sandwich design are to minimise overall depth and maximise accessibility without compromising the cost or performance of the subsystems involved. Depth of the sandwich is a function of the interface between HVAC distribution and structure and has consequences for first cost: the cost of *height* is reflected in stairs, lifts, vertical structure and external walling. This may be significant for buildings of small plan area which must rise several storeys.

5.06 Another important factor is the *density* of services over the area of the building and particularly at the transition from vertical to horizontal. Minimising vertical duct areas may well result in an unnecessarily deep horizontal distribution, simply to accommodate services at the point of entry to the floor sandwich.

5.07 Ease of *access* is the other major factor in floor sandwich design. Initial installation (see Routing control), alteration, maintenance and repair costs are all dependent on ease of access. The amount of space given and the location of service systems within the floor sandwich are resolved by a trade-off between the intrinsic requirements of the service systems and user requirements. The optimum sandwich configuration of structure and services may not be the same as the consultant's first choice based on performance and installed cost of the individual services. For example, a first choice of a double duct mixing box air distribution system may be revised to single duct reheat or multizone distribution to give simple distribution patterns and shallower sandwich depth. This might result in a high HVAC cost but a lower overall building cost.

6 Routing control and reserved zones

6.01 The services required in some form at the workplace for:

Comfort of the occupants.

Operation of equipment.

Performing tasks not associated with equipment (eg mail delivery, waste disposal).

In this context key questions are what are these services and by what means can they be delivered—by pipe, duct, cable, radio wave or messenger? Why can't the services go directly where they are needed?

What is the need for routing control and what is needed to provide control?

6.02 The answers to these questions will depend on the individual project; on the amount, size, complexity, maintenance, degree of modification and building volume involved. Nevertheless a generally applicable solution to routing control is provided by the concept of reserved zones within the service spaces of the building. The idea is simply to disengage the various service lines to permit services to travel through the building from source to user without interfering with each other, **9**.

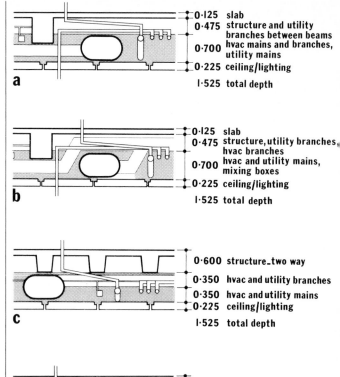

9 *Control of services routes may be achieved by reserved zones within the depth of the floor sandwich. The idea is illustrated by examples based on a 9·00 × 12·00 m structural bay.*
a *Beam and slab, single duct HVAC, 1525 mm total depth with bottom access.*
b *Beam and slab, double duct HVAC, 1525 mm total depth, bottom access. NB costly ductwork because of crossover.*
c *Waffle slab, single duct HVAC, 1525 mm total depth, bottom access. NB Structure occupies nearly 40% of available depth.*
d *Waffle slab, double duct HVAC, total depth 1875 mm, bottom access. NB additional depth required for crossover of branch ducts because of two-way structure.*

Obviously, providing for non-specific use of a building will require some redundancy in the servicing systems if high performance is sought. In office buildings, however, uses are specific, although they may change. The service systems, then, must accommodate scenery changes in the functional zone with a minimum of redundancy. Experience of hospital and academic buildings which house highly serviced, transient and specific functions, suggests that the best cost/performance combination is provided by service mains that suit 'all conditions' and branches that may be adapted to specific user requirements, **10**. This arrangement may entail a small degree of redundancy in mains, but this is more than offset by future savings on alteration costs.

6.03 The main reasons for reserved zone routing control should be summarised here.

1 For regular inspection, maintenance and emergency repair, it is important to:

Know where runs and equipment are located

Have ease of access

Be able to inspect all runs and equipment at a minimum number of access points

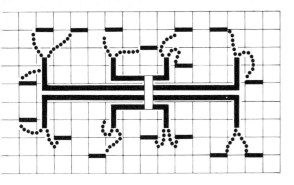

10 *Example of permanent main ducts sized and located to suit all conditions, feeding branch ducts that can be adapted to changing patterns of use.*

2 The space required for services routing adds up to a considerable volume, and overlapping services add to building height and thus to volume.

3 The 'first come, first fixed' attitude of services contractors provides simple fixing for early comers, while later trades have to thread around previous fixings. BSD analyses have shown that a considerable portion of routing cost and contingency is attributable to this arrangement.

4 Complexity of routing, or density, particularly where services group to enter a vertical core.

5 Later alteration of layout requires positioning of services to permit location, identification, and access, in order to reroute, remove or add branches and outlets.

6 Where an accelerated building programme is used, the layout of the offices may be decided after much services routing has already been installed.

6.04 In the context of services routing, many services required at the work place do not depend on centralised supply and can be localised. Some offices (eg speculative rental, or where there are height limitations) may benefit from a localised approach. Although the trade-offs need to be done for each case, localised services often result in lower overall building cost but higher component and maintenance costs. Greater disruption of work spaces during the life of the components is also likely.

Routing control will depend not only on considering the relationship of services to each other and to the structure, but also the 'travel cost' of different routes. Clearly, the shorter the distances the less the first cost. However, when office layouts are not known in advance, or when low alteration costs are important (eg for owner-occupied buildings) the considerations may differ, so the most general solution that has an acceptable degree of over-provision built into the initial layout will probably be preferred.

7 Delivery to workplace

7.01 Bringing services to the workplace depends on the services themselves, the configuration of the building, the constraints imposed by the structure/service model, and the intended use of the building.

Irrespective of whether the building is owned or leased, its configuration will imply patterns of workplace servicing. Shallow plan buildings will tend to depend on perimeter and core servicing requiring little lateral distribution. Limitations on potential alternate layouts due to plan form suggest that little provision of adaptability is worthwhile, and workplace servicing can generally be achieved through exterior walls and partitions.

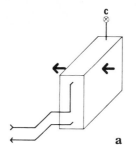

11 *Control of heating, ventilating, and air conditioning :*
a *Fan coil terminal unit : receives steam or heating water and chilled water from a central plant, air from outside via wall louvres or from central ducted system. Control : by thermostat located either in return airstream or on a wall controlling air flow or water valve.*

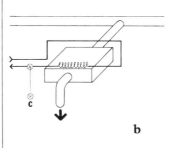

b *Single duct-terminal reheat : Single duct from central air-handling equipment delivers cool air throughout the building, re-heated as necessary by hot water pipe or electric coil on branch duct. 'Variable volume' systems may also reduce volume of air delivered. Control : room thermostat controls terminal unit to vary air volume and/or reheat the cool air.*

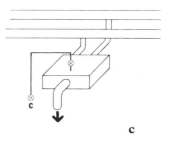

c *Double duct-central plant : centrally located equipment supplying two ducts one with cool air one with warm. For each control zone a branch duct is taken from each of the main ducts, through a terminal mixing bore and to the room in a common duct. Control : a room thermostat controls the mixing box to blend warm and cool air.*

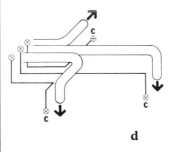

d *Multi-zone central plant : centrally located equipment. Warm and cool air blended by dampers at central air handling and distributed via small ducts to each control zone. Control : room thermostat operates unit mixing dampers to control the supply air temperature to each zone.*

7.02 Deep plan buildings will require longer lateral services distribution and a higher level of lighting. Potential flexibility of plan form may need to be matched by flexible workplace servicing. The basic and still largely unresolved problem is finding economical flexible routing from service space to desk top. By and large, the simplest and most economical routings within the office space are least acceptable aesthetically.

7.03 Workplace services can be considered as being needed at high level or low level. High level would normally include general lighting, heating and ventilating and air conditioning (HVAC), clocks, public address system. Low level includes local lighting, communications (telephone, intercom, CCTV) power supply for equipment, data terminals, lighting control, HVAC control, alarms. Discussions below of HVAC and cable borne services will serve to illustrate the main points.

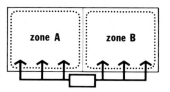
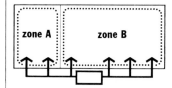

12 *Effect of changing layout may be to complicate balancing of air distribution unless HVAC system is also adaptable.*

8 Heating, ventilating and air conditioning

8.01 The problems of supply, return and control are interrelated. Particularly important is possible change of configuration of enclosed spaces on a floor. **11** shows how different HVAC systems relate to their control systems. The optimum size of control zone varies for each system, and serious problems of balancing and controlling air distribution can be created if outlets cannot be relocated to suit new office layouts. In **12** the effect of a new layout on control zones is shown. Even in this simple example, balancing the new layout would be difficult. In more complex mixtures of open and cellular space it may be impossible, unless lateral ducts and outlets are relocatable as well as partitions.

8.02 Choice of air outlet and return systems has to be considered at the same time as choice of partitions and ceiling/lighting system, particularly where cellular offices are involved. Common design faults are the arrangement of outlets so that some rooms can get no air supply except through the door; even provision in corner offices (particularly where under-window terminal units are used); and use of linear diffusers combining with the ceiling grid which must also accept partitions (resulting in flanking sound transmission between rooms).

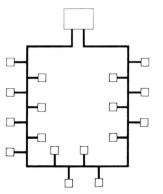

13 *Basic attributes of different systems need to be considered early on for capacity, routing and ease of access.*
a *Electrical distribution: many-to-many systems.*

9 Cable-borne workplace servicing

9.01 A basic distinction between electrical and communications services, which affects routing design and capacity is shown in **13**. Costs of disruption to workplace for later alteration or additional capacity may be higher than overprovision in initial cost. For many years in the USA it has been the practice to provide spare capacity wiring back to floor distribution boards in first cost, and with deeper and more flexible space this is now becoming necessary in this country.

9.02 Four basic modes of final delivery to workplace are shown in **14**. Both horizontal and vertical systems present problems of trade-offs between flexibility, economy and aesthetics. Horizontal systems may use the perimeter, reaching the workplace directly, through partition skirtings or over the floor finish. Perimeter servicing is suitable only for shallow plan buildings. For deep buildings distribution may be in the ceiling with power column or free drop to workplace. **15** shows two arrangements. The close spaced grid can be justified only in situations of extremely frequent change, while flexible connections from junction box to outlet entail more labour in alteration.

9.03 More common is floor distribution in trunking in the screed or feeding up from ceiling space below. This arrangement is convenient for desk access but interrupts

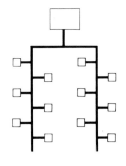
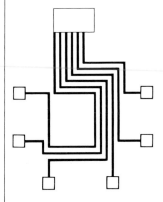
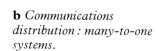

b *Communications distribution: many-to-one systems.*

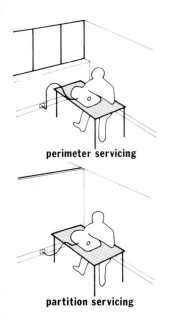

perimeter servicing

partition servicing

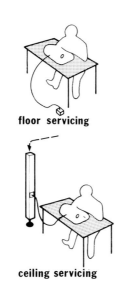

floor servicing

ceiling servicing

14 *Four modes of services delivery to the workplace.*

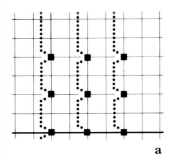

a

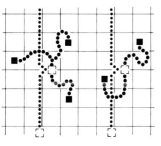

b

15 *Ceiling distribution:*
a *Ceiling socket outlets at regular intervals to accept power poles.*
b *Flexible connections from junction boxes to outlets.*

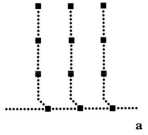

a

b

16a *Underfloor trunking to surface outlets. Outlets located in junction boxes in trunking within floor screed. Interrupts floor finish, but most covers are now designed to accept matching finish.*
b *Use of flexible conduit below raised floor. Free movement beneath access flooring requires less redundancy in initial layout and provides for easy relocation. Outlets mounted flush within access panel or proud of floor at joint between panels.*

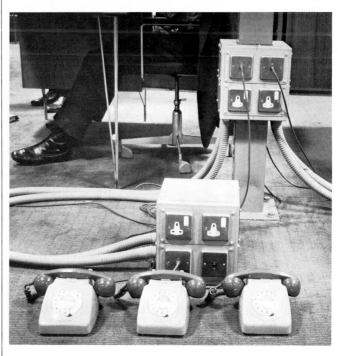

17 *American power pole by Wiremold carrying telephone and electrical circuits.*

18 *Outlets at low level from power drops in structural stanchions, at IBM Cosham.*

floor finish. Greater flexibility and economy is provided when raised access floors are used because cabling can go where it is needed and outlets need only be provided where they are wanted—ease of access makes alteration economical, **16**. Unfortunately economical access floors for general use are slow in coming to the market place, although they will probably be normal practice in offices within 10 years if the growth of cable-borne services continues.

9.04 Vertical delivery systems from ceiling to workplace are becoming more popular in the UK as in the USA and Scandinavia for deep plan buildings. The simplest approach is to use a free drop which may be housed in decorative conduit, but some find this aesthetically unsatisfactory. Partition drops may be used as well, where there are cellular offices, and these may incorporate service panels for several cable-borne systems. The most popular form of vertical distribution for deep space, however, is the service column, which may be on or off the ceiling grid. At present there are few products available in the UK which provide this facility. A good US example is Wiremold's Tele-power Poles, **17** which can be contrasted with Norman Foster's home made affair for IBM at Cosham which is incorporated in the stanchions, **18**.

10 Alteration and disruption

10.01 In designing integrated services systems it is hard to gauge realistically what the implications for alteration will be. Building configuration, structure/service model, floor sandwich, routing and delivery will all affect alteration cost. The aim should be to find systems which trade-off skilled labour requirement, cost and disruption to office work. A practical approach is to set up an initial plan for part of the building and two hypothetical changes it might undergo. Cost and time taken for the changes using different systems designs are then worked out in detail, as well as the number of days of disruption caused in the spaces being altered and in the adjacent space all round. Different systems designs produce a remarkably widespread and varied breakdown of alteration costs. Such an exercise is strongly recommended for buildings where cumulative capitalised costs (book value) are considered important.

11 Conclusion

11.1 In this study it has been impossible to cover all aspects of integrated services design. The wide variety of criteria in office design makes each building a case for individual treatment. The main point, however, is that the increasing proportion of cost attributable to services argues the need for a systematic approach to design. The essence of the approach outlined here is that it admits the *intrinsic* requirements of the services themselves, rather than treating them as something to be knitted into the building after the design has been done.

Section 6: The office environment

Acoustic factors

Noise pollution is a problem which offices have more than a fair share. AUSTIN BAINS examines the special acoustic problems of both conventional and landscaped offices, provides criteria for evaluating good acoustic conditions and describes techniques for achieving satisfactory working conditions.

1 Introduction

1.01 The most important office activity is communication: without it no form of organisation can exist. Internal communication in an office is mainly by word of mouth and much external communication is by telephone. Noise levels at the ears of a listener determine the levels that sounds must reach before they become audible and, in the case of speech, the standard of speech communication for a given voice level. Office acoustics is therefore basically the design of an efficient speech communication system which allows simultaneous use of many inputs and outlets and it is this simultaneous aspect of office speech communication that creates all the problems.

1.02 Since the acoustics of offices are rather special, there is no space in this article for a full discussion of the usual source/receiver annoyance problem encountered in offices and in buildings generally. (For that, the reader is referred to AJ Handbook Building Environment, section 5, Sound, which should also be taken as a general introduction to what follows.)

2 A method for evaluating speech intelligibility

2.01 Three problems of speech in an office need to be considered:

1 Speech communication, both between groups of people and over the telephone, must be reliable.

2 Some conversations will be confidential in the sense that it will be important that they are not overheard and understood by other people.

3 Overheard conversations should not distract people working alone.

To enable these to be discussed on a quantitative basis, an estimate of speech intelligibility is needed which can be calculated from first principles.

2.02 Speech consists of a series of sounds of varying intensity and frequency. In any short passage of speech there will be some contribution to the sound intensity at most frequencies in the audible range, and at any one frequency the intensity will fluctuate over a range of approximately 30 dB. Consonants are combinations of sounds of different frequencies while vowel sounds are more localised, mainly at the lower frequencies, but the consonants are the more important for determining intelligibility. Since a typical noise control technique will affect different frequencies to a greater or lesser degree, one needs to be able to calculate the intelligibility of speech for each band of frequencies and to sum the contributions.

2.03 It is possible to measure speech intelligibility by an articulation score: a list of syllables, words or sentences is read out and those that are intelligible marked. Such measurements made over narrow bands of frequencies when added together do not give the articulation score measured over the full frequency range, so an additional quantity is required. The articulation index (AI) was derived from articulation score measurements in such a way that AI can be added. The AI takes values ranging from 0 to 1 corresponding to completely unintelligible and completely intelligible speech respectively.

2.04 A graphical representation of the way the several parts of the speech frequency range contribute to speech intelligibility is shown in **1**. The example refers to the special case of face to face communication which will give the maximum AI at a given distance. Each dot represents a 1 per cent contribution so that, for example, the band of frequencies centred on 1000 Hz contributes 7 per cent of the total, that on 2000 Hz 11 per cent etc. The spread of dots vertically represents the 30 dB range of normal speech. The levels will fall off with distance from the speaker and the appropriate correction can be made using design charts **2**. In noisy conditions, some of the speech may be masked and the contribution of a band may be less than that shown in **1**. The reduction will be equal to the proportion of the intensity range that falls below the level of the background noise measured over the same frequency band.

2.05 Suppose a speaker and listener are 3 m apart in the open air. The levels at the listener will be 20 dB below the PWL. If the background noise is NC 45 then we add the correction of 20 dB to the levels appropriate to NC 45 and plot these on the dot field **3**. This has been done on **4**. Counting the dots and dividing by 100 gives the articulation index. In this case, there are 23 dots above the curve so the AI is 0·23.

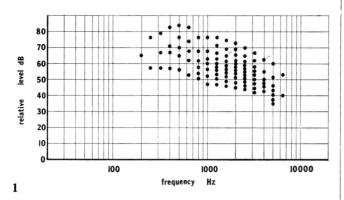

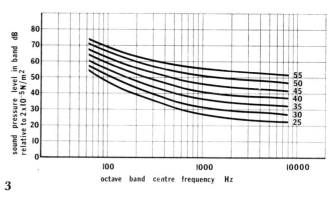

1 Graphical representation of contributions to speech intelligibility. Each dot represents a contribution of 0·01 to the articulation index. Frequencies between 700 and 5000 Hz account for 80 per cent of speech intelligibility; frequencies between 1000 and 2500 Hz for 50 per cent.

2 Design chart for finding the SPL due to a non-directional source in a room. Example A: in a room of 1000 m³, with average conditions the sound pressure level at 2 m = PWL − 12 dB.

Example B: in the open air at 2 m, SPL = PWL − 17·5 dB.

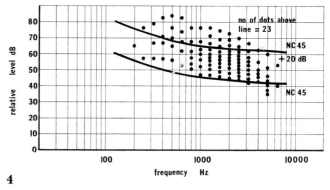

3 NC curves. To achieve a given NC rating noise levels must be below the appropriate curve at each frequency.

4 The number of dots above the line is 23. The articulation index is derived by dividing that number by 100.

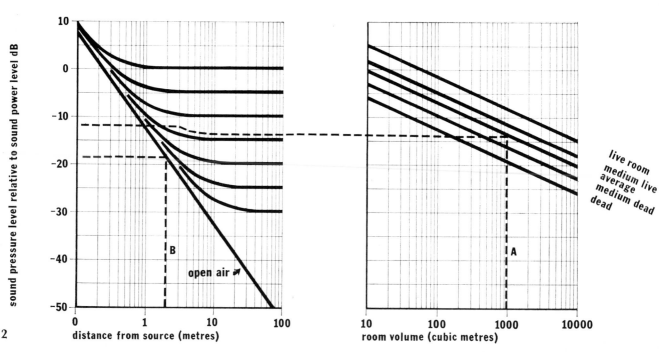

2.06 The concept of an articulation index was originally developed as a means of rating electronic speech communication systems, and a system is usually considered satisfactory if the AI is above 0·30 which corresponds to a sentence intelligibility of 90 per cent. It should therefore be possible to carry out a reliable conversation if the AI is no less than 0·30. It has also been shown that satisfaction with speech privacy is related to the AI. Occupants of a private office were asked to judge the level at which overheard speech would interfere with their everyday work. It was found that most people based their judgments on the point where the speech begins to be intelligible, and for the 10 per cent most critical people, this level was found to give an AI of 0·10. When asked in a second test to assess the privacy they required for the most confidential work, knowing their conversation would be heard as clearly as the speech they were hearing, the 10 per cent most critical people were satisfied if the AI was below 0·05.

3 Background noise

3.01 Noise within an office is the combined effect of a number of sources both inside and outside the building.
It is possible to specify maximum noise levels for a particular standard of speech communication and one of the most widely used rating schemes makes reference to the series of noise criterion (NC) curves shown in **3**. The following values are commonly recommended:

Table I 'Maximum noise levels'

Situation	Background noise level
Executive office ⎱ Conference room ⎰	NC 25
Private office	NC 30-35
Large open office	NC 40-45
Secretarial area ⎱ Drawing office ⎰	NC 50

3.02 There are several disadvantages in this approach, the biggest being that no indication of the desirable level is given. An NC curve generated electronically sounds far too sibilant and would be objectionable. This is not usually a problem in practice since a procedure designed to reduce noise at middle frequencies tends to be even more effective at higher frequencies and the spectrum of the background noise falls off much more rapidly than an NC curve above 1000 Hz. This means that when an NC curve is used to predict the articulation index, the result will always be an under-estimation of the situation in the completed building. An alternative series of curves is presented which were derived by modifying the high frequency portion to fall off parallel to equal annoyance contours 5. These curves, called BNL curves, are numbered by the level in the

1000 Hz octave band. The BNL curve closely follows the spectrum of a well-designed ventilation system, and when the curve is generated electronically it is a neutral, unobtrusive sound. The curve forms a basis for recommending desirable, as well as maximum, noise levels and should give better values of the articulation index.
3.03 The second objection to the recommendations in the table is that these values are based purely on the needs of speech communication and take no account of speech privacy. As the background noise is reduced, the privacy problem becomes more acute, and on economic grounds it may become necessary to compromise. A more flexible scheme that will allow this is required and the calculation of the articulation index is the best method currently available.

4 Cellular offices

4.01 Traditionally, the requirements of speech communication and privacy were reconciled by the use of heavy, airtight partitions. Lightweight partitions have many advantages for modern methods of building construction, and demountability is an attractive proposition for the client. Demountable partitions, however, are not airtight, so the sound reduction of which they are capable is limited. Most standard partitioning systems are unable to give confidential speech privacy at a background noise of BNL 35, and improving the performance by increasing the weight of the partition is expensive. Sealing the partition to make it airtight loses the advantage of demountability, and a wet construction system would be cheaper from the outset. The alternative is to raise the background noise level to a point where privacy is acceptable but this lowers the standard of speech communication within each office. At BNL 45, conferences of more than five or six people would not be possible, and telephone use would be occasionally difficult. BNL 40 would not normally be considered particularly noisy. The minimum level of background noise required can be calculated by using the manufacturer's data for the performance of the partition and the dot field **1**.

Partitions
4.02 An office for an example is divided into 3 m × 4 m × 3 m rooms. The sound pressure levels in an average 36 m² room are 3 dB below the PWL—see **2**. Partitions are taken to be proprietary demountable, with two skins of plasterboard on studs and the transmission loss figures have been plotted as the lowest curve seen in **6**. The middle curve is obtained by adding the correction term and the upper curve is obtained by adding an arbitrarily chosen background noise (BNL 30). The AI is 0·26. By calculating

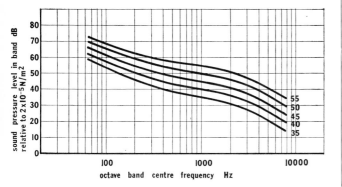

5 BNL curves : used to specify desirable noise levels (to mask outside noise) which should lie on the band defined by adjacent curves at each frequency.

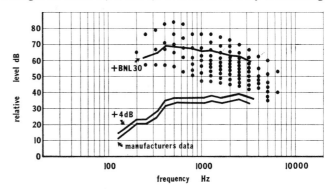

6 Calculation of privacy through a partition, see **4.02**. The lowest value comes from the data; the next takes into account the room correction − + 4 dB;

the top curve is obtained by adding the chosen BNL—in this case 30.

the AI for background levels of BNL 35 and 40, one can plot a graph of AI against background noise **7**. To give

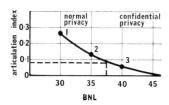

7 *Calculation of privacy through a partition. Point 1 was obtained by using the procedure set out in fig 6; points 2 and 3 by changing the BNL to 35 and 40 respectively.*

'normal privacy' the background noise should be at least BNL 37 and for confidential privacy at least BNL 41.

4.03 The manufacturer's figures are not always good indications of the performance of a partition in the field since the data usually refer to a laboratory test on a specially constructed partition whose area may be only a few square metres. The test partition may not include, for example, standard skirting and ceiling details. Field tests on partitions are not commonly available, so it is essential to try to ensure that the partitions erected conform as closely as possible to those used in the original tests. Particular points to watch are the seals at floor and ceiling and the skirting, which is often used as trunking for telephone and electrical cables and may be incorrectly replaced after removal for access. Electrical services are often a problem because switches and socket outlets are wired back to back in adjacent rooms with a hole straight through the partition.

4.04 An otherwise good partition may also be spoilt by substitution of non-standard panels such as a single sheet of glass at high level. Single glazing can give a reduction of around 25 dB when well sealed as opposed to 40 dB for a good proprietary demountable partition. In many offices, plywood or asbestos board substitute for standard panels where a gap of 100 mm or so has to be filled between a column and a wall or between the end of a partition and a window mullion; in such cases the infill may give a reduction of less than 20 dB. A strip 100 mm wide × 3 m high of 20 dB panel in a 3 m × 3 m wall that would normally give 40 dB will transmit three times as much sound as the rest of the panel put together.

Heating

4.05 Perimeter heating systems cause many detailing problems. The only way to seal around a pipe that passes through a partition is to pass it through an oversize sleeve which is made good to the partition with plaster. The inside of the sleeve is then packed with a flexible, airtight material. Continuous convectors will require a sealed panel inside the casing.

Ceilings

4.06 When partitions stop at the underside of a suspended acoustic tile ceiling, the sound transmitted by the ceiling and the ceiling space may be greater than that transmitted by the partition. Some mineral tile ceilings have a reasonable transmission loss, and the ceiling path is comparable with an average partition. Metal tiles with a backing pad are much worse. To raise the path through the ceiling to the standard of the partition, plasterboard should be laid over the back of the ceiling tiles with the joints taped. This creates problems when the ceiling is used as a return air plenum and the only satisfactory solution may be to use a ducted extract.

Ventilation ducts

4.07 Ventilation ducts are an important source of flanking transmission, especially when the ductwork includes lengths of flexible duct. Sound can then enter the system through the duct walls almost as easily as through the

diffuser. Losses in the ductwork can be increased by adding silencers before each outlet, which involves considerable cost. By preventing the background noise from becoming too low, silencing requirements are reduced. The cross-talk silencers are a constraint on the flexibility of the office space and partitions cannot be taken down and erected elsewhere without modification to the ventilation system in the new area. Installing silencers before each outlet in case they should all be included in the office space at some later date might be a wise precaution.

5 Landscaped offices

5.01 In an open plan office the wall area is so small in relation to floor and ceiling that sound is not significantly reflected back towards a source and there is no build-up of reverberant sound. The intensity of reflections off floor and ceiling and the intensity of direct sound both fall off with increasing distance from the source, so direct and reflected sound are always of comparable magnitude. The total sound intensity will also decrease continuously with increasing distance. This is much more like the behaviour in the open air than that in a normal room: noise sources are not confused by reverberation but are heard clearly and easily located.

5.02 The actual value of the sound reduction with distance depends upon the absorption of the two principal surfaces: ceiling and floor. In an open plan area with a suspended absorbent ceiling and a carpeted floor as shown in **8** a

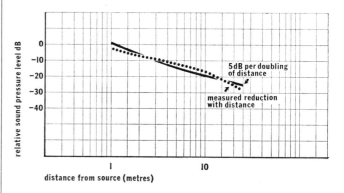

8 *Measured sound reduction with distance in an open office at 125 Hz; the measured reduction is very close to the theoretical value in the 1 m to 12 m area.*

reduction close to 5 dB/distance doubling has been measured and the average absorption (sum of the absorption coefficients of floor and ceiling) at the frequency of the measurements (125 Hz) was 0·65. In the open air the average absorption is unity, and in this case the reduction is 6 dB for doubling of distance, so the question naturally arises as to whether the sound reduction could be increased to the open air value and also what would be the effect if the absorption were greater than unity. It has been found that when the absorption is increased to unity, the reduction with distance does become 6 dB. It is not very easy to achieve an absorption much above unity since at high frequencies the absorption of ceiling tiles is rarely above 0·8 and a carpet of the quality and type that would be used in an office has an absorption coefficient of 0·3, which gives a total of 1·1. However, extra absorption can be introduced using ceiling baffles or using absorbent screens, and in such a way quite high values of absorption can be achieved. In these cases, it is found that the sound reduction is indeed greater than 6 dB for distance doubling and may be as great as 11 dB. This is a very significant increase, and, as we shall show later, represents a considerable reduction in the distance over which a noise remains audible.

5.03 In an open office many different activities take place simultaneously in the same space, producing a variety of noises, of which the most widespread are probably speech and typewriter noises, with more local intermittent noises such as copying machines and telephone bells. The result is that in an open office the level of noise varies throughout the day according to the activity inside and outside the office; it can rise quite considerably, as when the occupants prepare to leave for lunch, or drop when a group of people in one area gather for a meeting. Noise levels in dB(A) measured during two hours in a large open office with a 'quiet' ventilation system are shown in **9**. The equivalent

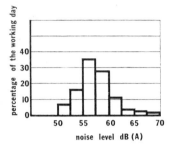

9 *Variation of noise level with time measured in an open office. Noise levels measured in an open office with a quiet ventilation system. A range of 10 dB(A) covers 63 per cent of the observations, but the total range is more than 20 dB(A).*

BNL levels will be approximately equal to dB(A) levels – 7.

5.04 If a source gives noise levels at a listening position that are quieter than the background noise, the source will not be clearly audible and is said to be masked. When source levels are louder than the background noise, the source will be audible. Levels at any listening position depend on distance from the source and absorption in the office. At busy periods only the few nearby noise sources will be audible, but at quiet periods sources that are quite a long way away will be clearly heard. That variations in the background noise level of 10 dB(A) during the day are not exceptional is seen in **9**. If we can achieve a sound reduction with distance doubling of 6 dB by the addition of suitable absorption, then the distance over which noise sources can be heard would increase by a factor of 3 as the background noise varies over this 10 dB(A) range. If noise sources are evenly distributed, the number of sources within audible range would increase by a factor of nine. Clearly this is very unsatisfactory and there should be some control over the minimum level of background noise independent of office activity, so that masking of distant sources is effective at all times. The higher the minimum level of background noise, the more effective would be the masking, but if the background level is too high, it can itself become a source of annoyance either because it is considerably above the average of the level of activity noise, or because it interferes with speech communication or use of the telephone.

5.05 Relationships can be plotted between distance from a speaker, BNL and AI **10**. A normal male voice at a conversational level is assumed, and the reduction with distance corresponds to absorption of a conventional mineral ceiling tile, and a conventional ceiling with 305 mm (1ft) deep baffles. In an open office one envisages conversations taking place between small groups of up to five or six people, and these should be possible provided that the background noise is low enough to allow reliable conversation (AI=0·3) over a distance of 2 m. This should be possible if the background noise does not exceed BNL 47 as seen in **10**. With the tile ceiling and at this background noise level, however, overheard conversations will still be distracting to anyone working alone up to a distance of 10 m. If the absorption were increased to that of a tile ceiling with 305 mm deep baffles, speech will not be distracting at distances greater than 5 m from the speaker.

There is, even so, a large area from 2 m to 5 m over which overheard speech will be distracting.

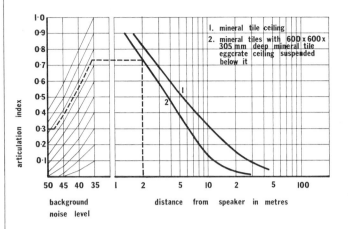

10 *Relationship between AI, distance and BNL in open offices; with people 2 m apart the BNL must not be greater than 47 to allow intelligible conversation—AI 0·03.*

5.06 The success of the open plan arrangement will depend on the density of occupation. If the density were around 25 m² per person, good conditions could easily be achieved. Unfortunately a figure of half this is more typical in offices. Local increases in density where privacy is not really important will allow greater spacing of working positions in more critical areas, and can be more successful than an even distribution of working positions throughout the office. Between departments where there is a considerable amount of telephone use and noise and the quieter departments' circulation areas should be used as buffer zones over which there is a steady fall in levels. Circulation around the perimeter should be avoided since it forces the density in office areas to increase.

5.07 If the BNL is increased by 6, then the intrusion of distracting speech is reduced almost by half **10**. Unfortunately, the distance over which conversations are reliable would be reduced by a similar factor, so that increasing the background noise is not a promising solution. The upper limit to the background noise will, in general, be determined by the speech communication requirement rather than with regard to achieving satisfactory privacy. If the background noise has the shape given in **5**, then levels of BNL 40-45 are found to be acceptable in an open office, and at busy periods activity noise as shown in **9** will lead to higher levels. However, if the background noise is above BNL 50, then the background noise itself is likely to become a source of annoyance.

5.08 A decrease in sound levels over that resulting from distance alone can be achieved by using a screen. A screen works by reducing the transmission of direct sound, but sound will still reach the listener by various indirect paths, ie reflections off the ceiling and other screens and by diffraction (or bending) of sound waves over the top and around the sides. The relative importance of reflection and diffraction and transmission through the screen, will depend upon the design of the screen and its position relative to both source and listener and objects in the area. Transmission through a screen is usually the least important propagation path and adequate reduction of the direct sound can be given by any non-porous layer such as a sheet of hardboard. In the case of low screens, the limiting path is diffraction over the top which can be reduced by increasing the screen height. The reduction of the screen is eventually determined by reflections around the screen, the most important reflections being those off the ceiling, even when it is highly absorbent. The AI calculated for a simple screen configuration is set out in **11**. A seated male speaker and a seated listener are 3 m apart without a screen, and with screens 1·2 m, 1·5 m and 1·8 m high, each 1·2 m wide. The ceiling is 3 m above floor level and is of mineral tiles, ie ceiling 1 in 10. To reduce speech to an AI of 0·3, the screen would need to be 1·8 m high and the background noise at least BNL 45.

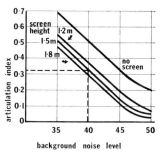

11 *AI with 1·5 m-wide screens for various background levels at 3 m from a male speaker; with BNL 40 a screen between persons 1·5 m high will give an AI of 0·33.*

5.09 The layout of screens is of considerable importance. It is tempting to use them to divide areas into small enclosures to give complete visual privacy. This can, however, cause the enclosure to behave as a small room in which there will be a build-up of reverberant sound so that the overall reduction from source to listener is reduced. This situation can also be caused by large pieces of furniture such as filing cabinets and cupboards. To reduce the level of reflected sound screens should always be faced with an absorbent material such as a perforated wood fibreboard. It is also tempting to reduce the number of screens by grouping all occupants of the office who require privacy into one area with screens, leaving the remainder of the office completely open. This is not advisable since in a large area kept aside for executives there will be less activity noise caused by typewriters and general circulation, so that background noise can become obtrusive. This is just the area, however, where masking noise is the most critical.

5.10 Near the office walls there will be an increase in all noise levels caused by reflections off them. In particular, there will be an increase in the levels of speech, and hence intelligibility, over those at the same distance from a speaker in the rest of the office. Working positions near the walls especially near corners will be worse than positions in the middle of the office, but these positions will be sought after because of their relative seclusion and their external views. Some improvement can be made by making walls absorbent and by curtaining windows. There will be a significant reduction in the performance of a screen near a wall, so people requiring a standard of privacy which can be achieved only with a screen should not be within 3 m to 4 m of walls. Screens less than 1·5 m high have a very small screening effect. However, the sound reduction with distance within the office does depend upon the absorption that can be put on the ceiling and floor and the use of low absorbent screens is an effective way of increasing the absorption in the office and it may be worth using low screens for this purpose alone.

6 Generation of background noise

6.01 There are two practical means of maintaining the required minimum background noise level. Most large, open offices are air-conditioned or mechanically ventilated and noise produced by the ventilation system can be used to provide the background level in the office. A typical spectrum of ventilation noise, which follows closely the desired shape shown in **5** is seen in **12**.

6.02 The noise results from two separate phenomena: at low frequencies fan noise predominates, at high frequencies

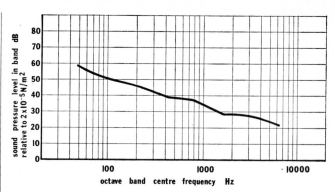

12 *Typical ventilation noise spectrum. The shape happens to be close to that of a satisfactory BNL curve.*

diffuser noise. The fan noise will depend essentially upon the fan duty and type, but there will be some attenuation along the ductwork and the resulting noise levels in the office can be estimated to within about 3 dB. The noise generated at a diffuser outlet will depend upon the airflow through it. If the noise from the ventilation system is to maintain a minimum noise level, then outlets must be capable of giving this level and ideally there should be a margin in the damper settings so that the system can be rebalanced with higher velocities if the levels are too low. The noise levels in the range 1000 to 4000 Hz are most important in masking speech, and this is just the range where the diffuser noise is greatest. Diffuser noise is consequently more effective than fan noise in masking speech, but the fan noise is essential if the background noise is to sound balanced and be acceptable. In cellular offices, the cross-talk silencers required for speech privacy will also reduce the fan noise, and this must be taken into account when designing the total silencing on the fan. It would be difficult to use a high velocity system to produce a good masking noise since the terminal units give a high attenuation and the fan noise will be low.

6.03 It is possible to introduce noise electronically using a noise generator and an array of loudspeakers. This does, of course, entail some not inconsiderable extra costs. The loudspeakers, in box enclosures, must be capable of radiating power at low frequencies and must give a wide beam at high frequencies to avoid poor distribution between speakers; ordinary paging system loudspeakers are not good enough. To give a background noise level of BNL 45 over a large area requires a lot of power and large amplifiers are required. One disadvantage is that there may be objections by a few individuals to noise which they consider 'artificial' especially if they ever experience the office empty with the noise generator switched off. However, it should be much easier to achieve the correct spectrum shape using this system, and the levels can easily be altered after completion. It should also be possible to contour the noise level to suit particular areas of the office which are put to different uses.

7 Noises other than speech sounds

7.01 So far we have been exclusively concerned with speech sounds within the office and conditions for speech communication and privacy. There are many other noise sources both inside and outside the building, but because they tend to be peculiar to individual buildings, full discussion will not be justified.

7.02 The most important external noise sources will be aircraft and road traffic. Prediction schemes such as the BRE method for estimating levels of traffic noise exceeded for 10 per cent of the time (L_{10}) can be used to assess the magnitude of the problem and work out insulation requirements. In severe cases, such as buildings close to an airport or in the centre of a city, measurements will be more useful.

Mechanical plant

7.03 Noise from mechanical plant will need to be considered in detail. Ductborne ventilation noise should be reduced by fitting silencers after the fans which should be in the section of ductwork passing through the plant room wall to prevent plant noise breaking into the duct after it has been silenced. Vertical shafts used for duct distribution should be sealed at each floor level. A high standard of sound insulation will be required between ventilation plant room and office. The tendency to put plant on the top floors of buildings can increase the problem since higher floors are often used for executives in whose offices low noise levels are desirable. In most cases, it will be impossible to achieve noise levels suitable for executive offices (NC 25) directly underneath a plant room; the amount of concrete required, even with a double floor, would be prohibitive. A non-office floor such as a restaurant or an archive/storage area could be used as a buffer zone where noise levels could be allowed to rise to levels 5 dB greater than those in the rest of the building.

7.04 Cooling towers do not usually lead to excessive levels of airborne sound in the office itself, since the air-conditioned areas are likely to have sealed glazing. They can cause structure-borne noise problems and need to be effectively vibration-isolated. Resilient mounts with a large deflection are needed to deal with a cooling tower on a light roof; isolation at the fan speed is not sufficient since much of the vibration is associated with falling water. As airborne noise from cooling towers may be excessive for surrounding buildings (particularly dwellings), silencing may be required. Forced draught towers with centrifugal blowers are the easiest to silence since the fans can cope with the extra resistance of the silencer, otherwise it may be necessary to oversize the tower.

Lifts

7.05 Lifts are also a source of structure-borne noise, but are rarely vibration-isolated in offices. Motors and generators are straightforward; the difficulty lies with the sheaves and pulleys and the easiest way to isolate these is to mount them all on a steel frame which is then isolated as a whole, using pads of a resilient material. In some cases, isolation of the guides may also be necessary.

Typewriters

7.06 Within the office itself, careful choice of equipment can give a useful reduction in noise. For example, the noise levels of three models of typewriter by the same manufacturer differ by 10 dB **13**. The variation between manufacturers will be even greater. Any typewriter on a thick felt pad will be quieter than one directly on a desk. In an open office telephone bells are not really needed, a buzzer or light would be adequate and much quieter. The necessary modification to a standard telephone would be fairly simple. The organisation and layout of an office is important. In an open office it is better to distribute typewriters, copiers and calculating machines throughout the area rather than group them together. This prevents the noise in one area becoming excessively high and affecting a large part of the surrounding office, but helps to keep the general level of activity noise from becoming too low. A screen near a typewriter to reduce local annoyance would be useful. In cellular offices, standard demountable partitioning systems will usually need modification to separate a large typing area from a private office and the

reduction required can be reduced by using less critical spaces to separate the two.

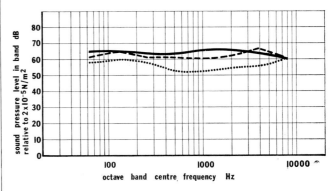

13 *Sound pressure levels from three models of electric typewriters made by the same manufacturer. The measurements were made under identical conditions at 1 m from the typewriter but the levels differ by up to 14 dB at 1000 Hz. The two upper paths show readings for golf-ball machines; the sliding carriage model is quieter.*

Glossary of terms

Sound power level (PWL)
The power of a source in watts is generally low (eg only 10 watts for a large orchestra) but the variation between sources is large (eg from $\frac{1}{100\,000}$th of a watt for a normal voice to thousands of watts for a jet engine). To reduce these powers to more easily handled quantities, the sound power level (PWL) in decibels (dB) is defined as
$$10 \log_{10} \frac{\text{actual power}}{\text{reference power}}$$
The reference power is generally 10^{-12} watts, so that $\frac{1}{100\,000}$ of a watt becomes 70 dB re 10^{-12} watts; $\frac{1}{100}$ of a watt becomes 100 dB re 10^{-12} watts and so on.

Sound pressure level (SPL)
The sound pressure level in dB is defined as
$$10 \log_{10} \frac{\text{sound pressure (N/m}^2)}{\text{reference pressure}}$$
reference pressure is 2×10^{-5} N/m² which is the threshold of hearing at 1000 Herz. Under normal conditions of temperature and pressure, sound intensities and sound pressures are numerically equal. The reference for sound intensities is chosen to maintain this equality through to intensity levels and sound pressure levels.

Sound intensity level (IL)
The sound intensity level in dB is defined as $10 \log_{10} \frac{\text{intensity (in W/m}^2)}{\text{reference intensity}}$
the reference intensity being 10^{-12} W/m².

dB(A).
The reading on a sound level meter using the 'A' weighting scale which reduces the relative importance of low frequency sounds.

Octave band spectrum
A graph of sound pressure level or sound power level against frequency plotted as though all the sound in an octave band were concentrated at the centre frequency of the band.

Articulation score
The percentage of words, sentences or syllables in a list which are heard correctly.

Articulation index (AI)
A quantity taking values between 0 and 1 calculated from the levels of speech relative to the background noise.

Speech interference level (SIL)
The average sound pressure levels in the octave bands centred on 500, 1000 and 2000 Hz.

Noise criterion curves (NC)
Curves specifying maximum noise levels which are numbered according to their speech interference level.

Background noise curves (BNL)
Curves for specifying desirable noise levels. They are numbered by the level in the 1000 Hz band.

Frequency band
Frequencies lying between two limiting frequencies. For an octave band, the upper limit is twice the lower limits. A band is usually designated by the centre frequency, the geometric mean of the band limits. The internationally standardised octave bands have centre frequencies at 63, 125, 250, 500, 1000, 2000, 4000, 8000.

Section 6 : The office environment

Thermal factors

The thermal range desirable—and possible to achieve—in an office is a matter for continuing debate. Certainly the concept of the ideal environment has come under increasing attack. ROGER HITCHIN surveys the current state of the art and offers guidelines for achieving a tolerable working environment.

1 Preface

1.01 Decisions made by the architect have implications for the thermal environment which have been described in general terms in AJ Handbook Building Environment,[1] Section 4 Thermal Properties and Section 8 Heating Installations, Mechanical Ventilation and Air-Conditioning. Thermal problems which arise in offices may also occur in other types of building and some parts of this text are concerned with expanding points made in the Handbook and pointing out their particular relevance to offices.

2 Background

2.01 A healthy human body is constantly producing heat at a rate which depends, among other things, on the physical exertion of the individual. For office work, this amounts to about 100 W per person. Within certain limits, the body can adjust the rate of heat loss by physiological means (such as sweating or shivering) to maintain body temperature at a safe level. A fundamental requirement of any human thermal environment is to ensure that these limits are not exceeded. For thermal comfort there are much stricter requirements—the heat loss must be fairly uniform in each direction and a balance must be maintained between the various avenues of loss—convection (dependent on air movement, temperature and clothing), radiation (dependent on the temperatures of surrounding surfaces), evaporation (dependent on relative humidity and air temperature), and conduction (dependent on the temperature and thermal properties of material in contact with the body) **1**.

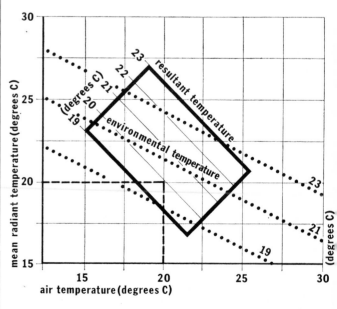

1 *Thermal comfort zone for sedentary work (from IHVE Guide) ; where the mean radiant temperature is* *20°C and the air temperature 20°C the resultant temperature is 20°C.*

2.02 When an office (or any other enclosed space) has steady heat gains, the temperatures of the surfaces and air of the office rise until increased losses balance the gains. Heat is lost by ventilation and through the roof, floor and external walls at a rate depending on their U-values.[2] There may be losses to adjacent spaces but, as these may be experiencing similar or greater gains, this cannot be relied upon. Long-term steady heat gains are not common in offices (permanent artificial lighting is probably the least unsteady, and this is usually switched off for part of any 24-hour period). Unsteady heat gains have a more complicated effect. When there is an increase in heat gain, some of the heat is absorbed by the surface layers of walls, ceilings, furniture etc, and this results in an increase of the temperature of the surface (and to a lesser extent of the rest of the structure).[2] This capacity to absorb heat gains is known as 'thermal admittance' of the surface (or Y-value) (see Table I). In practice, the heat exchanges in a room subject to fluctuating gains are complex, and admittance depends on the rate of change of the gain but, with certain simplifications, it is possible to estimate the magnitude of the effect.

Table I Thermal admittance values (from IHVE Guide)

Structural element	Admittance (W/m²°C)
Windows (typical)	
Single, unshaded	5·6
Single, internal blind	5·6
Double, unshaded	3·2
Double, mid-pane blind	3·2
Walls (more than 75 mm thick)	
Lightweight blocks type B or C (BS 2028)	3·0 to 4·5
Brickwork 4½in and 9in	4·5 to 5·0
Two fibreboard sheets with an air space	2·0
Floors	
Concrete	6·0
Concrete with carpet or woodblock	3·0
Suspended timber	2·0
Suspended timber with carpet	1·5
Ceilings	
Plastered concrete	6·0
Plasterboard on underside joists	3·0

3 A range of environments

3.01 Conditions necessary for office machinery are usually less demanding than those required by their users—comfort (or rather, lack of discomfort) of occupants is the primary aim. It is sometimes assumed that thermal discomfort reduces productivity, though experiments on the effects of temperature on schoolwork have produced erratic results. The ideal environment for an office is probably one which is stimulating without being uncomfortable.

3.02 Even if it were possible to define precisely the ideal office environment, it would certainly not be achieved in practice. Conflicting pressures, including capital and running costs, are traded off against each other until a compromise is reached which is less than ideal but lies within acceptable limits. Legal requirements are generally so low that thermal environments which satisfy but do not exceed them are generally considered unsatisfactory.

3.03 Design values rather give the impression of defining (and perhaps even ensuring) an ideal environment, but they will only be achieved in certain hypothetical conditions—in practice the various environmental parameters vary from point to point in the office and are constantly changing. This is not necessarily a bad thing—steady conditions are rather unstimulating, but there is a point where stimulation becomes discomfort. This point varies from person to person and from time to time. Design conditions define only a target environment. It is important that the fluctuations around this target which inevitably occur do not cause discomfort to a significant proportion of the occupants. It is impossible to please everyone all the time—or even at one time (see table II).

Table II Satisfaction with office heating*

Method of heating	% Occupants satisfied
Radiators	55
Electric fire	53
Floor warming	51
Warm air	49
Ceiling heating	42
Skirting heating	40
Cill heating	38

* Based on Langdon, Thermal conditions in modern offices, *RIBA Journal*, January 1965.

American laboratory studies suggest that, at best, 95 per cent of occupants will class themselves as comfortable in summer conditions. In offices, the maximum percentage of workers comfortable at any given air temperature is about 80 per cent, while figures of 55-65 per cent appear to be typical for overall assessments of comfort in summer in modern office buildings.[3] In winter, rather fewer people admit to being satisfied with office heating. These low figures probably reflect inadequate controls in many cases, although it is also generally true that the defects of thermally inefficient buildings can be only partially corrected by mechanical services.[4, 5]

Ventilation

3.04 Fresh air is required to supply oxygen for breathing and to remove products of respiration and other by-products of occupation, specifically odours and tobacco smoke. Ventilation is also very useful as a means of removing unwanted heat or moisture.

3.05 The volume of air per person needed to keep the level of carbon dioxide produced by respiration to a harmless level is only 1 litre/s. The minimum requirement for odour removal is often said to depend on the density of occupation (and habits of the occupants) and vary from 4 litres/s with 12 m³ air space per person to 11·3 litres/s with 3 m³ air space per person (for 'sedentary American adults of average socio-economic status').[3] Minima for offices recommended by the IHVE[2] are listed in table III. Greater rates than these may be required to prevent overheating or (less commonly in offices) excessive condensation. The dependence of minimum ventilation on room volume per person seems to be a result of adaptation to odours. Where unadapted people are likely to enter the space—the case in offices generally—the lowest rates should not be used.

Table III 'Minimum fresh air rates'*

Space	Assumed smoking	Litres/s per person
Open office	Some	8
Private office	Heavy	12
Conference room	Some	18
Executive office, board room	Very heavy	25

* Based on *IHVE Guide*.

3.06 The Offices, Shops and Railway Premises Act requires adequate supplies of fresh or artificially purified air, without defining the various terms used. The London Building Act requires, for offices, a minimum fresh air supply of 6 litres/s per person or per 4·7 m² floor area, whichever provides the greater ventilation rate (a waiver may be obtained to reduce this to 4 litres/s fresh air plus 2 litres/s recirculated if adequate air-conditioning is provided).

Air movement

3.07 The feeling of freshness or stuffiness of an environment is related to the air movement at head level. The sensation is dependent on the temperature of the moving air, but generally speaking, velocities below 0·1 m/s give rise to feelings of stagnation, while velocities above 0·2 m/s are likely to result in complaints from office workers [2].

Relative humidity

3.08 Relative humidity has very little effect on the comfort of sedentary persons, provided that extreme values (either high or low) are avoided. At 'normal' office temperatures of around 20°C, the range 40 to 70 per cent is generally acceptable. As the temperature rises, and heat removal from the skin depends more and more on evaporation, high humidities become more noticeable. High indoor humidities can result in condensation on metal window frames or single-glazed windows in cold weather **3**.

3.09 A disturbing side-effect of low humidity (which can easily occur in naturally ventilated offices in winter) coupled with the use of carpets (particularly those made from synthetic materials) is a build-up of static electricity in the body. This discharges as a spark, usually from a finger, when the person goes to touch a metal object, such as a filing cabinet or door handle. Spray-on coatings exist which reduce this by increasing the conductivity of the fibres of the carpet.

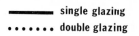

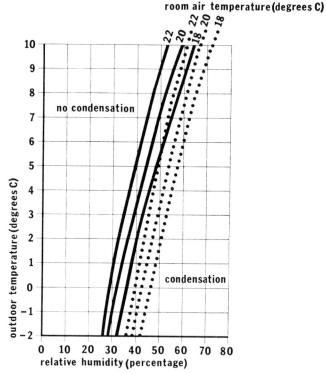

3 *Condensation on glazing. Condensation is likely to occur on normally exposed glazing under the conditions shown.*

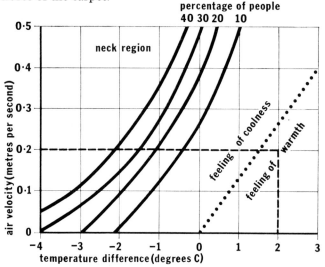

2a *Sensitivity to air movement at head level; if the air velocity is 0·2 m/s, people feel warm only if the moving air is 2° warmer than the general room temperature.*

These require re-application after shampooing and often make the carpet more easily soiled.

3.10 The London Building Act requires that, if the ventilation is reduced because air-conditioning is installed, the installation must be capable of maintaining a relative humidity of 50 to 55 per cent at all times.

Temperature and thermal indices

3.11 Although thermal comfort depends on a number of factors, traditionally, air temperature is taken to be the relevant indicator. A variety of thermal indices have been proposed, attempting to combine several of the component factors to predict an overall sensation. Among the better known indices are *globe temperature, equivalent temperature* and *resultant temperature*. In most conditions which one might reasonably expect to find in offices, these three have very similar values. The *IHVE Guide*[2] suggests that resultant temperatures of 19°C to 23°C are normally acceptable in winter and 20°C to 24°C in summer. The seasonal difference is basically due to the clothing normally worn, though an element of acclimatisation may also be present.

3.12 *Resultant temperature*, defined as 'the temperature recorded by a thermometer at the centre of a 100 mm diameter blackened globe', can usually be taken as the average of the mean radiant temperature and the air temperature, although it is also influenced by air movement.

3.13 When room surfaces are used for heating, care is necessary to ensure that this does not lead to excessive thermal radiation at head level (in the case of heated ceilings) or uncomfortably warm floors (with floor heating). In practice this means that floor temperatures should not exceed 25°C (or 27°C if this is reached only occasionally). Ceilings can be 5-10°C warmer, depending on height and area.

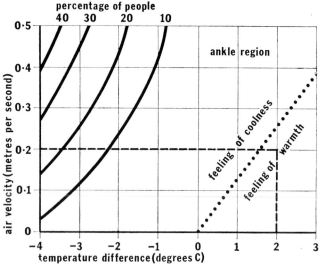

2b *Sensitivity to air movement; in this case, at foot level, if the air velocity is 0·2 m/s, the moving air has to be only 1/5°C warmer than the general temperature to avoid discomfort.*

3.14 Vertical temperature gradients should be small to avoid feelings of stuffiness. It is generally held that it is preferable for the head to be slightly cooler than the feet. In practice, this is rarely the case. However, the increase of temperature with height should be less than 1·5°C/m.

3.15 It is often convenient and economical to allow internal temperatures to vary during the course of the day. It may be possible to avoid the need for mechanical cooling by this means. It has been suggested that a reasonable standard is to allow a deviation of ±2°C from a mean of 24°C (ie, temperatures between 22 and 26°C during a day) with a 'borderline' standard of 25 ±4°C (ie, from 21 to 29°C). These extremes should only occur on days of high heat gain, and then only for short periods.

3.16 It is undesirable for surface temperatures to be more than a few degrees cooler than the air temperature (this is most likely to happen with single glazing in winter). Low surface temperature produces a lowering of perceived temperature in the direction of the surface and also results in currents of cold air which flow down the surface and may continue into the room as cold draughts **4a, 4b**. The 'cold radiation' effect depends on the angle subtended by the surface, and therefore on the surface area and the closeness of the observer. Cold down draughts are affected by the height of the surface.

3.17 If a temperature difference of more than 5°C is expected in summer between office and outdoor temperatures, entrance lobbies may be maintained at an intermediate temperature to provide a gradual transition on entering or leaving the building. Much greater temperature differences occur in winter, of course, and although it is not unusual for entrances to be heated to a lower temperature than offices, there is a greater difference between indoor and outdoor clothing which, to some extent reduces the effect of the differential. Greater familiarity of occupants with the idea of the building being significantly warmer than the surroundings probably also mitigates the shock.

3.18 The Offices, Shops and Railway Premises Act requires that a reasonable temperature be maintained, at least 15·5°C for sedentary workers. A thermometer must be provided on each floor.

3.19 Thermal radiation should not exceed an intensity of 50 W/m² from any given direction. (This is equivalent to a rise in radiant temperature of about 3°C at normal office air temperatures.) In practice, the only significant short-wave source of such radiation in office design is the sun. Direct solar radiation can increase the mean radiant temperature by up to 20°C (in addition to indirect effects caused by increased air and surface temperatures). Since the radiation is from one side only, the radiant temperature in that direction is higher still. Protection from solar radiation is essential for any working position close to windows. In contrast, short-wave radiation from general lighting, even with lighting levels of 1000 lux, is unlikely to raise the mean radiant temperature by more than 0·7°C. Increases of this order may be compensated for by a decrease in air temperature. Spot lamps may produce local radiant intensities approaching the acceptable limit.

4 Office design

4.01 It is useful to distinguish between 'deep' office spaces which require permanent artificial lighting and mechanical ventilation, and 'peripheral' offices for which daylighting and natural ventilation are possible (though not always advisable). Deep office spaces can be divided into internal areas remote from external walls and perimeter areas which have some features in common with peripheral offices.

4.02 The construction of walls, floor and ceiling influences thermal conditions in all types of areas. Poorly insulated

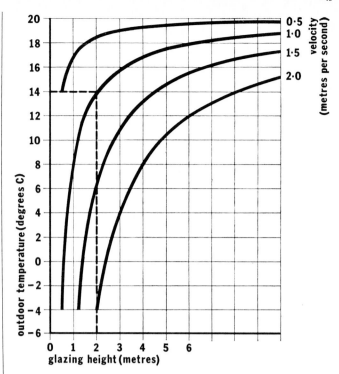

4a *Downdraught velocity, single glazing (room air temperature 20°C); with glazing 2 m high and the outdoor temperature 14°C, the velocity is 1 m/s.*

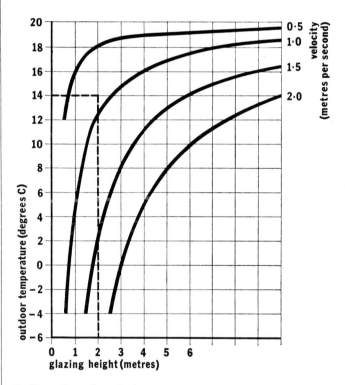

4b *Downdraught velocity, double-glazing (room air temperature 20°C); in this example, with the glazing 2 m high and the outdoor temperature 14°C, the velocity is reduced to 0·8 m/s.*

surfaces increase heat gains and losses. These can, of course, be offset, at a cost, by extra heating and cooling, but the room surfaces in winter also become cooler than if they were insulated. This reduces comfort by decreasing the mean radiant temperature (see para 3.11). Positioning insulation on the room side of the structure causes the space to respond quickly to changes of heat gain or loss, placing greater demands on the heating or cooling system. It is not, therefore, recommended, even though the preheating or cooling time required before occupation is reduced. (There may be special cases where rapid response is required, but this is not the case in most offices.) In practice, the building structure may largely be separated from the office air space by insulating layers of carpets and suspended ceilings.

Naturally ventilated peripheral offices

4.03 Mechanical services installations can be simplified if satisfactory natural ventilation is possible. Natural ventilation results from wind pressures and convection effects due to temperature differences between the air in the building and that surrounding it (*stack effect*). These forces are inherently variable and natural ventilation is therefore rather unreliable. Stack effect is generally small compared to wind pressure, except for tall buildings with unrestricted access between top and bottom storeys, and is not normally significant for the ventilation of individual levels except in very sheltered locations. It is significant, however, for lift shafts, and this may result in an unwanted ingress of air to entrance lobbies, making doors difficult to control. Revolving doors, which do not allow a direct flow of air, help to reduce this.

4.04 Exposed positions are conventionally taken to be:
Coastal and hill sites
Fifth and higher storeys in suburbs and country areas
Eighth and higher storeys in city centres.
Natural ventilation is difficult to control in these situations—and in any part of a building projecting above the general level of surrounding buildings. Tall buildings may give rise to increased air movement at ground level, which may make natural ventilation impracticable for even the lower storeys of nearby buildings. In any of these situations, only minimal opening of windows may be needed to achieve the required ventilation rate and this is likely to result in draughts which, as well as being unpleasant, may disturb papers.

4.05 There is also a conflict between winter and summer requirements. In winter, small openings at high level are preferable, to limit the inflow of cold air and direct the draughts away from occupants. In summer, large openings, preferably in more than one wall, are needed to maximise ventilation on still, warm days.[6] Openings should

be at a lower level to enable breezes of air movement to be felt on the face—though this can result in unplanned redistribution of paperwork, so accurate controls or paperweights are desirable.

4.06 Although natural ventilation is usually provided by opening windows, there are a number of proprietary ventilators available. These are more suitable for winter, and those which can be held partially open are to be preferred to those with only open/closed control.

4.07 The London Building Act requires an opening area of at least 2½ per cent of the floor area. This is aimed at providing smoke relief in the event of fire; for ventilation, 5 per cent should be considered an absolute minimum.

4.08 It is most uncommon for naturally ventilated offices to be cooled and so the ventilation needs to be capable of removing heat gains to prevent the air temperature rising to unacceptable levels. It is difficult to achieve the necessary ventilation rates (of the order of $10h^{-1}$) without also producing air velocities which would be considered unacceptable in mechanically ventilated rooms. Fortunately, the expectations of occupants are usually lower when natural forces are seen to be at work and higher velocities are more readily accepted as an alternative to higher temperatures. *Ventilation rate* is conventionally described in terms of 'air changes per hour'. This term is misleading since the introduction of a volume of air equal to the room volume does not normally cause the complete replacement of the room air—mixing of new air with the old takes place, and typically 30 per cent of the old air remains. Ventilation rate has dimensions h^{-1}. This is numerically identical to the usual air changes per hour.

4.09 It is not sufficient to provide openings that can be manipulated to provide the required ventilation; if the surroundings are noisy or otherwise polluted, they may not be opened. If problems are severe, sealed windows may be necessary. It is possible to design silenced or filtered openings for natural ventilation, but these may drastically restrict air change rates.

4.10 The principal source of heat gain in peripheral offices is normally the sun, and serious consideration should be given to the provision of solar radiation control in the building design—this can usefully begin with a check that the area of glazing is not greater than is needed 5 (see table IV). Methods of control of solar radiation have been detailed elsewhere[7] and comprise three main groups (reference to BRS Digest):

Table IV Recommended maximum percentage of external wall glazed (based on BRS Digest 68)

Type of location	Type of construction	
	Heavy	Light
Quiet	50	20
Noisy	25	15

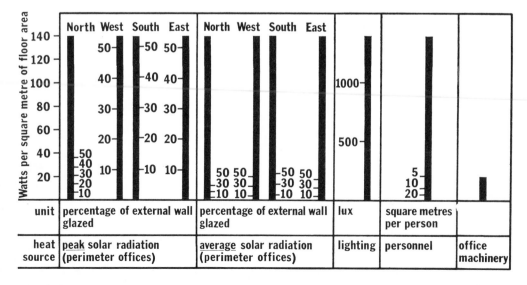

5 *Typical heat gains in offices. Thus, with peak solar radiation in a perimeter office, an external wall 40 per cent glazed on a west facing elevation allows a heat gain of 100 W/m².*

Internal controls (curtains, roller blinds, louvre blinds): reduce direct radiation on occupants but not very effective in reducing room temperatures unless highly reflective.

Special glasses and surface treatments: almost all reduce light more than heat, additional internal controls usually needed.

External controls (shutters, canopies, blinds, louvres, overhangs): can be effective but also expensive and difficult to maintain.

By their nature, peripheral offices have large proportions of their floor area close to windows, and blinds to reduce the intensity of direct solar radiation falling on work-places in these areas are essential where orientation or shading of the façade does not already do this.

4.11 As solar gains are variable through the day, the rise of internal temperature (or the cooling load) can be reduced by the use of surfaces with high admittance. Unfortunately, many common office surfaces, such as suspended ceilings, lightweight partitions and carpet, do not come into this category. Office furniture might be expected to add some admittance but, in fact, this is not necessarily so, because the thermal storage in furniture tends to occur at the expense of that in the more admittive surfaces.[8]

4.12 The other thermal property of furniture which is of interest is the coolness to the touch of some materials as compared to others (for example steel as compared to wood). This is a physically measurable phenomenon. When a (warm) hand is placed on the material, the temperature at the point of contact depends not only on the temperatures of hand and material, but also on the thermal properties of each. Steel, for instance, needs to be at a temperature of about 30°C to present the same warmth to the touch as wood at 19°C. With prolonged contact, the temperature of the point of contact reflects the material temperature and the heat flow from (or to) the hand more closely. On the other hand, there is no physical basis for the belief that some colours are warmer than others, except inasmuch as dark colours absorb solar radiation more completely than light and will therefore become warmer.[9] The effect (of occupants feeling that some colours are warmer than others) undoubtedly exists, and may influence the choice of colours (for example, north facing rooms which receive little sunshine may be decorated in 'warmer' colours). It is not recommended that this be allowed to influence the design of the heating or cooling system.

4.13 Heating may be provided in a number of ways in naturally ventilated offices, including radiators, convectors and floor or ceiling heating. Radiators and other heat emitters for which a choice of position is possible should be placed on the external wall. This offsets the influence of cold surfaces by providing a warm up-current to counter cold down-draughts and raising the mean surface temperature 'seen' in the direction of the window. To counteract down-draughts effectively, the emitter should be somewhat larger than the window.

4.14 Ideally, each office should have its own control, so that local gains from equipment or higher occupancy do not result in widely varying temperatures. Solar heat gains can still be large in winter, and separate control zones should be provided for all façades which differ in orientation or shading (this may include different levels with the same orientation). Possible future re-organisation of the offices should be borne in mind—it is by no means unknown for control zones to be subdivided, leaving the heating in one area controlled by conditions in an adjoining (but now unrepresentative) space. This seems particularly prone to happen when an organisation with a policy of individual offices for small groups of employees occupies a speculative building which has been designed with control systems suitable only for an open office plan.

4.15 Off-peak electric underfloor heating is not to be recommended as the sole source of heat unless solar heat gains are very carefully controlled and other incidental heat gains are known to be either small or steady. This type of heating can be satisfactory for background heating with another, more rapidly controllable, system providing a variable 'top-up'.

Mechanically ventilated peripheral offices

4.16 If opening windows are not practicable, ventilation can be provided mechanically. This is more expensive, but provides a known ventilation rate of filtered air and gives more uniform air movement than natural ventilation. It is usual for the total ventilation rate to be kept constant and the proportion of re-circulated air varied according to outside conditions. The supplied air needs to be warmed in winter to prevent cold draughts, and it is convenient to provide all the heating by this means. (This means that the advantages of below-window radiators are lost.) Occupants of mechanically ventilated buildings tend to assume that full air-conditioning is provided, and to base their expectations of comfort on this false assumption.

4.17 Closer control of air temperature and humidity can be achieved with air-conditioning. The choice of cooling system is basically between those systems which employ a unit in the room (which may or may not be the means by which fresh air is introduced) and those in which air is cooled remotely and ducted to the space. The former group includes, in addition to self-contained units, systems involving pipework and some central plant. The comments made in previous paragraphs concerning control of heating apply equally to cooling (and to heating with mechanical ventilation).

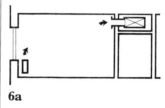

6a   **6b**

6c

6a *Mechanical ventilation of perimeter offices—supply below window—introduces heating or cooling close to main source of winter heat loss and summer heat gain, reduces duct-work in ceiling space but can result in poor air movement. Extract into ceiling space of corridor.*

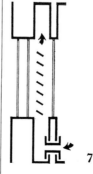

7 *Ventilated cavity window. In summer, solar radiation heat is absorbed by blind in cavity and transmitted to cavity air and removed without entering the office.*

6b *Supply from ceiling diffuser—occupies ceiling space. Extract into corridor can be undesirable as a source of extraneous noise.*
6c *Supply and extract by ceiling diffuser—may result in 'short circuiting' of air.*

In winter, warm office extract air raises temperature of cavity and inner leaf of glazing, reducing 'cold radiation' and downdraughts.

4.18 Air (whether cooled or not) may be introduced into the office in various ways. A suspended ceiling is generally most satisfactory for air distribution and movement, but other methods require smaller floor-to-floor distances **6a, 6b, 6c**.

4.19 Air is sometimes extracted via the cavity of double- (or triple-) glazed windows **7**. This slightly increases the cold surface temperature in winter. It is also an effective solar radiation control if blinds are fitted in the cavity, since heat produced in the blind by radiation is removed before it reaches the room.

Interior offices

4.20 Interior offices comprise windowless spaces and, more commonly, internal areas of open offices. There is, in practice, no distinct boundary between perimeter space and interior but, as a rule of thumb, the influence of windows may be taken to extend for a depth equal to $1\frac{1}{2}$ times to twice the ceiling height.

4.21 Permanent artificial lighting results in large heat gains in addition to those from occupants and equipment. In internal areas, it is not practicable to remove this heat by ventilation alone without temperatures rising unacceptably high in warm weather. Cooling must therefore be provided. Mechanical ventilation is essential because of the distance from openings (in single-storey buildings, roof ventilators and rooflights are possible—and may give better light/heat ratios than artificial lighting—but air distribution and movement will not normally be acceptable for office work). It is usual to have an 'all-air' cooling system.

4.22 Cooling is expensive, and any steps which can be taken to reduce it are worth considering. By extracting air through lighting fittings, some of the heat of the lamp can be removed before it enters the room. Much of this heat still has to be extracted by the cooling plant, and savings come indirectly, from a reduction in the volume of cooled air required to maintain the desired room temperature. It is possible to export some of the surplus heat, in winter, to perimeter areas which require heating. The higher temperature of air extracted via light fittings makes it useful for this purpose, though not for heat recovery in summer. Another method of preventing the heat from lighting fittings from entering the room is to use water-cooled fittings. Heat extracted in this way does not have to be handled by the cooling plant; provided that water temperatures can be suitably arranged, the heat can be rejected to the atmosphere via cooling towers or, just possibly, offered to the heating system. There is some doubt as to the practicability of achieving suitable water temperatures at present, but this is likely to be removed if high temperature light sources become widely used.

4.23 Since the heat gain from lighting is steady, there is even less scope for reducing cooling load by the use of high admittance surfaces than in peripheral offices. Also, such surfaces as there are tend to be lightweight or relatively well-insulated and therefore of low admittance.

4.24 It is common in this country to use the space above the suspended ceiling as a plenum for extracted (and therefore warm) air. This heats the ceiling and retransfers heat back into the room. An alternative, using the ceiling space as a plenum for (cool) supply air and ducting the extract is more commonly used abroad.

4.25 The lack of permanent partitions in open offices causes problems in the provision of reasonable air movement. It is difficult to arrange distribution from the ceiling to provide sufficient air movement at seated head level but not too much at standing head level. In conventional offices, it is possible to discharge air from ceiling diffusers, largely across the ceiling, allowing it to be deflected down the walls, with extract at low level. In open offices, there are few walls, and extract openings also have to be in the ceiling, which can lead to short-circuiting from supply to extract, by-passing the main body of the room. This can be reduced by placing supply and extract diffusers close to each other and directing the supply of air away from the extract opening. In the extreme case, this results in combined supply and extract diffusers, extracting in their centre and supplying from their periphery. A solution sometimes adopted is to supply air only to part of the space and extract only from the rest, so that the office is divided into supply and extract zones; this is not to be recommended unless extract zones can be placed in non-critical areas (for example, extracting via toilet areas).

4.26 Care is needed when louvred ceilings are used, to ensure that baffles do not impede the supply of air—generally, supply diffusers should be at the lower edge of the baffles, while extract can be from the space above. On occasions, hollow baffles have been constructed and air supplied through them, discharging through numerous small openings in the lower edge. This is unlikely to produce enough air movement in the space, although linear diffusers in this position may be satisfactory.

4.27 Since conditions in interior offices are relatively steady, the temperature of the supply air is also less variable than for peripheral offices. This, in turn, means that variations of air distribution due to changes in the buoyancy of the supply air are reduced. The exception to this is the pre-occupation pre-heat period, when the hot air introduced to raise the temperature can be so buoyant as to leave the temperature near the floor much cooler.

4.28 There is a temptation to suppose that an open office will be a uniform one, and therefore to control large areas as single zones. Different densities of occupation and heat gains from equipment can occur in areas occupied by different departments (or grades) of the same organisation, and open areas may be subdivided by usage even though there are no physical divisions.

Perimeter areas

4.29 Perimeter areas of deep offices share the problems of peripheral offices, except that windows are not normally expected to provide natural ventilation. They share with interior zones high heat gains from lighting and air distribution problems. Windows are provided as a visual link with the outside world rather than for daylighting, and a relatively small area of well-shaded glazing may provide this more effectively than a large area of venetian blind, with a consequent reduction in solar heat gain.

References

1 AJ Handbook Building environment [(E6)]

2 IHVE, Guide. London. 1970. £10·50 [(I) (J)]

3 ASHRAE guide and data book 1972. New York. 1972. 3 vols. $30 [(5–)]

4 LANGDON, F. J. Thermal conditions in modern offices. *RIBA Journal*. January 1965. [32 (J2)]

5 BLACK, F. W. and MILROY, E. A. Experience of air conditioning in offices. *IHVE Journal*, vol 34, p88. 1966. [32 (I)]

6 MANNING, P. Office design—a study of environment. Pilkington Research Unit. Liverpool. 1975. 30s. [32]

7 Window design and solar heat gain. BRS Digest 68 (second series) HMSO 1966 5p [(31) J2)]

8 KELLES, G. J. The influence on furniture of cooling loads. *Building Services Engineer,* vol 40, p79, 1972

9 BILLINGTON, N. S. Building physics: heat. Oxford 1967, Pergamon Press, £2·25 (Paperback £1·50) [(J)]

Section 6: Office environment

Office environment checklist

ANDREW RABENECK reviews below the major stages in designing services for office buildings in a checklist format. He also lists many key references.

Function:	To determine:	Consideration given to:	Basic references
Microclimate	Implications of local climate for building design	Air: temperature and humidity Wind: direction and intensity Pollution: natural and man-made Precipitation: rain duration and intensity, snow Radiation: sunlight Topography: exposure, slope, attitude	Meteorological Office climatological data published by HMSO Building Research Establishment Digest 127 *An Index of exposure to driving rain*
	Effect of building design on local climate. Air movement over and around new buildings	Nearby buildings and other physical features External shape of proposed building Positions of chimneys and ventilators Position of entrances, projections etc Types of roofs and walls proposed Building erection problems	BRE Digest 119 *The Assessment of Wind Loads* BRE Digest 141 *Wind Environment around tall buildings*
Lighting	The effect of direct sunlight	Limitations imposed by site Insolation of alternative building layouts Need for outside sunlight Control of inside sunlight Glare and solar heat gain	BRE Digest 68 *Window Design and Solar Heat Gain*
	The quantity and quality of indirect sunlight as natural daylighting	Legal requirements via enforcement of Daylighting Code Need to restrict admission of daylight Need for daylight indoors Impact of new building on daylighting on existing rooms Daylight factor distribution Size and shape of windows and rooflights Relation of daylight to electrical lighting	MHLG Planning Bulletin 5 *Planning for Daylight and Sunlight* BRE Digests 41 and 42 *Estimating Daylight in Buildings* BS CP3 Chapter 1: Part 1 (1964) *Daylighting* Illuminating Engineering Society *Code* London 1973
	The performance and types of electric lighting	Classes of visual tasks in new building Atmosphere to be created by electrical light Need for emergency or security lighting The contribution of daylighting to overall lighting conditions Source of electric lighting Illumination levels sought Limiting glare index Assessment of heat gain from fittings Selection of fittings Control of lighting; switching, blackout, dimming Operating and maintenance costs of installation	Illuminating Engineering Society *Code* London IES Technical Report 4: *Lighting during Daylight Hours* IES Technical Report 10: *Evaluation of Discomfort Glare* BRE Digest 76 *Integrated Daylight and Artificial Light in Buildings* BRE Digest 138 *Operating Costs of Services in Office Buildings*
Power	Size of electrical load	Lighting installations Heating, ventilating and air conditioning Water heating installations Cooking installations Small power: tools, office equipment, local lighting Heavy power: lifts etc Emergency supply (standby generators) Telecommunications installations Future demands	Jay and P and Hemsley J *Electrical Services in Building* Elsevier London 1968
	Method of supply and distribution of electric power	Supply Authorities' requirements Location of mains entry, transformers, switchroom, telephone exchange, battery rooms Location of principal distribution panels Wiring systems and routing of wiring Switching and control zones	*Electricity Supply Regulations 1937* Institution of Electrical Engineers: *Regulations for the Electrical Equipment of Buildings*
	Selection of appliances and fittings	Requirements for permanent installations Intended scope of office equipment and furniture systems Fittings relating to workplace servicing	BS CP 321:1965 Electrical Installations Jay P and Hemsley J *Electrical Services in Buildings* Elsevier London 1968

Function:	To determine:	Consideration given to:	Basic references
Thermal	An appropriate thermal environment inside a building	The characteristics of the outdoor thermal environment Overall performance requirements of the indoor thermal environment Specific attributes: temperatures, air change, air movement, relative humidity, ventilation, thermal indices Anticipated type of construction Incidental heat gains (eg lighting) Window design	Planning Office Space: *Thermal Factors* (p.140 on) Institute of Heating and Ventilating Engineers *Guide* 1970 Offices, Shops and Railway Premises Act 1963 BRE Digest 108: *Standardized U-Values*
	How to maintain the desired thermal environment	Performance required of heating, ventilating and air conditioning systems Population, nature and use of building Thermal behaviour of building fabric Internal heat and moisture gains Criteria of zone control Local distribution system: heat transfer medium Local distribution system: source of heat Main distribution system: heat transfer medium Evaluation of fuels and plant type; boilers and refrigeration Recovery and use of waste heat	Offices, Shops and Railway Premises Act 1963 IHVE Guide 1970 BS CP 341: 300-307: 1956 *Central Heating by low pressure hot water* BS CP 352: 1958 *Mechanical ventilation and air conditioning in buildings* *ASHRAE Guide* and *Data Books* published by the American Society of Heating, Refrigerating, and Air Conditioning Engineers
Acoustics	The best possible basis for special communication within the office	Evaluation of speech intelligibility related to space types Suitable background noise levels The requirements of cellular offices for privacy The requirements of open office space Effects of traffic, plant and equipment noise	*Planning Office Space:* Acoustic Factors (p.133 on) BS CP3: Chapter III: 1960 *Sound Insulation and Noise Reduction* Parkin P H and Humphreys H R *Acoustics, noise and Buildings* Faber London 1958 Reprinted since
	The control of noise in offices	Partition design Flanking sound transmission via walls, ceilings, floors ducts Selection of absorbent surfaces Vibration isolation of plant Generation of background noise	
Communications	Selection and design of a telecommunications installation	The types of communication required; internal/external Relay or recording of information Telex and data transmission Audio-visual systems Location of apparatus Economy of distribution systems Equipment rooms and ducting Power demands of system Acoustic implications	The Post Office: *Facilities for Telephones in New Buildings* Institute of Electrical Engineers: *Regulations for the Electrical Equipment of Buildings* 1974 BS CP 327.102: 1952 *Telephones and telegraphs, private services* BS CP 327.402: 1951 *Staff Location Systems* Consult BSI Yearbook for specialised publications
Security	Measures to ensure environmental safety and building security	Fire, theft, flooding Building form and fire requirements; fire compartments within building; means of escape Resources for firefighting and access Systems of fire alarm, fire-fighting equipment, emergency lighting	Consult local fire authority The Building Regulations 1965 Part E Offices, Shops and Railway Premises Act 1963 BS CP3: Chapter IV: *Precautions against fire Part 3: 1968 Office Buildings* GLC Code of Practice: Means of escape in case of fire, 1974
		Clients' requirements for security planning Alarms, locks, safes and strongrooms Possibility of flooding	Consult local police authority and clients insurers. No regulations on burglary
Waste disposal	Provision of drainage and sewage disposal	Normal flows from sanitary appliances Surface water flows Location of existing drains and sewers Location of toilets and kitchens within building Collection of foul water within building, horizontal and vertical Collection of surface water around building Loading of drains and sewers	Public Health Act 1961 The Building Regulations 1965 Part N. Offices, Shops and Railway Premises Act 1963 Shops and Offices, the Sanitary Convenience Regulations 1964 BS CP 301: 1950 *Building Drainage*
	Disposal method for solid waste	Nature and quantity of waste (mainly paper) Cleaning and housekeeping system anticipated	Public Health Act 1936

Function:	To determine:	Consideration given to:	Basic references
		Frequency and timing of collection Storage and access for disposal Storage for collection of high grade paper waste (eg computer) Routing and collection equipment within building	
Movement	Movement systems for people	Building population and types of uses including handicapped visitors to building Pattern of occupancy by time, location Travel times and distances Flexibility and future expansion Related needs of escape Design of stair access between floors Design of mechanical circulation: lifts and escalators	Only legislation concerns means of escape from fire. Offices Shops and Railway Premises Act 1963. Sections 28 *et seq* BS CP 3: Chapter 1V; Part 3 1968 Office Buildings The Building Regulations
	Movement systems for goods	Nature of demand for movement of post, stationery, documents, kitchen deliveries, furniture, trolleys, wheelchairs Patterns of use within building now and in future Appropriate mechanical systems: pneumatics, document conveyors, hoists Implications for core and duct design	
	Movement systems for services	Quantity sizing and grouping of building services Ventilation of core rooms (eg stores, toilets) Sizing and location of service ducts, vertical and horizontal Need to segregate services within ducts Acoustic and fire separation within ducts Support systems and expansion provision	BS CP 3 Chapter VII: 1950 *Engineering and Utility services*

Page 151: photographer Richard Einzig.
American Express, Cannon Street, London, designed by Duffy Lange Giffone Worthington

Section 7: Office facilities

Entrances and reception areas

The function of the reception and entrance is not only to control but also to impress the visitor with the identity of the occupant. COLIN CAVE examines various types of reception, describes their functions, and the problems associated with their design.

1.0 Principal types of reception

1.01 This information is concerned with the design of three main types of reception facility: main, deferred, and staff and/or goods. The first type will generally suit buildings in single occupancy while the buildings in multi-occupancy will tend to have the second type.

1.02 Main reception, principally for visitors and staff, is usually fairly prestigious and is at street level, **1**. Very large firms may also require separate departmental reception facilities.

1.03 Deferred reception compromises a two-stage activity in which all that is required at the main entrance is a commissionaire or good signing system to direct the visitor to further reception points within the building. These points are provided probably on a tenancy or departmental basis, **2**.

1

2

1 *Typical main reception area in a prestige office building.*
2 *Typical deferred reception point, in this case at the entrance to a separate tenancy within the building.*

1.04 Reception for staff and/or goods is often necessary for security or functional reasons to control the entrance of goods and/or staff into the buildings by separation from visitors or other members of the public. This is obviously the case with banks, for example, but is also true of many other building types.

2.0 The main elements

2.01 Reception areas are where a company meets its public and normally involve most, if not all, of the following, **8**:
1 receiving;
2 waiting;
3 exhibition and display;
4 storage for goods and for coats;
5 lifts and/or stairs.

Receiving

2.02 Briefing should include information on:
1 *Staffing:*
how many people?
what roles (eg commissionaire, receptionist, receptionist/telephonist/typist, messenger, demonstrator, etc)?
2 *Services:*
what services are to be provided?
announcing visitors;
conducting visitors to other locations;
answering personal enquiries (what technical level of inquiry, and how long and often?);
issuing publicity material and information;
sale of products;
collecting payments;
receiving post and certain types of deliveries.
3 *Security:*
what degree of security is required?
do staff and/or visitors require passes?

Waiting

2.03 The waiting area should be close to reception to avoid any visitor being 'forgotten', but should not cause visitors to feel 'exposed'. Possible embarrassment or anxiety may be increased or reduced by the layout, type of seating, and the provision of things to do, eg magazines, displays, an active view (street scene), etc.

2.04 Brief discussions may take place in the waiting area, and representatives or salesmen may be seen here. In some companies sensitive to industrial espionage no representative or visitors are allowed to progress beyond the entrance area, in which case some form of layout space may be required. Telephone and lavatories for visitors are desirable and should be located adjacent to the reception/waiting areas.

Exhibition/display

2.05 A badly executed or maintained display may be unconvincing and counter-productive to a firm's image and it may be preferable to have no display. The selection or design of display equipment should be determined by the following considerations.
1 Nature and size of display: two-dimensional items, (photographs, posters etc, slides/films etc); three-dimensional objects (models, manufacturers' products, etc); is the display unattended or attended?
2 Is the display permanent, semi-permanent, or occasional? If it changes, how often, in what way, and who is responsible for its erection and removal?
3 Is display to be visible to the outside or inside of the building, or both? Who is it for—passers-by outside, casual visitors inside, accompanied visitors inside?

Storage for goods and coats

2.06 Many people call at reception points merely to leave or pick up small parcels. For security reasons the commissionaire should be responsible for handling and storing these. In many cases it will also be necessary to provide for storage of visitors' coats and hand luggage. It should be remembered that often these coats will be wet.

Lifts and/or stairs

2.07 Both the size and capacity of lifts and stairs are important, as well as their siting in the entrance hall. Lifts should be visible from the entrance and reception areas, and sufficient waiting space should be provided in front of the lift doors.

3.0 Planning

3.01 Many reception and building entrance areas are not planned, but just happen. Frequently they are squeezed into the smallest possible space, particularly in the case of speculative office buildings where large entrance areas would mean less office area. Even in more spacious entrance areas the relationships between the four elements discussed earlier are not always thought out. Figures **3** and **4** show the major elements in the entrance areas of two office buildings. Figures **5** and **6** show how a reception area was re-organised to provide better facilities and better security. Table I is a guide to sizing the public areas in buildings, taken from the *AJ Metric handbook*.

Table I* Area per person to be allowed in various circulation areas

Occupancy	Area per person (m²)
Overall allowance for public areas in public-handling buildings	2·3 to 2·8
Waiting areas, allowing 50 per cent seating, 50 per cent standing without baggage, allowing cross-flows (eg airport) lounge	1·1 to 1·4
Waiting areas, 25 per cent seating, 75 per cent standing, without serious cross-flows (eg waiting rooms, single access)	0·65 to 0·9
Waiting areas, 100 per cent standing, no cross-flows (eg lift lobby)	0·5 to 0·65
Circulating people in corridors, reduced to halt by obstruction	0·2
Standing people under very crowded conditions—acceptable temporary densities	Lift car capacities: 0·2 m² (four-person car): 0·3 m² (thirty-three-person car)

*Table V *AJ Metric handbook*, p51.

Doors

3.02 Entrance doors are normally a pair of single or double swing leaves. Large banks of doors are rarely necessary and cause confusion as most of them are usually locked.

3.03 Revolving doors, often difficult to negotiate, **9**, should be used with additional swing doors and a draught lobby. A draught lobby is necessary because the revolving action draws dust-laden air into the building.

3.04 All doors should be fitted with springs to prevent them being left or blown open. Air pressures round tall buildings can be large and changeable. There are many examples of swing doors having to be replaced by revolving doors or electrically operated sliding doors because they tended to be blown or sucked open.

3.05 Air curtains or automatic doors should be considered where traffic is heavy or a permanent opening is desirable. A full air curtain traps dirt or rubbish in a floor grille.

Disabled persons

3.06 Often access for the disabled is not considered in the design of office buildings, in spite of the fact that legislation requires both the employment of a certain proportion of disabled persons[1] and the provision of access for the disabled.[2] Not all disabled persons are wheelchair-bound.

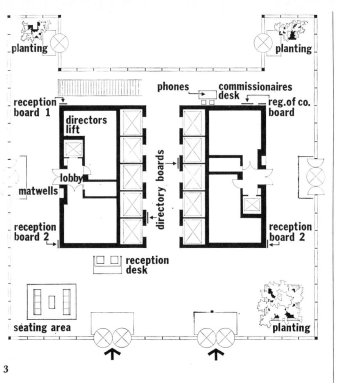

3

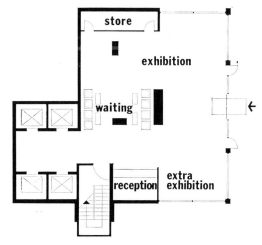

4

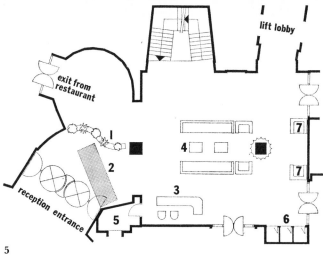

5

Key
1 Space divider: waist high planter.
2 Mat: too small.
3 Reception desk: awkwardly placed, does not have visual control of whole area.

4 Seating: two long bench seats, two armchairs; two low tables.
5 Storage for coats and goods: too small.
6 Telephone booths.
7 Guest telephones.

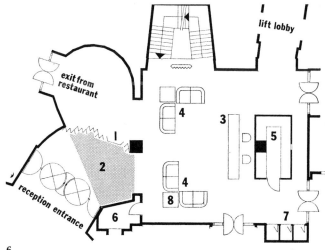

6

Key
1 New space divider: 1·75 m high and continuous, forces all visitors to enter reception area proper and walk towards commissionaire.
2 Enlarged mat.
3 Reception desk gives visual control of whole space, particularly entrance.

4 Seating: now more intimate, in full view of commissionaire.
5 Additional storage for goods and coats.
6 Locker facilities for commissionaire in old store.
7 Telephone booths.
8 Guest telephones.

3 *The expensively furnished reception area of an insurance company in London. Although at one side there is a commissionaire's desk and at the other a receptionist's these two points cannot supervise at least two of the six entrances. At the main entrance the relationship between the receptionist, doors and waiting area is good. No exhibition space is provided. The floor finish is durable but inadequate matting was provided in the first instance and had to be increased later.*
4 *Reception area in a government building providing good access for the disabled but little or no draught or dirt control. Extensive area provides a variety of arrangements of exhibition and waiting*
areas. Reception point, however, is partitioned off for security and to minimise the effect of draughts. This means that from the normal seated position the receptionist has no visual control of part of the exhibition area, the lifts and one entrance door. There is no easily accessible lavatory—because of the occupancy pattern of the building the closest wc is on the tenth floor.
5, 6 *How a reception area was reorganised to provide better facilities (more storage for goods and coats, better seating arrangements), better security (lockable store, all-round visual control), and better cleaning and maintenance (enlarged mat area).*

4.0 Environment

Heating
4.01 Where the reception area is the main entrance area special heating may be required to counteract draughts and heat losses through doors and any large areas of glass. Local heating may be provided for receptionists, and in the waiting area.

Lighting
4.02 Adequate local lighting should be provided for the receptionist and waiting areas. Otherwise lighting may be designed to achieve special effects and the desired external appearance of the building. Lighting for exhibition or display may be mounted on the building fabric or incorporated into the display equipment for which local floor or wall sockets will be required.

Acoustics
4.03 Choice of materials will control reverberant sound levels, though conversation areas may be treated separately. A visitor in the waiting area should not be able to hear conversation in adjoining office spaces.

KEY

Exterior
1 Ramped access for the disabled.
2 Steps to interrupt wind-blown surface dirt and litter sheltered by porch.
3 Well-drained dust and oil-free pavement (scrubbed and/or vacuum-cleaned).

Primary cleaning
4 Mats to wipe feet and remove dust; to drain water from raincoats and umbrellas. Doors arranged to encourage turning foot movements and at least four steps (vacuum-cleaned mats and well). Extract ventilation.

Secondary cleaning
5 Moisture-absorbent and anti-static mats (laundry service). Positive ventilation pressure.
6 Storage for wet outdoor clothes, umbrellas and parcels.
7 Removable, absorbent carpet in lifts as an extension of secondary cleaning.

7

8

Air-conditioning
4.04 Apart from the controlled comfort which it can provide for both permanent and temporary occupants of entrance areas, air-conditioning should be seriously considered if it facilitates the control of airborne dust. To prevent penetration of dust the main entrance areas should be at a slight positive pressure and the lobby area should be at a slight negative pressure, that is, subject to extra ventilation which draws air both upwards and downwards.

5.0 Cleaning and environment
5.01 From the point of view of environmental control the entrances to a building are weak points. It is estimated that 80 per cent of dirt in office buildings is carried in by people: 50 per cent on shoes and the remaining 30 per cent on clothes. Thus not only should the number of entrances be kept to a minimum but they must be designed to trap as much dirt as possible so that it may be easily removed. In most entrances dirt can be intercepted at three points. First, outside the building. Intelligent planning of surfaces is possible in most situations. If visitors have to travel across a wet gravel area before arriving at the door more dirt will be tracked in than if they have to walk across a dry, easily cleaned surface. Second, the lobby can be thought of as a primary cleaning area where there are adequate mats to wipe feet and remove dust, and where raincoats and umbrellas can be drained. Third, a secondary cleaning area where further cleaning of shoes takes place should be provided, 7.
The primary areas should be fitted with scraper mats through which dirt and water can drop, and should also have some provision for wiping. The secondary area should consist of moisture absorbent and anti-static mats.
5.02 The choice of materials in entrance halls, for the floor surface is particularly important, not only for effect but also for easy cleaning and maintenance. Most forms of hardwood, almost all the stone-based group and some of plastics/rubber group are suitable. Plain unbroken colours, both dark and light, should be avoided as they show every footprint.

References

1 Disabled Persons (Employment) Acts 1944, HMSO, 1958.
2 Sections 9 and 10 of the *AJ Metric handbook* give basic ergonomic and anthropometric data on disabled persons.

9

7 *Diagram shows how the requirements of good cleaning procedures can be integrated into the planning and design of reception areas.*
8 *Main reception area in a headquarters office. Good relationship between main elements, coats and goods storage, and lavatories behind wall in background.*
9 *Revolving doors and steps are difficult to negotiate. Floor finish in main area should have some degree of moisture absorbency.*

Section 7: Office facilities

Conference and meeting facilities

Meetings vary from accidental contacts in the corridor to pre-arranged, highly formal and ritualised events attended by large numbers of people. JOHN WORTHINGTON examines the full range of meeting types and analyses their design problems and opportunities.

1 Introduction

1.01 'Meetings' are any form of face contact between people. They may vary from accidental meetings of people moving between workplaces, to pre-arranged, highly formal and ritualised events attended by large numbers of people.

1.02 If meetings are to be effective, appropriate conditions must be provided. With larger and more formal events this need is generally recognised and the necessary provision made. Facilities for smaller, informal and accidental meetings are often neglected despite the value of such meetings in providing the day to day personal contact which allows for the passing on of information that does not always find its way into memoranda. The traditional cellular office arrangement provides ideal conditions for the small informal meeting: a table and a few chairs with quiet and privacy. This requirement is more difficult to accommodate for middle management and below in open planned offices, and one of the characteristics of the landscaped office as originally conceived was to provide a range of meeting places in the open area varying from the informality of break areas to screened meeting areas for up to eight persons associated with individual groups, **1**.

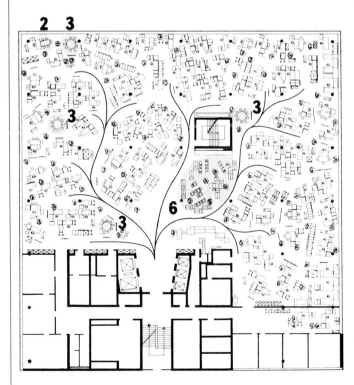

1 *Osram Building, Munich, planned 1962/63. Architects: Henn and Osram staff architects. Typical office floor showing range of meeting areas available in the open area.*

Key
2 Meeting area at the workplace
3 Meeting area for a group of workplaces
6 Rest area

These relate to the types of spaces given in table I.

1.03 The demand for a range of meeting places is confirmed by a number of studies. Stewart[1] has estimated that individuals in middle management spend 68 per cent of their time on personal contacts and 6 per cent on the telephone. Goddard[2] estimated that a third of the meetings attended by the senior business men he surveyed took place outside their workplace.

2 Types of meeting

2.01 Meetings may occur at the workplace, in a space attached to a group area, or in shared facilities common to all personnel within the building. Depending on the location, number of people present and the character of the event, meetings may be described as formal or informal. For the purpose of discussing meetings and conference facilities the range of spaces which may be necessary has been classified as follows: provision at the workplace; provision for a group of workplaces; provision for all members of staff.

Provision at the workplace
2.02 Meetings at workplaces generally involve few persons and are usually short. They can normally be accommodated by one or two visitors' chairs at the workplace; or, for more senior personnel, a separate table and chairs for a small group may be provided for longer discussions or entertaining, **2, 3**.

Provision for a group of workplaces
2.03 In planned open offices a meeting area may be provided near each working group. These meetings are often briefings, group discussions, or working sessions between some or all the members of the group and outside consultants. Meetings may last several hours. Space for between six to eight persons should be provided with some screening and with facilities for putting up charts and using a chalk board, **4**. The table is useful for laying out and discussing drawings and papers. Such a space may act as the focal point for the group and double up as space for collating information, layout of drawings and the location of the group notice and scheduling boards.

Provision for all members of staff
2.04 Where greater privacy is required or when it is felt desirable to have a higher quality environment for receiving visitors, special meeting spaces may be provided. These may be shared by all departments, and to ensure efficient use and that the space is properly prepared and refreshment provided, it is normal practice to have a pre-booking system. Such meeting spaces should be evenly distributed throughout the building, associated with the departmental work areas, but with direct access from the reception area for visitors. Provision for coat storage for visitors, and lavatory facilities should be adjacent. Since there are several kinds of meeting (formal, informal, interviews, large, small), a range of suitable spaces may have to be provided.

An important but often underrated occasion for the interchange of information is the office tea or coffee break. The policy in 'landscaped' schemes is to provide break areas on each floor served by vending machines and to allow staff to take a break at any time during the day, for unspecified amounts of time. The Centraal Beheer offices in Apeldoorn, Holland are designed around the principle of a central core of informal meeting and break areas with associated office areas.

2.05 Within most organisations there is the need for a space where all staff can meet. Meetings of this size are infrequent and are sometimes held in the cafeteria. Some firms may also need presentation spaces, lecture rooms, and con-

2

3

4

2 Proposed managers' work place standard. IBM Plant Administration Centre, Amsterdam. Space planners: Duffy Lange Giffone Worthington. Meeting table for six-person discussions and visitors' chairs for discussion at manager's desk.
3 Atlantic Richfield's New York headquarters. Space planners: JFN Associates, Board chairman's office with seating area for entertaining.
4 IBM Plant Administration Centre, Amsterdam. Space planners: Duffy Lange Giffone Worthington. Meeting areas for working groups in the open area.

Table I Types of meeting places, characteristics and requirements

Type of space	Number of persons	Typical space required per person	Type of use	Provision and equipment	Location
Provision at the workplace 1 Meeting at desk	2–3	2·00–2·75 m²	Short discussions, briefing subordinates, personal interviews.	1 or 2 visitor's chairs at work station.	Located in screened area if in planned open office environment.
2 Meeting area	4		Working discussion with the members of staff or visitors.	Conference table and chairs Related equipment—pinboard, chalk board.	
Provision for a group of workplaces 3 Meeting area	6–8	1·50–2·5 m²	Working sessions between members within group of personnel from outside involved with some project. May last several hours.	Conference table and chairs with some screening from surrounding work stations. Related equipment: flip charts, pin up space, chalk board. Provision of permanent notice board or chart board for use of group.	Located in group area adjacent to primary circulation, to limit disturbance of individuals.
Provision for all members of staff 4 Interview room	2–3	1·50–2·00 m²	Interviewing personnel or sales representatives. Discussions with members of public. Short periods of use up to ¾ hour.	Aural and visual privacy required.	Adjacent to main entrance and departments with major usage May require waiting area adjacent if used frequently.
5 *Meeting room*	8–12	1·50–2·00 m²	Meetings with outside visitors or internal policy making and planning meetings. 2–3 hour meetings.	Slides, overhead projector, flip charts, dimmer lights, good ventilation. Storage for drinks, audio-visual equipment.	Ease of access to all departments. Easily serviced with refreshments. Access for outside visitors without going through work areas. Coats area adjacent.
6 *Rest area*	12–18	2·25–4·00 m²	Primarily used for refreshment breaks, but may also to the area where general notices, scheduling charts etc can be displayed. This area may become an important point for the exchange of information and ideas. Used throughout day for short periods.	Vending machines, stand-up counters, low tables and easy chairs. Display board. Screening from work areas.	Adjacent to cloaks, wcs and rest room. Equally accessible to all personnel on each floor.
7 *Assembly area*	100–150		Infrequent meetings. Involvement of all staff.		May use cafeteria or recreation space.
8 *Board room*	16–24	1·50–2·00 m²	Formal board meetings, signing of contracts. Management meetings. Business lunches and entertaining. 2–3 hour meetings.	Formal layout. Audio-visual equipment. Good ventilation essential. Telephone extension. Space and facilities for stenographer.	Anteroom (for refreshments and leaving coats) attached. Easy access for refreshments. Two visits.
9 *Conference room*	15–20	1·50–2·00 m²	Presentations. Working discussions with outside visitors.	Audio-visual equipment. Dimmer lights and black out. Storage for equipment and furniture. Allow sufficient space for alternative layouts.	Easy access for visitors.
10 *Lecture room*	50–100		Large conferences, presentations, lectures and training sessions.	Closed circuit tv system. Control room for projector, lighting, curtains, tv and audio systems. Storage space for furniture display systems.	Adjacent area for audience to assemble before meeting. Several entrances.

ference facilities, with audio-visual equipment and space for between 20 and 75 persons. In smaller organisations there will normally be one conference room with audio-visual equipment to accommodate all requirements. To increase the flexibility of this facility it may be designed as a conference facility to seat about 20 people which can be sub-divided into two meeting spaces for eight to 10 persons, **6**.

2.06 The types of use, character, provision and location of meeting spaces are summarised in table I, **7**, **8**, **9**.

The number of spaces provided, amount of space per person, and quality and character of the space may vary considerably, depending on the type and size of organisation.

3 Character and provision of meeting places

3.01 A recognised function of the formal meeting spaces (eg the board room) may be to impress, or even intimidate visitors and represent the interests and financial stability of

5

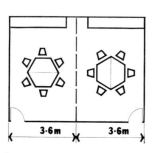

6

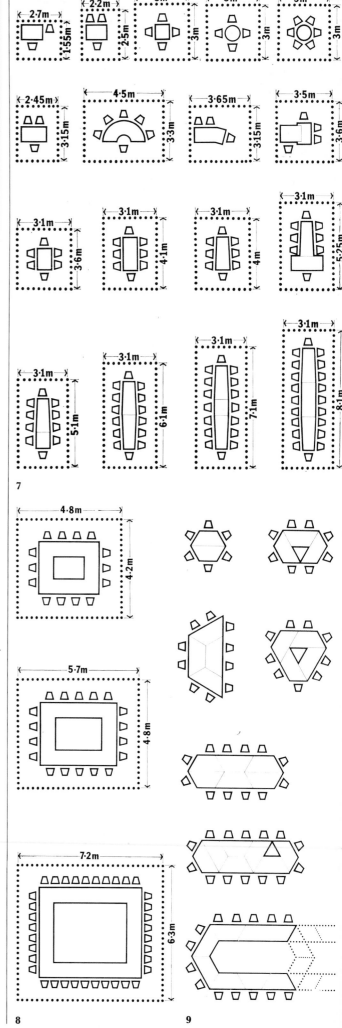

7

the company to the outside world, **10**. Equally other spaces may be used to put the visitor at ease, and create a *milieu* for creative discussion, **11**. The designer's role is to create a range of meeting environments in sympathy with the aspirations of the organisations, leaving individual users to provide appropriate settings for particular purposes.

3.02 Whether a meeting takes place in an individual's work area or in a separate meeting or conference space, the relationships between the participants[3] will be affected by:

1 the distance between, orientation, and relative heights of participants;

2 the use of the desk or table as either a shield or a common focus for interaction, **12**.

3 Each person's seating position in relation to external distractions (eg window, glass screens, the door, or the open office area); seating positions in relation to the major axis or orientation of the space or table;

4 the type of furniture, decor and lighting,[4]

Each of these factors can be manipulated to produce given effects in certain situations. Meetings in the same space may require quite different seating arrangements so that contacts with different purposes may all achieve maximum effect, **12**.

A manager, for example, may be expected to interview applicants, issue reprimands, hold a discussion with a colleague or visitor, as well as deal with the personal

5 *Provision for chair storage in a meeting room.*
6 *Diagram of facility for subdivisible meeting space for 12–16 people with chair storage attached.*
7 *Space requirements for*

informal meetings.
8 *Space requirements for formal meetings.*
9 *System of unitary furniture to allow for alternative layouts.*

8

9

10

11

problems of his junior staff.

Adaptable seating arrangements can be achieved by allowing sufficient space for furniture to be moved or by the provision of additional furniture and associated storage.

Size and allocation of meeting spaces

3.03 The number and size of spaces provided for meetings varies considerably with the type of organisation, depending on:

1 the size of the organisation: larger or more specialised organisations, especially those with a headquarters function, tend to require large meeting spaces for training sessions, presentations to outside visitors and entertaining;

2 the degree of bureaucracy: firms with a wide range of grades of personnel, and a high proportion of managerial staff tend to demand a greater number of formal meeting areas;

3 the number of outside visitors: firms such as advertising agencies who spend a great deal of time working with clients and also have a security problem of keeping clients' work separate, require a high proportion of secure meeting rooms separate from work areas;

4 the type of work being undertaken: project orientated groups where problem defining and solving sessions are frequent require a greater number of meeting areas than clerical staff;

5 whether the arrangements are open or cellular plan: cellular offices by their nature are full of convenient meeting places; open planning introduces a greater need to plan for both informal meeting areas in the open offices and for secure, private meeting spaces elsewhere.

3.04 Typical meeting area provision based on a selection of projects is summarised in table II.

3.05 Richard Davies in his study for the Civil Service on comparative space standards in open offices[5] (summarised in table III) analysed 12 planned open offices and drew conclusions on the percentage of the net area available that was devoted to separate meeting facilities.

Table III Percentage of space allocated for meeting areas as a percentage of total net area (based on study of twelve open plan offices)

| Support spaces | Space allocation expressed as a percentage of total net area | | | |
	Average of all offices	Average of office using 'Kew' furniture	Average of other 'general' offices	Average of drawing offices
	%	%	%	%
Meeting spaces	3	3	4	2
Storage	4	4	6	2
Refreshment/rest	5	3	6	—
Cloaks	2	2	2	—
General services	7	7	4	8
Circulation	18	15	19	15
Total support spaces	31	34	29	31

10 *English & Continental Property (Holdings) Ltd. Consultants: Duffy Lange Giffone Worthington. Formal board room also used for business lunches.*
11 *English & Continental Property (Holdings) Ltd. Informal meeting area.*
12 *Alternative seating arrangements at the work place, using the desk as either a shield or a common focus for interaction.*

Seating arrangement and condition

1 Informal situation with both parties working on an equal basis

2 Informal situation. Probable difference in status between parties involved

3 Interview or briefing with subordinate

4 Formal interview

12

Table II Meeting area provision for different types of organisations based on a selection of projects

	Meeting area at workplace	Meeting area serving a group of workplaces	Meeting rooms 6–8 persons	Lounge/rest areas	Meeting room 12–16 persons	Meeting room 16–20 persons	Conference room 22–28 persons	Lecture room 100–150 persons
Headquarters accommodation for an engineering organisation (population 1200)	1 per 15 office staff	1 per 10 office staff	1 per 80 office staff	1 per 280 office staff	1 per 120 office staff	None	1 per 1200 office staff	1 per 1200 office staff
Manufacturing administrative organisation (population 400)	1 per 40 office staff	1 per 12 office staff	1 per 45 office staff	1 per 80 office staff	None	1 per 60 office staff	1 per 200 office staff	None
Headquarters accommodation for a clerical organisation (population 1400)	1 per 18 office staff	1 per 26 office staff	1 per 55* office staff	1 per 400 office staff	1 per 280* office staff	1 per 230* office staff	1 per 1400 office staff	None
Consultancy organisation (population 80)	1 per 16 office staff	1 per 20 office staff	None	None	None	1 per 80 office staff	None	None

* apportioned to separate companies on each floor

13

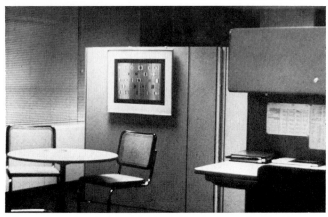

14

9 5 5

15

Key

2 Meeting area at the workplace	5 Meeting room 8-12 persons
3 Meeting area for a group of workplaces	6 Rest area
	9 Conference room

13 *JFN Associates, New York. Forum, general meeting area in the open space where personnel can sit, relax and entertain visitors.*
14 *JFN Associates, New York. Meeting facilities at workplace.*
15 *Offices for JFN Associates, New York. Shows the range of meeting spaces provided.*

4 Examples of the provision of meeting spaces

Offices for JFN Associates, New York, 15

4.01 Firm of designers and space planning consultants, with approximately 100 personnel. Required spaces for small working discussions, and project meetings with contractors, outside consultants, and client representatives.

Range of spaces provided:
conference room (board room)—seats 15-20 people, has audio visual facilities;
small meeting rooms—seat eight to 10 people for two to three hour working sessions that require privacy; these spaces can also be used as areas for individual quiet work as required;
rest area forum—general space where personnel can sit, relax and talk, and visitors may be taken. Work schedule, office notices etc are located in this area, **13**.
individual meeting area—four-person conference table adjacent to work station and shielded from outside distraction by screens, and secretarial position for controlling entry; **14**
group meeting area—conference table associated with six to eight stations and acting as a focus.

Central Electricity Generating Board, Generating Division, Barnwood, 16
4.02 Headquarters group largely composed of engineers with a staff of approximately 1400.
Range of spaces provided:
conference room for 24 persons;
conference room for 18 persons;
anteroom for conference facilities;
subdivisable meeting space for 24 persons;
lecture facility for 130 people, subdivisable into two smaller spaces;
break areas to seat approximately 50 persons at any one time;
meeting room for 12 persons;
individual—meeting space associated with workplace;
individual meeting table associated with workplace;
group meeting space.

American Express Banking Corporation, European Division, London, 17
4.03 Executive group of European Banking Section deals directly with clients discussing corporate finance arrangements. Approximately 12 personnel. The concept was to provide offices for the senior vice presidents and for the bank executives to be in the open areas with two luxurious meeting areas adjacent where clients could be entertained.
Range of spaces provided:
conference room—room for eight persons with kitchen facilities attached and sideboard for drinks. This space is used for business lunches, discussing business of a private nature, and finalising contracts;
informal meeting areas, **18**—for entertainment and discussions with clients. Aska globe swivel chair has a phone attached for clients to make private telephone calls. Reference book cases used to define the space and provide common service for the group;
visitors' chair at work place for casual discussions with visitors, or the secretary to take dictation;
meeting space in individual offices—low table and easy chairs, for informal discussions with visitors or members of staff.

16

17

References

1 STEWART, R., *Managers and their jobs*, London, Macmillan, 1967, £2·25.
2 GODDARD, J. B., 'Office communications and office location', *Regional Studies*, vol 5, p263, 1971.
3 SOMMER, R., 'Further studies of small group ecology', *Sociology*, vol 22, 1965, p337 (reprinted in *Communication in face to face interaction*, editors Laver, J. and Hutcheson, S., Harmondsworth, Penguin, 1972.)
4 JOINER, D., 'Office territory', *New Society*, vol 18, no 471, 7 October 1971.
5 DAVIES, R., '*Space standards for planned open offices*', DOE unpublished internal report, April 1971.

Key to 16
2, 3, 5 Meeting areas
5 Rest area
9 Conference room
10 Lecture room. These relate to the types of space given in table I.

Key to 17
1 Meeting at desk
2 Meeting area at the workplace
3 Meeting area for a group of workplaces
5 Meeting room 8-12 persons

18

16 *CEGB divisional headquarters, Barnwood. Architects: Yorke Rosenberg Mardall. Plan shows the range of meeting spaces available. In the open planned spaces meeting tables for the use of groups are provided adjacent to section heads' workplaces.*
17 *American Express Banking Corporation, London. Space planners: JFN Associates (UK) Ltd. Plan of executive accommodation.*
18 *American Express Banking Corporation. Informal meeting area in the open area for discussions with clients.*

Section 7: Office facilities

Storage and distribution

The provision of storage spaces in offices is often neglected by architects and the user. It is assumed that it can be accommodated within the furniture. This can be a misconception resulting from the lack of a clearly defined brief for the distribution needs of an office, and the conflict between purpose built single occupancy designs and those for leasing and multiple occupation. JOLYON DRURY shows that storage is only part of an overall materials distribution strategy that applies to every kind of office, large or small.

1 Background to the design of storage and distribution systems

1.01 The storage and distribution of office material is a function of office management policy and the nature of the firm. The important principle for designers to grasp is that stores distribution, handling and transport of work, or files, and internal transport methods (by hand trolley or conveyor) are an integral part of normal circulation and should be considered at an early stage in the planning of the building.

1.02 There are two basic parameters to consider:

1 The type of user: an office for a manufacturing company will use storage provision in a different way from that for an insurance group.

2 The types of storage that the class of user will require: this is a question resolved by detailed study of requirements.

2 Types of storage

2.01 Whichever type of user is involved it will usually be possible to distinguish what has to be stored, where it should be stored, how much space it will occupy and the speed of access required.

Storage has a hierarchical structure and can be considered either as an aspect of office work or as an aspect of maintenance:

1 *Storage as a dynamic aspect of the office work.*
Storage at the workplace.
Storage at the group.
Storage for a floor, a number of groups.
Storage for an organisation.
Recording/archives for a firm or group.

2 *Storage as an aspect of maintenance.*
Storage for a group.
Storage for a floor.
Bulk storage for a firm or group, either in-house or decentralised.

2.02 Designers should attempt to draw up an inventory with the client, formalising what articles are required at each of these levels of operation, and the necessary speed and frequency of access. This question should involve the company's policy towards material purchase and distribution, and whether any active form of stock control is involved.

Files are often only a small part of a user's storage needs but the proportion of the office to service function will vary with the size of the office, the number of operatives involved, and the type of business. The growth of service to office storage space rises in proportion to the increase in the number of occupants.

2.03 The inventory of office function material includes:
Work in progress.
Stored records for immediate access.
Stored records for historical back-up.
Stored records as a security function.
Stationery and supplies for immediate user.
Stationery and supplies with limited availability (security or cost).

2.04 *Bulk supplies*
Stationery
Cleaner's supplies and furniture for immediate use. This category includes catering supplies, which are discussed elsewhere in the handbook[1]).

2.05 Waste should also be considered. This involves: immediate waste for frequent collection, kitchen waste, disposable cutlery, non-recoverable paper and office waste. Repository; bales of waste paper for re-sale, security of shredded stock for incineration. The storage of waste will become and increasing problem as more financial pressure is exerted to conserve material for recycling.

3 Storage, handling and access

3.01 Storage and handling techniques for work in progress in the form of paper and files are well documented and are covered as part of the study on furniture.[2] Active work storage will differ for the levels of user and nature of the business. For example, checking clerks will seldom require more than one file at a time, whereas product managers will often require a number of files simultaneously for cross referencing and historical information. Poor provision for middle management is a frequent failure experienced with open planning particularly where the designer of the layout has been less than rigorous in his user requirement studies. This failure is reinforced by the widely held belief that proprietary furniture systems are more flexible and elastic than is the case.

3.02 Position of stored records should be related to circulation and speed of access, and to the number of users for whom the stored data is relevant. In some cases it will be preferable to decentralise document storage for security and to relate it to the user group. Conversely, for the large single company user with multiple access requirements, it may be preferable to consider a central store for all access speeds, with document conveyor links.
The decision to install conveyors fixes the layout of a building, and thus the means of work. Document conveyors take several forms, but are basically split into those serving individual desk positions, and those serving groups, **1**. In planning terms, the former employing paper sheets or files implies a linear layout, where the latter, using bins or cassettes defines nodes and secondary (usually pedestrian) distribution systems.

Deep storage

3.03 The deep storage of historical records again depends on the nature of the business. For many companies records need not be retained after a certain period except for some basic abstracts and summaries and these can and should be within the work area for rapid access. Examples of this type are small manufacturing companies. Some other companies need to keep numbers of records, for example of designs, product test results and sales figures, but will accept microfilm techniques to reduce deep storage volume to a minimum. Insurance companies and building societies have a complex operation due to the number of clients and the confidential nature of their business. It is in this sector where the limits of deep storage become blurred. At the Halifax Building Society, the storage of files is treated as deep storage, but all types share equally rapid access via an automated storage and distribution system planned as an

1 *A Sovex selective document conveyor feeding files to desk positions from a central store.*

integral part of the building design.
Despite the use of computer and photographic storage techniques, in certain circumstances it is likely that large quantities of paper will still have to be stored but in minimal space and with provision for rapid access. Table 1 lists documents typically found in offices together with the length of retention.

Support storage

3.04 Office support stores include stationery, paper, equipment and much of it carries a high value. As materials costs rise, emphasis is being placed on controlled provision for dispensing stores to staff, and increased interest is being shown in stock control techniques by office managers. The position of office support stores should be based on frequency of access and security. In large offices, it is useful to use the analogy of retail outlets served by a distribution centre. The outlets are the user groups or individuals. For efficient operation, these stocks must not be allowed to drop below a certain level; equally, it is uneconomic and costly for offices to carry more stock than they need in the foreseeable future. Support stores must be planned equally with maximum volume use in mind.

Identification and speeds of use

3.05 Ease of identification of material, and separation of active from back-up bulk stock, should enable a rapid check of inventory to establish the need for reordering. In office stores there are varying speeds of use.
Fast movers: Paper, invoice blanks, carbons, scribble pads, computer stationery.
Medium movers: Typewriter ribbons, type obliterating, writing equipment, special stationery, files.
Slow movers: (often high value stock): Calculators, typewriters, file sections.
In a store, the ease of access should be related to the speed of movement of the stock. Tables 2, 3 and 4 identify typical items of storage and relate them to speed of access for three typical workplace types.
At the work station, immediate individual storage can be solved by a lockable drawer: working groups will have different requirements.

Table I Retention of documents

This list does not claim to be comprehensive. Moreover, certain documents have been included on a somewhat conservative and cautionary basis, although many companies either no longer use them or keep them for any length of time. The periods of retention suggested are likely to be the maximum and in practice it may well be possible to apply shorter periods in a number of cases.

Company documents (excluding share registration).

Certificate of incorporation	
Certificate to commence business (if any)	
Board minutes	
Board committee minutes	
Minutes of general and class meetings	
Trust deeds	
Circulars to shareholders	1 master copy to be kept permanently.
Notices of general and class meetings	
Resolutions (prints of) passed at general/class meetings	
Memoranda and articles of association	
Seal book	
Proxy forms/polling cards	If not used—1 month; if used—1½ years after meeting.
Proxy forms used at court-convened meetings	3 years.
Register of directors and secretaries	
Register of directors' share interests	
Register of 10% holdings	1 master copy to be kept permanently.
Register of mortgages and charges	
Register of members	
Register of debenture holders	

Share registration documents

Application forms	
Acceptance forms	All originals permanently or 12 years if then microfilmed
Allotment letters (renounced)	
Renounceable share certificates (renounced)	
Allotment letters (lodged for exchange)	All originals 2 years.
Share and stock transfer forms	All originals permanently or all originals 12 years plus permanent full microfilm record (see Note 3).
Letters of request	All originals permanently or all originals 1 year plus permanent full microfilm record.
Allotment sheets	
Return of allotments (page 1 only)	
Redemption/conversion discharge forms or endorsed certificates	All originals permanently or all originals 1 year, plus permanent full microfilm record.
Signed forms of nomination	
Letters of indemnity for lost records	All originals permanently, unless microfilmed.
Annual return	Front page with capital and other particulars—permanently for record purposes.
Powers of attorney, stop notices and similar Court orders	1 photocopy of each—permanently.
Dividend and interest payment lists	'Bulk' lists 12 years. 'Direct' lists can be disposed of when an extract of outstanding warrants has been made.
Paid dividend and interest warrants	Originals 12 years after date of payment.
Dividend and interest mandates	Originals 4 years from closing of account.
Unclaimed dividend/interest lists	Until cleared or forfeited, whichever is earlier.
Cancelled share/stock certificates—no endorsement	2 years (see Note 3).
Notification of change of address	2 years.
Transfer receipts and balance receipts (if issued and returnable)	2 years.

Agreements and related correspondence

Major agreements of historical significance	Permanently.
Contracts with customers	
Contracts with suppliers	
Contracts with agents	
Licensing agreements	6 years after expiry.
Rental and hire/purchase agreements	
Indemnities and guarantees	
Other agreements/contracts	

Property receipts

Deeds of title	Permanently or until property disposed of.
Leases	12 years after lease has terminated and all terminal queries (e.g. dilapidations) settled.
Agreements with architects, builders, etc.	6 years after completion of the contract.

Patent and trade mark records

	Permanently.
Reports and opinions	10 years.

Accounting records

Books of accounts giving information sufficient to comply with Companies Acts 1948 and 1967	Permanently.
Supporting schedules and ancillary books	
Stock inventories	10 years
Plant records and capacity charts	
Investment schedules and documents	10 years (see Note 1 below).
Published accounts	Signed copy permanently. Spare stock needed for several years to meet casual requests.
Periodic accountancy reports, e.g. to Board	File copies for 10 years.
Auditors' reports	Permanently.
Taxation returns and books	

Banking records, including GIRO

Cheques, bills of exchange and other negotiable instruments	
Bank Statements	6 years.
Instructions to banks	

Employee records

Patent agreements with staff	16 years after employment ceases.
Staff personal records	7 years after employment ceases.
Personal records of company's important executives	Permanently for historical purposes.
Applications for jobs—unsuccessful	Up to 1 year.
Payrolls	12 years.
Salary registers	Up to 5 years.
Salary revision schedules	Up to 5 years.
Tax returns	Permanently.
Expense accounts	7 years.
Labour agreements	Permanently.
Works Council minutes	Permanently.
Time cards and piece work records	2 years.
Wage records (including overtime details)	5 years.
Medical records	12 years.
Industrial training records	6 years.
Accident books	12 years.

Pension records

All trust deeds and rules	
Trustees' minute book	
Fund annual accounts and Inland Revenue approvals	Permanently.
Investment records	
Actuarial valuation reports	
Contribution records	
Records of ex-pensioners	6 years after cessation of benefit.
Pension scheme investment policies	12 years after final cessation of any benefit payable under the policy.
Individual life policies under 'Top Hat' schemes	12 years after settlement of claim or final cessation of benefit.
Group health policies	12 years after final cessation of benefit.
Group personal accident policies	

[Where pension schemes are not self-administered but insured with an Insurance Company, there may well be no practical need for a company to hold duplicate copies of documents already in the possession of the Insurance Company.]

Insurance

Policies	3 years after lapse.
Claims correspondence	3 years after settlement.
Accident reports and relevant correspondence	3 years after settlement.
Insurance schedules	10 years.

Technical and research

Records and reports	12 to 15 years after requirements have ended.
Drawings and other data	

Shipping documents

Outwards and inwards	5 years after shipment completed.
Customs and Excise returns	5 years.

Donation and subscription records

Index of donations granted	6 years.
Deeds of Covenant	12 years after final payment.
Correspondence re donations granted (not covenanted)	1 year.
Correspondence re donations refused	3 months.
Subscription records	3 years after cessation of membership.

Transport records

Drivers' log books	5 years after completion.
Vehicle mileage records	
Vehicle maintenance records	2 years after vehicle disposed of.
M.O.T. test records	
Registration records	

Investments

Certificates and other documents of title	Permanently or until investment disposed of (see Note 1).

Notes

1 Any investment records which may be required for capital gains tax purposes should be treated as taxation records and retained permanently as advised under 'Accounting Records'.
2 Attention should be paid to the possible historical importance of any document before any decision is taken to dispose of it.
3 The suggested periods for retention of share transfers and cancelled certificates may be reduced if the Articles of the company are suitably amended to allow a shorter period of retention.
This table is reproduced by permission of the Institute of Chartered Secretaries and Administrators.

Table II Secretarial use

	Very frequent	Twice daily	Daily	Several times weekly	Weekly
Stationery	Filing cabinets and shelves	Filing cabinets and shelves	Filing cabinets and shelves	Filing cabinets and shelves	Filing cabinets and shelves
	Tote boxes	Tote boxes	Tote boxes	Stationery in store or lockable cabinets	Stationery in store or lockable cabinets
Type ribbons, carbon etc	Filing cabinets or tote boxes	Filing cabinets or tote boxes	Filing cabinets or tote boxes	Filing cabinets or tote boxes	
				Tote boxes in store	Tote boxes in store
				Stamps in lockable cabinet	Stamps in lockable cabinet
Typewriters Calculators etc (a high pilferage rate)	In lockable store	In lockable store	In lockable store	In lockable store	In lockable store

Table III General office use

	Very frequently	Twice daily	Daily	Several times weekly	Weekly
Computer software Tapes	Racks in computer rooms	Racks in computer rooms	Racks in computer rooms	Racks in computer rooms	Racks in computer rooms
				Racks/mobile cabinets	Racks/mobile cabinets
Printouts and punched cards	Special filing cabinets	Special filing cabinets	Special filing cabinets	Special filing cabinets	Mechanised cabinets and mobile cabinets
				Mechanised cabinets and mobile cabinets	
Files, records	Personal desks	Personal desks Filing cabinets Mechanical cabinets	Filing cabinets	Filing cabinets	
			Mechanical cabinets	Mechanised cabinets and mobile cabinets	Mechanised cabinets and mobile cabinets
Microfilm/fiche	Personal clips and carrels	Personal clips and carrels	Personal clips and carrels		
			Cassette racks and special cabinets	Cassette racks and special cabinets	Cassette racks and special cabinets
	Document handling system	Document handling system	Document handling system	Document handling system	Document handling system
Drawings/plans	Personal clips	Personal clips	Personal clips	Personal clips	
				Mechanised cabinets	Mechanised cabinets
				Rolls: microfilm and microfiche	Rolls: microfilm and microfiche
Catalogues, trade literature	Filing cabinets Bins Shelves	Filing cabinets Bins Shelves	Filing cabinets Bins Shelves	Filing cabinets Bins Shelves	Filing cabinets Bins Shelves

Table IV Management use

	Very frequent	Twice daily	Daily	Several times weekly	Weekly
Files	Personal lockable drawers/and cabinets	Personal lockable drawers/and cabinets	Personal lockable drawers/and cabinets		
			Safes and high security store	Safes and high security store	Safes and high security store
	Document handling system	Document handling system	Document handling system	Document handling system	Document handling system

In strategic storage terms, office supplies are no different in concept from parts for a manufacturing process, and the same storage methods can be used to great effect: some of these are covered later in this chapter. The proprietary office furniture manufacturers offer various methods of dispensing paper from drawers to shelves.

3.06 Do not underestimate the provision for back-up stocks: with rapidly rising prices, the most economic stationery purchase is often by the pallet load, about a tonne at a time. A pallet of paper takes up a 1200 mm cube. Remember also that the bulk storage of paper products affects the fire rating, and possibly demands for compartmentation.

3.07 Much of what is said here about the storage and retrieval of information in the office, will be affected by the decisions on whether or not to use microfilming. Certain kinds of documents, particularly those which are very numerous and have a standard format, may be microfilmed and consequently a great deal of storage space can be saved. The equipment for microfilming and for viewing is not particularly bulky and can easily be accommodated in the office, some of it on the desk top. Simple attachments provide hand copy from microfilm viewers.

Whether or not a microfilming programme is economically justified depends on the type and quality of material handled, on the kind of retrieval that is required, on the rate of retrieval and on legal requirements for the preservation of the original documents. The client organisation will want to look very carefully into these matters and since the decision may well affect major design decisions it may be advisable to take professional help before an investment is made in expensive equipment.

Maintenance storage
3.08 There is an access hierarchy for maintenance stores similar to that for office support stores, but its scale depends on how cleaning and office maintenance are to be organised. Increasingly this work is contracted out, but there is always a need to store essential items like furniture, toilet rolls, soap, waste sacks, light tubes and carpet tiles. Discounts for bulk buying are now so attractive that even the smaller user can be expected to buy by the case. Establish at an early stage whether the user will employ a contractor.

Waste storage
3.09 Although paper recovery costs at present exceed the return offered by the recycling companies, except for the output from the largest offices, this can be expected to change in the next few years. There will be a demand to segregate recoverable paper waste from general disposal material. Office cleaners most frequently use a plastic sack for collection: this method proves equally effective for all scales of office. There is a point at which the storage space required for uncompressed sacks justifies the purchase of a waste paper baler. The space savings are often 20:1, and these machines are comparatively cheap, but such a purchase must depend on whether the local authority or contractor collecting the waste will provide a daily, weekly, or intermittent service. It is also important to establish at an early stage what daily magnitude of waste is involved, considering any relevant trends in the office's development; for example, a change to on-line transmission of data may drastically reduce the need for waste paper storage. The storage of uncompressed waste paper and baled material carries a hazard fire rating.

Loading space
3.10 One of the most frequently neglected areas of office design is the provision of unloading space for suppliers' vehicles. Too often the normal operation of an office is disrupted by barrowloads of material being trundled through the main door, lobby and work space from a vehicle that has had to obstruct the road or pavement. In large offices the loading bay with segregated truck access should be adjacent to the store or to the goods lift feeding it. Most stores do not arrive in light vans; pallets of paper are often delivered as part loads on the maximum size vehicles of haulage contractors employed by the supplier. If the office is big enough to justify full pallet loads of stores, and also if similar bulk buying is involved in the catering, a raised loading dock is necessary. With a bridging plate, a pallet truck (generally useful in a large office) can unload pallets direct, or the vehicle can be discharged manually onto trolleys at the same level. Alternatively, a hydraulic scissor lift can be provided comparatively cheaply, to raise a pallet truck or trolley to any vehicle level. This is a more flexible solution, as all types of vehicles can be easily handled; mobile scissor lifts are available that can be moved quickly out of the way. Useful too, and suggested as a basic part of any size of office with a vehicle delivery point, is the extendable, gravity roller conveyor (Flexiveyor); these fold up into a very small space when out of use, and pull out, bend round corners and can have adjustable angles of fall in either direction by settings on the supports, **12**. Unloading access is not just for storage but for furniture and equipment. In the case of electronic equipment, vehicle access is required and the doors must have 1800 mm clearance.

4 Environment
4.01 Lighting in storage areas. Provide 400 lux in file stores: take care not to produce a glare situation off the cabinets and the code tags.

Fire control
4.02 Valuable company records must be protected from fire. Sprinklers are normally employed, but water often does more damage than flames and heat. There is no substitute for immediate detection in the storage area: if numbers of picking staff are employed, gas cannot be used. In an automated store, a localised gas discharge can be effective. If there is no alternative to sprinklers, these can also be used with face-to-face mobile racking, with special jointed mains, see **5**.

Back-up stock: long-term storage of stationery
4.03 Most papers including photocopying and tracing papers are packed in barrier wraps: these are impermeable, and so sprinklers are acceptable. The client's insurers should be contacted for any special storage requirements. Note that with uncompacted waste paper storage the fire officer should be contacted: waste paper has a higher hazard rating than stationery. Waste paper comes into storage hazard group C2. Stationery has a sprinkler rating of 0H3 and a Cl storage hazard.

Security
4.04 Both files and equipment are subject to theft from intruders, especially in multiple-occupancy buildings. Apart from the need to keep file stores secure against industrial espionage, high on the pilferage list are electric typewriters, pocket electronic calculators, and desk top copying machines. Spare machines should have a place to be securely locked away: this is usually a corner of the long-term stationery store.

5 Specialised storage equipment. . short term storage

5.01 Files
1 Drawer cabinets.
2 Circular file stores.
3 Mechanised filing.

5.02 Stationery
1 Steel cabinets.
2 Adjustable shelving.
3 Tote boxes.

Drawer cabinets
5.03 The usual type of filing cabinet, with files suspended on rails at the edges of the drawers. Lockable and fire-resistant. They can be used to delineate spaces in open plan offices but can impede circulation space when the drawers are open.

Circular file stores
5.04 These offer higher accessibility than drawer cabinets. File pockets are suspended from racks, arranged in tiers around a central spindle. The whole level can be rotated to locate a file **2**. This method saves space in high access situations, with all-round access allowing several levels to be picked simultaneously. Up to five tiers of files are available: as well as files, containers can be suspended for books and stationery.

Mechanised filing
(See also long-term storage)
5.05 Files are placed in bins on a single level at desk top height: they are rotated on a track by an electric motor **3**. The secretary remains seated and rotates the stock until the particular file comes to hand.

Steel cabinets
5.06 These are available lockable and fire-resistant with adjustable shelves and dividers. They are not very elegant and are noisy **4**.

Adjustable shelving
5.07 Several manufacturers offer runners to be set into the wall or partition, from which shelving is cantilevered on brackets: this type of shelving is well known to designers. For office use, lockable cabinets are available in some ranges, but there is a weight limitation on the support hooks or brackets, and on the fixing of the runners.

Tote boxes
5.08 These are open-ended boxes in various sizes, made out of plastics or paper. Plastic tote boxes have been employed in the electronics industry for some time for small parts storage during manufacture. They are beginning to be recognised as a flexible storage method for open plan offices; they can be sized to carry paper, clips and all the other equipment a secretary may need. Being moulded in bright colours, they can be used for colour code identification of a product or a department. They stack with enough room for a hand to be inserted between them, or they can be cantilevered from a louvred metal panel **5**. The panel can either be part of a modular furniture layout, or mounted on a trolley base, for instance for typing pool supply.

2 Circular file store. An option is a fireproof cabinet. Installed free standing, access can be from all sides.

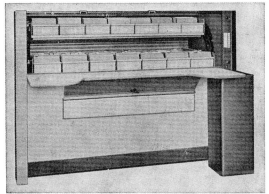

3

4

3 A mechanised filing cabinet. Herbert Zippel UK Ltd.

4 Double and single door steel cabinets. These cabinets have adjustable shelving. Welconstruct Co Ltd.

5

5 *A tote box cabinet, offering theft and fire security. The tote boxes are mounted on louvre panels. Note the wide variety of boxes and holders that are available.*

6 Storage equipment – long term

6.01 This section is concerned with the long-term storage of files and computer software. This cannot be separated from document retrieval: the planning and density of their storage depends upon the method and speed of access required.

Storage for stationery and supply goods
6.02 These systems can be satisfactorily used:
1 Adjustable timber shelving.
2 Slotted angle shelving.
3 Steel pigeon hole shelving.
4 Steel long span shelving.
5 Long span cantilevered shelving.
(See *Building and planning for industrial storage and distribution*, page 107.)

Files and software
6.03 These can be stored in
1 Drawer cabinets.
2 Suspended file cabinets.
3 Mobile cabinets.
4 Mechanised filing.
5 Automated file stores.

Drawer cabinets
6.04 These are still used by some offices for long-term storage. They are only fairly efficient for access, but provide fire and robbery protection.

Suspended file cabinets
6.05 The gangway obstruction caused by drawer-type cabinets and the time taken to select files is avoided by using instead lateral filing cabinets. Files are suspended in pockets in stacked rows, usually 5 or 6 vertically. Either the whole row swings forward for file selection, or the pockets are unclipped by a double motion **6**. The file ends are fitted with coded tags. Some cabinets are supplied with lockable roller shutter doors for security. Computer tapes can also be stored in this way but they rest on swing-out rails.

The most efficient way to plan is to form aisles with cabinets placed back to back. To allow optimum circulation the most used files should be placed nearest to the entry to the store, so that each aisle is organised into fast, medium and slow access sections.

Mobile cabinets
6.06 To gain a higher density of storage, suspended file cabinets can be placed on mobile bases, as can conventional shelf units. There are two methods available—*lateral* or *face-to-face* movement. With lateral movement three lines of cabinets are placed in parallel either side of an aisle. A space the length of one cabinet is left free in the first two rows either side of the aisle, so that the cabinets can be slid to expose the picking face required: three depths of file face are always available on each side of the aisle. The arrangement gives easy access, but the overall density is lower than that of the alternative. Face-to-face mobile cabinets are more usual. These allow only two sides of an aisle to be picked at a time, but very high volume efficiency is achieved with only one aisle width necessary within the stack. Motion can be powered or manual **7, 8, 9** (*Building and planning for industrial storage and distribution*, page 97).

Horizontal rotating stock
6.07 For open plan offices, files, tapes or cards are stored in bins in a horizontal cabinet, similar to the unit described in short-term storage section, but larger **10**. The bins are mounted on a motor-driven track, giving uninterrupted rotation: quick retrieval is possible by keying-in a files code.

Vertical rotating filing
6.08 More often used than the horizontal rotating stock, here pockets or bins are suspended from bars attached to a vertical chain. This system is designed to combine dense storage with fast retrieval. Versions are available that fit most common storey heights. The operator either rotates the store until the file becomes visible or the keys in a file code: the store will then automatically present the correct file. At the most sophisticated level, a computer serves a group of cabinets and selects which cabinet is involved, and the direction of rotation for the quickest delivery. Combined with a pneumatic tube order system, and a selective document conveyor to user positions, this method can produce fast retrieval at a comparatively low cost **10**.
6.09 Note that all these methods impose considerable weight on the floor: check that the structure is designed to accept heavy local loadings.

Automated file stores
6.10 Large central offices of companies, have found that automated filing and document conveying is an economic proposition. Two companies, Rand and Roneo-Vickers, offer what are really miniaturised automated warehouses, the Randtriever and Conservatrieve **11**. Operators key in requests from carrels outside the store; alternatively, the user can key-in a request from a desk top terminal. The files, suspended from rails in racking, are picked by a miniature stacker crane, and are placed on a selective document conveyor at the end of the aisle. The file is automatically routed by the computer control to the inquirer, whether at the carrel outside the store, or through

the document conveyor network to the user. Later developments are likely to include random storage in the racking.

6.11 The disadvantage of these systems is their cost, the time it takes to install them, and the risk of breakdown. This can be offset against the speed of retrieval and the service level provided for a large number of requests, and the high density of the storage. Twenty or more levels high is no problem, and the aisles are only just wider than the length of the files. However, these installations are a fixture in the building, usually at basement level because the floor loading is heavy. There is a possibility of employing structural racking, but this reduces flexibility.

8

6 *Suspended files in lockable cabinet. For large installations, cabinets are arranged laterally in aisles. Herbert Zippel UK Ltd.*
7 *Hand-cranked mobile shelving for storing stationery. This installation allowed three-and-a-half times more storage than a comparable conventional shelving arrangement.*
8 *Timber-framed mobile racks for computer tapes. Bruynzeel Wood Products Ltd.*

6

9

7

9 *Steel mobile shelving stacks, incorporating adjustable shelves. Used here to form pigeon holes for loose files.*
10 *A vertically rotating mechanised file store. Dense storage is combined with rapid retrieval. Herbert Zippel UK Ltd.*

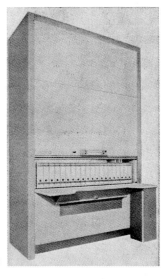

10

11 *Automated high-density file storage. The store is a scaled-down automated warehouse, linked to a selective document conveying system. Roneo Vickers Ltd.*

References

Generally the reader is referred to:
FALCONER, P. and DRURY, J., Building and planning for industrial storage and distribution. Architectural Press, London and Halsted Press, New York, 1975.
1 LAWSON, F., Eating, p. 169
2 GIFFONE, L., Office Furniture, Section 8, p. 191

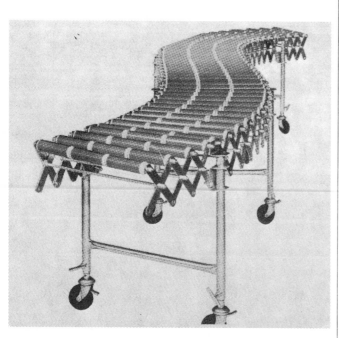

12 *Where space is at a premium, a flexible roller conveyor can solve many problems. This can be routed round obstructions, and can be concertinaed into a very compact unit for storage. Flexiveyor Products Ltd.*

Section 7: Office facilities

Eating

Regulations control standards for catering in office buildings. But decisions on whether to provide them or not and on the quality of what is provided remains very much with the client. FRED LAWSON sets out the factors to be considered in providing a full range of catering services from tea to all the meals of the day.

1 Requirements

1.01 In the UK legal requirements for the provision of eating facilities in office buildings are contained in:
Offices, Shops and Railway Premises Act, 1963, Section 15 requiring suitable provision to be made for the taking of meals where these are to be taken on the premises.
Food Hygiene (General) Regulations, 1970. (S. R. & O. 1970; 1172) specifying standards of construction, services and equipment in the interests of hygiene.
1.02 The range of facilities is extremely wide. At one end of the scale a small office unit—whether alone or part of a multi-tenanted building—may require no more than simple domestic equipment for the preparation of meals or beverages by the staff while, at the other end, a large organisation may need to serve several hundred meals within a $2\frac{1}{2}$ hour lunch period and meet various other demands. Facilities of this kind are often designed for use as social and reception areas.

2 Size and variety

2.01 The main factors which determine the size and complexity of the eating facilities are:
1 the numbers of employees who are likely to take meals on the premises
2 the periods in which meals will be required
3 the individual preferences and other influences which affect choice.
The number of meals required is not necessarily the same as the number of employees but depends very much on the circumstances and on alternatives available. In carrying out preliminary surveys of demand, account must be taken of the following:

Size of organisation
2.02 Number of employees, visitors and others who may require meals.

Alternatives available
2.03 Other restaurants in the vicinity, taking into account their convenience and suitability in terms of capacity, range of choice and price. An inducement to use these may be deliberately provided by subsidies such as luncheon vouchers: or the employees may go home for lunch.

Exceptional circumstances
2.04 For example, the use of office buildings for conferences or business exhibitions, and at times outside the normal work period such as shift work or evening duties.

Company policy
2.05 To a large extent, the range of provision will be dictated by the employer's social and financial policies. Some pay heavy subsidies while others charge the full economic costs of the catering service to the employees.

The numbers taking meals are clearly affected by these price variations. In leased premises, the size and type of catering facilities and conditions of tenancy must influence policy.

Peak meal period

2.06 The number of meals and the period over which the main meal period extends—usually two to two and a half hours—indicates the greatest pressures on equipment, service and dining space.

Choice

2.07 Apart from the question of costs, the range of choice to be offered may be affected by the proportion of employees in different age groups and occupations.

3 Beverages

3.01 Tea and coffee service during mid-morning and afternoon tea breaks may be operated independently or use part of the main facilities. In the latter case, arrangements are usually made for the counter line to be shortened or by-passed to allow faster service. Table I indicates the physical requirements for alternative provisions of tea or coffee service **1, 2, 3, 4a, 4b, 5**.

Table I Requirements for tea and coffee services

Main uses	Physical requirements
Self-preparation facilities For small numbers of staff and those working outside normal hours, eg, for security and servicing.	Staffroom fitted with sink, drainer and cupboard/worktop. A domestic electric or gas-heated kettle is normally required. Alternatively, an instantaneous water boiler or simple coffee machine (eg, of the Cona type) may be installed.
Vending machines More appropriate for larger numbers of staff, particularly in multi-lease premises with varying periods of occupation. Vending machines are most economical when breaks are taken at irregular times. Machine variations include heating (up to 3 kW) and/or refrigeration for hot and cold drinks. Up to nine choices are usually provided. Other vending machines may be used for snack items and for hot or cold meals. Daily cleaning and replenishment of containers and materials is usually necessary—the cup storage capacity of machines varies from 200 to 1000.	Should be mounted in a central position with adequate space to provide a waiting area without obstructing any corridor route or doorway. The number of machines required is determined by: Maximum number of people who require beverages over a break period of, say, 10 minutes.

Number of persons	Machines required
50	1
100	2
150	3

Distances to be travelled may warrant a larger number of machines dispersed throughout the building. Typical machine sizes range from 1400 mm high × 600 mm × 450 mm to 2000 mm × 850 mm × 650 mm. Smaller table models are also available. The price range of beverage machines is from £500 to £800 but vending installations are often hired and operated under contract.

Power—13 amp, single-phase 240 volt socket outlet. A 300-400 lux level of illumination is also necessary.
Water—13 mm mains drinking water supply with stopcock. The maximum and minimum pressures may be specified.

Spillage proof finishes, impervious and easily cleaned, are necessary in the vicinity of the machine.

A tidy bin for the disposal of cups is essential, preferably with a self-closing lid. Typical size 450 mm diameter × 750 mm high. A change-giving machine may be installed (size 890 mm × 215 mm × 115 mm).

Main uses	Physical requirements
Trolley service This is traditionally preferred by some offices. However, a trolley service is expensive to operate, time-consuming (particularly if cash is taken) and of limited availability. There is the likelihood of spillage and obstruction to corridors, lifts and doorways. Beverages are generally of better quality than from vending machines, ceramic cups can be used if preferred and food can also be sold from the trolley.	Corridors, lifts, doorways and circulation routes must be carefully planned to ensure easy wheeled access without obstruction. A central area must be provided for preparing the food and drinks, trolley-loading and parking, storage of ingredients and utensils, and washing facilities. The design requirements for this area are similar to those for other food rooms and must comply with the Food Hygiene Regulations. If the canteen kitchen is used for this purpose, enough space must be allowed for trolley movements and parking. In this area, bulk water heaters are normally installed and must be accommodated on stands or brackets to permit direct filling of the trolley urns. The electric loading of water heaters is about 0·1 kW per litre (equal to four to five cups capacity). Tea trolleys range in size from 900 mm × 600 mm × 900 mm high (most common) to 1200 mm × 700 mm × 900 mm high and they house one or two insulated urns, trays for cups and saucers or cartons of disposable cups.
Coffee and snack bars Coffee bars may be used to supplement the main meal service or to provide light meals where there are enough alternative restaurants in the vicinity.	Usually a purpose-made counter is provided, with an automatic water-boiler. A café set may be installed. Alternatively, coffee may be supplied from a service unit or glass percolators. A covered display case for cakes and sandwiches may be required and, in more complex arrangements, refrigerated counters may provide salads and cold puddings.
Cafeteria A beverage section is usually installed as part of the main serving counter. This is positioned at the end of the counter line to reduce the risk of spillage and delay.	Beverage counters are purposely designed units incorporating automatic water boilers. These may be of the: 1 *pressure type* which is housed under the counter or 2 *expansion type* mounted on the counter. Depending on the size and rating, automatic boilers have outputs from 40 to 140 litres/hr. A 13 mm water connection and 38 or 50 mm waste pipe to the drip tray are required. The pressure-type boiler needs to be supplied through a feed tank 5 to 8 m above the counter. Electric and gas-supply connections are required with loadings of about 0·1 kW per litre/hr. Counter units are formed from stainless steel sheeting—to facilitate cleaning and provide storage for cups and stands for pots.

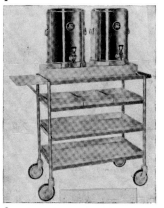

1 *A typical coffee percolating unit suitable for a small office establishment. (Cona Coffee Machine Co Ltd.)*

2 *Automatic water boiler of the pressure type supplying a cafe set. (Oliver Toms Ltd.)*

3 *Typical tea trolley with two insulated urns and space for cups, etc. (Tea Service Equipment Co Ltd.)*

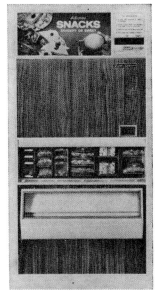

4a, b *Examples of vending machines for hot and cold drinks and for snacks. (GKN-Sankey Ltd.)*

5 *The Micro-Vend Buffet incorporates refrigerated storage for food and a micro-wave oven for reheating meals as required. (GKN-Sankey Ltd.)*

4 Meals

4.01 Meals for office employees may be provided through self-preparation facilities, vending machines or canteen services.

Self-preparation facilities

4.02 Facilities may be provided which enable the employees to prepare their own meals where:
1 there are few employees
2 where other choices are limited because of the location or time—as with, eg, night staff and security personnel.
Usually this provision is limited to tea- or coffee-making (see para **3** Beverages) for use with packed meals brought in by the employees. In more elaborate arrangements, a domestic refrigerator and cooker may also be installed but unsupervised equipment of this kind may be subject to some abuse. In all cases where meals are taken, it is necessary to provide chairs and tables or counters.

Vending machines

4.03 Apart from supplying beverages, snacks and packed cold meals, automatic vending machines can be used to provide a wide choice of hot meals. The storage cabinet—which is refrigerated—houses several meals on plates in separate coin-operated compartments. Individual meals are removed and heated as required, in a microwave oven which forms part of the unit. Meal-vending machines have similar uses for self-preparation facilities and can also be installed in small canteens as an automatic service facility or as a supplement to the normal counter service during and outside the main meal periods.

4.04 Requirements for vending machines include a 300 to 400 lux level of illumination and an electrical connection for the refrigeration unit and microwave generator. The larger microwave ovens require a 30-amp supply with an isolator switch. Careful siting is necessary to allow space for use and for cleaning and servicing without causing congestion. The number of machines needed depends on the peak demand for meals. Although a vending machine ensures that meals are available over a longer period, it is relatively slow compared with counter service. To extend the range of choice, alternative snack and beverage vending machines may be installed in the same grouping.

Table II Number of machines

Meals per 10 min	Machines
5-10	1
10-20	2
20-30	3

Vending machines are filled with prepared pre-cooked food supplied from a kitchen on the premises or by catering contractor.

Canteen services

4.05 Large office complexes often include a canteen service for staff, particularly if the choice of commercial restaurants is inadequate or inappropriate. Canteen arrangements may include:
1 Self-service cafeteria—for rapid service to large numbers. A number of alternative counter layouts improve the speed and efficiency of service.
2 Waitress service—for executive staff, directors and visitors. This also provides a facility for business discussions over lunch or dinner. The restaurant may also be used for conventions and meetings.

5 Location of catering facilities

5.01 In multi-storey buildings the catering unit may be located on any floor where space is conveniently available. A canteen on the top floor provides a more pleasant outlook and simplifies ventilation and security. Ground floor positions reduce the need for a service lift to transport food and waste through the building; there is also less difficulty in supporting, and gaining access for, the installation and replacement of heavy kitchen equipment and in providing drainage. Kitchens should be located to the north or north-east of the building for the coolest conditions.

6 Kitchen planning

6.01 The space requirements and equipment for storage of food and preparation of meals depends very much on the catering policy. Traditional methods of meal preparation need relatively large kitchen and storage areas. This work tends to be laborious and a large amount of equipment must be installed to facilitate the food preparation. Where food is supplied already prepared for use, considerable economies in space and equipment can be made but the initial food costs are higher. Many of the so-called 'convenience' foods are supplied in a frozen state to extend their storage life and, for this purpose, low-temperature cold rooms or refrigerators must be installed with sufficient storage capacity to allow for the normal delivery periods (usually three or seven days) with a reserve for emergency use.

7 Self-service cafeteria

7.01 Self-service is the most practicable way of serving meals to a large number in a short period—usually about two or three hours. The serving counter must be easily and directly accessible from the entrance but set back sufficiently to avoid congestion from customers waiting in this area. Menus and prices must be clearly displayed both before and over the serving counter. Tray stands should be located at the beginning of the counter line while cutlery and other requirements are usually positioned to one side of the route from the counter to the dining areas, **6, 7, 8, 9**.
7.02 The normal serving arrangement is a straight counter line with alternative choices in the order of their sequence in a meal—soups, main courses, sweets, beverages—followed by the cashier section. At the start of the counter, cold salads and snacks are often displayed to attract impulsive choice and provide a quick alternative to the main meal. This can be facilitated by allowing for by-passing of the main counter queue, particularly if there are delays in service.
7.03 The speed at which meals can be collected is determined by the slowest point of service—usually the cash desk or beverage counter. To accelerate the service, the cash desks may be duplicated and the beverage section removed from the counter line and replaced by vending machines or other facilities elsewhere in the room. Or for large numbers the whole counter line may be duplicated.

Design of counters

7.04 Serving counters are made up from purposely designed units, usually formed out in stainless steel, assembled in line and fitted with a tray slide. The counter units may be heated (hot-cupboards) with a heated top for container inserts (*bain-marie*), or refrigerated with a recessed top for chilled sweets, etc (dole plate), or fitted with a display case. Unheated counters are used for sandwiches, made-up sweets and cakes, etc, and should give some protection from contamination—for example a sneeze guard.

6

6 *Grill bar counter with display and heated bain-marie sections. Infra-red lamps are positioned over counter and behind servery are wall-mounted cooking units for meals to order. Counter is to one side of main food hall (in background) which operates on 'free-flow' principle. Catering equipment installed by Oliver Toms Ltd for the Plessey Co Ltd, Ilford.*

7 *Office dining facilities, Mercedes Benz (Agam), Utrecht, Holland, designed by Concorde Catering Equipment Co. Part of self-service counter for main cafeteria on first floor. Separate dining room is provided for senior staff and visitors and overlooks car showroom as a focal point of interest. Both serveries are supplied from a kitchen on the ground floor by elevator.*

7

8

9

8 Example of double self-service layout with two identical counters from each end to the centre. Cash desks are some distance from counter line to avoid congestion. In rear wall of servery are pass-through units for food to be transferred directly from the kitchen. Scheme installed for Kodak Ltd, Hemel Hempstead by G. F. E. Bartlett Ltd.

9 Small service counter incorporating bain-marie, hot-cupboard and cafe set. Unit serves directors and senior staff dining rooms for an office complex of DOE. Operating with waitress service, counter layout can be relatively simple. Installation carried out by Glynwed Foundries Ltd.

The normal length of counter line to provide a choice of two to three main meals and sweets is 7 to 10 m. With a single cash desk, the rate of meal service to the office employees is about six to nine meals a minute.

Free-flow systems

7.05 The 'free-flow' or multi-counter system is a development to increase the rate of self-service by adopting the 'supermarket' approach. Instead of one continuous counter, a number of small counters are installed each offering a different choice of meal. The employee can obtain a meal from any one of these, depending on the type of meal required and the number of other people waiting there, then leave the food servery through any one of several cash exits on route to the dining area. While increasing the speed of service, this arrangement is appropriate only for the largest premises since the layout of the counters and their associated circulation space occupies a considerable floor area.

Mechanical systems

7.06 Meals may be conveyed to the servery by mechanical equipment such as rotating turntables or carousels which together serve as the display counter. This method has some applications in serving snacks and cold meals but is usually less satisfactory for hot meals.

Collection of used tableware

7.07 This is usually the most difficult problem in catering operations and lack of organisation and planning can be unhygienic and lead to unsightly congestion. Alternative arrangements include:

1 Trolleys collecting the used dishes from the tables and conveying these to the dishwashing area.
2 Self-clearance—the employees taking their trays and used dishes to collection points.

To facilitate trolley collection, it is essential that the tables are arranged in rows with adequate space between the rows and at each end to allow for both trolley and customer circulation. The route to the dishwashing area must be short and unobstructed, **10**.

Self-clearance of tables is not likely to be satisfactory unless the users are familiar with the system. The design of the receiving area for used trays and dishes is a critical feature since this must be hygienic and convenient.

The most common arrangement is a bank of slotted spaces into which the loaded trays can be inserted from the canteen side and, subsequently, removed for washing up from the other. More elaborate systems involved the use of conveyors to take the used trays to more distant wash-up areas. Where disposable cups, plates and cutlery are used these will also need to be collected—either by self-clearance arrangements or by the table cleaning staff.

Planning

7.08 To avoid the risk of congestion or collision—particularly where trays are being carried and attention may be distracted—the routes followed by the employees entering and leaving the servery must not cross. Tray stands, cutlery stands, drinking water points and other requirements must be provided in conspicuous places where they are convenient for use but do not obstruct the circulation areas. To a large extent the routes taken by the employees using the servery and dining areas can be directed by the careful placing of screens and other visible obstacles and by the layout of the tables into groupings.

Seating area

7.09 In large establishments two of the primary considerations are to facilitate convenience and cleanliness, bearing in mind the fact that the seats and tables will probably be occupied two or three times in succession during the mid-day meal period. For this purpose laminated plastic table tops and similar coverings—such as vinyl—on the chairs are usually most practicable. Although moulded polypropylene chairs may be used, upholstered seating is generally more acceptable in this situation. The flooring may be in polyvinyl or composition tiles or be carpeted—depending on the level of sophistication desired.

7.10 The layout of the dining room has to take into account two, apparently conflicting, needs:

1 To ensure that the area is used to provide the maximum seating capacity while allowing sufficient corridor spaces for access to and from the tables, including space for trolleys where used and
2 To provide a suitable décor which will provide a relaxing contrast to the work environment, **10**.

The first may be obtained by arranging tables in regular rows while an appropriate atmosphere can be created by the use of dividers, screens and other design features to relieve the monotony of such a layout. Vacation of seats in

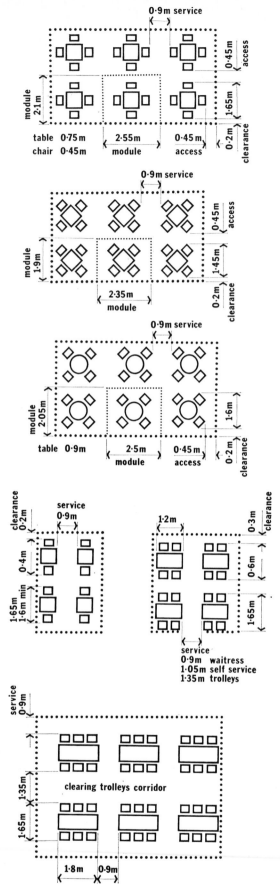

10 *Module dimensions for various seat groupings around rectangular and circular tables with aisle spaces for: waitress service; self-service; trolleys for table clearance. (Reproduced from 'Restaurant planning and design')*

11 *Example of staff catering facilities based on use of frozen foods needing minimum preparation. Equipment installed by Oliver Toms Ltd. (Reproduced from 'Principles of catering design')*

the dining room may be encouraged by providing a coffee lounge.

Waitress service

7.11 Waitress service is operated from a counter similar to that used in self-service but relatively simple in design. This is normally screened from view and has no merchandising value. Provision may be made for some of the serving operations, for example, pouring beverages, to be done by the waitress. Space is required for used dishes and this is most convenient before the serving counter and adjacent to the dishwashing area.

8 Food preparation and storage

8.01 Careful planning of the arrangements for delivery of food and for the removal of food waste and débris is necessary. This usually involves access and turning space for the delivery and refuse vehicles, an unloading area, checking and weighing facilities for food deliveries and provision for the storage of refuse awaiting collection.

8.02 Storage rooms for food must be near to the kitchen and, if this is not at ground level, consideration should be given to the installation of a goods lift to transport food and equipment, etc, to and from the stores. The types and sizes of food storage areas required depend again on the catering policy. Size is dictated by the number of meals to be served each day measured against the frequency of food deliveries, **11**. Types of food storage are shown in table III.

Table III Types of food storage

Store rooms	Foods
Vegetable store	Fresh vegetables, salads and fruit
Dry goods store	Dehydrated, canned, bottled and packaged foods
Chilled store	Perishable items—meat, eggs, dairy products, etc
Deep-freeze store	Frozen food items stored more than 3 to 7 days

Both chilled and deep-freeze storage must be refrigerated to maintain temperatures of about 3 to 5°C (chilled food) and −18 to −10°C (deep-frozen food). The relative sizes of the storage areas depends on the nature of the food. If, for example, the catering is based mainly on pre-cooked frozen food, a large coldroom or refrigerator is required but other storage can be reduced to the minimum.

9 Preparation and cooking of meals

9.01 The same considerations which determine storage requirements apply to the preparation and cooking sections of the kitchen. In most modern office buildings, where space is at a premium, the tendency is to use frozen food because of the cost and complications of large-scale meal preparation on the premises. This is particularly so in the case of staff shortages.

9.02 Food preparation equipment includes sinks for various purposes, benches, tables, utensils, and machinery to facilitate the routine work, such as mixing, weighing, mincing, chipping and slicing **12**. Modern kitchens now use forced-air convection ovens, microwave ovens, high-intensity infra-red heaters, grillers, deep fat fryers, and other sophisticated equipment for speed and ease of control.

9.03 The kitchen area normally requires heavy engineering services—three-phase electricity, gas mains, cold drinking water and domestic hot-water supplies, waste water connections and drainage (including grease traps where necessary), a high level of illumination, space heating and ventilation. The latter must include a high rate of extraction over the cooking, dishwashing and servery areas with provision for grease filters and damper controls. Handwashing facilities to comply with the Food Hygiene

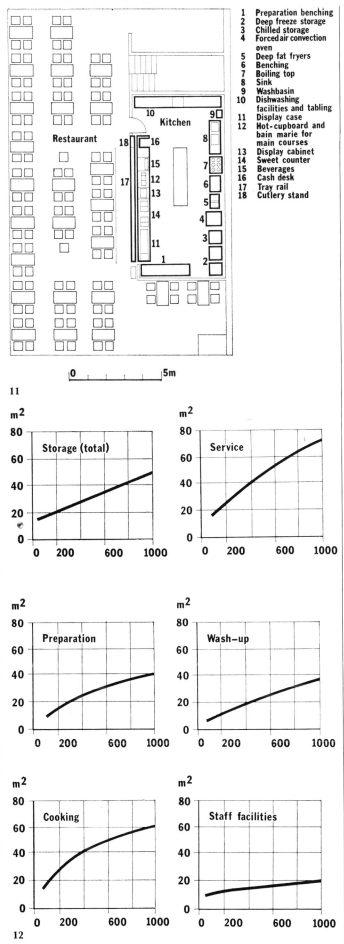

1 Preparation benching
2 Deep freeze storage
3 Chilled storage
4 Forced air convection oven
5 Deep fat fryers
6 Benching
7 Boiling top
8 Sink
9 Washbasin
10 Dishwashing facilities and tabling
11 Display case
12 Hot-cupboard and bain marie for main courses
13 Display cabinet
14 Sweet counter
15 Beverages
16 Cash desk
17 Tray rail
18 Cutlery stand

11

m² Storage (total), Service, Preparation, Wash-up, Cooking, Staff facilities

most common form of construction for large-scale operations because of their durability but laminated plastic sheeting on walls and plastic floor coverings, including epoxy resin surfaces, may be used as appropriate.

10 Dishwashing

10.01 In the kitchen area, some provision must be made for pan and utensil washing and in small catering units this may also serve for washing up tableware. In larger installations, the wash-up area is usually separated from the kitchen to reduce the effect of noise and splashing on the other areas. A semi- or fully-automatic dishwashing machine is almost always installed—its size and complexity being determined by requirements—and needs water, drainage and, often, ventilation connections.

10.02 Sufficient table or bench surface for piling used dishes, scraping off food débris and loading the machine must be provided while, at the other side, more surface is needed for unloading, draining and drying before removal. In most cases, the clean dishes can be loaded directly onto trolleys for transport back to the servery for re-use.

11 Storage of utensils and linen

11.01 A room or cupboard space must be provided for the storage of table and cooking utensils, cloths and other stocks. As well as the items in use, a similar quantity is usually kept in reserve as replacements. Separate storage is needed for cleaning materials and equipment.

11.02 The number of catering staff needed to operate even a simple service is normally at least one for each 40 meals served and may be double this number where there is part waitress service and shift work. Suitable lavatory and changing facilities for the catering staff must be provided and, although it is sometimes practicable to combine these requirements with the general facilities provided for the office staff, a separate changing area, with lockers, is usually necessary.

12 General

The design of catering and canteen facilities for offices is a subject which requires particular attention to practical details. This summary outlines the points to be considered in the preliminary planning stages. For more specific design requirements reference should be made to the publications listed below.

12 *Space requirements in a conventional kitchen for storage, preparation, cooking and service of food, dishwashing and staff facilities. Areas based on numbers of meals served at lunchtime. If food is delivered ready prepared for use, area needed for storage, final preparation and cooking is reduced by 50 to 60 per cent. (Reproduced from 'Principles of catering design')*

Bibliography

Directory of members 1973-74. Catering Equipment Manufacturers Association, London, 1973. £5·25
Annual survey of canteen prices, costs and subsidies. The Industrial Society, London, 1973. £4·00
LAWSON, F. R., Principles of catering design. The Architectural Press, London, 1973. £9·25
LAWSON, F. R., Restaurant planning and design. The Architectural Press, London, The Whitney Library, New York (as Designing Commercial Food Facilities), 1973. £9·25. Van Nostrand Reinhold, New York
MEDLIK, S., Profile of the hotel and catering industry. Heinemann, London, 1972. £4·00 (paperback £2·00).

(General) Regulations must be provided for the employees.
9.04 The constructional surfaces of the kitchen must resist mechanical damage, frequent cleaning with strong detergents, heat, steam and condensation. All internal surfaces must be well insulated and sealed against water vapour. Glazed wall tiles and quarry floor tiling are still the

Section 7: Office facilities

Hygiene facilities

COLIN CAVE discusses the factors which influence the provision of hygiene facilities and rest rooms and the fixtures and equipment which should be provided in them.

1 Provision of hygiene facilities

1.01 The following factors will affect a decision to provide centralised or dispersed hygiene facilities or a combination of the two:

1 length and directness of route to the facilities for users;

2 total numbers of males and females to be provided for and the size of the office area they occupy;

3 the possibility of the relative or total numbers of male and female users changing;

4 the limitations on future re-arrangement of office activities, especially if certain activities/users have hygiene facilities provided *en suite*, eg directors' suite, boardrooms, reception and waiting areas, rest rooms, eating and recreation areas;

5 occupation of the building by more than one firm and the possibilities of letting space in varying amounts and shapes, eg entire floor or floors, self-contained suites, a room or rooms; to what extent shared facilities are possible or satisfactory and who will be responsible for their maintenance, supply and cleaning;

6 economies from grouping serviced facilities and additional costs for isolated facilities.

Legal requirements

1.02 The Offices, Shops and Railway Premises Act 1963 lays down minimum standards for the provision of lavatory facilities. However, it should be noted that these are minimal and some authorities recommend different and better standards.[1]

Water closets men

1.03 The legal minimum for men (Offices, Shops and Railway Premises Act (OSRP), chapter 41, sections 9 and 10) is shown in table I.

Table I Legal minimum of water closets for men

Number of men	Number of water closets	Number of urinal stalls
1–15	1	
16–20	1	1
21–30	2	1
31–45	2	2
46–60	3	2
61–75	3	3
76–90	4	3
91–100	4	4
Over 100	4	4
		plus 1 closet for every 25 persons (or fractions of 25) in excess of 100 Every fourth additional closet may be replaced by a urinal

Water closets women

1.04 For women (and for men where urinals are not provided), the legal minimum is shown in table II.

Table II Legal minimum of water closets for women

Numbers regularly employed at any time	Number of water closets
1–15	1
16–30	2
31–50	3
51–75	4
76–100	5
Over 100	5 plus one additional closet for 25 persons in excess of 100 (a fraction of 25 counts as 25)

Wash basins

1.05 The Offices, Shops and Railways Premises Act 1963 requires washing facilities to be provided on the scale shown in table III (where there is no exemption from the requirement concerning running water). Section 10 requires hot and cold running water, soap and towels or other means of drying.

Table III Scale of washing facilities to be provided

Numbers regularly employed at any one time (or where separate accommodation is required for each sex the number of males or females)	Number of washbasins to be provided
1-15	1
16-30	2
31-50	3
51-75	4
76-100	5
Over 100	5 plus 1 basin for every 25 persons (or fraction of 25) in excess of 100

Where troughs or washing fountains are provided instead of basins, 2ft of length of a trough, if rectangular, or 2ft of the circumference of a washing fountain or circular or oval trough, counts as one wash-basin for purposes of the scale.

2 Space requirements

2.01 For men allow 0·32 m² a person for wc and urinal accommodation and 0·12 m² a person for handwashing accommodation. If these are combined, then 0·33 m² may be sufficient.

For women allow 0·3 m² a person for combined wc and handwashing accommodation. The minimum space allowed for a wc cubicle is $1 \times 0·8$ m, but $1·83 \times 0·9$ m is more usual and offers far easier access.

Rough guide

2.02 As a guide: each water closet occupies 1·67 m²; each urinal occupies 0·929 m²; and each wash-basin occupies 0·743 m².

These areas do not include outer walls, lobby allowance, and so on, but the urinal and wash-basin areas include space for user to stand.

2.03 Space should be allowed for vending machines, incinerators and waste bins (see drying and miscellaneous equipment under 4·05 and 4·06 below).

2.04 Arrangements must be made for hanging up or otherwise accommodating personal clothing not worn during working hours and working clothes not taken home. In each case, such arrangements as are reasonably practicable must be made for drying clothing (OSRP section 12).

3 Disabled persons

3.01 Disabled persons require special provision. Details are given in *Designing for the disabled* (see bibliography), but to summarise, wheelchair access to both the lavatory area and the cubicle, and a means for a disabled person to hoist himself from the wheelchair on to the fitting must be provided.

4 Equipment

4.01 *Urinals:*
Can be slab, stall or basin types made of porcelain, stainless steel or plastic with visible or concealed cisterns. Provide ashtrays. Special floor treatment for slab and stall types may be needed. Allow adequate access for concealed cistern.

4.02 *Wcs:*
Can be floor mounted or wall hung and have visible or concealed cisterns.

Provide adequate access for concealed cistern. Check partition strength for wall-hung wc.

4.03 *Wc cubicles:*
a in-situ (brick/block, wood plasterboard);
b prefabricated (metal, plastic, wood, terrazzo).
Provide ashtrays, toilet roll holder, (lavatory brush holder), coat hook. Compare b for cost, partition thickness, cleaning hindrance at wall and floor strength and durability.

4.04 *Washbasins:*
a individual basin;
b range of basins;
c hand spray basin;
d fountains and troughs.
Wall mounted taps aid cleaning and basin replacement. An individual basin is easier to replace than one in a range. Some form of vanitory unit may be provided for women (it may be a separate facility). A soap holder or dispenser is necessary.

4.05 *Drying equipment:*
a personal towels;
b cloth roller towel dispenser;
c paper towel dispenser;
d hot air dryers;
e mirrors.
With a and b, a laundering service is required; c requires regular replenishment; d needs regular servicing to avoid inconvenient breakdowns (NB some models are hand dryers only). With b and d, one unit should be provided to 2-3 basins. Used paper towel receptacles are required. Allow adequate-size mirrors for short and tall people and locate away from basins.

4.06 *Other facilities:*
a sanitary towel vending machine;
b sanitary towel disposal incinerators;
c contraceptive vending machine;
d soap, handcream and barrier cream dispensers;
e waste bins;
f clothes-hanging provision.
Replenishment of a is required. For b gas is most efficient, but there may be no other requirement for gas in many parts of a building; servicing is also required. For used paper towels receptacles may be needed. Means of disposal for sanitary towels are required where more than ten females are employed.

5 Cleaning and maintenance requirements

5.01
1 Wall and floor surfaces—hardwearing, impervious and easy to clean with corners and angles coved.
2 Trapped outlet in floor to assist cleaning.
3 Electric socket outlet outside wet area.

5.02 The regulations require that lavatories should not be located within spaces where persons other than attendants are working, nor must access be directly from such spaces unless effective mechanical ventilation discharging directly into the open air is provided.

6 Rest rooms

6.01 Rest rooms are not a statutory requirement but are generally provided in single-tenancy and custom-built buildings. They are used for short periods of time by people who are temporarily unwell. Their location is not critical, apart from a need to be away from major sources of noise. Where no full-time nursing attendant is provided, some awareness of other people should be possible to avoid the occupant feeling that he has been forgotten. Some means of contacting people should be provided.

6.02 Lighting (electric and daylight), heating and ventilation should be easily and obviously controllable by the room occupant.

6.03 In very large offices, separate rest rooms for males and females may be necessary. Males and up to 100 females need one couch. Where there are over 100 females present an additional couch will be required. (A very large switchboard may necessitate a separate rest room for telephonists.) In the case of multi-occupancy office buildings agreement will have to be obtained as to who will be responsible for maintaining the rest room.

6.04 Where full-time or part-time professional medical staff are provided (doctor, nurse, etc) proper facilities will be required as well as or instead of those outlined. Stretcher access will be required from the rest room, possibly using lifts, to ambulance access.

Civil Service scale of provision

6.05 Of all office-occupying organisations in the UK the Civil Service probably has the most codified standards. In the Civil Service standards and provisions for first aid rooms are calculated on the basis of staff numbers to give the following scale of provision.

Buildings with over 2000 staff: normally within $37 \cdot 2$ m² in two rooms plus a treatment room and a separate lavatory and wc.

Between 1001 and 2000 staff: $23 \cdot 2$ m² in two rooms plus a treatment room, a rest room and a special lavatory and wc.

Between 501 and 1000 staff: $18 \cdot 6$ m² divided by a screen into separate treatment area and rest area. Normally sited close to the women's lavatory.

Between 41 and 500 staff: $11 \cdot 2$ m² combined treatment and rest room. This may, if necessary, be provided as a portion of a room partitioned to the ceiling. Normally sited close to the women's lavatory.

Between 10 and 40 staff: $5 \cdot 6$ m² which may if necessary be provided as a 'screened-off' portion of a room.

Less than 10 staff. First aid box with chair and leg rest.

7 Equipment for first aid or rest rooms

7.01 The following equipment may be required:

1 divan or couch;
2 bedside table;
3 easy chair;
4 upright chair;
5 first-aid cabinet—this is a statutory requirement under the Shops and Offices Act Chapter 41;
6 linen cupboard (where a proper bed is provided, arrangements will be needed for laundering of linen, otherwise blankets only will suffice. Towels will require laundering in any case);
7 toilet facilities should be provided, preferably integral with the rest of the room, otherwise a washbasin should be provided within the room. Drinking water should be available;
8 telephone or other device;
9 screen, where two couches are provided.

Bibliography

1 *Shops, Offices and Railway Premises Act 1963,* HMSO.
2 GOLDSMITHS S., *Designing for the disabled,* London, 1967, RIBA.
3 McCULLOUGH W., *Physical working conditions,* London, 1973, Gower Press [(E2p)], £1·75.
4 McCULLOUGH W., *Lavatories and washrooms in factories and offices,* 1966, Industrial Society, Library, 48 Bryanston Square, London W1 £1·75.

Section 7: Office facilities

Automatic data processing

Computer rooms are an important part of many modern offices. GEOFFREY HUTTON describes the layout, environment and services required for automatic data processing equipment.

1 Introduction

1.01 The size of computers and computer peripherals varies widely between manufacturers and for this reason no attempt is made in this study to categorise the sizes of equipment or operating spaces. Those items of equipment which are mainly electronic (eg central processers, memories) are tending to become progressively smaller. What once required an area of 10 square metres can now be accommodated in one side of a 450 mm drawer. Those items of equipment which are mainly mechanical or involve fixed dimensions (eg punches, chain printers, keyboards) have an optimum size but nevertheless tend to vary widely between manufacturers, depending on cabinet design and combination with other equipment. A further tendency is for small computing equipment to be combined with other business machines (eg the visual record computer) and with various types of terminal to be used in normal offices. Large computer installations should be regarded as a special design problem requiring investigation of the machinery and process with the consultants and manufacturers concerned.

1.02 A computer installation consists of a central processer, back-up stores and input and output devices, **1**. All these items are normally contained within one room, unless the installation is very large or computer time is shared by means of telecommunication. Often, when computer time is shared, input/output devices and controls are separated from each other for ease of use and data security.

Additional areas are required for data preparation, storage for magnetic media files, storage of consumables and maintenance. Normal staff and office facilities, and external communications, are also required but do not generally need special consideration.

1.03 Small computers of the desk-top type are not particularly sensitive to temperature and will operate in a normal office environment, **2**. They are, however, a source of heat, and, in small rooms, can produce rather high temperatures.

As desk-top computers do not require a controlled environment, parts of this data sheet will be inapplicable to them. However, they have the same problems as the larger machines with regard to peripherals, data preparation, consumables and safety.

1 *A complex multi-computer installation : IBM*   *Information Service, Havant, Hampshire.*

2 Relationship between spaces and functions

2.01 A data-processing installation generally has two main areas. One is for the computer and the equipment which is connected to it. The other contains the preparation equipment which can work independently of the computer.

2.02 The on-line equipment requires two adjacent subsidiary areas. The first is a maintenance area, 25 to 40 per cent of the computer equipment area. This room should be at the same temperature and humidity as the computer room. The supply and maintenance areas should be at the same level as the computer room to allow easy access by trolley. Computer manufacturers will specify benches and any power points required for the use of service engineers. It is preferable to deliver new or replacement equipment to the maintenance area rather than direct to the computer room. If a lift is required, it should be at least 2 tons in capacity. The second area is for storage of stationery and tapes for the peripherals: it need not be so closely controlled for temperature or humidity. Shelving should be sufficiently strong and not too high, as both paper tapes and lineprinter paper in bulk are heavy. Floor loadings must be taken into account. Access to this area for restocking should be direct, not through the computer area.

3 On-line equipment

Power requirements

3.01 A mini-computer consisting of a central processing unit (cpu), high-speed punch and reader visual display unit (vdu) and Teletype would require a supply of about 2 kVA, single phase, at 240 volts (less than a single 13 amp supply). A larger computer with, for example, cpu, 246k memory, 15 magnetic-tape handlers, 10 magnetic-disc handlers, various input/output devices and a remote terminal could use a 75 to 100 kVA 3 phase supply. Allowing for 50 per cent future expansion installations over 700 kVA would require inputs of over 1000 kVA initially. Obviously, the scope of the equipment to be installed must be known in order to assess the power required. It must be remembered that a large proportion of this power is dissipated as heat to be removed by the air-conditioning.

Environment

3.02 The following conditions provide the optimum environment for most equipment:
temperature, $21 \pm 3°C$;
relative humidity, (RH) 50 per cent ± 10 per cent.
Normally the equipment will continue to operate satisfactorily within the limits 15 to 32°C and 20 to 80 per cent RH with a maximum wet-bulb temperature of 25°C. At no time should the temperature fall below 10°C and standby heating must be provided when the computer installation is shut down, for example, for holidays. Heating should also ensure that the room never reaches dew-point.

Layout of units

3.03 The computer manufacturer will very often be willing to advise on layout of the computer room. The following points should be noted when making initial plans.
1 Magnetic-media handlers are usually grouped together along the wall, with storage racks adjacent. Fluorescent lights should not be too near these items.
2 Easy access to all peripherals should be possible from the control terminal which should be shaded from direct light.
3 Visual display units must be arranged to prevent reflections in the screen from interfering with viewing at the operator's eye level.

4 Paper-tape readers/punches must have space for bins to receive tape as it is processed.
5 There should be clear desk tops for spreading programs and data-checking.
6 Lineprinters normally require space on all sides for servicing and paper feed.

4 Off-line equipment

4.01 The equipment used for preparing input media for the computer requires a room at least as large in area as the computer room, operated on the same principle as a typing pool. It is often necessary to plan for twice as many machines and operators as might at first appear, as it is usual to verify input by re-keying, the second machine checking for differences between the new and original information.
Keyboard machines include paper-tape punches, card punches, magnetic-tape machines and magnetic-disc machines. Optical character readers take OCR typeface as input.

4.02 All these machines consume between 0·5 and 2·5 kVA single phase. If the room is not controlled to provide the same conditions as the computer room, there must be a temporary storage area within the computer room to allow output from the data preparation room to be acclimatised. This area should be capable of storing approximately three to five days' output. Punch mechanisms are noisy and

Table I Typical weights of paper consumables

Type and number	Size of carton (mm)	Weight kg	Density kg/m³ (in cartons)
Paper-tape rolls (10)	500 × 200 × 140	7	500
Lineprinter paper	510 × 290 × 150	11	530
Telex rolls (12)	350 × 250 × 230	11	485
Punch cards (10 000)	420 × 370 × 200	25	800

Table II Power requirements

Selection of on-line equipment

	kVA at 200-240 V	
Central processing unit	3	
Remote control terminal	3·5	3 phase
265 K memory	7	
Magnetic-disc storage unit	2·5	
Magnetic-tape storage unit	1	
Paper-tape reader	0·5 to 2·5	
Paper-tape punch	0·5 to 2·5	single phase
Punch-card reader	2·5	
Lineprinter	3·0	
Teletype	0·5	

2 *A mini-computer, with magnetic tape handler, operating successfully in the relatively dusty environment of a classroom.*

sound-absorbing surfaces are recommended. There should be enough room between machines (not less than 1·5 m) to allow access for trolleys with consumables and output media.

5 Construction

Floors

5.01 Because of the large number of electrical connections between the cpu and the peripherals and power supply to every piece of equipment, all but very small installations require a suspended floor. This allows for the tidy connection of devices, and often also acts as a plenum chamber for supplying cooling air to equipment through grilles. These floors are designed as a grid of removable squares over the whole area. The suspended floor (and the structural floor) carry quite high loads which should be allowed for. The weight of trolleys carrying consumables to the equipment, and of maintenance trolleys removing equipment for servicing and repair, is also critical.

5.02 The floor panels should be non-combustible, neither abrasive nor abradable (to reduce dust), and acoustically dead; **3** illustrates the main types of floor construction used. The floor types can be grouped as those in which:
1 the panels are supported only at the corners;
2 the panels are supported along two parallel edges;
3 the panels are supported along all edges.
The first type has the most rigid panels, requiring the least support and leaving the void below the floor relatively clear. The others use lighter panels at the expense of freedom for services below the floor.

5.03 In choosing the required type of suspended floor, the following points should be considered.
1 Strength should be checked for the anticipated load from equipment and stationery. For general floor design, an evenly distributed load of 3·5 kN/m² is recommended in BS:CP 3: Chapter V: Part 1: 1967, although it should be borne in mind that high concentrations of equipment or stationery may lead to very high local loadings of up to 50 kN/m². In addition, the adjustable feet on equipment may cause punching stresses on the suspended panels.
2 Type of structural floor, and its surface condition.
3 Extent of initial cable runs.
4 Minimum acceptable height specified by the computer manufacturer to accomodate the recommended minimum radii for supply cables to units.
5 Frequency of changes to equipment.
6 How well the panels are sealed when underfloor cavity used as air-conditioning plenum.
7 Ease of lifting panels, and cutting holes for cables and the passage of air.

Walls

5.04 The walls and floors enclosing a large data-processing area should desirably form a compartment isolated from external fire. Within the computer suite, partitions should be non-combustible with a low surface spread of flame. The computer room itself may incorporate sound-absorbing wall surfaces, if required. It is best to isolate visitors by providing a viewing room, with windows overlooking the computer room. In installations where security is important data may be passed through to the computer operators by two-way drawers. All openings in walls should be sealed as well as possible against dust and noise. Double glazing should be used in any external windows to prevent condensation. All surfaces should be neither combustible nor abradable.

Ceilings

5.05 Ceilings are often suspended; ideally there should be a clear height of at least 3 m, with a minimum height of

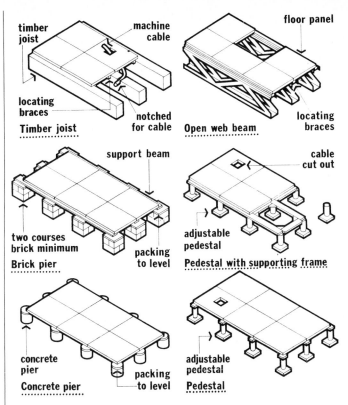

3 *Various types of suspended floor*

2·4 m. They should be sound-absorbing. They are often used as a plenum for the air-conditioning and can also accommodate recessed light fittings. If a suspended ceiling is used, temperature and fire sensors should be fitted. The acoustic panels should be non-combustible and should not produce dust.

6 Environment

Air-conditioning

6.01 The strict environmental control required by all but mini-computers, and the fact that computers produce heat in proportion to their power consumption, means that air-conditioning is a necessity. Some mini-computers in small rooms require forced ventilation or, preferably, refrigeration plant, to keep room temperatures comfortable for operators in summer.

6.02 For larger installations, there are three main options for air-conditioning.
1 *Window-mounted units*. Used in smaller computer installations, these are self-contained units, fitted in windows or hung on external walls. They are of re-circulatory operation, acting as coolers and driers. They also require humidifiers if the air is too dry, and they do not carry out fine filtration. Fresh air should be supplied by an auxiliary fan with efficient filtration.
2 *Packaged units*. These are freestanding and can be located within the computer room or adjacent to it, working through the wall. When they are within the computer room, their size must be allowed for. They are similar to window units as regards filtration and humidification. Water-cooled versions obviously require continuous water supplies, and a cooling facility (outside the computer complex) if the water cannot be permitted to run to waste.
3 *Central plant*. Used for large installations and high heat loads. This system is the most efficient, as it is usually purpose-designed with either underfloor or through-ceiling supply of filtered air at the correct temperature and

humidity. However, a plant room and adequate facilities for cooling are required.

6.03 An air-conditioning system should be as flexible as possible, to allow for changes in requirements, especially when the computer installation expands.

Dust

6.04 Computer equipment, especially magnetic-tape handlers, is very susceptible to dust. Air filtration is essential, except for some of the small machines. The slight pressurisation caused by the air-conditioning keeps dust entry to a minimum, but washable anti-static mats should be provided at all doors to the computer centre to prevent dust from being carried in on shoes. The mats can be cleaned by specialist laundry services.

6.05 Air filtration, often part of the air-conditioning, should be to BS 2831, test duct no 2 (95 per cent efficiency at 5 microns).

Light

6.06 The artificial lighting should be even and to a level of 500 to 600 lux, with minimum glare.

If there is a natural light source, care should be taken that direct sunlight does not fall on any of the operating consoles, making it difficult to see indicator lights. Dustproof enclosed fluorescent fittings, giving a daylight colour, are the best light source.

Sound

6.07 Peripheral equipment in a computer room can be very noisy, especially high-speed paper-tape readers and punches, and lineprinters. Any sound-absorbing materials ahould be located in relation to these machines. Sound-absorbing materials should be non-combustible, and free from dust and loose fibres.

Because of the hard floor and machine surfaces, the level of sound absorption required must be provided by the ceiling and, possibly, by the wall surfaces.

Mini-computers in an office need acoustic screens round noisy peripherals, such as lineprinters, punches and readers, to help reduce sound levels.

7 Services

Power supplies

7.01 IBM computers, for example, require power supplies within the following limits:

3 phase 368 to 448 V (UK standard 400, 415)
1 phase 212 to 258 V (UK standard 220, 240, 250)
frequency 50 $\pm$0·5 Hz (UK standard)

7.02 Monitoring devices normally activate alarms at 2 per cent voltage and $\pm$0·1 of a cycle. They should give warnings in the computer room and the appropriate supervisor's office, but should not disconnect the supply to the computer. Although within the limits for some machines, 440 volts, 3 phase can cause problems with some computers. If the supply is 440 volts, the computer manufacturer should be consulted to check whether transformers are required. All electrical supply, through switchgear to the computer connection point, is normally the responsibility of the building owner, as well as power points adjacent to all peripheral equipment, either in the walls or under the floor.

7.03 A typical input switchgear arrangement is shown in **4**. The supply to this should be direct from the incoming mains, the computer manufacturer usually insisting on five-wire supply cable, separately insulated. On no account should conduit be used as an earth. The supply cable should allow for 1·5 to 1·75 times the initial connected load, for expansion of the computer system without the need to arrange a new supply. A single contactor must control the

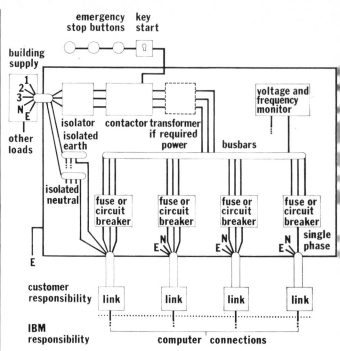

4 *Diagram of power connections required for an IBM computer*

supplies, with emergency 'off' buttons of the shrouded type located round the computer room. To restart, a key-operated system should be used and release of the 'off' button should not reconnect power. Fire alarms, electrical monitors and environmental monitors should not trip the power supplies off, but the use of a CO_2 fire-fighting system (sometimes called a carbon dump system) may be arranged to cut the power, as personnel will usually have no time to shut down the system themselves before evacuating the premises.

7.04 Where power cables cannot be arranged round the perimeter of the room within the floor void, care must be taken to see they do not run beneath other equipment.

Standby series

7.05 Computers are generally run on a double-shift basis for maximum return on the investment. Therefore, correct temperatures, humidity, filtration and power must be constant. The designer must consider the effect of failure to meet any of these requirements on the machine or operator.

7.06 Power failure is the most serious, as it affects all the services. Because of the problems caused to a large computer installation by sudden total loss of power, it is normal to have standby generating equipment. Emergency lighting must be supplied to enable the computer operators to complete the run or shut down the computer correctly, and for escape in an emergency. Large installations will continue to operate throughout power cuts and will have enough generating power to maintain air-conditioning and lighting. Such installations have standby equipment for all the services to allow for maintenance and failure.

8 Protection

8.01 In most buildings, the computer installations represent the greatest security risk because of the value both of the equipment itself and of the stored information. Therefore, it should be very well protected from fire occurring both inside and outside the area, loss through theft, vandalism and industrial espionage.

8.02 Even with every part of the structure non-combustible, a data-processing area is still a great fire risk. Paper tape, lineprinter paper and magnetic tape, in plastic storage cans, are used throughout the installation. Waste is also produced in large quantities, as information is updated. Magnetic tapes and discs are re-usable but scrap paper presents two problems. First, it is a fire hazard, collected as it is in large bins or trolley, and second, all printed output, issued while setting up a run or reorganising data, is a potential security risk. In an installation where security is a consideration, a shredder is required. Quantities of punchings from paper tape can be spilt when containers are emptied and this can fall through cracks between panels, with dust, to form a highly combustible layer on the structural floor. It should be removed with a vacuum cleaner at regular intervals to reduce fire hazards.

Fire

8.03 Modern solid-state equipment has a much better record for internal fire generation than older computer systems using valves. Manufacturers often incorporate heat-sensitive switches in high-risk units.

8.04 In some buildings, overhead sprinkler systems must be provided to satisfy insurance requirements. If the system includes the computer room, this should be on a separate circuit operated at very high local temperatures so that the water will not do more damage than the fire. Hand-operated extinguishers should be of the dry CO_2 type, with one close to each piece of equipment. It is normal to provide a central, fixed automatic CO_2 protection system for large computer installations, connected direct to each piece of equipment and/or as a sprinkler-type system. Because of the risk of asphyxiation, warning systems must be incorporated to give personnel time to get away before the gas is activated. The switches should be of the shrouded type, clearly labelled and preferably located beside the emergency power-off switches. It is unlikely that a normal computer shut-down routine is possible in the time between warning and operation of the gas, so automatic shut-down is acceptable, linked to the power-off circuits. Any electro-magnetic locks which could trap personnel should also be automatically released.

8.05 If possible, the data-processing department should be subdivided with fire-resisting partitions extending through suspended ceilings and floors. All doors should be fire-resisting or fire-check, self-closing: this also helps with control of temperature and dust. All constructional materials within the computer area should be non-combustible and care taken to prevent spread of fire through service ducts and within suspended ceilings and floors.

8.06 Care should be taken to prevent possible flooding of the computer room by fire-fighting operations on floors above. All smoke and heat detectors in ducts and other concealed spaces should show on a console the location of the sensor but should not activate the power-off contactor.

Security

8.07 In most large organisations, the computer room has a special security rating. Often the computer itself will be barred to all personnel except programmers and operators. This calls for additional partitioning and security doors. However, locks of the electro-magnetic type, operated by identity card, are not recommended close to magnetic tapes.

9 Installation

9.01 The computer suite should be finished and the air-conditioning operating for several days before the manufacturer installs the computer. Some manufacturers insist on a minimum of one week.

References

Computer installations: accommodation and fire precautions, Department of Trade and Industry, HMSO London, Revised edition, 1972

Fire protection for electronic data processing installations, BSCP 95/1970 British Standards Institution, London 1970

Technical services division notes available on request from Technical Services Division, Central Computer Agency, Civil Service Department, Old Street, London.

Electrics 74/75, London, The Electricity Council, 1972. pp 588, £4·00. Computer centres, pp 503-510.

Electrical Review, 28 November 1969, 'Design and installation of electrical services for computers', pp 793-804.

AGACE, J., 'Computer room preparation', *Electrical Supervisor*, August 1966, pp 207-211.

Installation planning booklet, IBM data processing systems, IBM (United Kingdom) Limited.

SECTION 8: MANAGING OFFICE SPACE

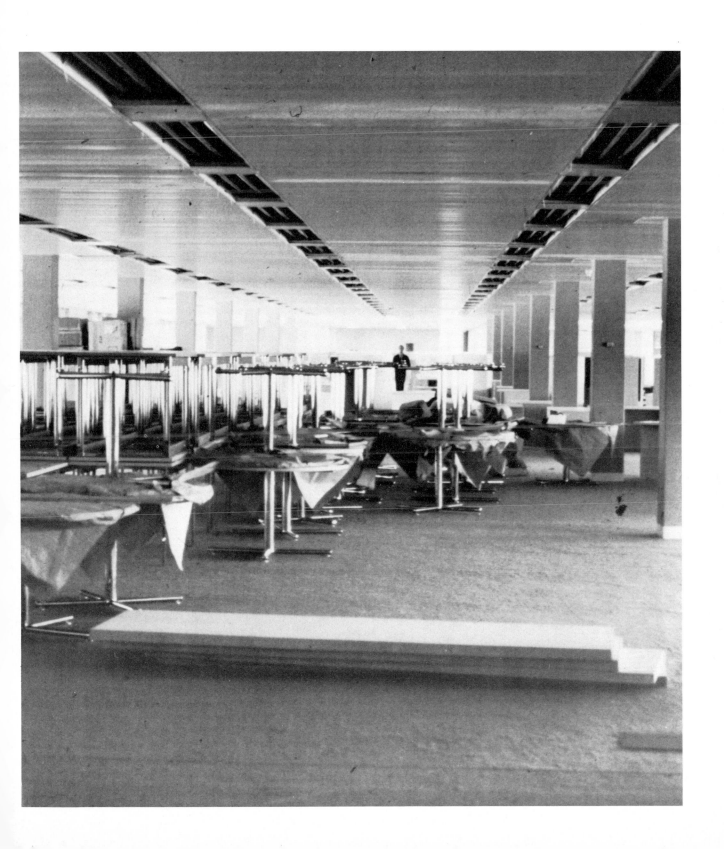

Section 8: Managing office space

Office furniture

Choosing a system of office furniture is an expensive and difficult decision. Over the last few years office furniture has changed dramatically, primarily as a consequence of the requirements of open office planning. LUIGI GIFFONE argues that more and more it is furniture and not walls which subdivide space. Increasingly the demands of different types of workplace are being met not by isolated items of furniture but by systems of interconnected parts.

1 Situations

1.01 Over the last few years the advent of office landscaping and the deep plan office space has resulted in quite new demands being made of internal walls and partitions and of office furniture systems. The differences between partitions and furniture have become increasingly blurred until we now have a situation where the furniture may be the partition and the partition part of the furniture.

While this may be easier for the architect, it creates problems for the furniture manufacturer in setting the limits of design specifications for any new product because he may have only a vague idea of the range of situations and spaces in which it will be used.

1 *So far, two different strains of office furniture have evolved (see para 4.05)*

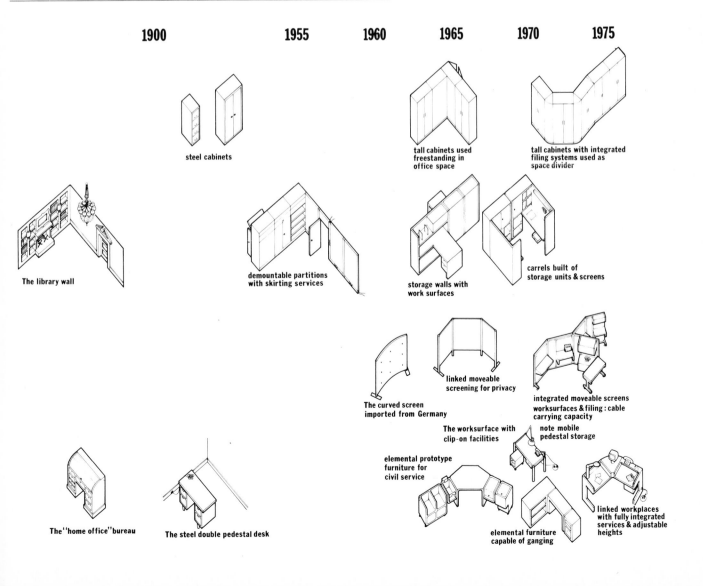

1900   1955   1960   1965   1970   1975

steel cabinets

tall cabinets used freestanding in office space

tall cabinets with integrated filing systems used as space divider

The library wall

demountable partitions with skirting services

storage walls with work surfaces

carrels built of storage units & screens

The curved screen imported from Germany

linked moveable screening for privacy

integrated moveable screens worksurfaces & filing : cable carrying capacity

The worksurface with clip-on facilities

note mobile pedestal storage

elemental prototype furniture for civil service

The "home office" bureau

The steel double pedestal desk

elemental furniture capable of ganging

linked workplaces with fully integrated services & adjustable heights

Table I Furniture ranges and potential arrangements

Range	Association and enclosure patterns						Properties — Storage provision					Display		Material					
	A	B	C	D	E	F	Full height	High level	Pedestal	Adjoining low	Mobile	Blackboard	Pinboard	Wood	Metal	Plastic	Filing systems available	Services integrated	Free standing units
	Isolated not enclosed	Clustered not enclosed	Ganged not enclosed	Isolated enclosed	Clustered enclosed	Ganged enclosed													
1 Abbess square one	●		●	●		●	●		●			●	●	●	●		●		●
2 Action Office	●		●	●	●	●	●	●	●	●	●	●	●	●	●	●		●	●
3 Intercraft Epsilon	●			●		●	●	●	●	●				●	●		●		●
4 Facit 80	●			●	●			●	●	●	●	●	●	●	●				
5 Fleximetric	●		●	●		●	●	●	●	●				●	●		●		●
6 Hille Office System	●		●	●		●	●	●	●	●	●			●	●			●	●
7 Lucas Inex	●			●	●			●	●	●	●			●	●				●
8 PU Work Station	●		●	●		●	●		●	●				●	●				●
9 MEP	●	●	●						●	●					●		●	●	●
10 Modulo 3	●		●	●		●	●		●			●	●	●	●	●			
11 Link 900	●		●	●		●	●	●	●	●				●	●		●	●	●
12 Plan System	●	●	●	●	●	●	●	●	●	●				●	●	●	●		●
13 Lucas Program	●	●	●	●	●	●	●	●	●	●					●				●
14 Richmond	●		●				●	●	●	●	●			●	●				●
15 Rymans Scope System	●		●				●	●	●	●	●			●				●	●
16 Stephens	●		●	●				●	●	●				●	●				●
17 Synthesis 45	●		●			●	●	●	●	●	●			●					●
18 NKR Team System	●		●	●	●	●	●	●	●			●	●	●	●			●	

Numbers refer to photographs on facing page

Deep and shallow space

1.02 In deep spaces there may be a need to provide some degree of enclosure without building artificially lit internal rooms. This may lead to the choice of furniture which includes some degree of screening. In shallow space where either small rooms or simple linear arrangements of furniture can be assumed, a need for screening is less likely.

Varying densities

1.03 In high density layouts there will be a strong need to put desks together to save space and to share working surfaces. But privacy may be critical and screening therefore essential. In low density layouts where ample space is available between desks, privacy can be provided by isolating workplaces.

Types of work

1.04 In some kinds of office, eg clerical or accounting offices, each workplace needs to be very closely related to the others because papers have to be passed or shared between workplaces. Close contact is essential. In other offices, the problem is the reverse, eg systems analysts require solitary working conditions for much of the time but occasionally require close contact between members of a project team around a group table.

1.05 All the possibilities cannot usefully be included here. In order to limit their number this chapter categorises the chosen furniture ranges into three levels of 'association', ie, the closeness required between one item of furniture and another to form a workplace or workplaces.

2 Categories and definitions

2.01 The three categories are:
Isolated—where the furniture forms a workplace quite separately from others.
Clustered—where a workplace is grouped with another or others to form a cluster.
Ganged—where adjoining workplaces are arranged in lines.

2.02 A whole range of new problems for the architect has also appeared, from 'where do lighting switches and power outlets go now the walls have disappeared?' to 'how much of a wall is this furniture system—and how much does it matter anyway?' The servicing problems are dealt with elsewhere in this book. This chapter deals mostly with the relationship between wall and furniture. A 'wall' may be anything which provides visual and acoustic isolation, from a freestanding mobile hospital type screen to a self-supporting unit carrying a desk and storage units. Providing it gives visual or acoustic isolation and comes as part of a furniture range, is constructed in such materials and available in such colours and style as are compatible with the remainder of the range, then it qualifies as a 'wall'. If it does not qualify, then the furniture range is described in the table as being one which 'does not enclose'; if it does, then as one which 'encloses'.

2.03 Combining the three conditions of association—isolated, clustered and ganged—with the two conditions of enclosure gives six different office furniture possibilities:

1

2

3

4

5

6

7

8

9

10

11

12

13

14

15

16

17

18

Isolated not enclosed **A**
Clustered not enclosed **B**
Ganged not enclosed **C**
Isolated enclosed **D**
Clustered enclosed **E**
Ganged enclosed **F**
Eighteen furniture systems have been examined (winter 1975) to see whether they can provide all these types of workplace.
Whether or not these ranges of furniture will meet requirements in these six categories is indicated in table I.
2.04 In addition, information is given in table I on: storage and display possibilities within each range; whether filing and document support systems are available from the manufacturers; whether any provision has been made for accommodating electrical wiring, power outlets and switches; whether all units are self-supporting or some support others, and of which materials each system is made.

3 Furniture selection

3.01 Assessing the right degree of association and enclosure required by an organisation is a matter of identifying the work patterns throughout the firm's structure.
3.02 The choice must also consider the 'fluidity' of this structure, in order to specify the degree of flexibility of the furniture system which is required to respond to the changes in layout, re-grouping, multiple use, etc.
3.03 The organisation's style and capacity of managing its environment and controlling its stock (investment and procurement policies, building maintenance, stocking and inventory systems, response to employees, feedback) are also important in the selection of a furniture system.
3.04 A high degree of user participation is also advisable in the selection process; test installations are a useful tool and *ad hoc* evaluation matrices can be prepared for filling in by various organisations' sample groups.
3.05 Recommending such care in selecting a furniture system may seem excessive but it should be viewed against the overall level of capital expenditure required and the far reaching effects it may have in running costs. The influence a furniture system can have on 'image' and employee morale and satisfaction are also not to be forgotten.

4 The future of office furniture

4.01 We have taken a synoptic view of the present furniture market and have attempted a typological classification of furniture functions and pointed out some important criteria for selection. Let us now consider the developments the product is likely to undergo in the future.
4.02 Two mainstreams of systems development can be immediately identified.
4.03 Desk and pedestal (equates with separation and individual filing).
4.04 Wall and cupboard (equates with separation and group filing).
4.05 The evolution of the two strains to this date is better described graphically, **1**. The two different levels of flexibility, at individual and group levels, should be associated with these two strains. The user's freedom to choose work surface height and orientation, access to filing, positions and level of lighting should prevail at desk level. The planner should be solely responsible for all changes in layout of the wall and cupboard elements to mitigate the effects of unwarranted alterations by users.
4.06 It is to be expected that these mainstreams will more and more merge producing fully integrated modular systems. At this point a third line of functions is already intertwining itself in the process: services, such as lighting,

power, telephone, video and printing terminals and the ever growing paraphernalia of the technology of communications must be catered for because their requirements may affect so deeply the nature and scale of the resulting hybrid in the future that we might well be referring to it as megafurniture or microarchitecture.
4.07 The repercussions of this increasing services penetration will undoubtedly affect the design of the office building. Once the function of distributing power to groups of work stations (rather than to each one individually) is satisfied by the megafurniture then the floor or ceiling power grid of the building shell could be spaced out. The same applies to lighting; extensive use of task light at work stations could allow a welcome and economical reduction of the general lighting levels. The actual progress of this evolution may be accelerated or slowed down by the willingness of the furniture industry to think and plan in architectural terms and to enter the field of building systems, as well as the ability of the architect to accept this intrusion and take the opportunity of looking at his building as a shell designed to house such scenery.
4.08 This evolution should produce savings in both shell and scenery: on one side the building could afford to revert to a less finished role of infrastructure, leaving the finishes to the scenery. This seems more appropriate for the very reason that in its new scale, the furniture has a more immediate visual impact on the user, and because taste and fashions change at a rate attuned more to the life span of furniture than that of a building.
On the other hand more sophisticated work-stations do not necessarily mean more expensive furniture if planning and modulating are thought of in terms of low technology, mass production, and if existing subsystems (ie power distribution ducting, light tracks) are cannibalised from other industries. Furthermore those cosmetic finishes inherited from the building could be more economically produced and more precisely controlled if mass produced within the furniture instead of being made to order in a labour consuming way as at present in the building industry.

5 Conclusions

5.01 It can not be emphasised enough that it is necessary to face the subject of furniture much more systematically. Management should do its homework in analysing, with or without outside help, its organisational needs and patterns of work. The architect should extend his professional interest from the building down to the furniture or, perhaps better from the furniture up to the building. He should ensure that the scenery that will fill his building will be well planned and well selected. Careful thought about scenery will inevitably influence the design of the building shell.

Section 8: Managing office space

Moving into an office

Moving into new office accommodation is sometimes a traumatic experience for all involved. JOHN WORTHINGTON discusses methods by which the move can be made easy. Explanation and staff consultation is essential. However, it should not be forgotten that the programming, design and revision of office layouts is a continuous process.

1 Introduction: Problems encountered during the move

1.01 Users moving into office accommodation can have a devastating impact on the way it is used unless they have been clearly briefed. The change of office is a traumatic experience and staff uncertainty may quickly lead to criticism of all aspects that are different from what existed before. Such criticisms are often concerned with organisational changes or transitory inconveniences due to settling in, and do not necessarily indicate fundamental objections to the design.

Nevertheless, at the time of the move the designer faces a number of human and organisational problems which, unless they are planned for, can create lasting antagonism to the new environment. The following are typical of the underlying causes of criticisms.

Changes in personal status

1.02 Personnel may be nervous, uncertain and antagonistic about moving. A move often entails not only a change in working conditions, but also a new relationship between home and office with new transportation systems to master and new routines to develop. The office move tends not only to expose those who have built up positions above their status but also to provide the opportunity for others to empire-build with the result that when they move into new accommodation they voice unjustified dissatisfaction.

Changes in organisational structure

1.03 A change of office invariably precipitates a change in the structure of the organisation. Redundant positions, inefficient practices and more direct lines of communication become obvious during reorganisation and changes of routine.

Concern for and understanding of user requirements

1.04 At the workplace level, individual users know most about their own requirements and are at their most vocal. In offices, unlike other building types, there is a very close involvement of the individual with his environment since most members of the firm have their own individual workplaces. On move-in day, layout plans become a series of personal territories to be defended and adapted to individual work styles.

2 Explaining the move

2.01 It is never too early to inform all levels of staff of any proposal to move or change the accommodation layout. At the early stages of a space planning programme rumours abound and great uncertainty may be felt by staff faced with the possibility of having to change their work patterns and maybe their homes. Staff should not hear of such proposals through unofficial channels. Much greater co-operation and goodwill will be developed if they are informed through gradual consultation and explanation.

2.02 As he will be seen in the offices and will be interviewing staff, a consultant's role should be fully understood by those who may be affected by it. To alleviate rumours and create confidence any consultant who is appointed to advise on office organisation should advise management to inform all staff of:

his own appointment and terms of reference;
the objectives of the project and the method of work;
the timetable of work and, if a move is planned, the proposed location of the new accommodation.

2.03 From the first stage it is a good idea if a member of staff is given responsibility for liaison between the consultants, members of staff and management. Eventually it may be advisable for the liaison officer to become accommodation manager with responsibilities for planning the move-in and managing the space afterwards. To support him and to ensure that the views of all parties are being considered a project team may be set up with:

a representative from each of the major departments;
a representative of the staff liaison committee;
a member of the client's own in-house estates division.

2.04 For ease of decision-making the project team should be no larger than eight to 10 people. On large projects some of the members may help consultants on survey work and liaise with the departments, on a full-time or part-time basis. The function of the team is to work with the consultant, architect, space planner or designer to reach decisions on matters such as the location of groups, workplace requirements and furniture, which can then be presented to senior management for approval. The value of such a team is that it is familiar with the proposals and can brief members of staff before move-in. The project team may eventually become responsible for decision making on the utilisation of space during the life of the organisation.

2.05 To assist the project team it may be desirable to arrange presentations and visits during the design process and help keep staff informed, table 1.

Initial design concept presentation
2.06 The design concept should be presented to staff in the early stages of the design process as soon as the initial programme has been developed. Depending on the size of the organisation either group heads or all members of staff should have the objectives and concept of the layout explained to them, preferably using illustrations of similar installations. Every opportunity should be given for questions to be asked and uncertainties aired at this stage so that fears may be alleviated. It is important that a concensus on the method of layout is reached at this stage if the design concept is not to be eroded when the move takes place.

Visualisation of design concepts
2.07 Many members of staff may find it difficult to visualise the environmental implications of deep space. If such space is being proposed visits may be organised to create a better understanding. Before making these trips, staff should be thoroughly briefed on what aspects of the layout they should look at, how to evaluate it and how to visualise their own organisation in similar premises. Wherever possible the consultant should have visited the examples beforehand and have basic statistics available on space allocations, and average densities for making subsequent comparisons. He should prepare a presentation or notes to brief the staff before visits.

Site and building orientation
2.08 For many staff, moving into new accommodation may mean a readjustment of their journey to work, house moving, and leaving what they have come to enjoy as a pleasant location to work in. It is advisable to introduce all staff to the new site as early as possible by a display showing transportation, facilities and amenities.

Detailed consultations
2.09 After the move and the design concept have been approved in principle, groups may be set up while final layout plans are being developed to discuss the following issues.

Detailed planning: a discussion should be set up with section heads to present detailed floor plans giving the specific location of various facilities and departments so that the original programme data may be verified.

Furniture systems: alternative furniture systems being considered could be displayed for staff comment. A thorough analysis of comparative advantages and disadvantages will be required in conjunction with any such consultation, **2**.

The use of open office space: if an open plan office is proposed presentations should be given to inform staff about detailed aspects of its use and to alert the project team to any additional problems. The presentations should be informal with at the maximum probably 50 people who, where possible, should be from the same department, to create confidence, **3**. Plans, diagrams and models should be used to explain the relationship of the individual to the layout, how he may personally adapt his space, and to discuss any problem areas such as noise, confidentiality and housekeeping. Again, each session should allow time for questions and answers so that all personnel have a sense of personal involvement and participation.

The accommodation manager should play a central role in these consultations and use them to explain his future role as well as to develop his earlier contacts with both staff and management.

3 Managing the move
Planning the move
3.01 All moves require painstaking planning to avoid disruption of services and unnecessary waste of resources,

Table 1: Synopsis of the types of presentations that may be undertaken during the design and implementation stage of a project				
Stage	Presentation	Purpose	Method	Effected by
Briefing	Management committee	Visualisation of design concept	Visits to existing installations	Project team Programmer
Completion of building shell design	All personnel	Explanation of proposed site and building	Display of model, plans, perspectives	Architect Project team
Sketch scheme for fitting out	Group heads	Briefing on internal environment	Discussion groups: final design concept material Sketch layouts	Architect Programmer Project team
Layout	Group and section heads Top management	Briefing on workplace mock up Presentation of alternative furniture systems	Conducted visits Evaluation questionnaire	Project team Programmer
Before the move	Managers	Presentation of space management procedures	Meetings	Project team Programmer
Before the move	All personnel	Removal procedures	Meetings Circulars Building description handout	Project team

Example from evaluation checklist for furniture systems

Flexibility
1 Are the dimensions and shapes of the components proper for accommodating the papers, forms, etc as well as machinery and equipment to be used?
2 Can the components be arranged in various combinations in order to serve multiple functions?
3 Are there a sufficient number of component types and sizes to provide for all needs?

Quality
Materials
1 Do the materials and construction appear to be sufficiently durable to withstand wear imposed by normal tasks?
2 Would the furniture units tend to cause damage or impressions on wall surfaces, carpeting and other floor surfaces?
3 Are the surface finishes related to the functions to be performed, such as smooth tops for writing, etc?
Stability
1 Will the hardware endure constant use and is it firmly affixed?
2 Are the components sturdy ie will they shake or vibrate from moderate impact? Will they yield to pressure?
3 Is the construction sufficiently strong to support the weight of persons, machines, etc?
Staff
1 Are finishes free from roughness which might cause injury to persons or clothing?
2 Are there sharp edges, corners or potentially injurious protrusions or legs?
3 Do the upholstery and carpeting tend to generate static?
Design
1 Does the overall appearance provide a pleasant working environment?
2 Would the various elements combined promote a logical natural and organised appearance?

1

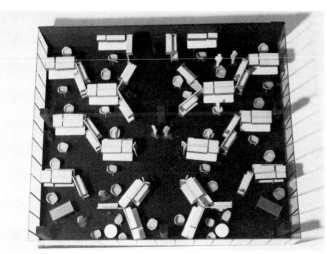

2

Subject	Person responsible
Deciding to move	Chairman/MD
Information for staff	MD/personnel
Packing up	Personnel
Memoranda	MD/personnel
Parking	Personnel
Loss of staff	MD/personnel
Recruitment	MD/personnel
Plan of the new office	MD/office manager
Coding	Office manager
Building	MD/maintenance
Tradesmen	Purchasing
Building maintenance	Maintenance
Stationery	Office manager
Design	MD/purchasing
The printer	Purchasing
A letter	MD/public relations
Notifications (general)	Co secretary
Professional advisers	Co secretary/PR
Taxation	Co secretary/accounts
Social security	Co secretary/accounts
Suppliers	Purchasing
Notifications to customer	MD's secretary
Furniture	Purchasing
Office equipment	Purchasing/office manager
Signs and nameplates	Purchasing
Rates on the move	Co secretary
Redirection of mail	Office manager
Telephones	Office manager/purchasing
The Offices Act	MD
Registration	Co secretary
Density	Office manager
Temperature	Maintenance
Toilets, etc	Maintenance
Fire precautions	Personnel
Removal	Purchasing
Inspection for access	Purchasing
The police	Co secretary
Insurance	Purchasing
Should the staff help?	Personnel
Wall-to-wall carpets	Maintenance/purchasing
Furniture destinations	Office manager
Contents of drawers and cabinets	Office manager/personnel
Gratuities	MD
Moved in a day	MD/personnel
Rubbish	Purchasing
Cleaning	Purchasing
Security	Purchasing/personnel

3

4. A critical path network or similar device should be prepared to relate the various events and parties concerned. The move may often be complicated by builders still being on site. Current high rents mean that firms are usually unwilling to keep two premises for very long and so they often move into new premises while building work is still in progress. This presents a great many problems: the design concept may be compromised, builders' work slowed down and staff expectations lowered, and the general uncertainty may have a detrimental effect on productivity and morale.

3.02 Before the move a furniture survey should be made to decide:

> items of furniture and equipment to be discarded;
> items to be renovated and moved into the new premises;
> items to be moved as they are;
> items to remain in the existing premises.

From this information a schedule of the new furniture and equipment required should be developed, and items allocated to each workplace. A list of suppliers and a specification of furniture, equipment and accessories may be compiled for the use of the accommodation manager after the move.

Telephones should be located, a special note made of any additional requirements for key and lamp or intercom units and a directory drafted.

Because of extended delivery times both furniture and telephone requirements may have to be settled many months in advance and care should be taken to update requirements immediately before the move.

Briefing the parties involved in the move
Staff notification
3.03 Briefing will normally be the responsibility of the accommodation officer. A few weeks before the move staff should be formally notified of the arrangements. In large firms it may be possible to provide them with a brochure describing the new accommodation, **5**. The final information they are given should include:

> the location of the new building and main transport routes;
> detailed timetable for the move;
> instructions covering the security of personal belongings, clearing of desks and filing cabinets, packing of files, and the labelling system to be used;
> details of departments, office services and amenities;
> housekeeping rules, tea break routines, mail procedures, handling of confidential documents;
> procedures for complaints or demands for additional space or equipment.

At about the same time as this information is circulated key members from each group may be taken to visit the new accommodation to orientate them to the way the building is organised and help them to visualise the implications of the plans already presented.

1 *Example of an extract from an evaluation checklist that may be provided to staff when comparing different furniture systems. The main headings for evaluation are: dimensions, access and ease of operation, flexibility, quality and materials, stability, safety, appearance, capacity, cost.*

2 *Scale models of components used in pre-planning the test installation of Action Office II at Herman Miller's headquarters office.*

3 *Responsibility within the company for aspects of the move, from the 'Black Arrow removal guide' published by Black Arrow Leasing Ltd, 66 Long Lane, Aintree, Liverpool L9 7BL*

Location	Map of area showing transport facilities. Full address and telephone number.
Access	Description of location of staff, visitors' and delivery entry points. Hours of opening. Means of access outside normal working hours.
Location of building facilities	Description of lift services, and alarm system. Location of toilets.
Visitors	Directions for visitors and special requirements for security.
Meetings	Location of meeting areas, and description of facilities available. Procedure for reservations and ordering refreshments.
Staff common room	
Staff restaurant and tea making	
First aid	Location of first aid room, list of volunteer first aiders and method of contact.
Fire precautions	Location of equipment and instructions for use. Description of fire drill sequence.
Car parking	Regulations for use of building car parking facilities.
Housekeeping rules	Hanging of notices including fire escape and other statutory requirements. Disposal of waste paper.
Messenger services	
Typing services	
Reproduction services	
Office manager	Location and name of office manager. Procedure for initiating changes and for complaints.
Cleaning services	Method of giving special instructions to cleaners. Procedure for complaints.
Heating and ventilating	Description of system and controls.

4 *Example of contents of handout describing accommodation.*

Suppliers

3.04 The process of moving in and organising the space will be greatly helped if furniture and equipment suppliers are clearly instructed where to locate items. Suppliers should be given:

floor layouts with the location of furniture keyed;
a list of furniture on each floor specified according to component and finish;
standard workplace forms, specifying components with type and colour of fabrics;
instructions on delivery and completion times and on where containers should be unpacked, items assembled and used packing cases stored.

Removal firms

3.05 The removal firm should be clearly told the origin and distribution of all the items to be moved and be given instructions for tidying up both the old and the new premises.

3.06 Keeping the firm running is of vital importance to organisations with a constant turnover of routine work, such as banks or advertising agencies, who will normally have to change premises out of normal working hours. To ensure a smooth flow of work the sequence in which items are moved may be critical. In open plan spaces the large elements such as full height storage units should be moved in first to define spaces. Care should be taken to phase the furniture suppliers and removal contractors so they are working at different times or on different floors.

3.07 Finally, sufficient time should be left for the space to be cleaned, and for the planning team to check the layout and equipment of each workplace for final adjustments before staff arrive.

Staff should find the following at their workplaces:
personal items and filing from old premises; telephone directories;

keys for furniture (for safekeeping these may be taped to the underside of the item);
post baskets.

Dealing with complaints

3.08 After the move the accommodation manager and consultants should be ready to receive complaints and suggestions, and should make a point of visiting staff in their new workplaces. Quick and sympathetic attention to initial problems, however trivial, will do much to secure acceptance of the new environment. The minor irritant left unattended often generates the greatest dissatisfaction.

3.09 A few weeks later, after personnel have had time to settle, a formal evaluation of the new arrangements may be desirable to establish any areas of staff concern, and so allow for future adaptations, 5.

Extract from office questionnaire

C Workplace function cont'd.
6 Satisfaction with my workplace as I found it at the time of move-in.
7 Amount of change of my workplace since move-in.
8 Assistance I received in suiting my workplace to my needs.
9 Satisfaction with my workplace now.

D Personal needs
(These items are designed to determine the extent to which your office suits you personally. Again please place a 'X' at the appropriate point along each scale.)
1 Compatibility with my personal taste.
2 Compatibility with the image the company should project.
3 Appropriateness of my workplace as a reflection of my position in the company.
4 Protection from distraction by others.
5 Extent to which my productivity is lowered by distractions by others.
6 Protection from being overheard by others.
7 Need for protection from being overheard to do my work.
8 Sense of privacy at my workplace.
9 Need for privacy.
10 Changes in my style of work required to adapt to the new space.

5 *Extract from an office use questionnaire designed to determine the extent to which the office layout has met objectives. The subjects covered were: planning process, physical environment, workplace function, personal needs, atmosphere, overall evaluation and comparison. Recipients were asked to indicate their degree of satisfaction on a seven point scale.*

Section 8: Managing office space

Management of office space

1 Programming, design and space management

1.01 Organisations are seldom static. Personnel leave or are promoted, new recruits are engaged and, even more fundamentally, management objectives and styles of operation continuously evolve in response to market conditions and other external forces. Such developments usually result in changes in spatial requirements and equipment. If a company is to use its accommodation effectively over a long period of time it needs to know its requirements and have a clear statement of objectives which are reasonably permanent and yet sensitive enough to respond to changing needs. A rigorous programming or briefing process is needed to obtain this information.

Programming

1.02 Programming is the process of ascertaining requirements in order to specify design solutions. The term programming is used in preference to brief writing to embrace the concept of response to changing circumstances over a period of time. The programme comprises written statements of standards for each level of staff; special group and departmental requirements; a plan for growth and change; and a statement of interdepartmental relationships and requirements for equipment and common facilities, **1**.

Programming furnishes the data for the *design concept* to the owner planning new accommodation and his architect. It also enables the client after he has moved into his new accommodation to review his changing requirements in the light of defined standards.

The programme may be prepared by the architect, the client or a professional programming specialist. In the last case the programmer may act as an intermediary between client and architect.

1.03 Two points are important. First, the role of the programmer is distinct from that of the architect even if the architect takes on this task. The rationale of the design concept arises from the requirements of the organisation: the programme should not be formulated to meet the design concept. Second, the programme continues after the client has moved into the space. As requirements are satisfied in use, it is only after moving in that the programme is fully tested. At this point the client's accommodation manager or some other person must monitor the programme in use and see that adjustments are made when necessary.

This view of the programme as a continuous process which involves the client's active participation is in contrast to the view of the design of offices as a sequence of operations which stops when the client moves in. At this point the client is often abandoned by the designer to manage his accommodation to the best of his ability. This ought not to be so. Throughout the whole process the client should have been involved in all strategic decisions taken on his behalf and should be fully aware of how the space can be used to his best advantage. If necessary he should also have been helped to train staff to take responsibility for the management of the space in use.

1 *Examples of documentation included in a programme:* **a** *schedule of departmental space requirements;* **b** *typical space standards;* **c** *typical adjacency diagram.*

Space management may be defined as the skill of matching user requirements to management objectives within the constraints of built form. It is a continuous process throughout the life of the user organisation. In this study JOHN WORTHINGTON describes some problems based on his experience of programming requirements for new accommodation and evaluating the existing accommodation of a number of major organisations. He shows how the architect's traditional role interlocks with the role of the accommodation manager.

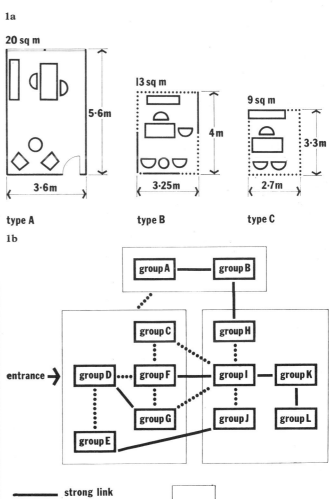

1a

1b

type A   type B   type C

1c

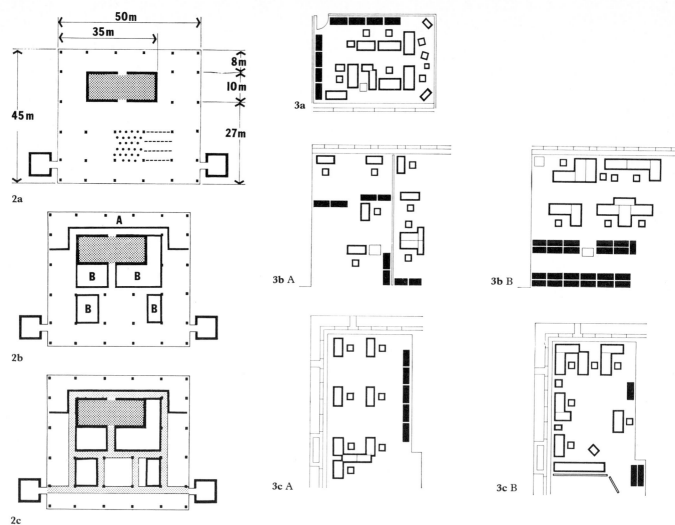

2 *Diagrams of a planning concept showing the possible location of individual offices and group areas :*
a *The empty shell 50 × 45 m has a structural grid between 10 and 11 m in both directions. Power and telephone outlets are at 2 m centres staggered (dotted)* *and lighting is at 3·6 m centres (dashed). The largest space is 27 m deep, the smallest 7·2 m.*
b *Offices for senior management at perimeter of zone A, and offices for section heads and support activities confined to zone B.*
c *This overcomes inherent* *disadvantages of limited accessibility to perimeter. Additional advantages are, first, that variety of open office spaces is greater and reduced to manageable proportions; and second, that it provides an obvious basis for economical and direct circulation.*

3 *Plans showing* **a** *overcrowding;* **b** *increased filing—A the design concept, B actual layout after a period of occupation;* **c** *ad hoc planning—A the design concept, B the actual layout after a period of occupation.*

The design concept

1.04 The programme is usually supplemented by a *design concept* which is a clear statement of how the design is intended to meet user requirements. The design concept may consist of a simple diagram showing the relationship of cellular to open office space; location of filing, and group facilities; zones for expansion; positioning of primary, secondary and tertiary circulation; and suggested zoning for different activities, **2**. It should be formulated by the designer and programmer early in the project as a datum to which future changes can be related.

The space management programme

1.05 The space management programme goes beyond both *programme* and *design concept* to formulate rules and procedures for the accommodation manager to apply in all likely eventualities during the life of the space. The space management programme will be concerned with two levels of responsibility, *housekeeping* and *strategic space management*. The accommodation manager will be responsible for the day to day running of the space. He will make decisions about the location of staff, the use of reserves of space, the

modification of layout, minor changes to partitioning and lighting etc. Most of these responsibilities are of a fairly routine nature and can be compared to *housekeeping*. However, an entirely different level of decision will occasionally be necessary. He should advise management on such strategic decisions as the reduction of the number of staff or the amount of space needed, the taking of new space or the commissioning of a new building. This is *space management* in its fullest sense.

If there is no policy for continuous planning, and if *ad hoc* changes are allowed to occur, the following results are likely.

An erosion of the standards proposed in the original brief.

With pressures on space caused by certain areas of the organisation growing faster than others the tendency will be for work spaces to be squeezed up to allow additional personnel and furniture to be accommodated, **3**.

An inefficient use of overall space available.

Ad hoc planning creates pockets of overcrowded space while leaving relatively under-utilised space in other parts of the building, **3**. Without an overall planning strategy major departmental reorganisation will be instigated only when the situation has become unbearable.

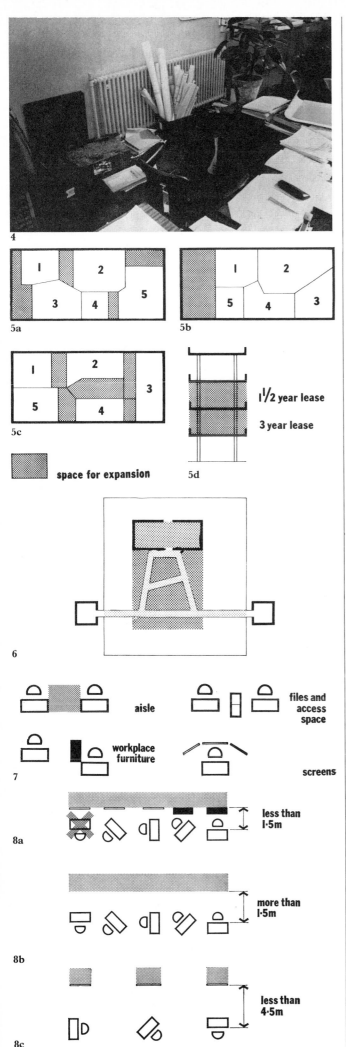

4

space for expansion   *5d*

I½ year lease

3 year lease

aisle

files and access space

workplace furniture

screens

less than 1·5m

8a

more than 1·5m

8b

less than 4·5m

8c

An inefficient use of the resources available.

Without an overall view of each department's requirements and the space available, new work processes may be badly accommodated and inappropriate technological solutions used. The need for additional filing and storage in certain departments could suggest the use of a space saving centralised filing system or microfilm rather than adding to an existing space consuming system, **3, 4**.

1.06 Armed with the right programme, a design concept and well designed space management procedures, both staff and management will be able to:

respond to change on a planned day to day basis;

review planning options in the light of agreed criteria;

assess the effects of changes in the longer term.

Without this basic data and the means to respond to change, many problems may be solved by short term expediency which in the long run will involve progressively more expensive solutions.

2 Implementing space management

2.01 The implementation of the programming and briefing process and the resulting space management programme will vary according to the kind of organisation. The chief factors which influence space management are the following.

Size of the organisation.

Entirely different problems occur in firms of 100 and 1000 people. Large organisations are more likely to have specialised departments dealing with accommodation.

Rate of growth and change.

A rapidly growing and changing firm will have far more difficult space management problems than an organisation which is static or slowly declining in numbers.

Number of locations.

For an organisation one large building is far easier to manage than dispersed parcels of space in many locations.

Degree of centralisation.

Some organisations have a policy that the same practices and standards will be used everywhere. Others are less centralised and allow more discretion to local managers. The more centralised the policy the stronger the accommodation manager's role will be.

Budgetary control.

Perhaps the most important factor is whether or not the client departments pay directly to a centralised estates department for their space. If they pay, they will be more likely to resist controls imposed by the accommodation manager in order to cut corners and achieve short term savings. However, payment may also have the effect of reducing extravagant and wasteful use of space.

In the notes which follow, the assumption is made that the accommodation manager works for a large and growing organisation with highly centralised control situated at

4 Poor housekeeping: filing systems allowed to decay and the wrong kind of storage.

5 Diagrams of four alternative layout strategies for growth: **a** *expansion space adjacent to each group;* **b** *expansion space for groups combined at one place on each floor;* **c** *expansion space clustered as pool of slack space;* **d** *expansion space centralised and sub-let on short term leases.*

6 Planning rules for block layouts—location of tall elements. Keep tall elements, eg screens and shelves within tinted area.

7 Planning layout within a group. Screen workplaces of conflicting function with available furniture.

8 Planning workplaces adjacent to aisles:

a, b *screen workplaces less than 1·5 m from primary aisles;* **c** *screen end of primary aisle if closer than 4·5 m.*

several locations. In other organisations the situation may be very different. The manager may be relatively insignificant, even sharing the role of managing space with several other jobs.

Types of change

2.02 The accommodation manager will be concerned with meeting a variety of types of change.

Changes initiated by individuals and which occur within the individual workplace.

These types of changes have no real effect on surrounding areas. They are concerned with rearranging existing components or placing a requisition order for additional components and should be dealt with through the departmental manager.

Changes initiated by individuals which affect adjacent workplaces.

These changes occur when a user wishes to move a common component (eg screen) or, in association with his colleagues, desires to reorganise the layout to create a more suitable workflow. Approval will be required by others affected and the department manager.

Changes initiated by groups or departments.

These may entail reorganisation of furniture to take into account new working patterns or expansion of boundaries. Approval should be sought from the other managers affected and the new plans developed by the space manager.

Changes initiated by senior management.

These will most probably be connected with organisational changes and may involve the space manager in major reshuffling.

Changes initiated by the accommodation manager.

By looking ahead at possible changes the accommodation manager may be able to forestall continuous small scale changes by relocating departments to allow evenly distributed pockets for growth.

The accommodation manager

2.03 The efficient utilisation and running of office space is dependent on the organisation appointing a member of staff (the accommodation manager) to be responsible for the planning, allocation and evaluation of space requirements. To function efficiently the accommodation manager will need to develop a strategic plan for growth and change, standards and rules for the layout of workplaces and procedures to initiate and monitor change, and to keep up to date records of how the space is being utilised.

2.04 The accommodation manager's proposed role may differ from the traditional understanding of this position in that there will be greater emphasis on the strategic planning of future use of space. It is suggested he should have a background of practical design and the ability to read plans, update them and keep schedules. He need not have a detailed knowledge of building construction or mechanical engineering. Maintenance can be in other hands. But he should understand the rudiments of these subjects and be able to liaise with specialists, anticipate problems and report failures clearly. The manager's most important task will probably be to collect and analyse information from department heads and the personnel department about projected space requirements. He should have a good knowledge of the whole company and be able to keep in informed touch with senior staff about their requirements. Finally he must have the authority and presence to resist pressure from superiors in rank who may wish to win space advantages for their departments against the best interests of the company as a whole.

The strategic plan

2.05 To use the space to the best advantage a strategic plan for growth and change should be developed as a part of the initial programming and planning process. The strategic plan:

locates space for immediate growth so that departmental expansion may take place with the minimum of upheaval. Such space may be allocated within each department, by leaving growth areas in strategic areas of the building, or by a combination of both, **5**;

takes account of long term growth by developing a programme of sub leasing of immediately surplus space so additional space comes available at regular intervals in the future;

may provide space on the site for building expansion.

Planning rules

2.06 To reduce the opportunity for conflict between staff, and to ensure the efficient use of the space available, the accommodation manager may adopt a set of planning rules based on the standards and design criteria developed in the original programme.

2.07 The overall objective of such a set of rules is to protect the 'rights' of the individual office worker while making explicit the planning criteria accepted and the processes involved in planning the move; to this end, many space management programmes contain not only arrangement rules but procedural guides.

2.08 Usually there are three levels of rules; those affecting the overall planning of the space, **6**, those for planning group areas, and those for planning individual working areas. Several examples of each are listed below[1]:

Rules for planning the whole layout.

Working groups will be arranged to follow patterns of work flow and interaction.

Careful distinction is to be made between primary circulation which generally links access and egress points and the major groups, secondary circulation which connects groups not adjacent to primary routes with primary routes, and tertiary circulation which is the circulation within the working groups.

Primary route widths will be not less than 2 m wide—increasing with the volume of traffic.

Secondary routes will be not less than 1·5 m wide.

Tertiary routes will be not less than 750 mm.

Group territory will be well defined and there will be no cross circulation between groups.

All routes will be kept 'clean' and defined by planters and screens.

Rules for planning group areas

Functions with the highest visitor content will be placed closest to primary or secondary routes.

Planting should satisfy a particular functional need such as a landmark screening, or as a barrier on circulation routes to block or direct traffic.

Conflicting functions to be screened with available resources such as aisle spacing, columns, planters or empty positions.

Rules for planning individual work areas

No person will directly face a circulation route, another person or storage furniture.

Each person should be able to see who is coming.

Procedures for change

2.09 The efficient management of space demands clearly defined procedures by which staff may initiate changes and the accommodation manager's staff may implement them. These procedures should include:

a clear reporting hierarchy for the sanctioning of changes;

a means of relating demands for space to budgeting and personnel plans.

To make sure that there is a rapid response to pressure, the accommodation manager will need to monitor the effect of *organisational changes* on both space and staff. He will thus need to be in contact with other company and staff representatives or associations.

Building records

2.10 The efficient use of accommodation requires continuous monitoring of how the space is being utilised. Accurate records can help to pinpoint areas of overcrowding, under-occupancy or insufficient storage. The records may include:

updated layout plans;
projections for current and future space requirements based on corporate planning and personnel projections;
an updated furniture inventory for each space;
allocation of space and equipment costs;
updated organisational chart and interaction diagram;
records of the frequency of use of building facilities, especially meeting areas.

3 Conclusions

3.01 This chapter has argued that architects should accept that there are certain new roles and processes involved in the design and management of office accommodation. Elsewhere in this book we have suggested that the architect is responsible for the extent to which spaces can be used long after the building is 'finished'. The shell/scenery ideas discussed previously[2] also support the concept of continuing design expressed in this study. The architect should ensure that he is fully informed and able to play a part in briefing an accommodation manager.

3.02 In the past the role of accommodation manager has not had the status it deserves. Space is an expensive resource which is easily wasted. Fortunately many companies are now waking up to the fact that poor housekeeping and space management can be expensive both in staff satisfaction and the inability to call on resources of space when they are required. These problems may be avoided or overcome when a manager has a specific responsibility for forward planning the use of space.

References

1 DUFFY, F. and WANKUM.
Office landscaping, London 1967, Anbar.
2 *Planning Office Space*
pp 3–7

Section 8: Managing office space

Three older office buildings

Office buildings are rarely constructed today with a planned lifespan in excess of forty years. In many instances, they will be torn down or become redundant before the forty years have expired. In this case study, COLIN CAVE examines three older office buildings, Lever Brothers at Port Sunlight, Surrey House in Norwich and Imperial Chemical House in London and analyses why they appear to be as successful today as when they were built at the turn of the century. His criterion of success is continuous effective use of office space. By tracing an occupational history, the author hopes to show that it was the initial design of the basic shell which determined the range of internal spaces available and thus the usefulness or success of the buildings over time.

1 Lever Brothers: Port Sunlight

Description

1.01 In 1888, in consultation with a Warrington architect, William Owen, William Lever chose the site on which he proposed to build this factory and model village. Much has been written about the model village, which was the work of several architects[1].

1.02 We are concerned with the factory and offices built in 1895 by William and Segar Owen and extended later by J. Lomax-Simpson who had become the company architect in 1910. The office building has an undistinguished, ornamented, stone frontage, and the plan, **1** was composed of two large office wings on either side of a split-level entrance hall. Behind, on the axis of, and leading off the entrance hall, forming a T-shaped arrangement, is the south wing of three storeys built by J. Lomax-Simpson in 1913-14. The south wing is built over the soaperies. Below the offices are the ovens, a fact which proved fortunate in 1967 (see later).

1.03 As can be seen, the three wings were almost identical: a large central, barrel-vaulted, top-lit office space with cellular offices on either side at the main office floor level and, in the case of the south wing offices, leading off a gallery at first floor level. For 70 years, the shell provided a spatial variety which suited the management style, the organisational structure and the working methods of the company, which was that of a largely routine clerical administrative adjunct to a manufacturing organisation with some accommodation for top management. The internal layout faithfully reflected the hierarchical structure of the company, **2**.

1.04 The most junior staff sat at one side of the open floor and progressed across the floor as they moved up the hierarchy until they reached the other side, where the supervisors' working positions were situated. The next step up (literally) was to the junior management cellular office space behind the supervisors. The next step was into the cellular accommodation at the other side which was a step above the main office floor. These were middle- and senior-management offices. They had private lavatories and outer offices for the secretaries.

1.05 By the 1960s, three factors had changed to such an extent that new office forms were required. The management style had become less autocratic, which was reflected in less direct supervision of the lowest grades. The organisational structure was being modified by an influx of

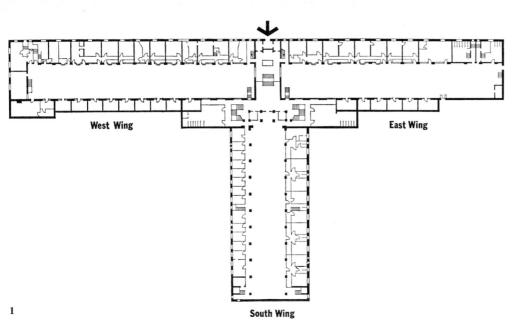

West Wing

East Wing

South Wing

1

1 Plan of Lever Brothers' building, Port Sunlight, showing addition of south wing. (Scale 1 : 1250).
2 Typical office interior in early 1960s, showing rigid geometry of furniture in central area and managers' offices at each side. Fluorescent tubes immediately below edge mouldings on vault.

new professionals, scientists of various disciplines, into the middle-management posts, a process which had started in the post-war years and continued through the 60s. The third factor was the improvement in working conditions in line with general practice.

1.06 Fluorescent tubes were added in banks in 1947 to supplement the natural daylight. The tubes were controlled by a photo-electric cell and were not entirely successful, **2.**

1.07 In 1967, it was decided to 'landscape' the south wing.

This involved clearing out the existing cellular offices, levelling the floor, changing the furniture, upgrading the finishes and the lighting levels, and installing an air-conditioning system of which the plant was neatly incorporated in one of the areas under the main floor. The work was completed in 1968 **3, 4, 5.** The two plans of the south wing are an interesting example of space utilisation; more people were accommodated in the 1968 plan than had ever occupied the ground floor before.

2

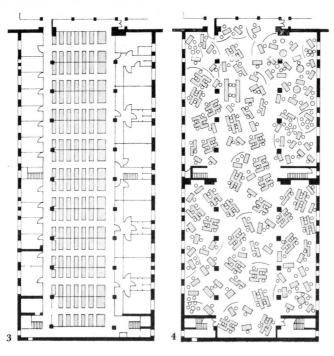

3 *Plan of south wing prior to 'landscaping', showing desk layout 1966.*
4 *Plan of south wing after 'landscaping', showing desk*
layout 1967.
5 *Interior view of 'landscape'. Managers have gravitated to the edges.*

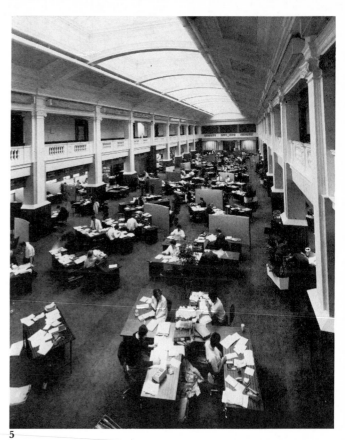

1.08 A particularly interesting feature of the building was that, in 1972, the three wings were a faithful representation of three different stages in its development: the 1947 layout, the pre-1967 layout, and the landscaped version. Since then the other two wings have been upgraded but neither has been totally landscaped.

2 Norwich Union: Surrey House

Description

2.01 The head office buildings of the Norwich Union Life Insurance Society were designed by a local firm of architects, Messrs A. J. & F. W. Skipper, in 1900, after several leading London-based architects had been rejected. The foundation stone was laid in 1901 and the building was occupied in 1906.

2.02 The souvenir of the inauguration of the Norwich Life Insurance Society declared that:

'Those only who have realised the inadequacy of the old offices where in strictly limited accommodation, every available inch of which was utilised, and with a rapidly growing staff, the increasing work of the Society was carried out under difficult and barely sanitary conditions can adequately appreciate . . . the completion of the well-arranged and ample New Offices which they have so long and anxiously looked forward to. It will be evident to those who inspect the New Building that in its design and construction the Directors have given very careful thought to the purposes of practical utility for which it was erected, while following the example of other leading companies in endeavouring to convey in their Head Office an expression of solidity, reliability, and permanence of the Society carrying on its operations therein. The size of the Building, the accommodation it gives, the labour-saving appliances it contains, its beauty, and the comfort in which it enables the Staff to discharge naturally lead one to contrast it with the Offices previously occupied by the Society . . .'

2.03 The exterior of the building is not particularly distinguished and is in a style which Pevsner calls *commercial baroque*[2]. Although the Norwich Union maintain that the details come from the 'purest Italian sources', the building bears a strong resemblance to the Amicable Society's building in Serjeant's Inn with which the company had merged 40 years earlier.

2.04 Internally, the building is much more exciting, as it contains some of the finest marble work in the country. The original design, a large hall surmounted by a dome with rooms arranged at the sides at both ground and first floors extending over about 1200 m[2], did not contain such splendid materials, but for some reason the marble originally destined for Westminster Cathedral found its way to Norwich **6, 7, 8, 9.**

2.05 One more quotation from the inaugural souvenir completes the description.

'The efficient ventilation and heating of the Building received very careful attention, and the system adopted has proved very successful. The air before admission is drawn through wet screens to free it from dust, smoke and other impurities, and when desirable, is passed over batteries of radiation to warm it to suitable temperature. Fans, worked by electric motors, have been introduced, of sufficient capacity to draw off, in twenty minutes, as much air as the building contains; so that it is always possible to keep the air perfectly fresh and of a comfortable temperature.'

2.06 The air is delivered into the central space through a 'font' device and is then deflected by a suspended baffle to all parts of the office.

The layout of working positions—lines of desks with central access—in the central hall has hardly changed throughout its life. The desks have changed from the stool and ledger type and more space is now allocated for an entrance area, but otherwise the space appears unchanged.

2.07 The Norwich Union soon grew out of the building, though the ground floor is still used for office purposes. The situation is unlikely to continue for long, as the long-term plan is to use Surrey House to accommodate the society's museum, and move the present occupants into a new office building constructed on the same site.

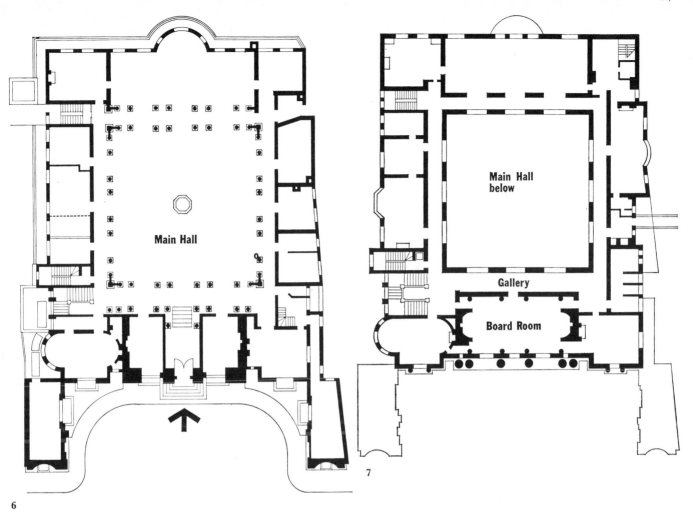

6

7

6 *Ground floor plan of Surrey House.*
7 *First floor plan of Surrey House.*
8 *Working areas at rear of office, 1970.*

8

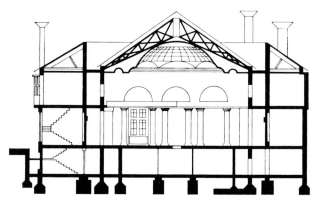

9 *Section through Surrey House.*

3 Imperial Chemical House

Description

3.01 Imperial Chemical House was designed for ICI by Frank Baines and constructed by Messrs John Mowlem & Co Ltd. Construction began in 1927 and was completed in 1929. The building was remarkable for its speed of erection, estimated at one-third of the time it would normally take for a building of that size.

3.02 There were 700 rooms occupying 2·8 ha, the total gross floor area being 34 000 m².

3.03 The plan form is a series of office spaces almost 18 m deep around central light wells **11**. The structural grid is 6·1 m × 3·6 m, resulting in extensive cellularisation of those dimensions; partition walls were of 100 mm hollow tiles plastered both sides. There was no air-conditioning, but heating coils were embedded in the ceiling and air was drawn from the offices into spaces above the ceiling in the corridor.

3.04 The building was occupied from 1929 to 1965 with virtually no change in the way the space was subdivided. By 1965, ICI was spread out in several buildings, some based in central London. As a result of a study by the management services division, all staff were to be centralised in IC House, and in Thames House North, **12**, which was constructed a little later than IC House and also fronts on to Millbank, on the other side of Horseferry Road. Leases were sold and the architects and estates sections had the job of fitting 800 to 900 office workers into a space previously occupied by 500 to 600 in IC House. This was an enormous remodelling job, claimed by the contractor, R. Mansell Ltd, to be one of the largest ever undertaken in the London area.

3.05 The principal device used was to open-plan several of the office spaces, in some cases from envelope to envelope and in others only the central space yielded by reducing the 7·2 m × 3·6 m spaces to 3·6 × 3·6 m. The cellular hollow tile partitions were largely replaced with glazed demountable partitions **10, 11, 13**.

3.06 Since 1966, progressive erosion of the open spaces has taken place. More and more cellular offices have been provided, sometimes because of re-organisation to meet legitimate spatial demands and sometimes as a reflection of the power of particular section leaders. Staff were more antagonistic than usual towards working in the open spaces.

3.07 The shell contains many types of space. One in particular can be identified. With the changes towards more group working, and away from the more autocratic management style towards a freer, more democratic and less heavily supervised style, some of the working groups and sections have defined their territorial boundaries more vigorously. So it is not uncommon to find a boundary partition around groups, usually along the line of the earlier corridor through which there is only one entrance to the group. Within that boundary, the group occupies a mixture of space types from the small cell for one person to the large space for several persons where more routine clerical operations are carried out.

3.08 In 1972, more pressure was exerted by higher management, as a result of another management services report, to contract from Thames House North back to IC House and to move some staff into lower rental accommodation.

3.09 IC House is fairly densely occupied, and a change from the 3·6 m space module is probably the only way of further increasing the density of occupation. Consequently, a new subdivision device is being explored which entails constructing a 1·2 m module space division system. The virtue of this module, it is argued, is that it will allow rooms of two modules, 2·4 m wide to be provided where previously 3·6 m had been the smallest sub-division. Theoretically this could provide up to 50 per cent more cellular spaces in the building. However, the 1·2 m module was abandoned on grounds of cost, particularly because the system would have involved extensive air-conditioning. Consequently, ICI has had to resort to converting space once used for other purposes to office space. For example, the gymnasium was taken over, a mezzanine floor inserted and used for a conference centre, strong rooms and stores were converted, double-module rooms divided down the middle and the restaurant was redesigned to release space previously occupied by the snack bar. The effect of this holding operation is to cope with immediate demands at slightly reduced space standards.

3.10 There is always pressure for additional single offices, which is explained by staff antagonism to open spaces and by the fact that ICI, in common with other organisations, envisages that increasing automation will slowly change the balance of jobs away from routine towards more decision-making tasks.* The effect is to increase the requirement for cellular space at the expense of open areas.

4 Appraisal

4.01 It is a central theme of this book that shell design is more than enclosing a given area on a given site. Successful shells respond to changing cycles of requirements. This study of three older office buildings attempts to show, by tracing occupational histories, how requirements have changed, and how the building shell has responded to these changes.

4.02 The single most important attribute of these three building shells is that they permit a variety of forms of subdivision. The number of possible subdivision alternatives appears to be related to the shell depth or, more precisely, subdivision alternatives are related to the dimension across uninterrupted office space. This theme is elaborated in sections 2 and 3 in this book, where it is explained that a building can contain a number of shell types and thus space depths.

This definition accommodates all three buildings. Both Lever Brothers and IC House contain basically one type of office space which is fairly deep, 28 m and 18 m while Surrey House contains two kinds of space some 5 m deep and some approximately 20 m deep.

4.03 Lever Brothers demonstrates the benefits to be gained from a 28 m deep shell. The ratio of enclosed to open spaces has consistently changed through the last 15 years. The particular arrangement of two bands of enclosed spaces at either side of an open, top lit, space makes an interesting comparison with IC House where the same arrangement is

---

* This assumption accounts for buildings such as the Hamburg Electricity Company in Hamburg designed by Arne Jacobson, where an entirely cellular building was demanded by the client just because of increasing automation.

10

13

10 *Single-person office in*
Imperial Chemical House.
11 *Typical plan of Thames*
House North.
12 *Typical plan of Imperial*
Chemical House.
13 *Open office space in*
Imperial Chemical House.

less successful due to less depth, barely 18 m and the absence of top lighting.

4.04 Although Surrey House contains a greater range of space types than either Lever Brothers or IC House, the spaces are less effective because of what the building symbolises rather than what it makes possible. It is the home and head office of a large organisation which considers itself to be one of the cornerstones of our financial apparatus, which is expressed through massive materials and expensive finishes.

4.05 Building shells which close options by reducing spatial variety, such as the 12 m deep typical speculative building, tend to become redundant more rapidly than those which do not. The contemporary reaction to this is to construct highly serviced deep shells, but few organisations can function well in these deep spaces unless a useful ratio of perimeter enclosed to open spaces is possible without resorting to internal rooms. Such internal rooms are generally unacceptable in Europe. Certainly this would be the case with the three organisations examined in this study.

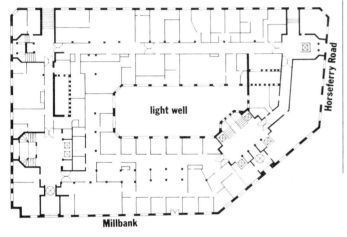

11

12 Millbank

References

1 PEVSNER NIKOLAUS, Ed.,
Buildings of England: Cheshire.
London 1971, Penguin, pp 303-
313, also DARLEY, GILLIAN,
Villages of Vision. London 1975,
Architectural Press.
2 PEVSNER, NIKOLAUS Ed.,
Buildings of England: NE
Norfolk and Norwich. London
1962, Penguin.

Section 9: A possible future

New projects

The design of office shells and scenery is changing as architects explore the potential of deep space, the demands of different kinds of organisation and the insistent pressures of change. JOHN WORTHINGTON reviews these trends in a number of new projects.

1 Introduction

1.01 This preview of office designs uses current UK practice and some of the more interesting office developments recently completed abroad to highlight the ideas discussed in the series. The schemes have been classified into four categories: custom designed offices, speculative offices, offices for local and central government, and renovations. Table I summarising these projects appears at the end of this introductory section. They are compared with developments abroad and discussed from the points of view of site planning, building organisation, space management and expansion and change.

2 Site planning

2.01 It is noticeable both here and abroad that the context and character of office development is changing. Increasingly large areas of the city are being developed comprehensively to integrate different land uses into complex building structures in which public space and tenants' space become intimately interwoven. Roche Dinkeloo's office retail complex for a Canadian city, **1**, shows such integration conceived on a monumental scale.

2.02 To gain the maximum use of urban sites, while keeping the continuity of the original building heights, there is a movement towards the use of deep planned office development. The Sedgwick Forbes head office building (Fitzroy Robinson & Partners), located to fill a complete block, is one of the first deep planned spaces for a specific client to be constructed in the City and is a possible prototype of how other city blocks might be developed (scheme 1).

2.03 Many offices being built for client occupation are conceived as a corporate or community symbol. Roche Dinkeloo's project for College Life Insurance on the outskirts of Indianapolis, **2**, creates an arresting set of sculptural forms that cannot be easily forgotten. A more conventional building form, Gunhar Birkerts Associates' Federal Reserve Bank of Minneapolis, has a similar impact on the city centre which will make Minneapolis impossible to forget.

2.04 The larger office complexes tend to be located in suburban or outer city centre locations, on office campuses or industrial estates with a wide range of amenities attached. This approach has been common for some time in America with such notable examples as SOM's Connecticut Life headquarters. In the United Kingdom the green fields headquarters complex and office park is only just gathering momentum. Warrington New Town Corporation is developing the concept of an office park aimed at research and development organisations (see also scheme 3).

The corporation aims to use the site for about 4000 administrative, professional, and technological staff on 30 hectares of land.

2.05 Several schemes are being developed for a com-

1 *Central city areas are increasingly being developed to integrate different land uses into complex building structures in which public space and tenants' space become interwoven; project for an office retail complex Canada (Roche Dinkeloo, architects).*

bination of commercial and industrial uses, often in the same building. The simple land use categories of office, warehouse or industrial are in practice difficult to distinguish, and a number of the buildings illustrated contain a combination of uses. Schemes such as PA Technical Services at Melbourn (scheme 2) include an integral mix of office and laboratory activities. In general, custom designed schemes have a substantial amount of space devoted to activities such as recreation, computer facilities, and training areas.

3 Building organisation

3.01 The development of deep planned buildings and the reduction of the number of cellular offices have tended to increase planning flexibility. However, the result of these larger open areas has often meant a loss of any sense of place, and led to major problems of orientation and control in the management of the space. To overcome some of these problems several new office developments have used split level sections, and varying volumes to create manageable sized spaces while continuing to allow for visual and physical continuity.

3.02 Raymond J. Cecil & Partners' proposal for a speculative block in City Road, London EC1, **3**, is based on the desire to design a sequence of spaces that can either be divided into small tenancies or used as continuous space by one organisation. The multi-level design operates as a conventional central core type building with the additional advantages that:

● unlike the traditional slab block, however many floors any one company occupies the core can always be a public area;

● companies choosing to occupy more than one level have a choice of circulation between levels;

● on each storey there are three separately serviced, lettable areas each of a different size, giving a permutation of over 50 different sized tenancies in the building;

● if more than one floor is let to a company, communications and the growth and change of working groups and services is greatly eased.

3.03 Herman Hertzberger's offices for the Centraal Beheer in Apeldoorn, **4**, is probably one of the most interesting attempts to personalise the quality of the deep plan space while still upholding its advantage of interaction. The

---

Table I Comparison of projects

Name of project	Number of floors	Type of office shell	Depth of predominant space type	Range of space types	Structural grid	Mullion grid	Telephone and electrical grid	Gross building area	Gross and net areas of typical office floor
Custom designed offices									
1 Sedgwick Forbes Fitzroy Robinson & Partners	8	Double zone split core	15·00 m	Shallow Deep	6·60 m	1·65 m	2·38 m	24 500 m²	2750 m² 2420 m²
2 PA Technical Services Piano & Rogers	2	Double zone split core	9·60 m	Shallow Deep	7·20 m	2·40 m	2·40 m	2868 m²	
3 G E Plastics, Warrington Chamberlin, Powell & Bon, Architects	2	Single zone mezzanine round double height space	7·00 m	Shallow Medium depth	9·00 m	1·28 m	2·41 m	1120 m³	
4 Editions Van de Velde Farrell Grimshaw Partnership	1	Double zone effect circulation round courtyard	6·00 m	Shallow	5·00 m 10·00 m	1·25 m	Suspended trunking	875 m²	760 m² 625 m²
Spec offices									
5 Arundel Court, Strand Frederick Gibberd & Partners	6 and 8	Double zone offset circulation	8·00 m	Shallow Medium depth	7·65 m 5·50 m	2·75 m	Perimeter and column	43 500 m²	4710 m² 3400 m²
6 Office building The Hague Yorke Rosenberg Mardall Groosman Partners Rotterdam	8	Single zone offset core	8·00 m 12·00 m	Medium depth	6·00 m	1·50 m	3·00 m at perimeter with subsidiary floor trunking	15 000 m²	968 m² 785 m²
7 Milton Keynes city centre office Central Milton Keynes Division	2	Double zone offset circulation	9·00 m	Shallow Medium depth	9·60 m	2·40 m	2·40 m	11 505 m²	11 505 m² 10 013 m²
Local and central government offices									
8 County hq, Worcester Robert Matthew Johnson-Marshall	3	Pavilions offset core	22·00 m	Shallow Very deep	10·80 m	1·80 m	1·80 m	20 000 m²	3580 m² 3460 m²
9 Town Hall extension Sheffield Civic Design Section of the Department of Planning & Design	3	Single zone offset core	10·00 m 19·00 m	Medium depth Deep Very deep	11·00 m	Windows in wall	3·00 m	21 390 m²	5460 m² 4830 m²
10 Portsmouth Civic Centre Teggin & Taylor	5	Double zone Central core	10·00 m	Shallow Medium depth	7·20 m	1·80 m	1·80 m	30 225 m²	3920 m² 3445 m²
11 Central government offices, Cathays Park Alex Gordon & Partners	5	Very deep Asymmetrical circulation offices round courts	26·00 m	Shallow Very deep	8·70 m	Windows in wall	Raised floor	40 744 m²	7300 m² 6100 m²
Renovation									
12 Bridge House, Southwark Renton Howard Wood Levin Partnership	6	Single zone Deep space	12·00 m	Medium depth Deep	8·00 m	1·35 m	Cavity floor duct system	4390 m²	725 m² 590 m²
13 12-18 Grosvenor Gardens Chapman Taylor Partners	6	Terrace Deep space Asymmetrical core	11·00 m	Shallow Medium depth Deep	7·50 m	Windows in wall	Perimeter and columns	6257 m²	

working areas consist of continuous space articulated by structure and voids in such a way that a group or an individual can appropriate and create comprehensible space for himself. The open wells with floors at different levels give a feeling of scale, interaction and belonging. This exploration of new sectional and plan forms is a welcome move away from the spatial drabness of the slab block developments.

4 Space management

4.01 Perhaps the greatest advance in the field of office building in the last decade has been the concern for interior planning and the management of space. With the reduction in the proportion of cellular offices, furniture systems have taken on a new role in dividing space and defining territory. Detailed thought has been given to the development of systems of components which can be applied to a number of different patterns of work. Systems such as Finnscape or Facit which combine both screening and freestanding tables and mobile filing units in one system can be used for individual private work stations as well as more open clerical layouts based on work flow.

4.02 The creation of large open planned floor areas is producing schemes where the office function is becoming more diversified and less formal. The new Topsikring headquarters in Ballerup, Denmark, **5**, is a huge single-storey space planned so that staff break areas, informal meeting places, socialising points, common reference facilities and decentralised office services may be found in one zone visually connected.

5 Expansion and change

5.01 The speed of technological innovation, and the increasing realisation by management that strategic corporate planning depends on the availability of space, has meant that the possibility for growth and change is now one of the major design determinants in office design. More common approaches to expansion and change are the adaptation of structures and the building of additions (see Editions Van de Velde, scheme 4) or the reorganisation of flexible furniture systems within an existing shell (see PA technical services, scheme 2).

6 Conclusions

6.01 Table I summarises and compares the data collected on the 13 schemes published. What is immediately apparent is the wide divergence in the choice of planning and servicing grids among the different schemes. Planning grids vary from 1·25 m to 2·70 m, but perhaps the most contentious choice is 2·4 m (Milton Keynes Commercial Building and PA technical services, schemes 7 and 2) which gives only minimum office width and reduces the user's options. Costs in the examples presented vary between £150/m² to £326/m². One reason for this divergence is the difficulty of finding a common method of comparison between buildings, some of which include many strictly non-office activities (such as car parking, laboratories etc), and the variation in tender dates.

6.02 The majority of buildings illustrated provide shallow or medium depth space with a few creating the very deep spaces that are most suitable for carrying through the principles of bürolandschaft planning. What does emerge from the analysis of the examples studied is that the majority of buildings yield a variety of space types by using either an offset core or primary circulation route. This emphasis on providing a variety of space types will increase future planning options and is a welcome development away from the more inflexible bürolandschaft plan form.

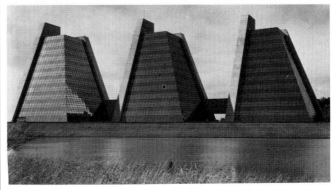

2 *Offices being built for client occupation may be conceived as a corporate or community symbol: College* Life Insurance headquarters *(Roche Dinkeloo, architects).*

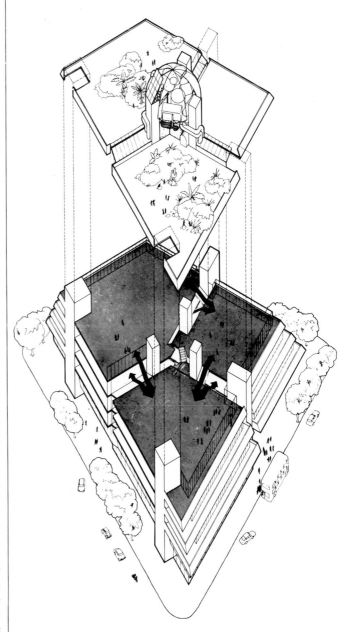

3 *Proposed speculative office block, City Road, London. Raymond J. Cecil & Partners. This project is based on the desire to* provide a sequence of spaces that can either be divided into small tenancies or used as continuous space by one organisation.

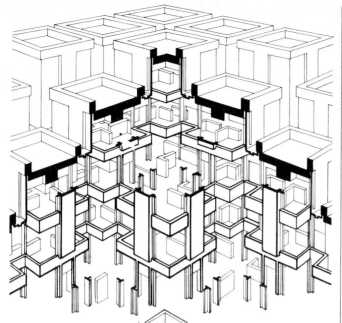

4 *Herman Hertzberger's offices for Centraal Beheer in Apeldoorn are an interesting attempt to personalise the quality of deep plan space while still upholding its advantage of interaction.*

5 *Topsikring headquarters, Ballerup, Denmark: 11 300 m² office building on two floors. Areas are defined by rest areas marked 'b'* *related to different types of garden: 1 flower, 2 tropical, 3 moss, 4 cactus, 5 water, 6 orchid.*

6.03 The speculative projects provide shallow or medium depth space, and in their design and location of cores and circulation routes are suggestive of a more open plan use of space. Because of site constraints and existing shell dimensions, medium depth and deep spaces may be provided in refurbishing examples developed for the speculative market. Such spaces are still treated with the greatest caution by developers and investment institutions in the new building speculative market. For the users' sake one must hope that this experience of leasing deep space will persuade developers that there is a demand and that it is a good investment.

CUSTOM DESIGNED OFFICES

1 Deep plan office space for insurance brokers

AT Aldgate, London
FOR Sedgwick Forbes
BY Fitzroy Robinson & Partners
SITE by Aldgate tube station and surrounded by Botolph Street, Middlesex Street and Aldgate High Street. The underground runs in a tunnel diagonally under the site.
CAR PARKING
Ground floor taken up by car parking for 18 cars, access, reception and loading bay.
BUILDING DESCRIPTION
Eight-storey reinforced concrete frame building, with granite faced sills and columns, two central cores with perimeter columns at 6·6 m centres. Distance from core to perimeter 15·25 m and 7·0 m. Overall dimensions of building about 40 × 60 m. Population of building approx: 1500.
COMPLETION DATE: March 1975

The Sedgwick Forbes Building is the first major deep planned space to be constructed specifically for a client in the City of London, and raises a number of planning, real estate and environmental issues that are likely to come increasingly to the fore in the future. The choice of a deep plan block 62 × 42 m has created a plan form that contradicts estate agents' concepts of viable leasable space; changed the massing of the building and scale of fenestration from that normally associated with the City; and in interior planning raised the issue of workplaces not being adjacent to windows. The issue of internal offices in deep plan space requires serious consideration by statutory bodies for it is clearly illogical in buildings which are totally air-conditioned and have high levels of artificial illumination to demand cellular offices to be on the perimeter for historical reasons of allowing natural light and ventilation. Moreover, many open planned working areas are denied a view because of the location of perimeter cellular offices. Although building deep plan space is more expensive in initial costs, the increased flexibility has already shown advantages. Soon after the beginning of construction the original clients, Sedgwick Collins, merged with Price Forbes. Individual offices are located at the corners of the building and internally adjacent to the core, **2**. The latter have required protracted negotiations with the GLC which require opening and direct lights for habitable rooms.

This is an important building in the context of the City of London, contributing a new dimension to the stock of space available, and creating a new scale and method of site planning more in keeping with the large clerical organisations that make up many City firms today.

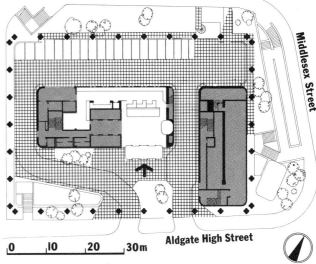

Botolph Street
Middlesex Street
Aldgate High Street

0　10　20　30 m

1 Vehicle access and parking located at ground floor under building block.

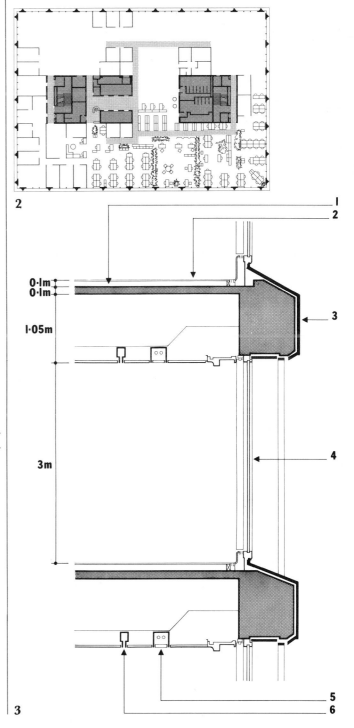

2
0·1 m
0·1 m
1·05 m
3 m
1
2
3
4
5
6

2 Typical office floor showing proportion of cellular to open plan space, internal offices and meeting areas.
3 Detail through perimeter wall.
1 Rc structural topping and pre-stressed trays on high-yield steel lattice beams at 1·65 m centres.
2 Cement and underlay on 1:6 cement/sand screed.

3 Scandinavian beige polished granite facing 38 mm thick in front of 27 mm air space.
4 Pilkingtons sealed glazing units: 6 mm antisolar, 10 mm air space, 10 mm clear float.
5 Twin tube comfort light fittings and air extract units at 1·65 m centres.
6 Continuous Moduline air-conditioning units at 1·65 m centres.

2 Technology and science centre

AT Melbourn, near Cambridge
FOR PA International Management Consultants Ltd
BY Piano & Rogers Architects
SITE
10 miles out of Cambridge and three miles north of Royston. The building is adjacent to the southern boundary of the site, allowing for possible future development of the front.
CAR PARKING
The local planning authorities' requirement was for 1 car per 22·0 m² of gross floor area. In order to leave as much site as possible for landscaping and future building, car parking for approximately 60 cars with a goods delivery point has been located underneath the building for phase 1.
BUILDING DESCRIPTION
Single-storey building 65 m long and 35 m wide supported on columns and having the workshop and plant room facilities, reception and car parking for 60 cars at the lower level, allowing maximum landscaped area and potential for future development. The building has rc columns at 7·2 m centres supporting a light-weight concrete waffle floor with structural steel roof support and wall cladding system on a secondary grid at 2·4 m centres.
COMPLETION DATE March 1975

PATS Centre's work is organised around projects which can vary between weeks and years duration, each project requiring a special mix of skills and expertise.
Unlike a normal office or laboratory the professional staff may require several work places where they can set up experiments and compile reports.
In order to accommodate the wide range of projects and servicing requirements Piano & Rogers proposed a frame structure with columns at 7·2 m centres with the services located directly beneath the floor slab and feeding through boxes in the floor, **1**. The planning concept for the main floor has been to locate the more permanent laboratory requirements (among which are the dark room, furnace room and clean room) in solid partitioned cores in the centre of the building, **2**. The more flexible laboratory areas are located between these cores and separated from the bürolandschaft office areas by removeable glazed partitions and sliding doors, **3**.

Planning for change
In sympathy with the dynamic nature of the client organisation the detailed requirements are varying during the building period. As new projects arise, additional equipment is required, and the demand for laboratory and meeting space increases. Liaison between the client and the architect has been provided by PA's Project Planning Division which has enabled decisions on these detailed requirements to be taken and implemented without delay. The concept of a flexible shell is meeting these demands, and the more complex, highly serviced laboratory requirements are being accommodated beneath the floor slab, thus leaving the main floor still as open as possible, **3**.
The concept of creating a well serviced shed where office and laboratory functions can co-exist would seem to be sympathetic to the demands of an organisation such as PATS. So far the strategy of concentrating on the need for well serviced flexible space, and not freezing on detailed requirements too early in the contract seems to be paying off.

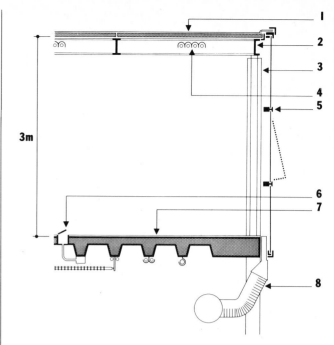

1 *Section through perimeter wall : 1 stressed skin plywood roofing panel with perforated soffit ; 2 180 mm deep two-way steel structure ; 3 precast concrete column ; 4 low brightness fitting 600 mm square ; 5 purpose made steel framing system to receive* 2400 × 1200 mm nominal *fixed glass, white vitreous enamel or pivoting toughened glass panels ; 6 telephone/electrical floor box ; 7 light-weight concrete coffered slab 400 mm deep ; 8 flexible H and V branch ducts.*

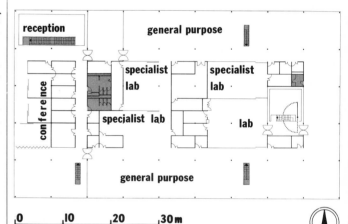

2 *Floor plan with general work areas at perimeter and specialist laboratories in centre.*

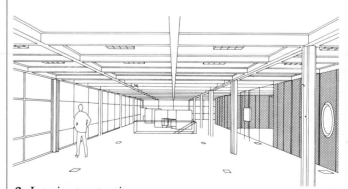

3 *Interior perspective showing general work areas and solid internal cores for specialist activities.*

3 Technical marketing centre

AT Risley Office Park, Warrington New Town
FOR General Electric Company of America,
Plastics Division
BY Chamberlin, Powell & Bon, Architects
SITE
The site is located in the Risley office park which is
part of the Warrington New Town redevelopment
area. The area of the site is 18 500 m².
CAR PARKING
Phase 1 provides 102 spaces.
Phase 2 provides an additional 36 spaces.
BUILDING DESCRIPTION
The office block consists of a two-storey
loadbearing reinforced concrete frame expressed
internally and externally. The external walling is
of aluminium patent glazing, bronze anodised,
with bronze solar glass. Internally the partitions
are non-loadbearing concrete masonry blocks. The
offices are fully air-conditioned, supplied by roof
level package units.
COMPLETION DATE August 1975

GE Plastics' projected offices, laboratories and warehouses
are an example of the space requirements of the new high
technology organisations that are beginning to develop in
this country and are already well established in America.
The GE Plastics scheme is intended as a prestige sales and
distribution headquarters to be occupied by their English
subsidiary, Engineering Polymers Ltd, 1. It will provide
technical assistance for existing and potential customers,
and it is expected that there will be a large number of
visitors who will also be invited into the laboratories.
Chamberlin, Powell & Bon's approach to the problem has
been to house the different activities of offices, laboratories
and warehousing in two distinct but connected buildings
which are located on the site in a formal setting. Additional
office space is planned in a separate office pavilion and the
warehouse and laboratory spaces will be extended.

Internal planning

The approach to the internal planning of the office space,
like the site planning, has an air of formality, 2. The
building is approximately 25 m across with a double
height, roof-lit space in the middle, reminiscent of Frank
Lloyd Wright's Johnson Wax, in which the clerical staff
will be accommodated. Surrounding this double height
space are private offices for directors, salesmen, secretaries
and conference rooms, 3. The accommodation provided is
conceived as being permanent.

1 Simple, formal building
intended to blend with
landscape.

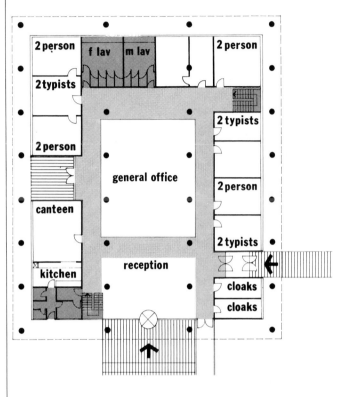

0   25   50 ft

2 Ground floor plan
showing double height
general office area and
single height perimeter
offices.

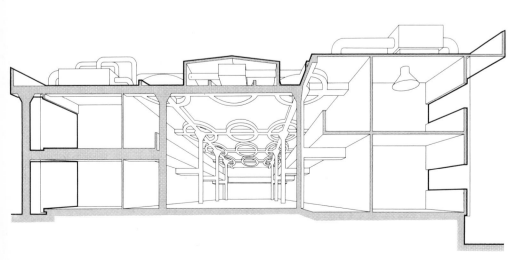

3 Perspective section
showing integration of
lighting—natural (at
column heads) and artificial
(below false ceiling)—with
structural system.

4 Music publishers' offices and warehouses

AT Tours, France
FOR Editions Van de Velde
BY Farrell Grimshaw Partnership
SITE
A cherry orchard on the outskirts of Tours. The building has been located at the rear of the site to retain existing trees.
CAR PARKING
Places for 15 cars on external hard-standing.
BUILDING DESCRIPTION
Single-storey building designed for an initial office accommodation of 25 persons with a possible maximum of 50.
Steel frame with insulated fibre glass cladding panels which are readily interchangeable with sheets of tinted glass where required.
Overall dimensions of building 25 × 25 m.
Structural bays at 5 m centres with 5 and 10 m spans.
Planning module 1·25 m, ceiling module 300 mm.
Subdivision of space with Hausermann partitions.
Continuous overhead power, telephone and lighting tracks suspended from roof.
COMPLETION DATE December 1974

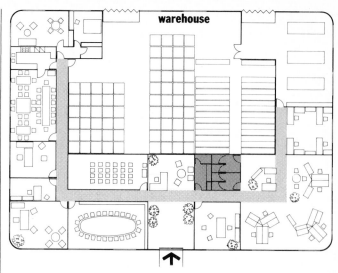

1 *Plan of phase 1 : single-storey building combining warehousing and offices.*

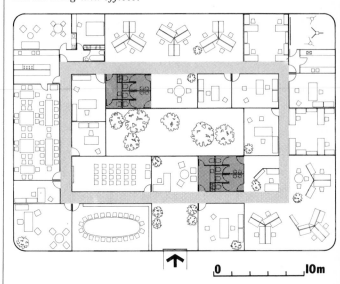

2 *Phase 2 : office accommodation expands around central courtyard ; warehousing on another site.*

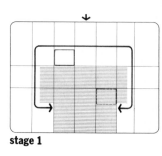

stage 1

Editions Van de Velde was a small family music publishing business based in the centre of Tours. Four years ago the firm purchased a site on the outskirts of the city for future expansion.

Initially the new accommodation required was office space for 25 staff, plus warehousing. It was envisaged that the organisation would expand rapidly as new fields of marketing opened up, and with this in mind it was proposed that the accommodation should be able to house up to 50 staff over the next five years, with a similar increase in warehousing.

Scheme

Farrell Grimshaw's scheme to meet these requirements is a single-storey building which in the first phase combines both warehousing and offices under the same roof, **1**. Then as each expands, the storage accomodation will be moved to another site and the office accomodation extended round a courtyard which is formed in the centre of the building, **2**. To achieve this degree of flexibility the substructure in the initial stages has been designed to allow for the drainage requirements of the final phase courtyard and the additional wc facilities, **3**. The Editions Van de Velde project gains from a flexible approach, which suits a new young management and a rapidly expanding and changing operation. It is expected to reach phase 2, **2**, over the next five years.

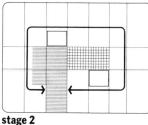

3 *Diagrams showing strategy for expansion. Intermediate stage 2 may not happen.*

stage 2

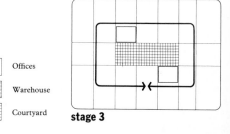

☐ Offices

▨ Warehouse

▦ Courtyard

stage 3

SPEC OFFICES

5 Arundel Great Court offices and hotel

AT Arundel Great Court, London
FOR Capital & Counties and Legal & General
Development in association with the trustees of the
Norfolk Family Estates
BY Frederick Gibberd & Partners
SITE
The site is bounded on the north by the Strand and
slopes down towards the river and Temple
underground station. The site, orginally four city
blocks, has been developed as a single block with
offices and a hotel arranged round a central
landscaped courtyard.
CAR PARKING
Basement parking for 215 cars is provided for both
the office and hotel users.
BUILDING DESCRIPTION
Six- and eight-storey office blocks arranged on
three sides around a garden court with a hotel on
the fourth side overlooking the river.
Structure: In-situ reinforced concrete frame on a
7·65 × 5·5 m grid, clad in Portland stone.
Depth of office block about 15 m.
Planning grid at mullion spacing 2·75 m, with
electrical and telephone outlets located on the
perimeter wall and columns.
COMPLETION DATE Early 1975

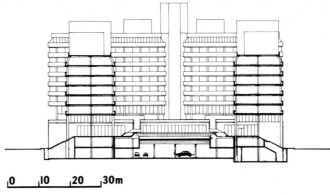

1 *Section through site*   *from surrounding streets to*
showing continuous   *central courtyard.*
pedestrian movement space

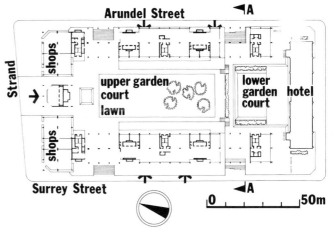

2 *Ground floor plan.*

The Arundel Great Court development shows a positive
attempt by a developer and his consultants to create open
spaces and building forms which will make a contribution
to the area.

Planning concept

The scheme proposed by Frederick Gibberd treats the four
original city blocks as one super block, and establishes one
major architectural composition of even height, that is in
scale with Somerset House and the Middle Temple
adjacent. The office blocks are placed round the perimeter
of a central courtyard, which at pedestrian level is open
with views and ways through to become part of its
surroundings. The objective was not to create an enclosed
space like a university cloister, but a central lawn open to its
neighbours and the public.
The original idea of the open lawn has been given
additional character by the north-south slope of the site to
the river, which has suggested two levels and the creation of
a lawn and sunken garden, with potentially very different
characters, **1, 2**.
For a speculative building the scheme is well provided with
access and toilet facilities and the frequent provision of
duct spaces means that additional executive lavatories and
kitchen facilities could easily be accommodated for small
professional firms, **3**.
The structure is a 7·5 m span with a central row of columns,
creating an off-centre corridor which would allow cellular
offices of 6 m × 2·75 m down one side and open planned
group areas of 7·5 m depth down the other. Shallow
cellular offices with an internal space for support staff or
completely open planned space could be provided. The
latter would be particularly suitable at the dead end
positions, **4**.

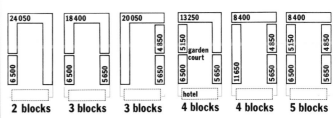

3 *Diagram showing*   *subdividing office space for*
alternative methods of   *various sized letting.*

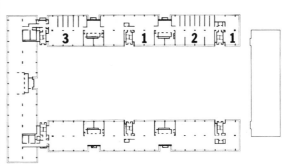

4 *Typical office floor*   *planned space; 2 cellular*
showing possible methods of   *and group spaces; 3 cellular*
office layout : 1 open   *and open plan spaces.*

6 Offices at The Hague

AT The Hague, Holland
FOR Argyle Securities, London
BY Yorke Rosenberg Mardall, London; Groosman Partners, Rotterdam
SITE
Bounded by the railway and main arterial road into the city.
CAR PARKING
Separate multi-storey car park adjacent to office building. Accommodation for 197 cars on eight half-levels staggered in section. Clad in vertical metal louvres.
BUILDING DESCRIPTION
Fifteen floors, ground floor being entrance and computer facilities. Reinforced concrete structure with flat slabs and columns on 6 m grid.
Offset core dimensions, core to perimeter 8 m and 12·5 m.
Internal partitions may be located on a 1·5 m planning grid.
Fully air-conditioned.
COMPLETION DATE November 1974

The activities of British property developers on the Continent has resulted in an increased amount of work being undertaken by British architectural firms in Europe. In this project Argyle Securities, the developers, felt it was important to use an English firm of architects to reduce their own communication problems by making sure the briefing stage and legal documents were in their own language.

Yorke Rosenberg Mardall's approach to working in Holland was to associate with a Dutch firm of architects to simplify many of the design communication problems, gain advice on the choice of components and construction techniques, ease the production of detailed construction documentation and give site instructions. In practice, as the job progressed, YRM found that many of the components and proprietary systems were the same as or similar to those in this country but under different names.

Planning concept

The building has been conceived in principle as a traditional depth, central core tower block, but there are several interesting aspects to the detailed planning of the reception floor. To create the maximum of usable floorspace it has been planned as internal space surrounded by rentable space on the perimeter, with an entrance tunnel on two sides, **1**. On a typical upper office floor the core has been planned as an offset block, the main vertical shafts (lift, stairs and ducts) being located in the geometrical centre of the building.

The core has access through it from each side, with no doors between the lift lobby and the main space. It is therefore possible to accommodate a high proportion of cellular offices or provide open plan layouts in the 12·5 m deep space, **2**. The floor plans also allow each floor to be subdivided into as many as four separate tenancies, yet when one tenant in in occupancy the open lift lobby allows a continuity of access from one side of the block to the other through the core.

As a speculative development the quality of this block is well above average. The planning of the core with through access and the possibility of subdivision for a variety of tenancies is a major development from the more traditional core with circulation round its perimeter. With such expertise exported to Europe it would be satisfying if the experience were passed back into British developments to improve the quality of speculative building in this country.

1 Building located in twilight area bounded by highway, railway, canal and run-down two-storey housing.

2 Typical floor plan. The off-centre core allows a combination of cellular and open plan space.

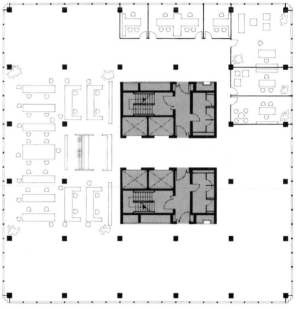

3 Detail through perimeter wall: 1 rc slab contains cast-in conduit for lighting power-supply. Carpet bonded to screed; 2 perimeter trunking containing power and telephone cables; 3 convector; low pressure hot water finned tube system behind stove enamelled steel convector housing/sill unit; 4 air extract via light fittings to ceiling void plenum; 5 variable input via linear diffusers.

0·056m
0·2m
0·425m
2·519m

7 Commercial building

AT Central Milton Keynes
FOR Milton Keynes Development Corporation
BY Central Milton Keynes Division
SITE in the city centre near the shopping centre.
CAR PARKING
The basic principle of the central area plan is to create publicly available peripheral parking space shared between adjoining developments. Parking is at ground level next to the building round the edge of the development block.
BUILDING DESCRIPTION
Two-storey development round two courtyards to house a wide variety of commercial activities.
Construction: reinforced concrete columns on a 9·6 m square grid. The frame is clad externally in grey Cornish granite.
Windows are of grey glass in black anodised aluminium frames.
Depth of office space: 16·8 m on first floor and 14·4 m on ground floor.
Planning grid for window mullions, reflective ceiling plan and telephone and socket outlets is 2·4 m.
COMPLETION DATE May 1976

Unlike the other speculative schemes illustrated, this building in the new Milton Keynes city centre is being developed by the corporation for renting in a commercially untested location. It is particularly interesting to view the scheme in the context of:

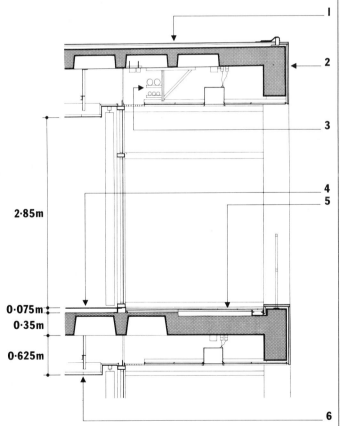

1 Section through gallery access and perimeter wall : 1 granite chippings 20 mm on bitumen dressing on layer of Permabit 60 roofing on building felt on 25 mm fibre board on 40 mm polystyrene insulation on vapour barrier ; 2 cladding of honed Cornish grey granite; 3 electric cables; 4 linotiles on sand/cement screed; 5 reconstructed granite paving tiles 300 × 300 × 25 mm to gallery; 6 suspended metal ceiling with integrated lighting and air handling units.

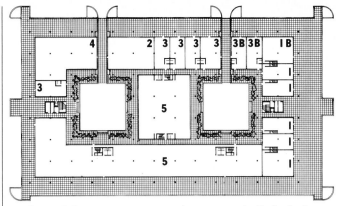

2 Ground floor : 1 two-storey office and commercial space (B is bank) ; 2 commercial space (restaurant) ; 3 single floor lock-up units; 4 public house; 5 speculative office space.

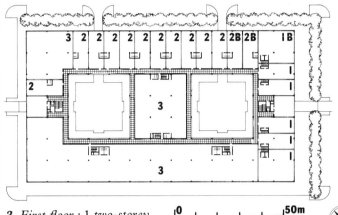

3 First floor : 1 two-storey office and commercial space ; 2 professional office space ; 3 speculative office space.

● how a rapidly growing new town has chosen to deal with its office building requirement ;
● what advantages new town office developments may offer compared with existing city centre schemes ;
● what advantages a scheme developed directly by the corporation may offer to the users who are usually restricted by the traditional requirements and standards of developers.

Planning concept
The scheme provides a variety of types of space, 2, 3.
1 Lock up spaces with self-contained service core varying in size from 100-200 m² with dual access from the pavement and courtyards. These units will be used for such businesses as a launderette, temporary grocer's shop and newsagent ;
2 larger spaces of approximately 800 m² at corner locations, usually on two floors, for the pub, restaurant and bank ;
3 small units yielding 200-400 m² with two floors of space and access from pavement and gallery ;
4 small office units yielding approximately 120 m² with access from the first floor gallery. These units might be used by small professional firms with a staff of 9-12 people ;
5 approximately 3300 m² of space with air-conditioning, integrated ceiling lighting and floor finishes, which can be subdivided into units of about 500 m² and connected over two floors, 1.
The office space provided, especially on the first floor, suggests a number of problems. The 120 m² office shells being built into the scheme appear unsuitable for small professional firms. The relatively narrow frontage of 7·2 m in relation to the depth of 16·8 m allows for only two or three private offices and an internal open planned area, yet professional offices tend to require a high proportion of cellular space for partners to confer with their clients.

LOCAL AND CENTRAL GOVERNMENT OFFICES

8 County administrative hq

AT Nunnery Wood, Worcester
FOR Hereford-Worcester County Council
BY Robert Matthew Johnson-Marshall & Partners
SITE
On the outskirts of Worcester on the road to
Stratford-on-Avon.
CAR PARKING (PHASE 1)
On open hard-standing 325 temporary car parking
spaces are provided.
At basement level 65 spaces are provided for
members, visitors and senior council officers.
BUILDING DESCRIPTION
Three-storey building designed as a series of
approximately 500 m² pavilions that in section and
height step down the site.
Phase 1: population for about 500 staff with
council chamber, committee rooms and members'
accommodation. Social and recreational facilities
to serve about 1000 staff. Final development should
allow for 1500 staff and a possible 200 additional
staff for the area health board.
Within each pavilion there is a central structural
grid of 10·8 m with columns at 5·4 m centres at the
perimeter.
COMPLETION DATE Summer 1977

The green fields approach of the project contrasts with the
city centre schemes of Sheffield and Portsmouth (schemes
9 and 10), and it was felt, would provide a pleasant working
environment, and room for expansion, which would
compensate for the degree of isolation and separation of
staff from city centre facilities at lunch time, **1**.

Briefing

In discussing the office environment the client's brief
carefully refrains from demanding either an open plan or
cellular solution and highlights the varied nature of local
government work. The brief suggests that 'the design of
the offices should allow for any normal office function to
take place, from typewriting to technical drawing.

Planning concept

From the client's informal and undogmatic attitudes
Robert Matthew Johnson-Marshall developed the concept
of a flexible open plan space. Since local government relies
on staff who stay for a long time and fit into a career
structure, it was felt that to attract and hold them the
physical environment and accommodation standards were
of the utmost importance. The architects proposed distinct
manageable areas of open plan space that would accommodate about 50 persons.
The reasoning behind this size of group was:
● the realisation that working groups which needed close
  interconnection were seldom greater than 40-50 staff;
● it was a size that was still socially comprehensible, as
  borne out by the average size of the school class or the
  army platoon;
● architecturally it produced an acceptable proportion of
  height in relation to width.
In addition it was felt that this size of grouping would allow
good views for all and a degree of control over the
environment, no work station being more than 12 m from
the perimeter, **2, 3**. The proposed scheme is based on a
planning unit of approximately 500 m² which allows for

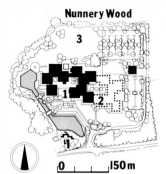

1 *Site located on city outskirts which has allowed pavilion planning in a landscaped setting : 1 phase 1 ; 2 projected phase 2 ; 3 site for further expansion.*

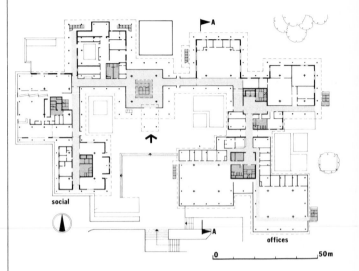

2 *Ground floor plan showing location of main circulation routes through pavilions.*

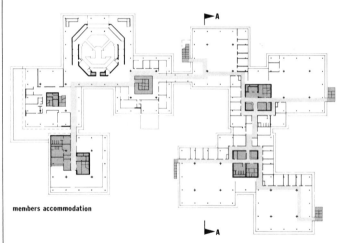

3 *Upper floor plan (level 2) showing possible location of cellular offices and circulation.*

4 *Section through site : printing and stationery store with offices above.*

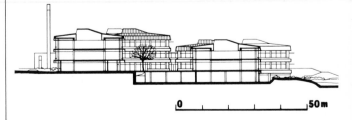

cellularisation of 10-35 per cent and forms a series of
interconnected pavilions on the site, **4**. Expansion would be
by adding additional pavilions.

9 Town hall extension

AT Sheffield
FOR City of Sheffield Metropolitan District Council
BY Civic Design Section of the Department of Planning and Design
SITE A glazed bridge connects the extension to the existing Victorian town hall, adjacent to the main shopping thoroughfares of Sheffield and overlooks an existing public garden on the north-west, and a new garden to the rear.
CAR PARKING
Accommodation for about 400 cars on basement and mezzanine levels.
BUILDING DESCRIPTION
Three-storey, varying depth block served by three central cores, with a penthouse floor for restaurants and plant. Reinforced concrete structure with columns on a diagonal grid at 11 m centres. Cladding precast concrete polished aggregate finish, 2·5 m wide storey-height panels. The lighting is on a 2·1 m grid with floor outlets located at 3 m centres, 3.
The offices have been designed for a total population of 1400 staff who initially are planned to be the housing, city treasurer's, and planning and design departments.
COMPLETION DATE July 1976

Like the majority of local authorities, the City of Sheffield has long outgrown its original Victorian premises and occupies a variety of accommodation in different parts of the city. Thought had been given since before the war to extending the town hall.
In 1968 the management consultancy firm of Urwick Orr was appointed to advise on the structure of the city's departments. One of its recommendations was that the city should develop new offices on bürolandschaft principles.

Planning concept
The concept for the new extension was to house all the departments that deal with the public under one roof, and as far as possible to accommodate all staff except department heads in open planned space. The building was designed so that the ground floor could be used for sections in constant contact with the public, 1. Upper floors were designed to create deep plan areas flanked by narrow depth offices for executives, 2.
The building was designed to have a specific proportion of closed offices to open offices and, like the majority of integrated environmental schemes of that period, separate ventilation and air-conditioning systems were designed for the cellular and open planned offices respectively, to save money. The result of this decision is that the flexibility of being able to vary the number and location of cellular offices has been negated, and it will now be a costly operation to vary the accommodation. It is interesting to compare the Sheffield approach with that of the new Hereford—Worcester headquarters (scheme 8) where great emphasis has been given to the amount of cellular space provided and the degree to which the proportion of cellular to open space may vary.

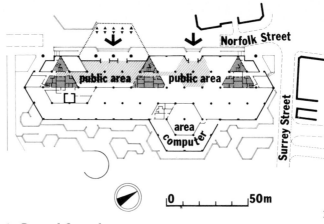

1 Ground floor plan: areas to be used for contact with public.

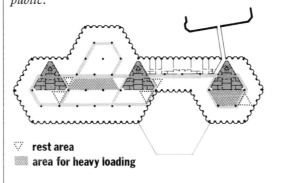

rest area
area for heavy loading

2 Typical upper office floor showing area given over to cellular offices and varied depth open areas.

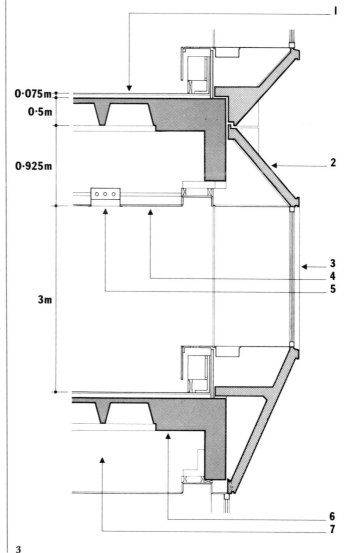

3 Detail through perimeter wall: 1 screed and finish; 2 precast concrete cladding units, ground external finish; 3 clear double glazed sealed units, 2·1 × 1 m; 4 patent suspended ceiling-fibre board fully accessible; 5 air handling fluorescent continuous light fitting; 6 in-situ concrete frame; 7 plenum void.

10 Civic offices

AT new city centre, Portsmouth
FOR City of Portsmouth Corporation
BY Teggin & Taylor
SITE In a redevelopment of a central area precinct of about 12·5 ha, the civic offices flank the north and east sides of a new pedestrianised Guildhall Square. The square is on two levels which has allowed pedestrian links to be formed from the civic offices to the Station entrance.
CAR PARKING About 220 cars are accommodated at lower ground floor and podium with pedestrian links to adjacent multi-storey precinct garaging.
BUILDING DESCRIPTION
Six-storey block with an additional floor at lower ground level for parking, storage and goods delivery. The ground floor is largely special for uses requiring easy public access.
The construction is a 300 mm deep flat slab supported on concrete columns at 7·2 m centres, the bracing being provided by the reinforced concrete walls of the cores. The structural elements are covered with ceramic mosaic tiles and the cladding is a painted aluminium frame with solar bronze glass infill. The depth of the building is 18·5 m to allow for a choice of open or cellular planning. The planning grid is 900 mm: telephone and electrical outlets at 1·8 m centres.
COMPLETION DATE April 1976

Unlike the Hereford–Worcester headquarters the form of the civic offices at Portsmouth was generated largely by the requirements of the master plan for the city centre precinct drawn up by Lord Esher with whom the present architects were in practice.

Because Portsmouth and Southsea lacked a central core which was both unmistakable and worthy of their size and importance, the redevelopment plan was intended to create a centre which would integrate existing activities round the Guildhall, and create a pleasant focus where people might congregate. Within this framework the civic offices have been conceived as buildings which reflect and enhance the Guildhall portico, provide enclosure to a bricked plaza, and by the careful positioning of the solid cores, present visual stops to vistas from different locations in the development.

Planning concept
When the design of the civic offices was begun in 1965 the architects envisaged a bespoke solution designed round the detailed brief of accommodation prepared by the town clerk's department based on a population of 1100 staff plus 10 per cent expansion. The project was later shelved and when design work was resumed in early 1970 it became apparent that some departments had expanded and others contracted. The population to be accommodated had risen to 1500 and with local government reorganisation other major changes could be foreseen.
The limitations of a bespoke building were realised and the local authority accepted the proposal to 'design and obtain approval for the erection of a flexible office structure in which the local authority could establish itself, but which, as circumstances demanded, could be sublet, altered or leased for other purposes'. The building shell which was finally conceived was 18·5 m deep, **2**, so allowing for:
● total cellularisation with a central zone of 5 m for circulation, storage, waiting and informal meetings;
● individual offices on one side of the block adjacent to open planned areas for groups of 8-12 people;
● open planned areas using the complete block width.

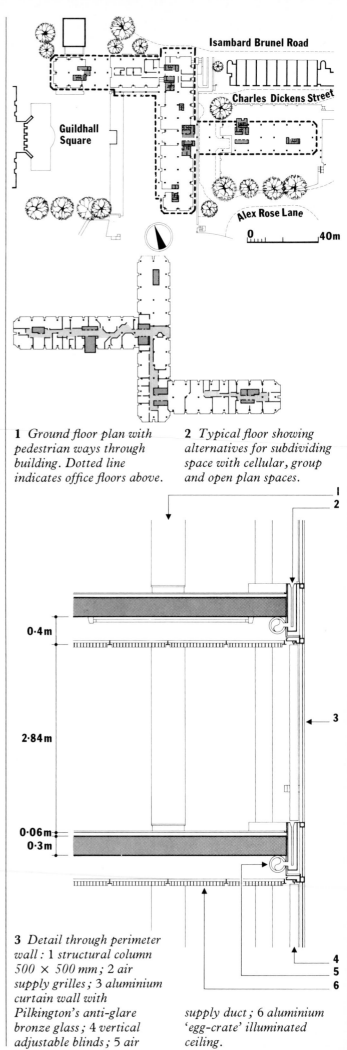

1 Ground floor plan with pedestrian ways through building. Dotted line indicates office floors above.

2 Typical floor showing alternatives for subdividing space with cellular, group and open plan spaces.

3 Detail through perimeter wall: 1 structural column 500 × 500 mm; 2 air supply grilles; 3 aluminium curtain wall with Pilkington's anti-glare bronze glass; 4 vertical adjustable blinds; 5 air supply duct; 6 aluminium 'egg-crate' illuminated ceiling.

11 New government offices

AT Cathays Park, Cardiff
FOR Property Services Agency
BY Alex Gordon & Partners
SITE
The new offices which are primarily intended for the Welsh Office are in the traditional civic complex near the city centre. They will be connected to the existing Welsh Office building and will be used partly by the Welsh Office and partly by other government department(s) yet to be selected.
CAR PARKING
Parking spaces for 495 cars are provided on two floors below ground level.
BUILDING DESCRIPTION
The proposal is for a five storey building which will provide accommodation for approximately 2500 staff mainly as planned open offices. The block is approximately 85 m wide by 120 m on its widest floor, with two internal courtyards, creating spaces on average 26 m wide. The structural columns are at 8·7 m centres, and the cladding will be of Portland stone and bronze coloured metal to relate to the existing building in Cathays Park. Lighting level reduced from 896 to 570 lux intended to give 20 per cent energy cost saving.

1 *Extension (sic) for Crown offices to original Welsh Office (on left).*

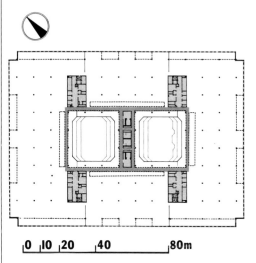

2 *Section showing internal courtyards and cantilevered facades to reduce* *massiveness in relation to existing Welsh Office.*

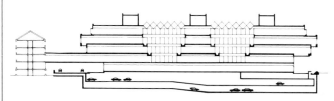

```
0  10  20    40            80m
```

3 *Typical floor plan. Dotted lines indicate possible locations for cellular offices.*

A five storey building will provide accommodation for approximately 2500 staff mainly in planned open offices, **1**. Cathays Park is one of a number of major offices for central government outside the London area which are under discussion at the present moment.

The scheme is interesting from the point of view of the massing of a building for 2500 persons, the overall dimensions being about 120×85 m with a typical gross floor area of 9323 m². The architects have stepped each floor to reduce the bulk of the facade, and created two internal courtyards to reduce the uninterrupted size of the interior spaces, **2**.

Planning concept

The planned open offices varying from 16 to 27 m in depth are deeper than present central government offices. The choice of such deep space is surprising in view of the fact that a large number of government departments tend to work in groups of 8-12 people, related to a more senior staff member who may well require private office accommodation. Group spaces about 16 m deep, a concept developed by the offices group at the DOE, would probably suit these requirements better.

The design allows flexibility as to the degree of cellularisation on any floor. Individual private offices have been planned to occur in the positions shown on the plan, **3**. Two categories of office are proposed, those with speech privacy and those in the internal zones with minimum speech privacy. A square coffered ceiling to be used throughout, **4**, will allow for complete flexibility in the location of individual offices and for the upgrading of the quality of speech privacy in the future.

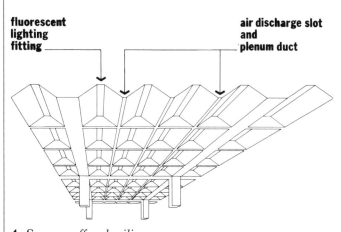

fluorescent lighting fitting
air discharge slot and plenum duct

4 *Square coffered ceiling integrating lighting and air-conditioning.*

RENOVATION

12 Bridge House

AT Southwark
FOR English Property Corporation Ltd
BY Renton Howard Wood Levin Partnership
SITE
The building occupies a visually important site on the southern approach to London Bridge. The building is within Southwark Borough's strategy plan for the Thameside area adjacent to, but not included in, the Hay's wharf sites.
CAR PARKING
Garaging for seven cars with access from Montague Close at the Cathedral precinct level.
BUILDING DESCRIPTION
The original building designed by Sir Robert Smirke has been gutted and a new structure threaded into the existing shell. An extension at the rear has been demolished and replaced by a new extension. The lower floors which are accessible from the Cathedral precinct have been allocated for use as a public house and restaurant. The upper floors with access from Borough High Street are designated for office use. The six storey extension at the rear has a concrete frame with areas of exposed aggregate finish and brick cladding below bridge level. The cladding above bridge level is lead faced spandrels with anodised double glazed fixed windows. The window mullions are on a 1·35 m grid. The power and telephone distribution is a cavity floor duct system to be wired up by the tenant.
COMPLETION DATE January 1976

The particular form of construction chosen for the renovation was determined by a need:
● to ensure stability of the structure during gutting operations without extensive external or internal shoring due to site limitations;
● to create the minimum loading so as to avoid the need for extensive foundation work which could disturb existing foundations.
The structural system is a light structural steel frame anchored to the existing external walls and threaded through holes cut in the existing timber floors, **1**. The flooring on top of the steel column and beam framework is of precast concrete planks with a structural screed topping. The timber beam joists and boarding are stripped out as the concrete floors are constructed.
The new extension at the rear of the site forms space which is approximately 14 m deep from the core and could be used for a totally open planned layout or as a combination of cellular and landscaped space, **2**.

The site layout should greatly improve the environs of Southwark Cathedral. The shallow depths in the renovated Bridge House combined with the relatively deep plan space of the new extension provide an attractive range of office space. It is easy to visualise an organisation with a requirement for both smaller good quality spaces and larger clerical areas finding this development very attractive. The executive and public areas could be housed in the conversion and the open planned areas in the new extension at the rear.

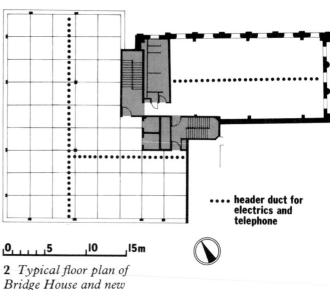

•••• header duct for electrics and telephone

0 ___ 5 ___ 10 ___ 15m

2 *Typical floor plan of Bridge House and new extension.*

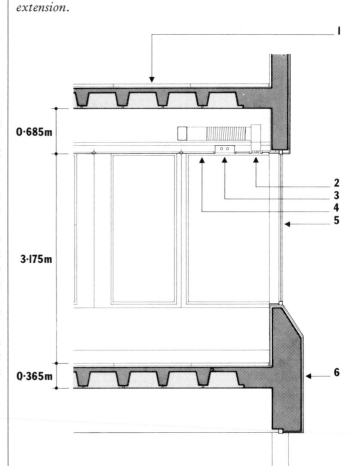

0·685m

3·175m

0·365m

1 *Diagrammatic section showing new floor system into existing sheet of Bridge House. Roof and fourth floor supported on existing walls. Steel frame carries intermediate floors and provides lateral restraint to existing walls.*

4
3
2
I
bridge level
UG
M
LG
B

0 ,3 ,6 ,9 ,12m

3 *Section through perimeter wall: 1 in-situ rc slab 300 mm with Spanform wood-wool infill units; 2 air supply grilles; 3 continuous lighting troughs in alternate bays; 4 special pvc-faced modular ceiling with* *partition accepting channels at 1·35 m centres; 5 sealed double glazing with anodised frames (40 per cent of windows open for emergency ventilation); 6 in-situ rc spandrel with no 4 lead on inodorous felt.*

13 12-18 Grosvenor Gardens

AT Grosvenor Gardens, London SW1
FOR Chesterfield Properties Ltd
BY Chapman Taylor Partners
SITE
Overlooking a mature London square in a strategic
location close to Victoria station.
CAR PARKING
Basement car parking for approximately 17 cars.
BUILDING DESCRIPTION
The development consists of a scheme to demolish
completely and rebuild behind the original
Victorian facade. The scheme consists of six floors
with an additional mezzanine at the rear. The
original party walls in three of the existing houses
have been removed to give a clear area of
approximately 24 × 24 m on the main floor. The
structure is an in-situ reinforced concrete frame
at approximately 7·5 m centres.
Electrical and telephone outlets are located in
floor trunking embedded in the screed
approximately 1 m from the perimeter walls and
on the columns. Light fittings are at 2·20 m centres.
COMPLETION DATE November 1975

Numbers 12-18 Grosvenor Gardens are part of a terrace
built in the 1880s in the French chateau style overlooking
its own residents' gardens.
The scheme graphically illustrates the degree of work
involved in converting and conserving existing office
accommodation.

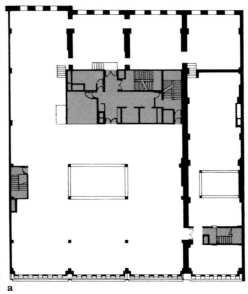

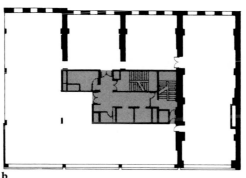

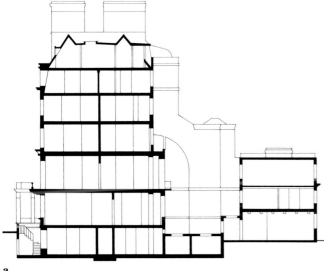

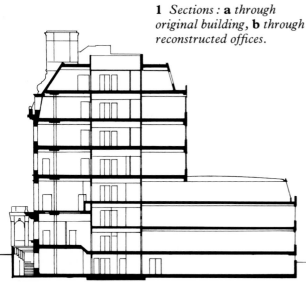

1 *Sections :* **a** *through
original building,* **b** *through
reconstructed offices.*

2 *Plans :* **a** *first floor,*
b *upper floors.*

The facades facing the garden were left standing, and the
building behind was almost completely dismantled so that
the frontage would not be affected. Behind the film-set
facade the office space was replanned and completely
rebuilt to create a more efficient ratio of net to gross floor
area, more easily usable floor space, and a better quality of
finish and environment than existed in the original blocks.
The developers' experience of this form of redevelopment
suggests that it is certainly no cheaper than total demolition
and building from scratch. It was also important to develop
two to three units at the same time to get the best ratio of
services and access to usable office space. The accommodation will suit organisations which require a high
degree of interaction in their method of work, although a
greater concern for the potential users' requirements could
have provided more effective space at little extra cost. The
location of light fittings on the reflective ceiling plan does
not seem to have been considered in relation to possible
partition layouts. In the deep space on the ground, first and
mezzanine floors socket and telephone outlets are located
on vertical surfaces at about 7 m spacing which may
severely limit the servicing of individual work places. The
heating and air-conditioning units at desk height round the
perimeter of the spaces encroach into the rentable area of
the building and reduce usable floor space, **2**.
This is nevertheless a welcome move in the development of
new office space. The character of Belgravia has been
retained, while well serviced high quality, usable office
space has been created, with an elegance, style and
character that new developments are seldom able to
achieve. Hopefully, as architects become more involved
with rebuilding existing structures, their understanding of
historical styles will develop, and more than merely the
original facades will be retained.

Section 9: A possible future

New directions

The main themes of the handbook are drawn together. THE EDITORS review the experience of the last few years and look forward to likely new developments in the design of office shells and scenery.

Introduction
1.01 The first AJ series on office design ended in the early 60s with the first news of office landscaping. For the next decade this idea dominated office design. It is appropriate at the end of this book to look ahead and to try to predict which new ideas are likely to influence design for the next 10 years.

Major themes
1.02 The two major themes which have run through this book are *shell and scenery*, and the emphasis on the *process* of office design and use. These themes stem from what has been learned from office landscaping in Europe, from real estate practice in the UK and the US, from the theoretical study of organisations and from the practical problems of maintaining and running large stocks of office space for growing and changing corporate bodies.

Shell and scenery
1.03 In offices it is important to be clear how long each design element is likely to last, to distinguish between long life elements, such as structure and core, and shorter term elements such as partitions and furniture. The main design problem for the shell is to keep many options open; the problem for the design of scenery is to meet precise but short term requirements.

Types of organisation and space
1.04 Deep down, the proponents of office landscaping assumed that all organisations were the same and that consequently office landscaping was equally appropriate in all circumstances. This cannot be so. In this book it has been argued that there are generic types of office organisation each with a distinctly different set of spatial requirements. In parallel there are distinct types of office shell and scenery each with different properties.

The space planning process
1.05 There exists a whole battery of standards and procedures to guide the consumer, the client, to choose the right amount and type of space to meet his requirements. Many of these are simply applied common sense. Others are closely related to organisational procedures. Sometimes decision making about design involves an interactive procedure with the client, either at the highest level or in the midst of countless departments and sections.

Space management
1.06 Architects are traditionally concerned with the design of single, new buildings. Much of our thinking is limited by this concern. We are less sensitive to the entirely different point of view of the organisational client who is less interested in 'projects' than in continually fitting a volatile organisation through time into a diverse and changing stock of space scattered in several places. The client's problem of space management is, of course, also a kind of design, although an unusual one, for architects; it is a continuing process.

2 Trends to watch

2.01 This is a very interesting moment in office design. The major themes which we have identified are potent agents for destroying simple minded allegiance to one kind of solution, for forcing to our attention the design implications of user requirements and user policy, for enlarging the traditional boundaries of architectural responsibility from one-off projects to planning the use of space through time, and for solving the problem of meeting precise user requirements in long term and often speculative office building shells. What new kinds of office design are likely to emerge?

2.02 Sheer size has been one of the most spectacular characteristics of modern office space. Partly this has been a consequence of the application of a superior building technology which has been able to make such spaces habitable. Partly it has resulted from arguments that size and openness encourage communications and permit flexibility. The scale of these spaces is best realised when comparisons are made between deep office space and other building types such as houses, large or small, **1**.

2.03 Most of the developments which seem imminent are a reaction against the size of these very deep open spaces. It is as if they are attempts to mediate between the individual and the organisation as a whole as it is represented by the bulk of the total building. Whether large centralised organisations will continue to be viable or appropriate is another question.

2.04 What is new in office design is often a commonplace in other building types. Certainly echoes of some of the major architectural ideas of the century can now be found in office planning, not as arbitrary devices but as responses to the fundamental user problem of expressing the significance of the individual and the small group while still preserving the integrity of the organisation as a whole. Several of these architectural precedents which are being put to new uses are illustrated below.

Intermediate elements

2.05 Older office landscaping and especially American open plan offices had very few separating elements between workplaces. Gradually more and more screens, storage units, large plants, etc, have been introduced until the degree of subdivision in basically open space has become very high. Screen based furniture systems have followed this trend since this furniture has taken on many of the functions of the old fixed partition. There are now examples of the introduction of fixed partitions, or fins, with no return, very like the walls in Mies van der Rohe's Barcelona Pavilion or his brick house project of 1923. The effect of this device is to create spaces which are separate

1

2

3

1 *Comparison of open office : Belgravia house converted to office use and a Parker Morris standard house, drawn to the same scale.*
2 *Effect shown by Mies van der Rohe's brick house project, 1923.*
3 *Same effect in Rietveld's sculpture pavilion, Arnhem, 1954.*

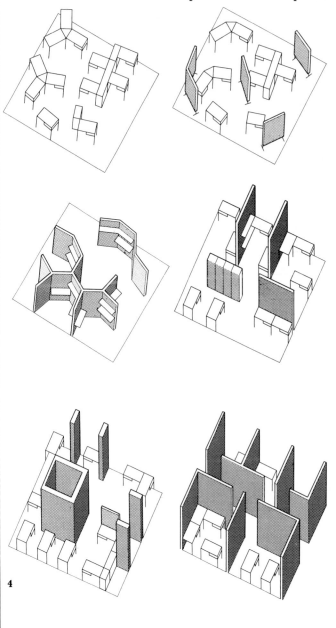

4

4 *The full gamut of possibilities of subdivision.*

but which flow into one another, and which are all connected to the outside view, **2, 3**. In this way working groups of various sizes within the organisation can be distinct but separate.

2.06 So far such effects have been achieved by the intermediate elements of short term scenery. There seems no reason why the core itself should not be 'shattered' to provide a similar interconnected stock of spaces. Figure **4** shows the full range from open plan, to screening, to screen furniture, to fixed fins, to shattered core, to cellular plans.

Modules of space

2.07 A similar desire to achieve distinct and separate modules of space which interlock into a whole is evident in Hertzberger's Centraal Beheer building in Apeldoorn, **5**. Again the basic theme is the relation of the individual to the organisation, an idea which has obsessed Hertzberger in a great many non-office projects. The novelty of this kind of solution in office design should not make us forget a long and respectable tradition of modules of space in modern architecture. Two examples are indicative: Louis Kahn's Richards Laboratory in Philadelphia, **6** and Aldo van Eyke's children's home in Amsterdam, **7**.

2.08 The significance of the modules of space approach compared with intermediate elements is that the impact on the shape of the building shell is far more drastic. For the first time for many years in office design the trend of the increasingly anonymous shell has been reversed and long term building elements are again doing much of the work of spatial separation. Architecture is coming back into office planning, **8**.

Reversible space

2.09 In Germany the reaction to very deep open plan spaces has taken the form of an interest in what is called 'reversible space', that is building plans which produce not one space but several, some of which can be either open or cellular, **9**. Apart from the obvious concern with the accommodation of small units within larger organisations, this German development shows how, in an economy in which custom built office buildings are almost the rule, the problem of keeping options open for future organisational change is being met.

2.10 The Anglo-Saxon tradition of the single flexible speculative office shell, which reaches its highest form in New York, is an entirely different response to the same problem. So is the traditional Japanese house, in which only the interconnecting spaces are positive and in which, by removing the 'scenery', spaces are indeed reversible, **10**.

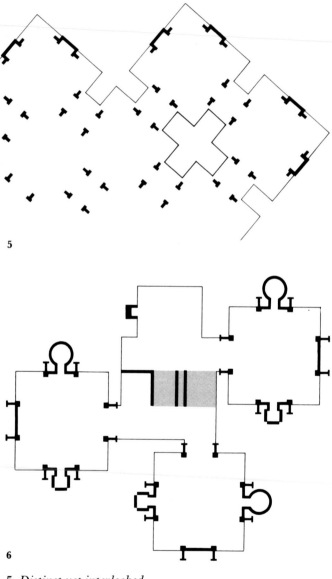

5

6

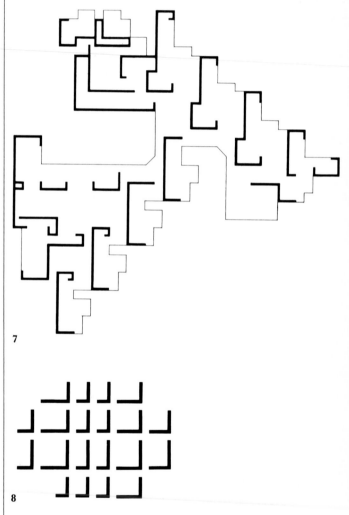

7

8

5 *Distinct yet interlocked spaces in office planning.*
6 *Early version of Richards Laboratory showing interconnected modules of space.*

7 *The same principle as **6** in Aldo van Eyke's children's home, Amsterdam.*
8 *Flexibility for groups changing size over time using a two-dimensional sheet of interconnected small rooms accommodates unpredictable number of changing working groups.*

(From C. Alexander, A pattern language which generates multi service centres, Center for Environmental Studies, Berkeley, California, 1968.

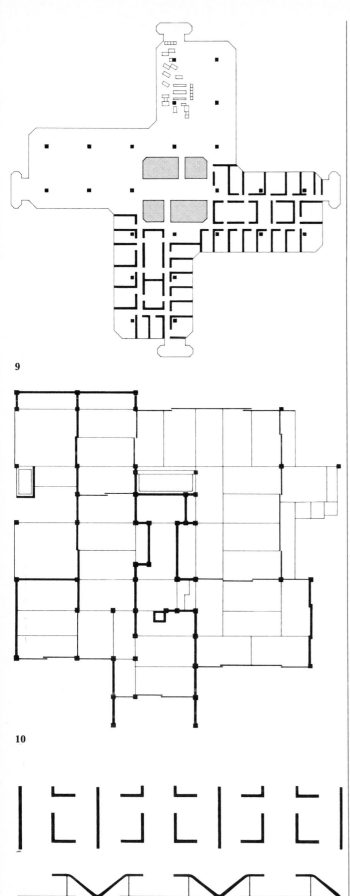

9

10

11

Conservation of energy

2.11 When the original AJ series began the energy crisis had not made itself felt. Undoubtedly deep open space has many advantages for office planning providing its limitations are understood. What we are less sure of now is its cost, in terms of energy. A new design problem has been posed: is it possible to achieve the flexibility and interconnectedness of deep space without unduly high energy costs? At least one study suggests that it is.[1] There will be many responses to this problem without simply reverting to mean and constraining, naturally lit and ventilated, speculative office floor plans. These responses may take the form of more elaborate sections or of the increased use of courts. Perhaps the solutions which emerge may owe more to school or hospital planning than to conventional office design, **11**.

3 Postscript

3.01 This handbook could be one of the last purely on office design. As office work becomes increasingly important in our economy, it becomes harder to define. Boundaries are crumbling; between home and office, between factory work and office work, between the realms of equipment, between computers and men.

3.02 However, we architects are in danger of being locked into older prototypes of what an office is. As we have tried to argue in this chapter, there may be very great and unexplored similarities between accommodation for office work and for other activities such as teaching, health care and living. Innovations seem to come from those who can leap over conventional boundaries and learn from one field what is likely to be useful in another. The fundamental task for architects is not simply design of buildings, certainly not of office buildings, but to understand and design the relationship between activities and space through time.

Reference

1 GORDON, A. 'Future office design: energy implications', *Journal of Architectural Research*, Vol 3, no 3, September 1974.

9 *Extension to Brunswick City Hall by Ernst Sieverts. Wings can be highly compartmentalised or open plan.*
10 *Shokin-tei tea pavilion, an extreme form of reversible space.*
11 *Plan and section of Venice hospital by Le Corbusier. Section manipulated to light and ventilate internal environment.*

Section 10

Design guide

Design guide

The themes of the book are combined here into a design guide for offices. The guide by HUGH B. ELLWOOD follows the RIBA plan of work to the production of final sketch design.

Contents

Introduction

The purpose of this guide is twofold: first to identify the more important aspects which the designer must consider in relation to office buildings and second to demonstrate the order of priority in the design process. This order is not just a sequence but a cyclical process in which the designer gives sufficient consideration to the right aspects at the appropriate time and returns to investigate and develop them further at later stages. Both the design and the brief are developed in parallel.

In this design process the architect may wish to refer to the RIBA plan of work or the *Job Book* for more detailed guidance in particular areas. The design guide sets out the design process up to the production of the final sketch design. References are given to further information in the earlier sections.

The design guide follows the theme set out in the book. It is neither likely nor is it desirable that the modern office block will be closely fitted to the client's requirements. Tenants come and go and organisations grow and change. Some office design decisions are long term, others are short term so that the architect is concerned with different levels of activity involving different timescales.

The shell	structure, core and skin which are intended to last as long as the building is useful, for 40 years or more.
The scenery	partitions, furniture and furnishings related to the life of a tenancy or a particular stage of an organisation's development and lasting perhaps five or seven years.
The set	the arrangement and rearrangement of office scenery to meet constantly changing short-term needs with the time scale sometimes measured in weeks.
The services	basic installations such as lifts or mechanical services will last 20 to 25 years. Services at a smaller scale, such as light fittings and electrical points, will change with the scenery and must be capable of accommodating the shortest term requirements of the set.

A Inception: general framework

1 Initial requirements

The object of this stage is to obtain sufficient information about the type of client and his overall requirements to assess quickly whether the project is a feasible proposition. This means ensuring that legislation will permit the required development on the particular site.

Section 2 The office shell
Section 5 The law and regulations

2 The client

The type of client involved in office building may be classified as:

An owner-occupier whose main purpose in building is to house a particular function;

Section 2 The office shell

A developer whose main purpose in building is as an investment. The developer may have no tenants at the outset or he may have a tenant already established who could play a role in the design process.

Section 4 The economics of building offices

Because of these two different types of client, each with his own purpose, there are in reality two different design guides. Each section of the guide will therefore indicate to which type of client it relates.

3 Type of building

The type of building activity may be classified as:

New building where an open site is developed or a building completely renewed;

Conversion where an existing building is reorganised or its use changed with a varying degree of structural alteration.

Section 8 Managing office space

Again, the architect must use the design guide according to the type of building activity.

The nature of the intended development will follow from the type of client, ranging from a simple office block in the case of the occupier client to possibly mixed developments for a speculative developer. In the latter case, where projects may include residential accommodation, shops and parking, the type and scale of accommodation has to be established.

Section 5 The law and regulations

4 Space requirements

With an occupier client an assessment should be made of his business activities and staff numbers to arrive at an overall floor area and some indication of how they might change and develop.

A developer client would normally already have assessed the broad feasibility of building the type of development and areas involved on a particular site.

Section 2 The office shell
Section 3 The office interior

5 Legislation

Consents and approvals will have to be obtained at various stages throughout the job from a variety of interested parties or local and national authorities. This will involve:

Section 2 The office shell
Section 5 The law and regulations

General legislation Town & Country Planning Act 1971, Public Health Acts 1936 *et seq*, Offices, Shops & Railway Premises Act 1963;

Legislation outside GLC area Building Regulations 1972, The Building Standards (Scotland) (Consolidation) Regulations 1971, Building Regulations 1972 E7;

Legislation inside the GLC area London Building (Constructional) By-law 1972, London Building Acts (Amendment) Act 1939.

At each stage the guide sets down which aspects of legislation have to be satisfied with the resulting effect on the design.

6 Office Development Permit

In London and certain areas of the South-east an Office Development Permit has to be obtained before any planning authority can consider a town planning application for more than 15 000 ft² of office space.
If an application is refused, then any further work is abortive.

Section 5 The law and regulations

7 Outline town planning

Once the ODP has been obtained, where this is necessary, then outline planning approval should be obtained. The purpose of planning regulations is to:

> determine the category of development permitted;
> determine the intensity of development controlled by the 'plot ratio' (the ratio of 'gross built floor area' to 'overall site area').

Within Greater London applications are also referred to the GLC for consideration under the Greater London Development Plan.

Section 5 The law and regulations

8 Management

Management is a vital activity which continues throughout the whole process of briefing, design, construction and occupation. It is a process which continues throughout the life of the new organisation and its functions and objectives are determined at each stage.
The occupier client may be a single individual or a group of individuals representing the many interests of a company organisation. The developer, too, may well be an amalgam of various interests and certainly may have as part of the team the services of specialist advisers such as solicitors, surveyors and letting agents. To ensure efficient communication and to establish clearly the bounds of responsibility and authority in the case of the corporate client there should be a single person or a small project team consisting of representatives of the interested parties who would:

> have authority to take decisions on behalf of all interested parties; have access to specialist advisers and more detailed consultation with members of the client organisation.

As a means of carrying out these functions regular project meetings should be held to:

> ensure that all information is disseminated both ways; obtain client approval at appropriate stages; establish and monitor programmes; determine all other objectives and their achievement.

Section 8 Managing office space

Section 4 The economics of building offices

9 Cost limits

For the occupier client who, in an expanding situation, may already have been in a number of previous premises the capital costs of the site and the building must be balanced between:

> space allocation;
> standard of building, governing maintenance costs;
> equipment and furniture.

The client's ability to fund the operation, the designer's ability to cost control and the consideration of cost-in-use will all affect the above.

Section 4 The economics of building offices

For the developer who sees the office as an investment, the building costs are just one part of the economics of developing and letting a particular commodity where non-architectural factors, such as market conditions, play a part. The developer will calculate what he can afford to pay for the site and the building.

10 Programme

The establishing of key target dates and their subsequent monitoring will enable the occupier client to:

organise his finances;
plan his office reorganisation;
organise the move.

For the developer the programme will be an essential element of the whole investment exercise.

Section 8 Managing office space

B Feasibility: general strategy

The object of this stage is to assess the client's requirements in broad terms, to see how these can be accommodated within the constraints of the site and relevant legislation and to recommend a particular strategy.

11 Existing situation

Where a client already occupies office premises an analysis of the existing situation will be useful in showing the client's business processes, its shortcomings and possible improvements, the reasons for any move and what will be required to be transferred. This analysis will lead to the development of the brief and should cover:

business methods and organisation;
personnel;
space standards and areas;
furniture and equipment.

Section 7 Office facilities
Section 8 Managing office space

See paragraph 12 below

12 The strategic brief

The brief should be seen not as a rigid set of instructions, but rather as a statement of intent which will develop with the design process, which at the early stages will not be too detailed and which will vary considerably with the type of client. At the feasibility stage only sufficient statement of intent is required to establish the overall strategy and to decide quickly on basic architectural elements (see below: 15 Feasibility report).

Section 2 The office shell
Section 3 The office interior
Section 8 Managing office space

Business activities	the type of work; services to be provided.
Personnel	number of staff & categories; relationships between individuals, groups and departments.
Area	areas per floor; gross area of building; floor to ceiling heights.
Equipment	any notable items such as computers or filing systems.

The developer will have a much broader policy. As an investor he will be adding to the stock of office space in a city to meet the demand of the users. He will therefore be taking a long term view on the uses to which his building might be put by as yet unspecified tenants.

13 Site investigation

The site appraisal is intended to elicit all information, demonstrating the advantages and restraints so that the architect can make all decisions in relation to the existing conditions. At the outset it must be decided whether the investigation is for the purposes of a feasibility study only or whether is should be the fuller information required for the detail design. The nature of the investigation will also depend on whether the site is an open area, is a site with buildings on it or is simply an existing 'building'. The appraisal should cover:

Site characteristics	location and land use; topography and geology; roads, access and transport facilities; public utility services.	
Physical constraints	existing buildings; boundaries; local hazards.	
Legal constraints	ownerships; restrictive covenants; prescriptive rights; interested parties.	Section 5 The law and regulations
Possible existing information	maps & plans; planning approvals; site surveys.	

14 Legislation

By this stage it should be clear that development will be permitted. From now on the designer must ensure that proposals conform to certain standards and these early considerations will cover:

Section 5 The law and regulations

Town planning	architectural design and surroundings; sunlight & daylight guides; building lines & improvement lines; density; building height restrictions; car parking; access to site.
Building Regulations	zones of open space.

15 Feasibility report

The architect should now recommend to the client what course of action to follow and what will be involved. This will first determine:

Overall strategy	whether to reorganise and adapt existing premises with or without extension; to rent other premises; to build his own premises.

Given the client's basic requirements and the limitations imposed by both the nature of the site and legislation interpreted in that context, the architect must make some fundamental assessments of the nature of the building itself.

Building shell	possible shape of building; number of floors; bulk and relationship to site; cellular or open plan.	Section 2 The office shell Section 3 The office interior

16 Cost feasibility

In assessing the capital cost of the total building project a number of factors in the design of the building shell can affect the costs:

Section 4 The economics of building offices

ratio of net (lettable) area
to gross floor area;
ratio of external wall to
floor area, a function of
plan shape and height;
artificial or natural
environment and services
required;
structure;
car parking.

An assessment should be made of all capital costs which will form, as a preliminary cost estimate, the basis of future cost planning. At this stage the programme for design and construction should be determined as this too will have an effect on the ultimate cost.

C Outline proposals: the shell

The object of this stage is to develop the building form on the basis of a more detailed assessment of the client's requirements, so that a clear indication of the design in architectural terms can be submitted to the client.

This stage is mainly concerned with the development of a new building. However, each paragraph is also concerned, to a lesser degree, with the consideration of the building shell where an existing building is being reorganised.

17 The shell brief

Having established the brief in broad terms during the feasibility stage the architect should now develop it in more detail and from the point of view of the building shell since the development of the client's ideas and policies is part of the development of the architectural design. This should cover:

Section 2 The office shell

General operational policies

distribution and storage of supplies, information and records;
waste disposal;
circulation of personnel and access;
communication both internal and external;
car parking.

Section 7 Office facilities

Visual environment

the choice of natural lighting, artificial lighting or a combination of both, will affect:

the permissible depth of building;
the heating and ventilation requirements and consequent amount of mechanical services.

Aural environment

In controlling noise caused by speech, a balance has to be achieved between the need for communication and the need for privacy. Noise from other sources such as external noise, plant, installations and equipment has also to be controlled. This control can be achieved by:

Section 6 The office environment

Planning

location of noise sources;
distribution and grouping of personnel.

Construction and finishes

Thermal environment

While certain standards of temperature and ventilation are required by legislation, these minimum standards will not satisfy the demands of comfort. At this stage the choice of natural ventilation, mechanical ventilation or air-conditioning is closely linked to:

Section 6 The office environment

the building depth;
the building section.

Flexibility

The concept of flexibility is inherent in the approach to the design of office buildings from the points of view of 'shell' and 'scenery' with their different time scales. Flexibility also covers other aspects all affecting the building form:

Planning

accommodating different tenants' organisations and requirements;

Phasing

a possibility with a large project;

Extensibility

foreseen and unforeseen.

18 Analysis of data

In formulating the policies during the development of the brief, a mass of data will have been tabulated. This must be analysed to establish the key issues and problems to be solved in the design process.

Space allocation

already assessed at feasibility stage to establish overall area;
now checked for individuals and groups.

Section 3 The office interior

	Relationships	matrix demonstrating relationships between individuals and groups; bubble diagrams developing arrangement and relationships of clusters.	
	Organisation	influence of type of organisation on office shell.	
	Schedule of accommodation	detailed list of rooms and specific areas.	

19 Legislation

At this stage the architect must interpret regulations which affect the form and internal layout of the building shell.

Section 5 The law and regulations

General	*Building Regulations*	fire rating; fire compartments and enclosures; unprotected areas.
	Offices, Shops and Railway Premises Acts	means of escape in case of fire; number and positions of staircases and exits; provision of sanitary accommodation.
GLC area	*London Building (Constructional) By-laws 1972*	fire compartments and enclosures; minimum amount of windows.
	London Building Acts (Amendment) Act 1939	means of escape in case of fire.

20 The building form

In the case of a developer client the building will be for unknown uses with unidentifiable requirements. An occupier client, while being able to identify his requirements, will still be subject to growth and change. For this reason the building shell should be designed with factors in mind other than those immediately apparent or requested in the brief and should cover:

Section 1 Planning office space
Section 2 The office shell

The shell	*Brief*	key issues resulting from data analysis.	
	Legislation	affecting form and internal layout.	
	The site	advantages and constraints.	
	Form	requirements for flexibility, phasing or extension; ratio of perimeter to floor and depth of building; heights and sections.	
	Planning	major horizontal and vertical circulation, cores; departmental and group relationships; multiple occupancy.	Section 2 The office shell
Services	*Content*	Volume of services required, depending on building form and standard of environment required.	Section 6 The office environment
	Distribution	relationship to circulation and user areas; system of horizontal and vertical distribution; requirements of change and growth at differing time scales.	
Structure	*The grid*	structural, constructional, servicing and planning grids.	Section 2 The office shell
	Demarcation	type and sizes of spaces; test layout of furniture.	

Scenery	*The section*	requirements of legislation for minimum heights; structural space, related to column spacing; accommodation of services, related to building depth.	
	Planning	physical space requirements; planning arrangements and grid.	Section 3 The office interior
	Servicing	requirements of services and relation to services grid.	

21 The site

In designing the site layout the architect is developing the context for the building shell comprising:

Legislation	town planning and Building Regulations;
Physical requirements	determined from site survey.
The brief	requirements of access and circulation.

22 Proposals

The architect should prepare a number of alternatives, showing how all the above may be resolved, and giving his recommendations about the building form. For the occupier client he should indicate how the client's functions are accommodated within the building form in terms of group relationships and typical planning layouts.

23 Costs

The costs can now be assessed more accurately as outlined above and checked against the original budget.

D Scheme design: the scenery

This stage is concerned equally with the design of a new building and the conversion of an existing one. A fully worked out design will be prepared based on the outline proposals and any subsequent modifications. For the occupier client the architect will complete the brief and the scenery design in detail.

24 Detail planning solutions

The preferred solution should now be developed so that the building 'shell' becomes finalised. The office space should then be evaluated showing how either:
1 the space could be subdivided into a series of tenancies and different sized rooms; or
2 the space is arranged in the agreed room layouts.

Section 2 The office shell
Section 3 The office interior

25 The scenery brief

All remaining detailed information should now be collected, agreed and assessed.
Business activities
Broad description of the office organisation and work
Detailed analysis of activities and work processes
Main and subsidiary office processes or functions
Assessment of services to be provided centrally or departmentally
Other special requirements
Administrative structure, procedures and requirements
Personnel
Numbers of staff in each group or sub-group and their categories
Relationships within the groups and between the groups
Contact with visitors and the outside
Office routine

Section 3 The office interior
Section 8 Managing office space

Space allocation	related to status; related to work function; related to furniture and equipment.

Equipment
Detailed analysis of all equipment in relation to work
Flow diagram
Description of items of equipment
Detailed analysis of equipment and furniture in relation to
individuals:

Section 7 Office facilities

> categorise staff by
> furniture requirements;
> note special requirements.

Facilities
Storage facilities
Filing systems
All other ancillary requirements

Environment
A more detailed analysis of the visual, aural and thermal
environment considered under paragraph 17 above.

26 The scenery

Having designed the long term office building shell to leave
options open in some cases for a variety of tenancies and in
all instances for a developing and changing organisation,
the architect must now design the office interior to be
quickly adaptable to short term requirements. He is
concerned at this stage with the elements of interior design
or 'scenery' and with their arrangements or 'sets'. The
scenery will include:

> partitions;
> fixtures;
> fittings;
> equipment;
> furniture;
> finishes;
> lighting.

27 The set

The arrangement and adjustment of the office interior is of
the shortest time scale, accommodating the building shell
to the immediate requirements of the office organisation
and taking into account:

Section 3 The office
interior

Organisational variation	differentiation, the degree to which workplaces are distinguished by area, position, furniture, etc; subdivision, the degree to which workplaces are physically partitioned.
Organisational structure	status, hierarchy, position, authority; communication, relationship.
Physical arrangement	depending on the above, the characteristics of scenery arrangement would be: cellular group spaces open plan landscaped.
Office layout	layout at the whole building level; specific furniture arrangements isolated clustered ganged.

Section 8 Managing
office space

At this stage the architect is concerned with the detailed
interaction of the:

Section 6 The office
environment

> planning grid;
> constructional grid;
> servicing grid.

28 Costs

Just as the incidence of the cost of the mechanical services
on the total building costs will have been determined

largely by the choice of the form of the basic building shell, so too the relative incidence of the costs of the elements of the scenery will be determined by the type of office layout as well as by quality.

29 Management

From this point onwards management will have two functions:

Project management	ensuring that the project is physically carried out according to the design requirements.	
Space management	the continual running and planning of the office space so as to preserve the original standards.	

Section 8 Managing office space

Bibliography

This bibliography cites some of the more interesting recent books and articles related to office design

K. Alsleben, *Neue Technik der Mobiliarordnung im Büroräum*, Quickborn Verlag Schnell: 1960
One of the first texts of the office landscaping movement
K. Alsleben et at *Bürohaus als Grossraum*, Quickborn Verlag Schnelle: 1961
Case study of one of the earliest landscaped offices
J. Batty (ed), *Developments in Office Management*, Heinemann: London 1972
Good guide to what interests the office manager
F. Black, 'Office Building: Needs of Small Firms' *Building* 8, 87-97, 1972
A. Boje, *Open Plan Offices*, Business Books Ltd: London 1971
Consultant's view of how to plan open offices
P. R. Boyce, 'Users' Assessment of a Landscaped Office' *Journal of Architectural Research* 3, 3, 1974
One of the few before-and-after studies of user satisfaction
P. Cowan et al, *The Office A Facet of Urban Growth*, Heinemann Educational Books: London 1969
The office in its urban and theoretical setting
P. W. Daniels, *Office Location*, G. Bell & Sons: London 1975
Excellent academic survey of office location
A. Dickens, *Structural and Service Systems in Office Buildings: a Background Review*, Cambridge Land Use and Built Form Studies Working Paper 35, 1970
A good survey of current practice
F. Duffy and A. Wankum, *Office Landscaping*, Anbar Publications Ltd: London 1969
Useful concise statement of arguments for office landscaping
F. Duffy, 'Role and Status in the Office' *Architectural Association Quarterly* October 1969
F. Duffy, 'Office Design and Organisations: 1 Theoretical Basis' *Environment and Planning B* 1, 1, 1974
F. Duffy, 'Office Design and Organisations: 2 The Testing of a Hypothetical Model' *Environment and Planning B* 1, 2, 1974
GB Department of the Environment, *Planned Open Offices Cost Benefit Analysis* London 1971
Attempt to justify open planning on cost-benefit grounds
GB Department of the Environment, *The Planned Open Office: A Primer for Management* London 1971
Sensible short survey of major problems in planning open offices
GB Department of the Environment (Gilbert Jones), *Local Authority Offices: Area and Costs* DOE: London 1965 nd
Fundamental work on how the shape of offices relates to costs
GB HM Treasury, *The Practice of O and M* HMSO: London 1965
Very clear exposition of how to carry out Organisation and Methods Studies
A. Gordon, 'Future Office Design: Energy Implications' *Journal of Architectural Research* 3, 3, 1974
Discusses the energy problems of servicing deep space
O. Gottschalk, *Flexible Verwaltungsbauten* Quickborn/Verlag Schnelle 1968
First class source of information about all aspects of office landscaping
V. G. Haines, *Business Relocation: A Guide to Moving a Business* Business Books Ltd: London 1970
What needs to be done in planning the move
R. Hohl, *Modern Office Buildings* The Architectural Press: London 1969
Good photographs and plans of office buildings of the 'sixties
I. Hoos, *Automation in the Office* Public Affairs Press: Washington DC 1961
Sociological study of the impact of automation on office work
Institute of Directors, *Better Offices* Institute of Directors: London 1964
Early editions are best. Good, serious information for clients
J. Joedicke, *Office Buildings* Crosby Lockwood Staples Ltd: London 1962
An excellent survey of buildings which were news in the late 'fifties
D. Joiner, 'Social Ritual and Architectural Space' *Architectural Research and Teaching* 1 (3), 11-22, 1971
E. C. Keighley, *Visual Requirements and Reduced Fenestration in Offices* Building Research Establishment, Current Paper 41/74
Interesting studies of preferred window shapes
F. D. Klingender, *The Condition of Clerical Labour in Britain* Martin Lawrence: London 1935

F. J. Langdon, 'A Study of Annoyance Caused by noise in Automatic Data Processing Offices' *Building Science* 1, 68-78, 1965
F. J. Langdon, *Modern Offices: A User Survey* National Building Studies, Research Paper 41, HMSO: London 1966
Superb survey of environmental conditions in post-war office buildings
D. Lockwood, *The Black coated Worker* Unwin University Books: London 1969
Important sociological study of the growth of clerical unions
L. Manasseh and R. Cunliffe, *Office Buildings* BT Batsford Ltd: London 1962
A good survey of best British practice in early 'sixties
P. Manning (ed). *Office Design: A Study of Environment* Liverpool University Press: Liverpool 1965
N. O. Milbank, J. P. Dowdall, A. Slater, *Investigation of Maintenance and Energy Costs for Services in Office Buildings* Building Research Station, Current Paper 38/71
How to estimate maintenance and energy costs
C. W. Mills *White Collar* Oxford University Press Inc: New York 1951
Classic sociological study of the office worker
J. Pile, *Interiors' Second Book of Offices* Whitney Library of Design: New York 1969
Interesting because it reveals the impact of office landscaping on American space planning
R. Probst, *The Office as a Facility for Change*, Herman Miller 1968
Facile but full of insights into how office work is changing
R. Probst and M. Wodka, *Action Office Acoustics Handbook* Herman Miller Research Corporation, 1975
Useful guide to acoustics in the open plan
H. A. Rhee, *Office Automation in Social Perspective* Basil Blackwell: Oxford 1968
Important and wide-ranging survey of the impact of automation on the office
K. Ripnen, *Office Space Administration* McGraw-Hill Inc: New York 1974
Down-to-earth guide to American space planning practice
M. Saphier, *Office Planning and Design* McGraw-Hill Inc: New York 1968
Slick but informative as a guide to New York attitudes to interior design
M. F. Schmertz, *Office Building Design* (2nd edition) McGraw-Hill Inc: New York 1975
Survey of a wide range of recent American (and other) office buildings. Good photographs and plans
J. Shelton, 'Landscaped Offices' *The Architects' Journal* 5 March 1969
An interesting comparative survey of services in some of the earlier German office landscapes
R. Sommer, *Tight Spaces: Hard Architecture and How to Humanise it* Prentice-Hall Inc: Englewood Cliffs, NJ 1974
Contains some interesting and perceptive comments on office interior design
F. I. Steele, *Physical Settings and Organisational Development*, Addison-Wesley, Reading, Mass., 1973
The office as seen by the psychologist interested in organisational development
P. Tabor, *Pedestrian Circulation in Offices* Cambridge Land Use and Built Form Studies, 1969
An analysis of pedestrian movement in relation to office planning
A. S. Tannebaum, *Social Psychology of the Work Organisation* Wadsworth Publishing Co Inc: Belmont, California 1966
Very good short survey of what social psychology has to contribute to the study of the work organisation
B. W. P. Wells, 'Subjective Responses to the lighting installation in a Modern Office Building and their Design Implications' *Building Science* 1, 47-48, 1965
B. W. P. Wells, 'The Psycho-Social Influence of Building Environment: Sociometric Findings in large and small office space' *Building Science* 1, 153-165, 1965
M. Wigginton, *Offices* AD Briefing, London Architectural Design, nd
Short survey of problems in office design

Special issues of journals
Progressive Architecture, November 1969
Official Architecture and Planning, April 1970
Architectural Review, October 1970
Progressive Architecture, March 1971
Built Environment 1, 7, October 1972
L'Architecture d'Aujourd'hui, 165 December 1972/January 1973

List of authors

Editors

Dr Francis Duffy, ARIBA. Partner of Duffy Lange Giffone Worthington, Architects and Space Planners, who specialise in brief writing and the effective use of space/time. Author of many articles. One of several people responsible for introducing office landscaping to the UK.

John Worthington, MArch, AA Dipl (Hons). Partner of Duffy Lange Giffone Worthington. He is particularly interested in user requirements and has written extensively on housing.

Colin Cave, DipArch (Hull), Architect. Associate in Duffy Lange Giffone Worthington, previously worked for Property Services Agency in the Directorate of Building Development and has returned to the Civil Service. He is particularly interested in user requirements and brief writing.

Contributors

Stephen Mullin, MA, DipArch (Cantab), RIBA. Architect currently working in local government on aspects of housing policy and is particularly interested in the social history of architecture.

Richard Davies, DipArch Hons (Kingston), Architect. Works for Property Services Agency and is particularly interested in the problems of briefing for complex buildings of large clients which he researched while working in the Directorate of Building Development.

Barry Booth, DipArch (Portsmouth), Architect. Works for Property Services Agency, researched office design while working in the Directorate of Building Development now interested in the production side of architectural design.

John Francis, DipAD (Int Des). Interior designer previously worked in Directorate of Building Development now working for Michael Aukett Associates.

Bevis Fuller, BSc(Soc), Dip Arch (Nottingham), Architect. Is particularly interested in sociology, working on housing in the Property Services Agency. His contribution was written while working in the Directorate of Building Development.

Bernard Williams, FRICS, AMBIM. He is a building economist and principal partner of Bernard Williams Associates who advise on financial matters related to building and development.

Bill Thomas, BSc (hons) Civ Eng, BA Hons, M Arch, ARIBA. Partner of Pollard Thomas and Edwards and is principally concerned with medium and low cost housing as well as office design.

Andrew Rabeneck, MArch, DipArch. Principal of Building Systems Development, consultants in system building in United States and United Kingdom. Particularly interested in developing integrated approaches to design and construction.

Austin Bains, BSc, PhD. Is a physicist and a specialist in noise control with Engineering Design Consultants. He is particularly interested in noise control within open plan offices and schools. He is also a co-author of *Acoustics in Educational Buildings* (Department of Education and Science Building 51).

Roger Hitchin, BSc, MIHVE. Previously worked for Engineering Design Consultants, now researching the relationship between building design and services, particularly heating, with the British Gas Corporation.

Jolyon Drury, MA, DipArch (Cantab), RIBA, MIMH. Architect in private practice especially interested in Industrial Buildings and production and storage planning. Co-author of *Building and Planning for Industrial Storage and Distribution*.

Fred Lawson, MSc, CEng, FIAF, FIPHE, MIHVE, MAEHO, MInstF. Currently at University of Surrey researching planned obsolescence and maintenance of buildings. Has written extensively on catering and eating. Author of *Hotels, Motels and Condominiums*, and co-author of *Tourism and Recreational Development*.

Geoffrey Hutton, DipArch, ARIBA. Architect in private practice specialising in building research and information systems.

Luigi Giffone. Partner of Duffy Lange Giffone Worthington. Experience in Industrial Design, Architecture and Space Planning, currently interested in translating user requirements into design decisions in Product and Interior Design.

Hugh Ellwood, PhD, BA (Hons) Arch, RIBA. Associate of Building Design Partnership.

Index